PROVERBS
A Commentary in the Wesleyan Tradition

*New Beacon Bible Commentary

PROVERBS
A Commentary in the Wesleyan Tradition

John E. Hartley

BEACON HILL PRESS
OF KANSAS CITY

Copyright 2016
by Beacon Hill Press of Kansas City

ISBN 978-0-8341-3530-7

Printed in the United States of America

Cover Design: J.R. Caines
Interior Design: Sharon Page

Library of Congress Cataloging-in-Publication Data

Names: Hartley, John E.
Title: Proverbs / John E. Hartley.
Description: Kansas City, Missouri : Beacon Hill Press of Kansas City, 2015.
 | Series: New Beacon Bible commentary | Includes bibliographical references.
Identifiers: LCCN 2015040219 | ISBN 9780834135307 (pbk.)
Subjects: LCSH: Bible. Proverbs—Commentaries. | Wesleyan Church—Doctrines.
Classification: LCC BS1465.53 .H37 2015 | DDC 223/.707—dc23 LC record available at http://lccn.loc.gov/2015040219

10 9 8 7 6 5 4 3 2 1

DEDICATION

TO DOROTHY LEONE ROBBINS HARTLEY
in celebration of our golden anniversary;
a most capable wife, truly God's gift as expressed in her given name
Prov 19:14; 31:10

COMMENTARY EDITORS

CONTENTS

GENERAL EDITORS' PREFACE

The purpose of the New Beacon Bible Commentary is to make available to pastors and students in the twenty-first century a biblical commentary that reflects the best scholarship in the Wesleyan theological tradition. The commentary project aims to make this scholarship accessible to a wider audience to assist them in their understanding and proclamation of Scripture as God's Word.

Writers of the volumes in this series not only are scholars within the Wesleyan theological tradition and experts in their field but also have special interest in the books assigned to them. Their task is to communicate clearly the critical consensus and the full range of other credible voices who have commented on the Scriptures. Though scholarship and scholarly contribution to the understanding of the Scriptures are key concerns of this series, it is not intended as an academic dialogue within the scholarly community. Commentators of this series constantly aim to demonstrate in their work the significance of the Bible as the church's book and the contemporary relevance and application of the biblical message. The project's overall goal is to make available to the church and for her service the fruits of the labors of scholars who are committed to their Christian faith.

The *New International Version* (NIV) is the reference version of the Bible used in this series; however, the focus of exegetical study and comments is the biblical text in its original language. When the commentary uses the NIV, it is printed in bold. The text printed in bold italics is the translation of the author. Commentators also refer to other translations where the text may be difficult or ambiguous.

The structure and organization of the commentaries in this series seeks to facilitate the study of the biblical text in a systematic and methodical way. Study of each biblical book begins with an ***Introduction*** section that gives an overview of authorship, date, provenance, audience, occasion, purpose, sociological/cultural issues, textual history, literary features, hermeneutical issues, and theological themes necessary to understand the book. This section also includes a brief outline of the book and a list of general works and standard commentaries.

The commentary section for each biblical book follows the outline of the book presented in the introduction. In some volumes, readers will find section ***overviews*** of large portions of scripture with general comments on their overall literary structure and other literary features. A consistent feature of the commentary is the paragraph-by-paragraph study of biblical texts. This section has three parts: *Behind the Text*, *In the Text*, and *From the Text*.

The goal of the *Behind the Text* section is to provide the reader with all the relevant information necessary to understand the text. This includes specific historical situations reflected in the text, the literary context of the text, sociological and cultural issues, and literary features of the text.

In the Text explores what the text says, following its verse-by-verse structure. This section includes a discussion of grammatical details, word studies, and the connectedness of the text to other biblical books/passages or other parts of the book being studied (the canonical relationship). This section provides transliterations of key words in Hebrew and Greek and their literal meanings. The goal here is to explain what the author would have meant and/or what the audience would have understood as the meaning of the text. This is the largest section of the commentary.

The *From the Text* section examines the text in relation to the following areas: theological significance, intertextuality, the history of interpretation, use of the Old Testament scriptures in the New Testament, interpretation in later church history, actualization, and application.

The commentary provides *sidebars* on topics of interest that are important but not necessarily part of an explanation of the biblical text. These topics are informational items and may cover archaeological, historical, literary, cultural, and theological matters that have relevance to the biblical text. Occasionally, longer detailed discussions of special topics are included as *excurses.*

We offer this series with our hope and prayer that readers will find it a valuable resource for their understanding of God's Word and an indispensable tool for their critical engagement with the biblical texts.

Roger Hahn, Centennial Initiative General Editor
Alex Varughese, General Editor (Old Testament)
George Lyons, General Editor (New Testament)

ACKNOWLEDGMENTS

I wish to express my appreciation to the editors of NBBC for the invitation to write a commentary on Proverbs. I am very grateful to the administration of Azusa Pacific University for the many ways support has been extended for producing this volume.

I have been privileged to teach the book of Proverbs to undergraduate students at Azusa Pacific University for several decades. Thus, the opportunity to produce this volume was gladly received, for it provided the opportunity to engage this biblical book with great intensity. Moreover, its numerous proverbs and instructions offer guidance for ordering one's life on the foundation of a strongly committed relationship to God. They provide guidance for dealing with the many aspects and puzzles of daily life. Pondering them leads to a blessed life, above all keeping one on the true path.

Since the numerous proverbs vary in style and approach, the interpreter faces many exegetical challenges. That is why there are wide variations in the interpretations of many sayings. Often these proverbs, primarily those in Sections II through IV, have been considered banal. Most fortunately in the last two decades several high-quality commentaries and monographs have brought to light the treasures present in this biblical book. These works have greatly impacted this volume. In particular I am deeply indebted to the superb commentary and articles of Professor Michael Fox. I have also benefited greatly from Professor Christine Yoder's lucid exegetical comments and her perception into the theological and ethical teaching of each unit.

I wish to express great appreciation to Mrs. Lark Rilling for reading the manuscript in its entirety and making numerous suggestions that have enhanced its readability. I also extend my gratitude to former students and colleagues for proofreading some chapters and making valuable suggestions: Daniel Eichelberger, Morgan Greer, Jake Evers, Paul Lehman-Schletewitz, and Barbara Hayes. Above all I am most grateful for the extensive support my wife, Dorothy, has provided. Besides entering numerous editions of the chapters into the computer, she has reviewed them very carefully.

To Dr. Robert D. Branson, the section editor, I extend high commendation for carefully and patiently shepherding the composition of this volume over many years. His guidance and suggestions have significantly enhanced this volume. Moreover, his words of encouragement along the way have been most welcomed.

John E. Hartley

ABBREVIATIONS

With a few exceptions, these abbreviations follow those in *The SBL Handbook of Style* (Alexander 1999).

General

→	see the commentary at
AD	anno Domini (precedes date)
BC	before Christ (follows date)
ca.	circa
ch	chapter
chs	chapters
e.g.	*exempli gratia*, for example
Eng	English
et al.	*et alii*, and others
f(f).	and the following one(s)
Gk.	Greek
HB	Hebrew Bible
Heb.	Hebrew
i.e.	*id est*, that is
lit.	literally
LXX	Septuagint
mg.	margin
MS(S)	manuscript(s)
n(n).	note(s)
NT	New Testament
OT	Old Testament
sg.	singular
Syr.	Syriac Version
v	verse
Vg.	Vulgate Version
vv	verses

Modern English Versions

KJV	King James Version
NASB	New American Standard Version
NIV	New International Version
NJPS	*New JPS Hebrew-English Tanakh: The Traditional Hebrew Text and the New JPS Translation.* The Jewish Publication Society. 2000.
NKJV	New King James Version
NRSV	New Revised Standard Version
REB	Revised English Bible
RSV	Revised Standard Version

Print Conventions for Translations

Bold font	NIV (bold without quotation marks in the text under study; elsewhere in the regular font, with quotation marks and no further identification)
Bold italic font	Author's translation (without quotation marks)

Behind the Text:	Literary or historical background information average readers might not know from reading the biblical text alone
In the Text:	Comments on the biblical text, words, phrases, grammar, and so forth
From the Text:	The use of the text by later interpreters, contemporary relevance, theological and ethical implications of the text, with particular emphasis on Wesleyan concerns

Old Testament

Gen	Genesis
Exod	Exodus
Lev	Leviticus
Num	Numbers
Deut	Deuteronomy
Josh	Joshua
Judg	Judges
Ruth	Ruth
1—2 Sam	1—2 Samuel
1—2 Kgs	1—2 Kings
1—2 Chr	1—2 Chronicles
Ezra	Ezra
Neh	Nehemiah
Esth	Esther
Job	Job
Ps/Pss	Psalm/Psalms
Prov	Proverbs
Eccl	Ecclesiastes
Song	Song of Songs/ Song of Solomon
Isa	Isaiah
Jer	Jeremiah
Lam	Lamentations
Ezek	Ezekiel
Dan	Daniel
Hos	Hosea
Joel	Joel
Amos	Amos
Obad	Obadiah
Jonah	Jonah
Mic	Micah
Nah	Nahum
Hab	Habakkuk
Zeph	Zephaniah
Hag	Haggai
Zech	Zechariah
Mal	Malachi

(Note: Chapter and verse numbering in the MT and LXX often differ compared to those in English Bibles. To avoid confusion, all biblical references follow the chapter and verse numbering in English translations, even when the text in the MT and LXX is under discussion.)

New Testament

Matt	Matthew
Mark	Mark
Luke	Luke
John	John
Acts	Acts
Rom	Romans
1—2 Cor	1—2 Corinthians
Gal	Galatians
Eph	Ephesians
Phil	Philippians
Col	Colossians
1—2 Thess	1—2 Thessalonians
1—2 Tim	1—2 Timothy
Titus	Titus
Phlm	Philemon
Heb	Hebrews
Jas	James
1—2 Pet	1—2 Peter
1—2—3 John	1—2—3 John
Jude	Jude
Rev	Revelation

Apocrypha

Bar	Baruch
Add Dan	Additions to Daniel
Pr Azar	Prayer of Azariah
Bel	Bel and the Dragon
Sg Three	Song of the Three Young Men
Sus	Susanna
1—2 Esd	1—2 Esdras
Add Esth	Additions to Esther
Ep Jer	Epistle of Jeremiah
Jdt	Judith
1—2 Macc	1—2 Maccabees
3—4 Macc	3—4 Maccabees
Pr Man	Prayer of Manasseh
Ps 151	Psalm 151
Sir	Sirach/Ecclesiasticus
Tob	Tobit\
Wis	Wisdom of Solomon

Egyptian Wisdom Texts

Admonitions of Ipuwer	Admonitions of Ipuwer
Amenemhet or Instruction of King Amenemhet	Instruction of King Amenemhet
Amenemope or Instruction of Amenemope	Instruction of Amenemope
Any or Instruction of Any	Instruction of Any
Merikare	Instruction for Merikare
Ptahhotep or Instruction of Ptahhotep	Instruction of Ptahhotep

Secondary Sources

ABD	*Anchor Bible Dictionary.* General editor, David Noel Freedman. 1992.
AEL	*Ancient Egyptian Literature: A Book of Readings.* 3 vols. Miriam Lichtheim. 1973.
DCH	*The Dictionary of Classical Hebrew.* 8 vols. Edited by David J. A. Clines. 1993-2011.
ISBE	*The International Standard Bible Encyclopedia,* Fully Revised. 4 vols. General editor, Geoffrey W. Bromiley. 1979-88.
JBL	*Journal of Biblical Literature*
JSOT	*Journal for the Study of the Old Testament*
JSOTSS	Journal for the Study of the Old Testament Supplement Series
NIDB	*New Interpreter's Dictionary of the Bible.* 5 vols. General editor, Katharine Doob Sakenfeld. 2006-9.
NIDOTTE	*New International Dictionary of Old Testament Theology and Exegesis.* 5 vols. General editor, Willem A. VanGemeren. 1997.
SubBi	Subsidia biblica
TDOT	*Theological Dictionary of the Old Testament.* Edited by G. Johannes Botterweck, Helmer Ringgren, and Heinz-Josef Fabry. 1974-2006.
WBC	Word Biblical Commentary

Greek Transliteration

Greek	Letter	English
α	alpha	a
β	bēta	b
γ	gamma	g
γ	gamma nasal	n (before γ, κ, ξ, χ)
δ	delta	d
ε	epsilon	e
ζ	zēta	z
η	ēta	ē
θ	thēta	th
ι	iōta	i
κ	kappa	k
λ	lambda	l
μ	mu	m
ν	nu	n
ξ	xi	x
ο	omicron	o
π	pi	p
ρ	rhō	r
ρ	initial rhō	rh
σ/ς	sigma	s
τ	tau	t
υ	upsilon	y
υ	upsilon	u (in diphthongs: au, eu, ēu, ou, ui)
φ	phi	ph
χ	chi	ch
ψ	psi	ps
ω	ōmega	ō
'	rough breathing	h (before initial vowels or diphthongs)

Hebrew Consonant Transliteration

Hebrew/ Aramaic	Letter	English
א	alef	'
ב	bet	b
ג	gimel	g
ד	dalet	d
ה	he	h
ו	vav	v or w
ז	zayin	z
ח	khet	ḥ
ט	tet	ṭ
י	yod	y
ך/כ	kaf	k
ל	lamed	l
ם/מ	mem	m
ן/נ	nun	n
ס	samek	s
ע	ayin	ʿ
ף/פ	pe	p; f (spirant)
ץ/צ	tsade	ṣ
ק	qof	q
ר	resh	r
שׂ	sin	ś
שׁ	shin	š
ת	tav	t; th (spirant)

BIBLIOGRAPHY

COMMENTARIES

Alter, Robert. 2010. *The Wisdom Books: Job, Proverbs, and Ecclesiastes*. New York: W. W. Norton.

Clifford, Richard J. 1999. *Proverbs*. The Old Testament Library. Louisville, KY: Westminster John Knox.

Dunn, James D. G. 1988. *Romans 9-16*. WBC 38B. Dallas: Word Books.

Fox, Michael V. 2000. *Proverbs 1-9*. Anchor Bible 18A. New Haven, CT: Yale University Press.

_____. 2009. *Proverbs 10-31*. Anchor Bible 18B. New Haven, CT: Yale University Press.

Kidner, Derek. 1964. *The Proverbs*. Tyndale Old Testament Commentaries. Downers Grove, IL: InterVarsity.

Koptak, Paul E. 2003. *Proverbs: The NIV Application Commentary*. Grand Rapids: Zondervan.

Lennox, Stephen J. 1998. *Proverbs: A Commentary in the Wesleyan Tradition*. Indianapolis: Wesleyan Publishing House.

Longman, Tremper, III. 2006. *Proverbs*: Baker Commentary on the Old Testament, Wisdom and Psalms. Grand Rapids: Baker Academic.

McKane, William. 1970. *Proverbs: A New Approach*. The Old Testament Library. Philadelphia: Westminster.

Murphy, Roland E. 1998. *Proverbs*. WBC 22. Nashville: Thomas Nelson.

Murray, J. 1965. *The Epistle to the Romans*, vol. 2: *Chapters 9-16*. The New International Commentary on the New Testament. Grand Rapids: Eerdmans.

Plöger, Otto. 1984. *Sprüche Salomos (Proverbia)*, vol. 17 of Biblische Kommentar zum Alten Testament. Neukirchen-Vluyn: Neukirchener.

Schreiner, Thomas. R. 1998. *Romans*. Baker Exegetical Commentary on the New Testament. Grand Rapids: Baker Books.

Van Leeuwen, Raymond C. 1997. *The Book of Proverbs*. Pages 17-264 in vol. 5 of *The New Interpreter's Bible*. Nashville: Abingdon.

Waltke, Bruce K. 2004. *The Book of Proverbs: Chapters 1-14*. New International Commentary on the Old Testament. Grand Rapids: Eerdmans.

_____. 2005. *The Book of Proverbs: Chapters 15-31*. New International Commentary on the Old Testament. Grand Rapids: Eerdmans.

Whybray, R. N. 1972. *The Book of Proverbs*. Cambridge Bible Commentary. Cambridge: Cambridge University Press.

_____. 1994a. *Proverbs*. New Century Bible Commentary. London: Marshall, Morgan & Scott.

Wilson, Gerald H. 2002. *Psalms Volume I*. The NIV Application Commentary. Grand Rapids: Zondervan.

Wright, J. Robert. 2005. *Ancient Christian Commentary on Scripture. Old Testament IX: Proverbs, Ecclesiastes, Song of Solomon*. Downers Grove, IL: InterVarsity.

Yoder, Christine Roy. 2009. *Proverbs*. Abingdon Old Testament Commentaries. Nashville: Abingdon.

MONOGRAPHS AND REFERENCES

Alonso-Schökel, Luis. 1988. *A Manual of Hebrew Poetics*. SubBi 11. Rome: Biblical Institute Press.

Alter, R. 1985. *The Art of Biblical Poetry*. New York: Basic Books.

Bauckham, Richard. 2008. *Jesus and the God of Israel*. Grand Rapids: Eerdmans.

Camp, Claudia. 1985. *Wisdom and the Feminine in the Book of Proverbs*. Sheffield: Almond.

Dunn, J. D. G. 1996. *Christology in the Making: A New Testament Inquiry into the Origins of the Doctrine of the Incarnation*, 2nd ed. Grand Rapids: Eerdmans.

Fretheim, Terrence E. 2005. *God and World in the Old Testament: A Relational Theology of Creation*. Nashville: Abingdon.

Hatton, Peter T. H. 2008. *Contradiction in the Book of Proverbs: The Deep Waters of Counsel*. Society for Old Testament Study Monographs. Hampshire, GB: Ashgate Publishing.

Hermisson, H. J. 1968. *Studien zur Israelitischen Spruchweisheit*. Wissenschaftliche Monographien zum Alten und Neuen Testament 28. Neukirchen-Vluyn: Neukirchener.

King, Philip J., and Lawrence E. Stager. 2001. *Life in Biblical Israel*. Louisville, KY: Westminster John Knox.

Lichtheim, Miriam. 1973. *Ancient Egyptian Literature: A Book of Readings*, vol. 1: *The Old and Middle Kingdoms*. Berkeley, CA: University of California Press.

Longman, Tremper, III. 2002. *How to Read Proverbs*. Downers Grove, IL: IVP Academic.

Murphy, Roland E. 1990. *The Tree of Life*. AB Reference Library. New York: Doubleday.

Rad, Gerhard von. 1972. *Wisdom in Israel*. Translated by James D. Martin. Nashville: Abingdon.

Schaff, Philip. 1996. *The Creeds of Christendom: With a History and Critical Notes*, vol. 1: *The History of the Creeds*. Revised by David S. Schaff. Grand Rapids: Baker Books.

Vaux, Roland de. 1965. *Ancient Israel: Its Life and Institutions*. Translated by John McHugh. New York: McGraw-Hill.

Washington, Harold C. 1994. *Wealth and Poverty in the Instruction of Amenemope and the Hebrew Proverbs*. Society of Biblical Literature Dissertation Series 142. Atlanta: Scholars Press.

Wesley, John. 1975. *Explanatory Notes upon the Old Testament*. Reprint. Salem, Ohio: Schmul Publishers.

Whybray, R. N. 1994b. *The Composition of the Book of Proverbs*. JSOTSS 168. Sheffield: JSOT.

Williams, James G. 1981. *Those Who Ponder Proverbs*. Bible and Literature Series. Sheffield: Almond.

Yadin, Yigael. 1963. *The Art of Warfare in Biblical Lands*. 2 vols. New York: McGraw-Hill.

Zohary, Michael. 1982. *Plants of the Bible*. Cambridge: Cambridge University Press.

ARTICLES

Baer, D. A., and R. P. Gordon. 1997. *ḥesed*. Pages 211-18 in vol. 2 of *NIDOTTE*.

Beyse, K.-M. 1998. *māšal* I; *māšāl*. Pages 64-67 in vol. 9 of *TDOT*.

Bilkes, Gerald M. 2009. Money, Coins. Pages 130-38 in vol. 4 of *NIBD*.

Brown, William P. 2004. The Didactic Power of Metaphor in the Aphoristic Sayings of Proverbs. *JSOT* 29:133-54.

Bryce, G. E. 1972. Another Wisdom-"Book" in Proverbs. *JBL* 91:145-57.

Call, M. W. 1979. Bank; Banking. Pages 408-9 in vol. 1 of *ISBE*.

Camp, Claudia. 1991. What's So Strange about the Strange Woman? Pages 17-31 in *The Bible and the Politics of Exegesis* (FS N. Gottwald). Edited by D. Jobling, P. L. Day, and G. T. Sheppard. Cleveland: Pilgrim Press.

Davies, E. W. 1980. The Meaning of *qesem* in Prv 16,10. *Biblica* 61:554-56.

Dell, Katharine J. 1997. On the Development of Wisdom in Israel. Pages 135-51 in *Congress Volume*, vol. 66 of Supplements to Vetus Testamentum.

Denning-Bolle, Sara J. 1987. Wisdom and Dialogue in the Ancient Near East. *NUMEN* 34:214-34.

Diamond, A. R. Peter. 1997. *d'g*. Pages 906-7 in vol. 1 of *NIDOTTE*.

Domeris, W. R. 1997. *'ebyôn*. Pages 228-32 in vol. 1 of *NIDOTTE*.

Elliott, J. H. 1991. The Evil Eye in the First Testament: The Ecology and Culture of a Pervasive Belief. Pages 147-59 in *The Bible and the Politics of Exegesis*. Edited by D. Jobling et al. Cleveland: Pilgrim Press.

Fee, Gordon D. 2000. Wisdom Christology in Paul. Pages 251-79 in *The Way of Wisdom: Essays in Honor of Bruce K. Waltke*. Edited by J. I. Packer and Sven K. Soderlund. Grand Rapids: Zondervan.

Fontaine, Carole. 1985. Proverbs Performance in the Hebrew Bible. *JSOT* 32:87-103.

Fox, Michael V. 1994. The Pedagogy of Proverbs 2. *JBL* 113:233-43.

_____. 1996. The Social Location of the Book of Proverbs. Pages 227-39 in *Texts, Temples, and Traditions: A Tribute to Menahem Haran*. Edited by M. Fox et al. Winona Lake, IN: Eisenbrauns.

_____. 1997. Ideas of Wisdom in Proverbs 1-9. *JBL* 116:613-33.

Franklyn, Paul. 1983. The Sayings of Agur in Proverbs 30: Piety or Scepticism? *Zeitshrift für Alttestamentliche Wissenschaft* 95:238-52.

Fuhs, H. F. 1975. *ghl, gehālîm*. Pages 461-65 in vol. 2 of *TDOT*.

Gertz, J. C. 2006. *tûšiyyâ*. Pages 647-50 in vol. 15 of *TDOT*.

Ginsberg, H. L. 1945. The North-Canaanite Myth of Anath and Aqhat. *Bulletin of the American Schools of Oriental Research* 98:15-23.

Gitay, Yehoshua. 2001. Rhetoric and Logic of Wisdom in the Book of Proverbs. *Journal of Northwest Semitic Languages* 27:45-56.

Goldingay, John. 1994. The Arrangement of Sayings in Proverbs 10-15. *JSOT* 61:75-83.

Grossmann, C. L. 2005. The Gospel of Billy Graham: Inclusion, *USA TODAY*, May 15. http://usatoday 30.usatoday.com/news/religion/2005-05-15-graham-cover_x.htm.

Habel, Norman C. 1972. The Symbolism of Wisdom in Proverbs 1-9. *Interpretation* 26:131-57.

Hanson, K. C. 1996. How Honorable! How Shameful! A Cultural Analysis of Matthew's Makarisms and Reproaches. *Semeia* 68:83-114.

Hoffmeier, J. K. 1988. Weapons of War. Pages 1033-43 in vol. 4 of *ISBE*.

Hossfeld, F. L., and E. Reuter. 1999. *nāśā᾽ II, maśśā᾽*. Pages 55–59 in vol. 10 of *TDOT*.

Janzen, W. 1963. *᾽ašrê* in the Old Testament. *Harvard Theological Review* 58:215-26.

Jobes, Karen H. 2000. Sophia Christology: The Way of Wisdom? Pages 226-50 in *The Way of Wisdom: Essays in Honor of Bruce K. Waltke*. Edited by J. I. Packer and Sven K. Soderlund. Grand Rapids: Zondervan.

Kletter, Raz. 2009. Weights and Measures. Pages 831-41 in vol. 5 of *NIBD*.

Kugel, James L. 1997. Wisdom and the Anthological Temper. *Prooftexts* 17:9-32.

Lichtenstein, Murray H. 1982. Chiasm and Symmetry in Proverbs 31. *Catholic Biblical Quarterly* 44:202-11.

Lyons, Ellen L. 1987. A Note on Proverbs 31:10-31. Pages 237-45 in *The Listening Heart: Essays in Wisdom and the Psalms in Honor of Roland E. Murphy, O. Carm.* Edited by K. G. Hoglund et al. JSOTSS 58. Sheffield: Sheffield Academic, 1987.

Malchow, B. V. 1985. A Manual for Future Monarchs. *Catholic Biblical Quarterly* 47:238-45.

McCreesh, Thomas, P. 1985. Wisdom as Wife: Proverbs 31:10-31. *Revue biblique* 92:25-46.

McKinlay, Judith E. 1996. *Gendering Wisdom the Host*. JSOTSup 216. Sheffield: JSOT Press.

Montgomery, David J. 2000. "A Bribe is a Charm": A Study of Proverbs 17:8. Pages 134-49 in *The Way of Wisdom: Essays in Honor of Bruce K. Waltke*. Edited by J. I. Packer and Sven K. Soderlund. Grand Rapids: Zondervan.

Müller, H.-P. 1980. *ḥākam, ḥākām*. Pages 370-85 in vol. 4 of *TDOT*.

Murphy, R. E. 1985. Wisdom and Creation. *JBL* 104:3-11.

Nel, Philip J. 1998. Juxtaposition and Logic in Wisdom Sayings. *Journal of Northwest Semitic Languages* 24:115-27.

_____. 2002. The Rhetoric of Wisdom's Ethics. *Old Testament Essays* 15:435-52.

Preuss, H.-D. 2006. *tô᾽ēbâ*. Pages 591-694 in vol. 15 of *TDOT*.

Smith, Mark S. 1992. Rephaim. Pages 674-76 in vol. 4 of *ABD*.

Steinmann, Andrew E. 2001. Three Things . . . Four Things . . . Seven Things: The Coherence of Proverbs 30:1-33 and the Unity of Proverbs 30. *Hebrew Studies* 42:59-66.

Van Leeuwen, Raymond C. 1986. Proverbs 30:21-23 and the Biblical World Upside Down. *JBL* 105:599-610.

_____. 1990. Liminality and Worldview in Proverbs 1-9. *Semeia* 50:111-44.

_____. 1992. Wealth and Poverty: System and Contradiction in Proverbs. *Hebrew Studies* 33:25-36.

Van Pelt, M. V., and W. C. Kaiser, Jr. 1997. *bhl*. Pages 611-12 in vol. 1 of *NIDOTTE*.

Whybray, R. N. 1992. Thoughts on the Composition of Proverbs 10-29. Pages 102-14 in *Priests, Prophets, and Scribes. Essays on the Formation of Second Temple Judaism*. Edited by E. Ulrich et al. JSOTSS 149. Sheffield: JSOT Press.

Williams, James G. 1980. The Power of Form: A Study of Biblical Proverbs. *Semeia* 17:35-57.

Wolters, Al. 1985. *Ṣôpiyyâ* (Prov 31:27) as Hymnic Participle and Play on *Sophia*. *JBL* 104:577-87.

_____. 1988. Proverbs XXXI 10-31 as Heroic Hymn: A Form-critical Analysis. *Vetus Testamentum* 38:446-57.

Yee, Gale A. "I Have Perfumed My Bed with Myrrh": The Foreign Woman (*᾽iššâ zārâ*) in Proverbs 1-9. *JSOT* 43:53-68.

Zobel, H.-J. 1986. *Ḥesed*. Pages 44-64 in vol. 5 of *TDOT*.

TABLE OF SIDEBARS

INTRODUCTION

PROVERBS

A. Composition and Importance of the Book of Proverbs

I. The Structure of the Book of Proverbs

The book of Proverbs has six sections. Each section, save for the last, is identified by a heading. The headings indicate that this book came together in stages over a long time span. As a result each section has distinctive characteristics.

The headings to Sections I (chs 1—9) and II (10:1—22:16) associate their contents with Solomon (mid-tenth century BC), Israel's premier sage. The references to Solomon are similar to references to David at the headings of several psalms. Rather than identifying Solomon as the author of these sayings, his name authenticates the sayings as genuine Israelite wisdom.

The brief headings to Sections IIIA (22:17—24:22) and IIIB (24:23-34) identify their contents only as "sayings of the wise." The Israelite sage who composed Section IIIA was well acquainted with the Egyptian text the Instruction of Amenemope, an instruction that a high Egyptian official composed to provide his son guidance for becoming a respected government official. After 23:11 the Israelite sage ceased drawing on the Egyptian text except for 24:11. The Israelite scribe, then, is to be viewed as the author of Section IIIA.

Section IIIB (24:23-34) has the title "these also are sayings of the wise." Nothing is known about its origin. This brief collection addresses three topics. They are organized into two parallel sets dealing with "courts" (vv 24-25, 28), "speech" (positive [v 26]; vindictive [v 29]), and work (well-organized [v 27]; a parable of a lazy farmer [vv 30-34]; Clifford 1999, 216).

The sages who composed the materials in Section III may have worked during the reign of either Solomon or Hezekiah, for both kings supported the pursuit of wisdom. The fact that both kings were heavily engaged in international relations would have provided these Israelite sages the opportunity to study in Egypt.

Section IV (chs 25—29) is a collection of proverbs associated with Solomon compiled by scribes who served under King Hezekiah (late eighth century BC). Those scribes attached this collection to the existing book of Proverbs. It is marked by some distinctive traits: the sayings are arranged topically; several concern the crown; many have vibrant metaphors.

At a later date the sayings of Agur and Lemuel, possibly two northern Arabian kings (chs 30; 31:1-9), were appended to the book as Section V.

A sage composed the encomium of the noble wife to provide this book a fitting capstone (31:10-31; Section VI). Supporting evidence for this view is twofold. (1) The encomium is an alphabetic acrostic. This style was highly prized by the ancient Israelites, being attested in several texts (Pss 9—10; 25; 34; 37; 111; 112; 119; 145; Lam 1, 2, 3, 4). This structure enhances the encomium's power. Thus, it is a fitting conclusion to a book of wisdom. (2) In praising the noble wife the poem also highlights the role of Woman Wisdom (section I). These two descriptions provide an elegant frame for the book of Proverbs.

2. The Compilation of the Book of Proverbs

During the monarchy a key leader in Israel recognized the importance of collecting Israelite wisdom sayings and recording them in a volume to become part of her literary heritage. Likely that leader was Solomon. His interest in wisdom is legendary. He spoke three thousand proverbs and composed a thousand and five songs (1 Kgs 4:32). He commissioned sages to collect, organize, and prepare an anthology of Israelite proverbs. Likely they included some of Solomon's sayings. Unfortunately, there are no criteria for identifying the ones he composed. The resulting anthology has become Section II of Proverbs.

Since the anthology is a collection of unconnected proverbs, the sages recognized that it needed an introduction (Section I) to provide guidance for using the proverbs. To serve this purpose they assembled several instructions that address key themes in greater detail. This suggestion is based on the variations in the style and length of the instructions. Six of them are essays that constitute the entire chapter (chs 2, 4, 5, 7, 8, and 9). But chs 1, 3, and 6 are a composite of short instructions on diverse topics composed in varying styles.

The language of both the instructions and the proverbs in Sections I through IV is classical biblical Hebrew, the Hebrew of the kingdom era (tenth to fifth century BC; compare Clifford 1999, 4-5). This fact supports the possibility that the first four sections of Proverbs came together sometime between the reign of Solomon and that of Hezekiah.

The book of Proverbs bears witness to the importance of the pursuit of wisdom in ancient Israel. That pursuit continued to be important during the Second Temple era as attested by the composition of several wisdom works: Ecclesiastes, Job, Ben Sira, Tobit, and the Wisdom of Solomon.

3. The Authority of the Book of Proverbs

In Section I several times sages refer to their instructions as "teaching" or "law" (*tôrâ* [Prov 1:8; 3:1; 4:2; 6:20; 7:2; compare 13:14; 31:26]) and "command(s)" (*miṣwâ* [2:1; 3:1; 4:4; 6:20, 23; 7:1, 2; compare 10:8; 13:13]). In the Pentateuch these two terms stand for the precepts and statutes associated with Moses' law (e.g., *tôrâ* [Exod 24:12; Deut 4:44; 29:21 (20 HB)] and *miṣwâ* [Exod 15:26; 16:28]). By using these terms Israelite sages were underscoring the authority of their instructions. In this spirit they exhorted their sons or students to memorize their teachings (Prov 2:1; 3:1; 6:20-22; 7:1, 2).

4. The Value of the Book of Proverbs for Christians

Christians relate to Proverbs in a variety of ways. Many ignore this book, often because of its apparent lack of unity. Others, aware that it contains valuable nuggets of insight, read part of a chapter or a section from time to time. However, seldom is this book read in a worship service. Few sermons are preached from it. Conversely, some key Christian leaders have integrated a chapter of Proverbs into their daily Bible reading to receive guidance for dealing more astutely with daily issues. Billy Graham reported, "I used to read five psalms every day—that teaches me how to get along with God. Then I read a chapter of Proverbs every day and that teaches me how to get along with my fellow man" (Grossmann 2005). Dr. Gayle D. Beebe, president of Westmont College, says,

> I read the chapter in Proverbs that corresponds to the number of the day on the calendar. Then I read one psalm and one parable. The proverbs remind me to have a moral orientation. The psalm reminds me to trust God, and the parable reminds me to look at situations differently and to undergo a perceptual reorganization if something seems "stuck."

Clearly, reading from Proverbs nourishes one's faith and provides guidance for dealing with daily tasks.

Those who read Proverbs enjoy the instructions in Section I. They take great delight in the euphoric tone and grand promises of ch 3. Consequently, this chapter is the one best known. Many who go on to read beyond ch 9 soon lose interest in the string of disconnected proverbs. While reading a chapter, they find their minds wandering. When they come to the end of a chapter, they have little memory of what they have just read. Becoming discouraged with reading further in Proverbs, they turn to another book of the Bible. There are a variety of approaches for working with Proverbs to avoid this tendency.

This commentary seeks to provide avenues for discovering rich insights in Proverbs. Recurring topics are identified in the overview section to each chapter in Sections II through V (10:1—31:9). The reader, certainly teachers and pastors, may scan this section to identify proverbs on themes of interest. Another way of identifying proverbs for contemplation is to scan the headings of the proverbs in a particular chapter. A heading, identifying the topic of a proverb and its structure, stands before each proverb in Sections II through V. By using either approach, a person will find two or three proverbs to focus on. These suggestions are in accord with the intent of a proverb: contemplation and reflection. Therefore, this biblical book needs to be approached differently from other biblical books. Through contemplation these sayings offer valuable insights into the daily aspects of life.

B. Characteristics of Hebrew Poetry in Proverbs

Poetry provides a more intense presentation than prose. It conveys ideas, emotions, nuances, and emphases by a play on terms and often on the sound of terms. Proverbs are composed in a poetic style referred to as Hebrew parallelism. This style is found throughout the OT, especially in psalms and prophetic oracles. A stanza may have many lines. However, the typical proverb as found in Sections II through IV has two lines.

Each line of a proverb usually has three or four Hebrew words: one or two nouns, a verb, or an adjective. The English translation has more words because some independent English words as articles, pronouns, and conjunctions are attached to a noun or verb in Hebrew. Therefore, in looking for three or four parallel terms, pronouns, articles, and helping verbs are ordinarily overlooked.

The second line of a proverb is formulated in relationship to the first line in one of three ways: it reiterates the idea stated in the first line, it states an opposite idea, or it develops the thought expressed in the first line.

I. Main Types of Parallelism

In this volume the three main types of Hebrew parallelism are identified on the relationship of the second line as **affirming**—restating an idea thereby providing it greater precision; **opposing**—stating an opposing idea; and **advancing**—developing the concept expressed in the first line (Wilson 2002, 39-57). In this commentary the style of each proverb is identified in its heading in Sections II through IV.

In the following examples of these patterns a capital letter (A, B, C, etc.) identifies each line. The core words in each line are identified by lowercase letters (a, b, c, d). The words in the second line receive the same lowercase letter plus a mark. The mark identifies the character of the relationship between the parallel terms: a word used with a similar meaning is marked by an acute accent ('), a word with an opposing sense by a minus sign (-), and a word that advances the idea by a plus sign (+).

a. Affirming

	a	b	c
A	I have taught you	the way	of wisdom;
	a´	b´	c´
B	I have led you	in the paths	of uprightness. (4:11 NRSV)

This saying is affirming because the three key terms in line B are synonymous with those in line A. Line B adds a dimension to the statement in line A. It brings out that a teacher also functions as a guide. More importantly it emphasizes the connection between acquiring wisdom and living righteously.

b. Opposing

	a	b	c
A	The tongue	of the righteous	is choice silver;
	a-	b-	c-
B	the mind	of the wicked	is of little worth. (11:3 NRSV)

Line B expresses an opposing idea to the statement expressed in line A. "Mind" (heart) and "tongue" have different roles. "The tongue" gives expression to the thoughts of "the mind"; that is, their functions are very different. "Righteous" and "wicked" are clearly opposites as are "choice silver" and "little worth." This proverb contains an element of surprise in that a person's mind is usually considered far more important than the tongue. But a righteous person's tongue has greater value than the mind or thoughts of the wicked.

c. Advancing

	a	b	c
A	It is not good	to be partial	to the wicked
	d+	e+	f+
B	and so deprive	the innocent	of justice. (18:5)

Line B continues the thought of line A by describing an appalling outcome that results from a judge's showing partiality to the wicked (line A).

2. Chiasm

Chiasm is a style that occurs often in Hebrew poetry. Chiasm is derived from the Greek letter *chi*, English X. This style is also identified as "a mirror" or "envelope" pattern. In a chiasm the three elements (a, b, c) in line A occur in an inverted order (c, b, a) in line B.

	a	b	c
A	Trouble	pursues	the sinner,
	c-	b-	a-
B	but the righteous	are rewarded	with good things. (13:21)

29

In a chiasm the emphasis falls on the center. This proverb, thus, emphasizes the different experiences of two people who are morally opposites, "sinner" in contrast to "righteous" (c). Their experiences in life, standing at the center, are underscored. The verbs give the saying color. "Pursues" conveys being relentlessly beset by troubles. The wicked have no way of circumventing this pattern in their lives. The righteous, however, "are rewarded." They are often pleasantly surprised by "good things."

Two proverbs may be structured in a chiastic pattern A:B::B:A; for example, Prov 15:28-29 (compare 28:13-14):

	a	b	c
A	The heart of the righteous	weighs	its answers,
	a-	b-	c-
B-	but the mouth of the wicked	gushes	evil.
	d	e-	a-
B+	The Lord	is far from	the wicked,
	e	c´	a
A+	but he hears	the prayer	of the righteous.

The outside lines, A and A+, express the main thought. The righteous reflect carefully before expressing their thoughts. Therefore, the Lord honors their integrity by hearing their prayers (A+). By contrast, the wicked speak a torrent of words without reflecting on what they are saying. Their intent is to conceal their true motives, for they do not desire to honor the Lord. This saying stresses that in speaking much the wicked show that they lack wisdom and are far from the Lord. Thus, their words are not only unreliable but also seek to harm others. By contrast, the righteous think carefully before speaking. Their demeanor honors the Lord. He, in turn, hears their prayers. The chiastic arrangement of these two proverbs signals that they are to be interpreted in light of each other.

3. Other Characteristics

a. Implied Words or Concepts

Another characteristic of this style of poetry is that a word or concept expressed in one line is implied in the other line.

	a	b	c
A	Listen,	my sons,	to a father's instruction;
	a´	d	e
B	pay attention	and gain	understanding. (4:1)

The sons are directly addressed in line A. That direct address is implied in line B. More importantly "a father's instruction" in line A is implied as the object of "pay attention" in line B.

b. Play on Sounds of Words

Another way that words or a concept are emphasized is by making a play on the sounds of key terms. This approach is very effective because humans "correlate sounds and perceptions" (Williams 1980, 45). An example is Prov 27:14: If anyone "blesses" (*měbārrēk*) a "neighbor" (*rē'ēhû*) "loudly" (*běqôl gādôl*) "early in the morning" (*běbōqer*), it will be viewed as cursing (*qělālâ*). The repetitious sounds *m + b + r + k, b + q + l, g + d + l, b + q + r* are focused in "curse" (*qllh*), the lead word in line B. These sounds capture the grating sensation that neighbor feels on hearing such a blessing!

c. Use of Metaphors

Several sayings employ metaphors. There is a concentration of this style of proverb in Section IV. Insights are gained by reflection on ways the images "rebound off each other" (Williams 1980, 42).

	a	b	c
A	Like a club	or a sword	or a sharp arrow
	d	e	f
B	is one who gives	false testimony	against a neighbor. (25:18)

These potent metaphors capture the devastating effect a neighbor feels whenever someone lodges a false accusation against him. In another example a metaphor captures the vulnerability of a person lacking self-control.

	a	b	c
A	Like a city	whose walls	are broken through
	d	e	f
B	is a person	who lacks	self-control. (25:28)

This proverb seeks to motivate such a person to overcome that flaw.

Giving attention to these patterns leads to seeing the artistry of Israelites in their poetry. Furthermore, awareness of these patterns enhances one's meditation on these texts. To assist the reader, these patterns are identified in the heading to the proverbs in Sections II through V.

C. Theological Themes

I. Wisdom

In Proverbs "wisdom" (*ḥokmâ*) references "a body of knowledge" and "reasoning ability" (compare Fox 2000, 32-34). In some texts wisdom is personified as Yahweh's companion. She serves as his representative in society (→ sidebar "Wisdom" at the end of 8:30-31).

Since God brought forth Wisdom as the first of his works, she was present observing him create the world. Her presence conveys that every aspect of creation has been made wisely (compare Fretheim 2005, 199). The entire creation bears witness to God's majestic wisdom. It is evident in the marvelous beauty present everywhere in the world, especially in the amazing varieties of plants and animals that fill the earth. Moreover, wisdom is hidden in the infrastructure that governs earth's dynamic environment that supports myriads of life forms. It is also evident in the dynamics that influence the ways humans form communities and build empires.

In Proverbs Wisdom as God's representative is pictured as moving throughout the city, a metaphor for human society (compare Van Leeuwen 1997, 88-89, 97). She visits the city's heights, the center of government, and the cult. She walks through the streets, stopping at the city square where humans assemble, conduct business, decide judicial cases, and share news (1:20-21 and 8:1-4). Thus, she is present where humans make transactions and enter into defining relationships.

While moving about the city, Wisdom calls out, inviting all to join her and gain prudence (1:20-21, 33; 8:1-11; compare 9:1-6). In those who accept her call she instills the desires to pursue knowledge, to live virtuously, and to fear Yahweh. These desires motivate them to choose the straight path and to be vigilant in staying on that path throughout life.

Wisdom equips her followers with reasoning skills: prudence, discretion, shrewdness, sound judgment, and strategic planning (1:2-6; 8:12, 14). These skills empower them in multiple ways. Most importantly they provide insight into justice. That insight enables rulers to compose just decrees, develop programs that promote the community's well-being, and render fair judicial decisions, especially in ruling on difficult cases (8:15-16; compare 1 Kgs 3:16-28).

With these intellectual skills humans investigate the natural and the social orders. Their research has produced extensive knowledge about various aspects of nature and the social world. With this knowledge humans have made thousands of inventions, profoundly impacting their ways of living.

These intellectual skills enable humans to record their discoveries as well as their thoughts and imaginations in a wide variety of mediums, including literature, art, film, and drama (Prov 1:6). By studying these works humans acquire knowledge that leads to enrichment of their respective cultures and expands their horizons. A major result of this knowledge has been the development of highly complex nation-states that support huge populations.

Wisdom endows humans with various talents (compare Exod 31:2-11; 35:20—36:1). Those who develop a particular skill gain a means of supporting their families as well as making valuable contributions to their communities. They discover new ways of doing things as well as developing means or resources for overcoming obstacles and handicaps.

On another level Wisdom cultivates in her followers virtues: integrity (Prov 11:1, 3a; 16:11), humility (11:2b), kindness (11:16a, 17a), patience (14:29; 15:18), dependability (11:13b), and graciousness (16:24; compare 11:16a). Those who develop these virtues gain self-confidence and a strong sense of self-worth.

Wisdom encourages the development of social skills. Etiquette is stressed far more in Egyptian instructions than in Proverbs. Nevertheless, there are a few proverbs on proper conduct, such as exercising proper manners at a royal banquet and in working with people (23:1-3, 6-8, 29-35). The development of social skills makes the workplace and social gatherings more pleasant, enhancing the interchange of stories and ideas that promote genuine rapprochement.

Above all, Wisdom's presence with her followers leads them to the knowledge of God (2:5-6); knowledge stands for a deeply committed relationship with God based on trust. This knowledge of or communion with God inspires humans to live honorably. As they travel through life their lives are marked by deeply meaningful interactions with God. Those interactions transform their lives, conforming them to the image of God. In this process their orientation to life moves from the self as the center to God as the center. As a result their lives become a continual conversation with God.

Given the presence of evil forces in the world, Wisdom is vigilant in protecting her followers from dangers that they encounter from time to time. In particular, she develops in them hatred for all forms of evil as pride, deception, perversity, and violence (4:24; 6:16-19; 8:13). In addition, she diligently endeavors to deliver them from the schemes of the wicked (2:12-15) and the allure of the adulteress (2:16-19).

Nevertheless, acquiring wisdom is an arduous task for several reasons. Humans must be diligent in acquiring knowledge so that they have a basis for learning how to think incisively about complex issues. In order to cultivate virtues they must follow strict disciplines. These disciplines require self-denial and resistance to natural inclinations to engage in foolish pleasures (see 3:11-12). Thus, the pursuit of wisdom requires persistent effort throughout life. That effort is comparable to the determined efforts of treasure hunters in their search for precious metals regardless of the cost or the obstacles (2:1-5).

To encourage their sons (students) to persist in the pursuit, the sages exhort them to love Wisdom (4:6). Those who exalt and embrace her will find that she responds by loving and honoring them (4:8; 8:17a). The joy they experience from this dynamic relationship energizes them to stay the course and to overcome all obstacles as they grow in wisdom (e.g., 2:10-12; 3:13-18, 21-26; 8:34-36).

Wisdom, thus, is the coherence of all knowledge intellectual, moral, judicial, and spiritual. Acquiring wisdom yields supreme benefits: "long life, health, prosperity, honor, favor, happiness, and protection" (Fox 2000, 349). Clearly, "wisdom is a power" (Fox 1997, 619, 627) that Yahweh makes available to all who fear him.

2. Characteristics of Proverbial Sayings

Anthropologists have found that proverbs are common to all peoples (Nel 2002, 436). From antiquity peasants, living close to the soil, expressed patterns they experienced in nature and in daily life in witty, short sayings, for example, "He who sleeps during harvest is a disgraceful son" (10:5*b*). When clans organized into tribes and empires, humans at all levels of society contributed sayings to their people's collection of proverbs.

Since these sayings are composed spontaneously and transmitted orally, most are anonymous. Their style and value make them memorable. Children pick them up from hearing them in daily conversations. Thus, they function as conveyors of a culture's values and customs.

The English word "proverb" has a more restricted use than the Hebrew term *māšāl*, "be like, comparable," which is regularly translated "proverb." The English term stands for sayings that present a poignant insight about life. Many are brief: "Money talks" and "Practice makes perfect." By contrast, *māšāl* references sayings that focus on a similarity between two items (Beyse 1998, 67). This term is used for a wide range of genres: saying, maxim, aphorism, parable, oracle (Num 23:7, 18), allegory (Ezek 17:2; 24:3), and taunt song (Ezek 14:8). As a result Hebrew "proverbs" vary greatly in length.

When the term is used in reference to the Bible, most people think of the short sayings found in Prov 10—29. In these two-line proverbs, the second line responds to the first in a variety of ways. Usually it restates, contrasts, or advances the thought expressed in the first line (→ "Characteristics of Hebrew Poetry in Proverbs" in the Introduction). Some proverbs are longer as is the case in 22:17—24:34: three lines (22:29), four lines (23:17-18), six lines (23:19-21), and eleven lines (24:30-34).

Seldom is the situation that gave rise to a proverb preserved. Lacking that information, some proverbs are viewed as irrelevant or bland. Nevertheless, since the sayings mainly deal with basic human traits, patterns in nature, or issues of daily life, they continue to offer valuable insights for living more prudently and virtuously.

Proverbs cover the spectrum of life. Many characterize people, define boundaries, or advocate moral behavior. Some set forth priorities such as "Look before you leap." Others describe a way that is better even though that way appears to be counterintuitive to human inclination; for example, "A penny saved is a penny earned." Some proverbs present insights that may be applied differently in different settings. This is the case with the saying "A bird in hand is worth two in the bush." This proverb advises a fowler that it is better to keep the bird caught rather than risk losing it by trying to catch another bird. From another perspective, however, this saying encourages a person to resist the strong human inclination to be greedy.

In a collection of proverbs there are usually contradicting proverbs. The classic example in the book of Proverbs is 26:4-5:

Do not answer a fool according to his folly,
> or you yourself will be just like him.
Answer a fool according to his folly,
> or he will be wise in his own eyes.

The sages deliberately placed these two proverbs back to back. A key reason was to alert youths to the fact that proverbs, save for those prescribing moral behavior, are not applicable to every situation. In fact, there are times or situations that require an approach opposite to what a well-known saying advises. It is essential, then, to exercise keen discernment before taking a course of action based on a particular proverb. To use a proverb judiciously it is essential to have a clear grasp of both the proverb's teachings and the situation to which it may be applied. This requires using the intellectual skills wisdom provides.

The distress that the devout experience on encountering contradicting proverbs may be eased by awareness of two reasons that such contradiction among proverbs in a collection is inherent to the genre. First, a proverb never states a contingency. Nevertheless, contingencies are inherent to everything humans do. When faced with a contingency a person often has to alter or adjust the approach being taken. Second, the insight that a proverb gives is valid for specific situations or times, not for all occasions, due to the constantly changing flow of life, that is, the movement of the seasons and experiences, as between summer and winter, between times of sowing and times of harvesting (see the polarities of human experience listed in Eccl 3:2-8). That is, proverbs that are appropriate in a time of joy are not fitting in a time of sorrow. In light of this reality, the presence of opposing sayings in the book of Proverbs is solid evidence that the collection transcends time by dealing with basic issues of life realistically.

A brief illustration may help clarify this point as well as illustrate the value contrasting proverbs have in prompting deeper reflection on an issue. Deeper reflection is clearly the goal of the sages, for it leads to making better decisions. Thereby a person is growing in wisdom.

On receiving a job offer a person has to decide how to respond. While pondering the offer, one is guided by the saying "Nothing ventured nothing gained." That saying encourages a self-confident person to accept the new job, viewing it as a step in an ascending career. On further reflection, however, the saying "A bird in hand is worth two in the bush" comes to mind. This saying prompts one to be cautious about leaving a secure job for a new one about which little is known. More importantly this saying motivates that person to search diligently for information about the new job, especially in regard to its demands, risks, and opportunities. That search will bring to light important information about the new job, providing a better basis for making a prudent decision. While neither of these proverbs offers definitive guidance, they promote deeper reflection on the better course to take. This reflection leads to a more confident decision.

Another characteristic that is troubling to some is two sayings that have a line in common:

Ill-gotten treasures have no lasting value,
> but righteousness delivers from death. (10:2)

Wealth is worthless in the day of wrath,
    but righteousness delivers from death. (11:4)

The repetition is intentional. It is to spur deeper reflection on ways that the different settings impact the sense conveyed by the line that is repeated. In both examples righteousness is far more valuable than wealth. Certainly this is the case with ill-gotten wealth. The second proverb presents a specific example that supports this assertion: wealth, regardless of its source, has no value in the day of wrath. Wealth is completely discounted when weighed against the value of righteousness.

A key role of proverbs is to encourage the development of virtues. An instance of this principle is demonstrated in the saying that a merchant needs to use true weights in settling transactions (11:1; 16:11; 20:10, 23). Other proverbs promote devotion to God as expressed in the book's motto: "The fear of [Yahweh] is the beginning of wisdom" (9:10). A deep reverence for Yahweh encourages the pursuit of wisdom and by implication the pursuit of wisdom deepens one's devotion to Yahweh. That is why the book of Proverbs and other wisdom texts are an integral part of the Scriptures.

This view, however, is counter to much of current intellectualism that operates on the premise that faith is counter to knowledge. This view holds that people of faith are unable to discover unvarnished truths. But ancient wisdom, being "thoroughly religious" (Clifford 1999, 9), was based on the premise that faith enhances genuine learning. In working with proverbs it is important, then, to keep in mind that the ancient Israelites did not separate life into secular and religious. Thus, Israelite wisdom works from the perspective that people need to exercise both faith and reason to have a rich or blessed life.

Proverbs, thus, supplements the revelation given in the Law and the Prophets, providing guidance for living wisely. They provide guidance for dealing with both routine issues of life as well as the unexpected in ways that respect people and honor God. In other words, they promote a person's moral and spiritual health while traveling life's course. Moreover, they give counsel from a communal perspective. There is no rugged individualism in this collection of wisdom. Rather, these sayings provide counsel for having a long, "blessed" life within one's community, especially a community of those who fear God (3:13-18; 8:34-35).

3. Retribution

Retribution, a prominent theme in Proverbs, holds that virtuous acts are rewarded and wicked deeds are punished. The sages emphasized this doctrine in order that youths might see the connection between a deed and its outcome (Nel 1998, 115). It is often referenced by the saying "one reaps what one sows" (see Gal 6:7-8). This aphorism gives the doctrine the sense of inevitability. But strictly causal relationships are not common in wisdom sayings (Williams 1981, 18). That is, a proverb describes a common pattern in life but does not take into consideration factors that may alter an outcome. Outside of reaping what is planted, a farmer has to deal with multiple factors that affect a harvest, causing it to vary, sometimes widely, from year to year. This is due to several factors: the quality of the seed and the soil (see Matt 13:4-8), the amount and the timing of rainfall, daily temperatures, and pestilences.

Likewise, many factors impact the outcome of human acts. Three major factors are human freedom, impersonal natural forces, and God's involvement. As a result life experiences are "not a matter of mathematical certainty" (Murphy 1998, 267). Variations in outcomes are also integral to the way God has designed the created order. Because humans have to deal with these variables, they have opportunities to discover ways of being more resourceful.

The doctrine of retribution greatly influences the way many interpret their experiences and how they judge others. They honor those who excel at a task and earn a good income. Conversely, they look down on those who are poor and/or are beset by hardships or losses. People tend to think that the poor and those beset by troubles are being punished for incompetence or wrongdoing. Such uses of retribution, however, frequently lead to misjudgments. Job's story is the classic case of a person who was wrongly judged as a brazen sinner solely because he lost all his wealth and became very ill. His friends who came to console him became convinced that he was guilty of some terrible sin. Consequently, they exhorted Job to repent so that he might regain his health and wealth. Their advice, though, tempted him to take a course that would have undercut his integrity. Their strong belief in retribution blinded them from grasping Job's real situation and offering him sound counsel. In somewhat the same way, sensitive people endure great distress by interpreting a misfortune or a setback as God's punishment for their having done something wrong, though sadly they have no idea what that might be. Thus, a clearer understanding of this doctrine is essential to prevent agonizing misuses of this belief.

It needs to be remembered that a proverb describes a pattern in life rather than stating a "formal concept of causality" (Williams 1981, 19). That is, proverbs do not function as natural laws. The numerous "better than" proverbs clearly show that outcomes are often counter to what is expected. That there are situations in which results may be better is clear evidence that deeds do not hold within themselves precise consequences; for example, many proverbs state that wealth attends wisdom (3:16; 8:18). That such is not always the case is supported by several better-than proverbs; for example, "better the poor whose walk is blameless than the rich whose ways are perverse" (28:6; compare 15:16, 17; 16:8, 16; 17:1; 19:22; 22:1).

Nevertheless, despite the limitations of the doctrine of retribution, it describes general patterns in daily experience. Students who study hard excel over those who take their studies casually. Employees who are reliable, diligent, careful, and courteous advance over those who are habitually late, careless, argumentative, and rude. Likewise, a community of hardworking, responsible citizens is stable, secure, and prosperous.

Thus, it continues to be prudent to teach youths that working hard leads to good results. They also need to be taught that there are occasions when the upright experience setbacks, but these may not be a direct result of some action. Such setbacks or losses are caused by a variety of forces independent of the integrity of their actions. Sometimes they become victims of unscrupulous people. Other times they experience losses randomly, such as the sudden loss of a home during a fierce storm.

It is also essential to instruct youths about Yahweh's role in their lives. This is expressed in the proverb "In their hearts humans plan their course, but [Yahweh] establishes their steps" (16:9). Yahweh's involvement in affecting the outcome of a person's plans serves as additional evidence that the deed-consequence pattern is not without exception.

Realizing these inequities, there are proverbs that speak of God's intervention in human affairs to correct injustices. For example, the sages believed that God defends the poor and the unfortunate when they are exploited (22:22-23; 23:10-11; compare 17:5). Unfortunately, none of the sayings in Proverbs describe the ways God provides this help. However, there are accounts in Scripture of God's protecting the weak. A superb example is God's enabling the widow of Zarephath, who showed kindness to Elijah, to survive a harsh famine by marvelously providing for her a continuous source of flour and oil (1 Kgs 17:8-16).

A sound understanding of this doctrine encourages those who fear Yahweh to plan carefully, commit their plans to Yahweh, put the plans into action, and let Yahweh affect the outcome. Working together with Yahweh strengthens their relationship (16:1, 3, 9).

4. Speech

Words are very powerful. They possess the power of life and death. It is little wonder that numerous proverbs deal with speech (18:21; compare 10:19). Well-spoken words are "a pre-eminent" source of blessing (Brown 2004, 145). They are likened to eating delicious fruit (18:21b) or honey (16:24). They are also described as a tree of life (15:4a). In the same vein the teaching of the wise is considered "a fountain of life, turning a person from the snares of death" (13:14; compare 10:11a).

Genuine praise motivates people to excel. Children certainly need to receive praise frequently to become confident adults. An additional great benefit of praising another is that one humbles the self, thereby building integrity. Flattering words, however, work ruin (26:28b). They are destructive because the design of flattery is to manipulate another person (29:5). As a result it demeans that person. By contrast, a person who offers a rebuke becomes more highly favored than a flatterer (compare 28:23). Thus, a judicious rebuke is well received by a listening ear like a gift of gold jewelry (25:12).

Wisdom equips a person with the ability to speak astutely and skillfully. Thus, people savor a wise person's words. Their words may be trusted, for they are based on wisdom's values. Furthermore, truthful words endure (12:19a). People look to the wise for guidance, especially when facing difficult issues.

In general humans enjoy speaking. Nevertheless, it is prudent to avoid speaking excessively. That is an irritating trait of fools (18:6-7). Talking too much has inherent dangers: pouring out vain thoughts, misspeaking, and betraying confidence (11:13a; 20:19a). An undisciplined tongue carries the potential of damaging critical relationships (11:9a). Misspoken words sometimes lead to strife (18:6a) or even to a beating (18:6b). There are times when speaking foolishly puts a person's life in danger (18:7; 10:10b).

Some people have sharp tongues. Their words are likened to sword thrusts (12:18a) or a scorching fire (16:27b). Harsh words not only inflict sharp pain but may also crush a person's spirit (15:4b; compare 11:9a). Sharp words arouse such anger that conflict breaks out in a community (15:18a; 29:22a; 30:33). Likewise, the warped speech of the wicked has the potential of destroying a city (11:11b). No wonder the prudent are careful to hold their tongues (10:19b).

People enjoy listening to eloquent speakers. Insightful words nourish their thinking (10:21a; Brown 2004, 142). A skilled speaker is able to motivate people to face difficult issues and take on the task of improving their circumstances.

Those who have the ability of using words well keep themselves out of trouble (21:23). They are able to speak in a way that calms those who are angry (15:1a). Their skill at speaking brings them honor (12:14). The power of a gentle tongue is captured in the saying: "Through patience a ruler can be persuaded, and a gentle tongue can break a bone" (25:15).

Both Proverbs (4:23) and Jesus (Matt 15:11, 18-20) stress that a person's words, flowing from the inner mind, reveal a person's true character. By speaking at length a person discloses deep attitudes, feelings, and convictions. By listening carefully to what a person says, it is possible to discern the person's true feelings about issues.

Aware of the tongue's great power, the apostle James passionately exhorts believers to control their tongues (Jas 3:1-12). He warns the pious that failure to control their tongues means that they are self-deceived and their piety is worthless (Jas 1:26).

5. Valuing Marriage

Several proverbs applaud strong marriages: "[A man] who finds a wife . . . receives favor from [Yahweh]" (18:22; compare 19:14); "A wife of noble character is her husband's crown" (12:4a; compare 14:1a). Such a husband has full confidence in his wife and entrusts her with many household enterprises (compare 31:11-12, 27). Yahweh plays a vital role in a man's having the good fortune to marry a talented woman. In fact, Yahweh's role is more crucial than that of one's parents (19:14). Given the patriarchal setting of these sayings, an era when parents arranged marriages for their children, Proverbs stresses the importance of a family's seeking Yahweh's guidance in finding a vibrant wife for a son.

In making a strong marriage a husband needs to honor his wife. Foremost he must be faithful to her. Given the power of lust, there are three instructions on the dangers that result from connecting with another man's wife (5:1-14; 6:27-35; 7:6-27). These teachings are balanced by the instruction that encourages a husband to keep his marriage vibrant by passionately loving his wife (5:15-20).

The instruction in 5:1-14 seeks to make a husband realize that the ecstatic joy of an erotic affair that lasts for a brief time is not worth the loss of honor. He also needs to understand that an adulteress has little concern for his well-being. In fact, she does not value life itself. In addition, several harmful consequences are likely to follow a tryst. That man makes himself vulnerable to extortion from those who oversee the adulteress (vv 9-10). They will spend that man's wealth on partying and luxuries. He also exposes himself to contracting an illness that will afflict him harshly as he ages (v 11). Additionally, deep regrets at having spurned the guidance of his teachers will trouble him the rest of his life (vv 12-13).

A second instruction warns against satisfying deep-rooted lust by romancing a neighbor's wife (6:20-35). This warning is supported by a vivid description of the dreadful consequences such an indiscretion brings. The sage highlights the inevitability of severe consequences with the proverb "Can a man scoop fire into his lap without his clothes being burned?" (v 27). This rhetorical question emphasizes the great pain, both physical and social, the man will have to bear when the woman's husband takes revenge (vv 33-34). Any thought this man has of escaping such harm by offering her husband compensation is sheer folly. The reality is that an offended husband will not accept any compensation (v 35). Consequently, the adulterer will have to endure shame the rest of his life (v 33).

In the third instruction (ch 7) a sage teaches naive youths the tactics of an experienced adulteress so that they might escape her destructive allure. From a haunt and protected by the shadows of the early evening she looks for a person who likely will accept her enticement. Catching sight of a naive youth, she walks up to him and begins to caress him as she speaks softly into his ear. She tells him that she has offered sacrifices that morning, bringing to his attention that there is an abundance of delicious meat at her house. She goes on to describe the luxurious setting where they may spend the evening making love. She assures him that they will not be caught for her husband has gone on a long journey and will not return for a couple of weeks. Greatly excited, the ensnared youth follows her like a deer stepping into a noose, unaware that "her house is a highway to the grave" (v 27). Joining her will cost him his life.

Given the dangers of engaging in extramarital affairs, the sages include an instruction (5:15-23) that describes how to keep one's marriage vibrant. The husband needs to love his wife passionately, becoming intoxicated with her love. A wife's love will satisfy his libido, squelching any desire to get involved with another woman. He will have no fear of a beating or of coming under the control of others. To underscore this counsel the sage adds the warning that Yahweh is constantly vigilant, observing all that a person does (5:21).

The unsurpassable value of a strong marriage is highlighted in the portrait of the noble wife (31:10-31). Highly talented, she manages her household adeptly. She cares for her children and skillfully guides the servants in their tasks, including the production of a variety of goods that are sold at the market. The noble wife is also engaged in expanding the household's enterprises. Her work enables her husband to serve as a community leader. The community responds by honoring both of them highly.

Additional honor is accorded women by the portrait of Wisdom in chs 1—9. At the house she has built, she prepares a grand banquet, inviting youths to dine with her and learn wisdom (9:1-6). This picture underscores her vital role in equipping humans with intellectual and moral skills.

The honor conferred on both of these women in Proverbs eases its patriarchal perspective. Nonetheless, there are times when women have to read this book against themselves (McKinlay 1996, 99). Those who are able to do so will find many treasures in this volume of Israelite wisdom.

These instructions continue to have a vital role for those who follow Jesus. They applaud the pleasures of sex. In fact, they offer counsel that leads to finding the highest pleasure in this aspect of life. Their guidance rings true against the media's continual claim that the best sexual pleasure is found outside of marriage. That position is false. The truth is found in the teaching of Proverbs: engaging in uncommitted sexual relations leads to regrets, loss of vigor, exposing oneself to painful illness, and potentially being harmed by one whose honor has been deeply offended by such activities.

6. Wealth and Poverty

According to several proverbs health, wealth, and long life accompany wisdom (e.g., 3:13-18, 21-24). These benefits enabled a peasant to support a large family. These rewards, however, are never quantified. Psalm 90:10 states that a long life spanned seventy to eighty years. In antiquity a person needed good health to live past seventy. Wealth was measured in the size of one's flocks and the produce of the fields. Through hard work and the prudent use of resources a family developed a lineage over several generations (13:22a;

19:14*a*). The wealth, though, was not the copious wealth esteemed in present-day industrial nations.

Gaining wealth is never presented as the highest goal in Proverbs. Although in her self-description Woman Wisdom says that wealth and prosperity are with her (8:18), she adds that her gifts of counsel, sound judgment, and discretion are far better than gold or choice silver (8:12, 14, 19). The emphasis on gaining wealth resides in the need to counter the harsh conditions that attend poverty (10:15*b*; 15:15*a* [Heb.]; 19:4*b*, 7).

Several proverbs encourage people to be industrious by emphasizing ways that produce wealth: working diligently (14:23*a*; 28:19*a*), maintaining one's household (27:23-24), and trusting Yahweh (28:25*b*). Other proverbs scorn character traits that lead to poverty: sloth (10:4*a*; 12:24*b*), talking rather than working (14:23*b*), love of sleep (20:13*a*), indulging in expensive pleasures like wine and luxuries (21:17), chasing fantasies (28:19*b*), and stinginess (11:24*b*). There are other causes of poverty, such as encountering a misfortune or being victimized (13:23).

Nevertheless, the poor are not forgotten by Yahweh. They experience God's compassion in various ways. Some receive gifts from the upright who are motivated by sayings such as "Blessed is the one who is kind to the needy" (14:21*b*; compare 22:9) and "Those who give to the poor will lack nothing" (28:27*a*). Other sayings encourage generosity: "One person gives freely, yet gains even more" (11:24*a*; compare 11:25) and "Whoever is kind to the needy honors God" (14:31*b*; compare 19:17). Moreover, the upright who are poor find consolation in knowing that Yahweh is their Protector, who will take up their case against the powerful oppressor (22:22-23; 23:10-11).

Those who begin to acquire wealth need to avoid the temptation to become obsessed with wealth. That obsession produces bad character traits such as pride (30:9) or overconfidence (28:11*a*) that lead one to place trust in riches (11:28*a*) and to hoard (11:26*a*). Others are beset by debilitating fatigue (23:4*a*) and/or anxiety over the possibility of losing what they have acquired.

The best antidote to avoid coming to trust in one's wealth is generosity. Giving to the needy honors God, their Maker (14:31*b*). By referring to God as the Maker of the poor (14:31*a*), this saying communicates that the poor and the rich have equal standing in God's sight (22:2; compare 29:13). That is why mocking the poor or turning one's back on them is an expression of contempt for God (17:5*a*; 14:31*a*). That attitude carries a heavy consequence: "Whoever shuts their ears to the cry of the poor will also cry out and not be answered" (21:13).

Several proverbs seek to counter an avid desire for wealth by emphasizing values that far surpass being wealthy: fear of Yahweh (15:16), wisdom (16:16), righteousness (16:8*a*), solid reputation (22:1), "a small serving of vegetables with love" (15:17), "a dry crust with peace and quiet" (17:1), integrity (28:6), and truthfulness (21:6*b*).

Some proverbs speak of the wicked becoming wealthy through corrupt means such as deception (21:6; see 10:2*a*). Those who gain wealth by fraud destroy their spiritual well-being. Such wealth is often fleeting, a deadly snare, and a potential source of harm (21:6; 11:17*b*; see 23:4-5). Moreover, riches have no lasting value; they are "worthless in the day of wrath" (11:4*a*).

Aware of the dangers that attend becoming wealthy, King Agur petitions God to cleanse him of any self-deception (30:7-9). He prays never to become poor or rich. He supports this petition by stating that his primary desire is to have food sufficient for the day. Otherwise if he becomes wealthy, he may deny God. Or if he becomes poor, he may feel compelled to steal, and thereby dishonor God.

7. Jesus and Proverbs

a. Jesus the Sage

A study of Proverbs sheds light on Jesus' teaching and his identity. Jesus was well versed in proverbial wisdom, both popular and Israelite. In responding to a situation he sometimes quoted or devised a proverb; for example, he told a new disciple who wanted to delay following him so that he might bury his father: "Let the dead bury their own dead" (Matt 8:22). On other occasions Jesus used this form to stress a key principle; for example, "In the same way you judge others, you will be judged" (Matt 7:2*a*) and "All who draw the sword will die by the sword" (Matt 26:52*b*). Jesus employs a proverbial style several times in the Sermon on the Mount; for example, "If the salt loses its saltiness, how can it be made salty again?" and "A town built on a hill cannot be hidden" (Matt 5:13*b*, 14*b*; see 6:21-24, 27, 34; 7:1-2, 15-20).

In that sermon Jesus emphasized that humans have to choose one of two ways: the broad path leading to destruction or the narrow path leading to life (Matt 7:13-14). Jesus used "way" (Gk.) as a metaphor to tie into its use in Proverbs. The term "way" or "path" frequently occurs in Proverbs for one's lifestyle or the course one pursues in life (e.g., 4:11-12). Whereas Jesus differentiates the ways by their width, Proverbs uses light: the path of the righteous is well lit, but the way of the wicked lies in deep darkness (4:18-19).

Jesus began the Sermon on the Mount with a number of beatitudes (Matt 5:3-11). He was employing a form found in several OT texts (e.g., Pss 1:1; 32:1, 2; Prov 3:13; → sidebar "A Beatitude" in overview for 3:13-20). Jesus used this form of commendation on other occasions (see Matt 16:17; Luke 10:23; John 13:17).

These examples show that Jesus was identifying his teaching with Israelite wisdom. This is confirmed by the way he concluded the Sermon on the Mount (Matt 7:24-27). He compared those who put his words into practice to a wise person who built a house on rock. When that house was struck by a terrible storm, it stood firm. However, those who fail to follow his words are likened to a fool who built a house on the sand. During a heavy storm it came crashing down. This conclusion echoes the proverb "The house of the wicked will be destroyed, but the tent of the upright will flourish" (Prov 14:11). After choosing twelve disciples, he gave them spiritual authority. Before sending them out on their first mission, he gave them instructions on how they were to conduct themselves. Given that they would be like sheep among wolves, Jesus reinforced the nature of his instructions with the saying "Be as shrewd as snakes and as innocent as doves" (Matt 10:16b). That is, they were to be prudent in the ways they responded to complex situations they would encounter. Jesus wanted them to display the characteristics of Wisdom as recounted in Proverbs.

Furthermore, several sayings of Jesus echo a proverb; for example, "No one who puts a hand to the plow and looks back is fit for service in the kingdom of God" (Luke 9:62). This saying is in accord with the proverb "Let your eyes look straight ahead . . . do not turn to the right or the left" (Prov 4:25a, 27a).

Like the ancient sages Jesus emphasized the importance of controlling the body rather than letting a body member compel a person to depart from his teaching (Matt 5:28-30). In Prov 4:20-27 the sage teaches his son to manage his entire body—ears, eyes (sight), heart, body, mouth, lips, gaze (lit. eyelids), and feet. Jesus' counsel on settling a matter out of court is in accord with the proverb "What you have seen with your eyes do not bring hastily to court" (25:7b-8a).

Jesus is renowned for his picturesque parables. This genre is included in the Hebrew term translated proverb (māšāl), "be like," even though there is only one parable in Proverbs (24:30-34). In several parables Jesus incorporated a saying or an idea found in a proverb. Many in his audience would have noticed the connections; for example, Jesus' teaching against taking vengeance is heard in the proverbial saying "Do not say, 'I'll do to them as they have done to me; I'll pay them back for what they did'" (24:29; see Rom 12:19). Jesus, however, raised the standard higher: "In everything, do to others what you would have them do to you" (Matt 7:12a).

Those who heard Jesus telling the parable of the prodigal son (Luke 15:11-24) would have recalled the proverb: "A companion of prostitutes squanders his wealth" (Prov 29:3b). Hearers of the parable of the sower (Matt 13:1-9) would have thought of the proverb "The one who sows righteousness reaps a sure reward" (Prov 11:18b).

In the parable that advises selecting a seat at a wedding prudently (Luke 14:7-11), Jesus counsels against acting overconfident in public by foolishly taking a seat higher than one's standing. When asked to move, that person will be deeply embarrassed. This counsel is expressed by the proverb "Do not exalt yourself in the king's presence . . . it is better for him to say to you, 'Come up here,' than for him to humiliate you before his nobles" (Prov 25:6a, 7).

The description of Wisdom's preparing a banquet and sending messengers to the city center to invite passersby to the banquet she is preparing (9:1-2) adds a dimension to Jesus' parable of a king's sending his servants to the street corners to invite people to come to his son's wedding (Matt 22:1-10).

Clearly, Jesus was grounding his teachings in Israelite wisdom. These connections encourage his followers to ponder Israel's wisdom in order to gain a broader context for understanding his teachings. In doing so they will discover the ways his teachings are new and superior.

b. Jesus the Wisdom of God

Jesus identified himself as the Son of Man and the Son of God. To understand Jesus' nature and his relationship to God the leaders of the early church looked to the OT for additional insight. They drew key insights from the role of Wisdom in Proverbs, especially 8:22-31, and other Jewish wisdom texts. These insights found expression in the early hymns that exalt Jesus (John 1:1-18; 1 Cor 8:6; Col 1:15-17; Heb 1:1-4). These hymns assert his existence prior to creation, his relationship to creation, and his ministry on earth.

Both Wisdom and Jesus are described as present in the world, communicating God's will to humans. Both are the source of life. Both empower humans with wisdom (compare Waltke 2004, 130). Nevertheless, there are key differences between Wisdom and Jesus. Wisdom was begotten by God as the first of his works (Prov 8:22), but Jesus is eternal. Wisdom is a personification of an attribute of God, while Jesus is the full revelation of God. Wisdom was present observing God create (8:30-31). However, all things were created in or by Jesus. Paul writes, "In him all things were created: things in heaven and on earth, visible and invisible . . . all things have been created through him and for him. He is before all things, and in him all things hold together" (Col 1:16-17).

In the prologue to John's Gospel (John 1:1-14) Jesus is identified as the Word. Since "wisdom" and "word" are virtually interchangeable, both terms are employed as names for Jesus. As Word Jesus is identified with the way God created the universe as recounted in Gen 1. Just as God created by speaking, Jesus' word has creative power. Jesus healed many by speaking a word. As God gave life to the first humans, Jesus resurrected the dead by calling them back to life (Luke 7:11-16; John 11:38-44). On the first day God said, "'Let there be light,' and there was light" (Gen 1:3).

Jesus identifies himself with light, saying, "I am the light of the world" (John 8:12; 9:5). On the sixth day, God created humans in his own image. Since humans are in the image of God, Jesus, the Son of God, was able to take on human form and live on earth as the Son of Man in order "to give his life as a ransom" for humans (Mark 10:45).

In the OT there are several accounts of God's speaking to humans. Similarly, Jesus, the Word, delivers long speeches as found in John's Gospel (e.g., John 6:25-59; 10:7-18). This is especially the case in his describing his unique relationship with God, his Father (5:19-47; 8:34-59). As the Word, Jesus reveals that humans must be born anew, that is, born of the Spirit, to have eternal life (3:1-21). This underscores the creative role of the divine word.

Furthermore, God's great wisdom has been revealed in his providing redemption for humans through the life, death, and resurrection of Jesus (1 Cor 1:24).

In the early centuries of the Christian era, the church fathers ardently debated the nature of the relationship between God the Father and Jesus, his Son. The Arians held that Jesus was created. They based this position on the LXX's translating the Hebrew verb *qānâ*, "acquire, possess" (Prov 8:22), with *ktizō* "create": "God created me" (i.e., Wisdom). Based on the LXX's reading of this verse, the Arians taught that Jesus was a distinct creation of God. They believed that even though Jesus is the most exalted creature, he is neither equal with God nor eternal.

Several bishops, by contrast, held that Christ is truly God, having the same substance as the Father, and that he is eternal. To win acceptance of their position as the position of the church, they had to counter the Arians' interpretation of Prov 8:22. Athanasius accomplished this goal by applying the term "create" to the incarnation. He reasoned that the creation of wisdom described in Prov 8:22 was wisdom's image being formed in those being born (Waltke 2004, 127). Athanasius wrote: "Being Son, [Jesus] is inseparable from the Father, and there never was a 'when' when he did not exist. He always existed . . . since he is the image and radiance of the Father, he also possesses the Father's eternity" (Wright 2005, 66b).

Athanasius' view was adopted by the Council of Nicea as the orthodox position. In its present form it states as enlarged: "And in one Lord Jesus Christ . . . begotten, not made, being of one substance with the Father, by whom all things are made" (Schaff 1996, 22-28). The wording "begotten, not made" is based on taking the Hebrew term *qānâ* to mean "beget." Proverbs 8:22-31, therefore, has had a profound impact on the Christology that the church adopted.

COMMENTARY

I. A COLLECTION OF WISDOM INSTRUCTIONS: 1:1—9:18

A. Title, Prologue, and Motto (1:1-7)

IN TH TEXT

1. Title (1:1)

■ **1** The title identifies this book as a collection of **proverbs** (*mĕšālîm*). This Hebrew term includes several genres such as short sayings, instructions, admonitions, numerical sayings, parables, and characterizations. It is used even to describe a few prophetic oracles (e.g., Isa 14:4; Mic 2:4). This wisdom collection is associated with **Solomon son of David, king of Israel**, because of his fame in composing three thousand proverbs and a thousand and five songs (1 Kgs 4:29-34). He had this ability because God endowed him with extraordinary wisdom (1 Kgs 3:10-14). He became known as the father of Israelite wisdom. The inclusion of his name in the title validates this collection as the finest Israelite wisdom. However, it does not convey that **Solomon** composed all of the sayings and instructions preserved in this collection. This view is supported by the titles at the head of the six sections (1:1—9:18; 10:1—22:16; 22:17—24:34; 25:1—29:27; 30:1—31:9; 31:10-31). Two of these titles identify the material within a section as "the sayings of the wise" (22:17; 24:23*a*). Since "wise" is plural, i.e., *wise men,* "the sayings" in these sections come from various sages. The titles at 30:1 and 31:1 identify the material in those chapters as coming from non-Israelites.

47

That the sayings and instructions in Proverbs have diverse origins is not surprising, for wisdom is an international enterprise. Many of the proverbs in this book are likely Solomon's. It is also easy to imagine that his proverbs and songs inspired other Israelites to compose proverbs and aphorisms. Some of those have likely been included in this collection. Unfortunately, there are no criteria for identifying the author of a particular saying or instruction other than those in chs 30 and 31.

2. Prologue (1:2-6)

OVERVIEW

The prologue sets forth five objectives of this collection. Each objective is introduced by an infinitive (vv 2-6) except for the exhortation in v 5. These objectives employ eleven words for the domain of wisdom. Being abstract terms, their precise definition is not possible. Since these terms have overlapping senses, they are used interchangeably. This characteristic leads to wide variations in the way these wisdom terms are rendered in English translations.

The prologue identifies two audiences. The first is "*the* simple" (*pĕtāyîm*) or "the young" (*na'ar*). Youths, being naive, are unaware of the complexities of life. Oblivious of the dangers they will face in life, it is urgent that they gain wisdom.

The second audience is "the wise" or "the discerning," those who have acquired a solid foundation in wisdom (v 5). In identifying the wise as an audience, the sages were aware that learning is a lifelong process. Through advancing in "learning" the wise become more adept at strategizing, particularly in giving "guidance." At this point it is important to note that the encouragement to gain wisdom is extended to everyone. The book of Proverbs makes no distinction as to a person's social status, mental aptitude, or professional goals in its instructions.

■ **2** The primary goal of this collection is that youths *gain* [*yāda'*] **wisdom and instruction**. To realize this goal they must dedicate themselves to pursuing **wisdom** diligently under a sage's **instruction** (*mûsār*; → sidebar "Reference to Liturgical Practices in Proverbs" at 3:9-10). Sages employed a variety of *disciplines* (*mûsār*)—physical, social, and mental—to overcome the innate resistance in students to change. Those who respond to **instruction** come to understand the **words of insight** (*bînâ*) recorded by the sages. A variety of genres preserve the *insights* of the sages (see the list in v 6). Youths need to be trained in skills for interpreting these genres.

Wisdom stands for a sound, comprehensive view of life. In particular it refers to ideas, concepts, and paradigms that provide perception into human experience. By pondering a sage's **wisdom** a youth develops a worldview for understanding and coping with the multifaceted aspects of life. That worldview includes insight into the relationship of the temporal and the eternal. Since God brought forth Woman Wisdom as the first of his works (see 8:22-31), **wisdom** is a true guide for equipping humans to live in a meaningful, productive way. Humans have the ability of benefiting from **instruction** in **wisdom** because they have been made in God's image.

■ **3** *Youths* need *to receive* instruction in prudent behavior (*haśkēl*). By learning to conduct oneself *prudently* a person gains self-confidence. That one also inspires trust in associates and acquaintances.

Prudence equips a person with the ability to develop strategic plans for dealing with critical or difficult issues. This is very evident in David's life. Soon after joining Saul's army as a youth, he had great success in defeating the Philistine armies. He was skilled at developing shrewd strategies that led to a series of victories over stronger Philistine forces. His skill inspired his soldiers, giving them confidence to fight fiercely. Consequently, David is described as "successful" (*yaśkîl* [1 Sam 18:5, 14-15, 30]). Therefore, Saul made him commander of the army (1 Sam 18:5).

Prudence gives insight into judicial and moral matters, being conveyed by three terms: **right, just,** and **fair** (Prov 1:3; 2:9). **Right** (*ṣedeq*) stands for that which conforms to an accepted standard, a precept on behavior that is in accord with the Law. In regard to material objects it describes that which is exact, such as a proper weight. **Just** (*mišpāṭ*) describes strict conformity to a standard. It is used to describe an accurate judicial decision and upright behavior. These two terms often occur together. Together they describe justice as the solid foundation on which to build a vibrant community. These qualities establish harmony in a community and inspire confidence in the leadership. **Fair** (*mêšārîm*; lit. **straight**) stands for honest, unbiased treatment of others in all matters. A **fair** decision is rendered free from bias or emotions such as anger. Thus, leaders who are **fair** rule reasonably and equitably, promoting a community's sense of well-being.

■ **4** Instruction in wisdom gives *the* **simple** a depth of character by equipping them with special intellectual skills: *cunning*, **knowledge**, and **discretion**. These skills are inherently amoral (Fox 2000, 61). Consequently, in acquiring these skills a person needs prudence to use them circumspectly. *Cunning* or *craftiness* (*'ormâ*) is the ability of devising clever strategies for dealing with complex situations such as devising a plan to increase the yield of the crops or a scheme for escaping an enemy's trap. This skill enabled David to continually elude Saul's efforts to capture him (1 Sam 23:22). This trait enables youths to escape being enticed into evil behaviors (Prov 22:3; 27:12). It enables the simple to reflect critically on their behavior and discover how to become more astute (14:8, 15). However, those who are wicked use this trait to concoct complex, deceptive schemes that trap even those who diligently seek to avoid getting caught in a scam. The Gibeonites, occupants of Canaan whom the Israelites were to drive out, used this skill to devise "a ruse" that tricked Joshua into making a treaty that allowed them to remain in Canaan (Josh 9, esp. v 4; see Exod 21:14).

By learning under a sage, youths acquire **knowledge**. The deeper and wider a person's **knowledge** about a wide variety of topics, the better one is equipped to formulate accurate generalizations and to deal astutely with all kinds of issues.

Another skill youths need to develop is **discretion** or ***shrewdness*** (*mĕzimmâ*). On the positive side, **discretion** gives a youth the resourcefulness for devising astute strategies to address complex problems or troubling situations. It equips a person for making better decisions and more appropriate responses in dealing with all kinds of situations. Jesus praised this skill, "Be as shrewd as snakes and as innocent as doves" (Matt 10:16). Like any skill, this trait may be used for selfish ends. In such cases it is rendered "schemes" (Ps 10:2).

■ **5** The style of the prologue shifts to an exhortation, a frequent style in Section I. **The wise** and **the discerning** (*nābôn*), those who have already advanced in the acquisition of wisdom, are exhorted to **listen**, that is, focusing one's attention to hear exactly what is being said.

The discerning are exhorted to ***acquire*** **guidance**. That is, they are to strive to improve their skills at strategic planning and providing insightful counsel for addressing complex issues (Prov 20:18; 24:6).

■ **6** "The discerning" (v 5) are to enhance their skills at interpreting various literary genres, including **proverbs, parables** or ***satirical sayings*** (*mĕlîṣâ*), **the sayings and riddles of the wise**. While the sense of many **proverbs** is clear, others are obscure. That obscurity is often difficult to penetrate given that **proverbs** circulate free from a context. Certainly applying a proverb to a specific situation requires discernment. An interpretation must be done adeptly, for misapplying a proverb may lead to an unpleasant outcome. Interpreting **parables** requires special skills of discernment. Jesus' disciples recognized that many of his parables were opaque. Often they asked him to explain the meaning of a parable he had just given (e.g., Matt 13:36; Mark 4:10, 13, 34*b*; Luke 8:9-10; see John 16:25).

Another skill is needed for solving **riddles**, that is, various types of word games. The key to a riddle often centers on a pivotal word or a phrase being used with a meaning other than the sense that first comes to mind. Until that distinctive sense is discovered, the riddle remains an enigma. Samson was highly skilled at composing riddles (see Judg 14:10-18). His riddles appear simple, but the key to their interpretation is so well hidden that the Philistines could not solve them. Numerical sayings such as those found in Prov 30:15-31 may be a type of riddle. A group at a gathering was asked to name a certain number of items that fit a category. After naming them, they were challenged to come up with one more.

3. Motto (1:7)

OVERVIEW

The motto is tied structurally to the prologue in that its last two nouns, "wisdom and instruction," form an inclusio with their presence in the first line of the prologue. It functions as the key theme of this volume. Standing here and in 9:10 this proposition encircles the first section of instructions. It also forms an inclusio with the final description in the book, that of the noble wife. She is portrayed as embodying the many traits that wisdom bestows on one who fears Yahweh (31:30).

■ **7** The fear of *Yahweh* is the beginning of knowledge (9:10). *Fearing Yahweh* means that a person has a deep reverence for Yahweh as a result of acknowledging Yahweh as the Holy One, the Sovereign of all creation. Since humans are inherently unworthy in the presence of the holy, their innate response is **fear**. Out of fear the sinful cringe in God's presence. But those who are devoted to Yahweh express fear in worship or devotion. Fear leads them to always address God with deep respect. They never relate to him presumptuously as in overstepping his word or in exalting the self before him.

The fear of *Yahweh* is the beginning or the basis of knowledge or wisdom. Devotion to God serves as the foundation on which all knowledge is erected. Those who fear Yahweh conduct themselves according to his commandments, for this fear "motivates and informs right conduct" (Yoder 2009, 7). Furthermore, this fear equips them to deal with situations, especially those not addressed by the Law, in a way that is morally right. For example, in Egypt the Hebrew midwives spared newborn Israelite boys despite Pharaoh's order to kill them. It was their fear of Yahweh that gave them the courage to disobey Pharaoh's contemptible command (Exod 1:15-22).

Fools, however, **despise wisdom and instruction**. Their self-centered, stubborn attitude makes them defiant. That defiance leads to contempt for that which is virtuous and for those who strive to live righteously. This attitude keeps them from accepting the call of Woman Wisdom. Moreover, their desire for pleasure and ease makes them stubbornly resistant to enduring the disciplines necessary to learn from **instruction**. Until that attitude changes, there is little hope for any *fool* to gain **wisdom**.

FROM THE TEXT

The phrase **the fear of *Yahweh*** describes devout followers of Yahweh. Trusting him fully, they strive to live righteously. They seek to lead their communities in following the standards God has given his people.

The wise submit their intellectual prowess to their commitment to Yahweh, recognizing his claim on their lives (see Deut 10:12-13). When there are tensions between their fear and their knowledge, they live with that tension in anticipation of a time when their insight will give perspective on that tension. Their fear is truly genuine when it is exercised in the face of doubt.

Without **the fear of *Yahweh*** the acquisition of knowledge often leads to a sense of self-sufficiency and pride. As one becomes recognized for extraordinary insight into a subject, one is tempted to feel superior. Yielding to that temptation leads to placing the self at the center of one's world. However, **the fear of *Yahweh*** alerts one's conscience to the danger of that attitude and prods

51

one to overcome it. Thus, *fearing Yahweh* nurtures in a person attitudes that build relationships. Consequently, Godfearers inspire others to be diligent in the pursuit of wisdom.

In the NT the descriptor of the devout shifts to faith in Jesus. God accepts their faith as righteousness (Rom 3:21-26). While faith or belief occurs a few times in the OT (e.g., Gen 15:6; Exod 14:31; Hab 2:4), it becomes the key term for a person's relationship to God in the NT. This change has taken place because Jesus redefined the character of his disciples' relationship with God. They are no longer servants but friends (John 15:9-17). Now believers have the assurance of their new standing with God because Jesus represents them before God in the heavenly temple (Heb 9:11—10:25). Consequently, for NT believers faith is the foundation of wisdom.

B. Instructions in Wisdom (1:8—9:18)

I. Instruction: Invitation from Sinners and Woman Wisdom's Calling (1:8-33)

OVERVIEW

This instruction has three parts: exhortation to listen (vv 8-9), counsel to reject the invitation of sinners to join their gang (vv 10-19), and counsel not to delay in accepting the call of Woman Wisdom (vv 20-33).

The sage addresses this instruction to a son or an apprentice, a person who is naive in regard to the intricate ways of folly and wisdom. He is alerting the son to the strong appeals that he will receive for his allegiance from sinners and from Woman Wisdom. He begins with a detailed description of the enticements sinners will offer, encouraging him to join their gang. The sage's goal is to embolden the son so that he will reject their appeals. The other call the son will receive is from Woman Wisdom. In this case the sage's goal is to motivate the son to overcome any hesitancy in accepting her call.

a. Introduction (1:8-9)

■ **8-9** The sage or parent opens by exhorting *the* **son** or the apprentice to **listen . . . to your father's instruction and . . . your mother's teaching** (*tôrô*). **Teaching** has a wide range of meanings from a very general reference as here to a specific body of authoritative material like the Pentateuch. That restricted meaning probably developed in the Second Temple era. It is possible that at some stage in Israel's history teaching came to stand for a collection of wisdom sayings like the Book of Proverbs.

Reference to *the* **mother's teaching** indicates that her instruction was highly regarded in wisdom circles. This is supported by the fact that **mother** parallels **father** seven times in Proverbs (4:3; 6:20; 10:1; 15:20; 23:22; 30:17; see 31:1). These references indicate that both parents played a significant role in raising their children to pursue wisdom. Also they suggest that the original setting for training a youth, either a son or an apprentice, was the home.

The son is to highly prize their **teachings**. He is to let them adorn his **head** like **a garland** or wear them about his **neck** like **a chain**. The sage is speaking metaphorically, drawing on the custom of high officials wearing clothing and jewelry that symbolized their position (see Gen 41:42; Dan 5:16). It is very possible that youths in training wore some kind of symbol that reminded them of their status and their parents' teaching.

My Son in Proverbs

A parent's or a sage's addressing an instruction to *a* **son** is found in the earliest wisdom instructions, for example, Egyptian Instruction of Ptahhotep (line 50, *AEL*, 1:63) and Amenemhet (1:1). In the Egyptian Old Kingdom high government officials, trained as scribes, composed instructions for training a son to succeed in the governmental bureaucracy. As the central government grew, it probably established schools for training scribes to serve throughout the bureaucracy. Even though the majority of students in these schools were males, **my son** is to be taken as gender and status inclusive (Murphy 1998, 12). The wisdom tradition recognized the essential role of women in teaching youths. While the instruction of women took place in the home, it is possible that some women served as teachers and advisers beyond the home in light of the references to wise women in ancient texts (2 Sam 20:16; Prov 14:1). In order to teach, these women certainly had been taught. This claim is based on the fundamental axiom that to teach, a person needs to have had formal training. The reference to the Queen of Sheba's coming to test Solomon's skill at wisdom is instructive (1 Kgs 10:1-10). Having such an interest in conversing with a person noted for his wisdom suggests that she had been highly trained in wisdom.

My son also functions as a literary marker in Section 1 of Proverbs. Frequently it identifies the beginning of an instruction (Prov 1:8, 10; 2:1; 3:1; 5:1; 6:1; 7:1; also **sons** in 4:1; 5:7; 7:24; 8:32). Within an instruction it marks a subsection (1:15; 3:11, 21; 4:10, 20; 6:3, 20). Once it stands after a digression to signal a return to the main theme (5:20; Whybray 1994a, 39). The frequent occurrence of **my son** in section 1 is solid evidence that these instructions were assembled to train youths for serving as officials throughout the government and religious centers.

b. Counsel to Reject the Call of Sinners (1:10-19)

OVERVIEW

The sage alerts the son to the enticing appeal sinners will use to sway him to join them. They will emphasize the great opportunities he will have: (1) exerting power over others (vv 11-12), (2) even exercising as much power as the grave or Sheol (v 12), (3) gaining wealth quickly and with little effort (v 13), (4) sharing fully in the loot (v 14), (5) shedding someone's blood (v 11), and (6) enjoying camaraderie in dividing up valuable items taken as spoils (v 14). Against this background the sage pleads with the son to reject their invitation (v 15). He supports the plea by describing in detail the cruel ways that a gang treats people. He also points out the terrible fate that will befall him if he joins up with them (vv 16-19).

This unit is closely knit by the repetition of several terms: "go"/"come" (*hālak* [vv 11*a*, 15*a*]), "blood" (*dām* [vv 11*b*, 16*b*]), "lie in wait" (*ṣāpan* [vv 11*b*, 18*b*]), *for no reason*/"useless" (*ḥinnām* [vv 11*b*, 17*a*]).

IN THE TEXT

■ **10** To make sure of the student's attention the teacher again addresses him directly: **my son**. He enjoins him **not *to* give in to** the efforts of ***sinners*** (i.e., gang members) to draw him into joining their gang. The teacher is aware that a youth may be prone to accept their offer out of curiosity. They want to experience how sinners live. To counter this thought the sage seeks to make the youth aware that sinners will not easily let him leave the gang. They do not want anyone who knows their whereabouts and plans outside of their control. Clearly, the sage is motivating the son to exercise caution in yielding to their call. If *the* son reflects on the sage's counsel, he is likely to heed the admonition: **do not give in to them**.

■ **11-12** The teacher apprises the son of specific incentives sinners will use to lure a person to join them. They offer the exciting opportunity of ***lying* in wait** to shed ***an* innocent *person's*** blood ***wantonly*** (*ḥinnām*). That is, he will be able to participate in a dastardly deed just for the thrill of flaunting his power. Committing such a crime will give him a sense of invincible power. He will boast of having power like the fiends of the grave, those who transport souls **to the pit**, the abode of the dead (see Job 18:11-14). But such arrogant boasting reveals degraded morals.

■ **13-14** Sinners will add the enticement of ***sharing*** in whatever valuables they take from their victims. With little chance of a youth's having a way to earn much money, this offer is very enticing. They make it even more enticing by adding that he will receive from their take **valuable things** to **fill** his ***house***. For the first time in his life he will be able to take pride in his house. An even greater appeal is the opportunity of ***sharing*** the loot (lit. ***one purse***). When the **loot** is divided up, no preference will be shown (Whybray 1994a, 40). A youth gets excited at the chance of being on par with members of the gang. The sage quickly adds that for him to share in the spoil he has to **cast *his lot* with *them***. This idiom means that he must make the gang his family. It also means that there will be no easy exit from the gang. Moreover, he will be placing himself in jeopardy of being subject to harsh penalties society inflicts on gang members for violent deeds.

■ **15-16** To get the youth to focus his attention, the sage addresses him again as **my son**. He sets before him two prohibitions: **do not go along with them; do not set foot on their paths**. The son must firmly resist the powerful draw of these enticements. He must not even consider taking one step in their direction.

Appealing to the youth's morals, the sage points out that **the feet** of these sinners **rush into evil**, even **to shed blood**. By mentioning **the shedding of blood** the sage is seeking to get the youth to realize that these sinners commit heinous crimes. They act impulsively. Spurred on by malicious emotions, they commit very cruel acts.

■ **17-18** Using an analogy the sage seeks to impress on the youth the utter folly of connecting with sinners. A fowler knows that it is **useless to spread a net** in full view of *birds* he wishes to catch. *Birds* are sufficiently aware to avoid jumping about on a net placed in front of them. But that is not the case with gang members. Their bragging is similar to a fowler's spreading a net before what he hopes to capture. As a result of their boasting, they take bold risks. They become more careless in their daring exploits. As a result, their behavior alerts observant citizens that they are about to make a heist. Therefore, these citizens set a trap to capture them in the act of committing a crime. Thus, their bragging puts them in jeopardy of shedding their own **blood**. These sinners *are ambushing* themselves (see Ps 35:4-8). The sage is basing this argument on the principle of retribution, namely that those who scheme to harm others wantonly will suffer greater harm than they planned to inflict.

■ **19** The teacher concludes this topic by describing the sinners' demise. With this picture he is making an earnest effort to persuade the son not to yield to their invitation.

The end of all who grasp greedily for gain is forfeiture of their own lives. They need to be aware that **ill-gotten gain . . . takes away the life of those who get it**. The sage is making the son aware of the high price that comes with keeping company with a band of renegades. It is likely he will forfeit his own life. That price is far too steep for a youth to give any consideration to their invitation.

c. The Urgency of Accepting the Call of Woman Wisdom (1:20-33)

OVERVIEW

Woman Wisdom, pictured as walking throughout the city, calls out to the simple (vv 20-21). She urges them to cease delaying their acceptance of her invitation (vv 22-23). To motivate them to change course she depicts the shameful consequences they will bear for having rejected her call (vv 24-27). She goes on to warn them that if they call out to her later, she will not answer because they have refused to fear Yahweh (vv 28-29). Their refusal will bring on them serious consequences (vv 30-31). She concludes by emphasizing the vastly different outcomes that attend rejecting or accepting her call (vv 32-33). Astutely she states the benefits in the last line.

■ **20-22** *Woman Wisdom* walks through the city *calling out* to everyone. Her going throughout the city is accented by four terms: **the open, the public square**, that is, places where people congregate to converse, *the head of noisy streets*, and **the city gate**. She directs her call to *the* **simple** (*pĕtāyîm*), **scoffers** (*lēṣîm*), and **fools** (*kĕsîlîm*). It is remarkable that **Woman Wisdom** also directs her call to stubborn **fools**, for they are viewed as incorrigible in wisdom texts. Possibly she still holds out some hope that they will respond to her invitation.

It is noteworthy that *Woman Wisdom* searches for followers rather than merely setting up a booth in the marketplace where people may come by and talk to her. Her approach corresponds to many scriptural descriptions of God's reaching out to humans (Deut 7:7-8). This is seen in Jesus' saying, "[I] came to seek and to save the lost" (Luke 19:10). In fact, Jesus personally called those who became his closest disciples. This picture of God's calling out heartens all who hope to find wisdom.

To those within hearing *Woman Wisdom* poses two probing questions. Of *the* **simple** she asks, **How long will you . . . love your simple ways?** Of *scoffers* she inquires, **How long will** you **delight in** *scoffing*? **How long** brings to their attention her distress at their having failed to respond to her call. Forthrightly she declares that the reason they have not accepted her call is because they *take* **delight in** folly and **hate knowledge**. It is a marvel that humans continually crave that which is distorted and unfulfilling over that which is good and wise. Her addressing *hardened* **fools** (*kĕsîlîm*) warns *the* **simple** as to the kind of persons they will become if they persist in ignoring her call (Waltke 2004, 203).

■ **23** At this point Woman Wisdom forcefully implores them to change direction: *turn on the basis of* my **rebuke**. They must *turn* from the folly they delight in and *turn* to accept her **rebuke**. By describing her call as *a* **rebuke** she underscores the necessity of their making a radical change. That change will be an enlightening experience. It will cause them to adopt a completely different way of viewing the world order (see Van Leeuwen 1990, 114).

Woman Wisdom promises to enable them to make such a radical turn. She **will pour out** *her* **thoughts** (lit. *spirit* [*rûah*]) on them. **Pour out** describes the gushing of water from a spring (see Isa 44:3). This imagery means that she will generously give her *spirit*. This picture is similar to the description of the outpouring of God's Spirit at Pentecost (Acts 2:17, 18). Her *spirit* will open their minds to grasp fully the meaning of her *words* or **teachings**. Her *spirit* will create in them attitudes, values, and desires that are like hers. With this promise Woman Wisdom reveals that she will enable those who follow her to overcome their craving for folly and empower them to pursue wisdom. Her *spirit* will give them a depth of understanding that comes only through God's presence in a person's life.

■ **24-27** The attitude of these fools reveals that they are *refusing* **to listen when** she *calls* and to *pay* **attention when** she *stretches* **out** *her* **hand**, a gesture that signals that she welcomes them to join her. In fact, they **disregard** her **advice and do not accept** her **rebuke**. Therefore, Woman Wisdom seeks to change their stubborn attitude by calling to their attention that they are at risk of being *overtaken* by **disaster** and **calamity**. The certainty of punishment is underscored by these two terms standing in a chiastic pattern: **disaster:calamity::**

calamity:disaster (vv 26-27). These terms stand for natural catastrophes: a *powerful* storm like a tornado and **a whirlwind**. Any who are caught in such storms suffer great losses and possibly personal injuries. If they continue to reject her call, they set their own fate.

When Woman Wisdom sees them facing **disaster**, she will rejoice triumphantly. Because they have mocked her, she **will mock** them **when calamity overtakes** them. Her taunting will add to their misery. In antiquity taunting was a common way of heaping shame on the arrogant who were finally getting their comeuppance. From the perspective of retribution, shame is the appropriate punishment for pride, especially for those who pride themselves in the pursuit of folly. By underscoring their shame, Woman Wisdom hopes to alert the simple to the critical importance of responding to her call without further delay. She earnestly desires to keep them from such an ill-fate.

Mocking as a Form of Punishment

Woman Wisdom's response seems cold and uncivil to a contemporary audience. Nevertheless, she is justly venting her fury caused by their continued rejection of her invitation. It is important to remember that mocking was and remains a common practice in many cultures. References to mocking are attested in various scriptures. In the Song of Moses, which recounts Israel's victory at the Red Sea, the singers taunt the fallen Egyptians (Exod 15:9-10). Mocking is also heard in the Song of Deborah. The poet mocks Sisera's mother by picturing her as looking out a window watching anxiously for her son's return. Unaware that he has been killed in battle, she imagines that he has been delayed in returning solely because he is enjoying the spoils of the battle (Judg 5:28-30; see Isa 37:22-25). In some psalms God's sovereign power is exalted by describing him as mocking Israel's foes (Pss 2:4-5; 37:13; see Ps 52:6-7 [8-9 HB]).

Taunting is still present in a variety of ways in Western cultures. E.g., when a prize fighter defeats a vaunted foe, he boasts of having decimated his opponent. Here Woman Wisdom mocks fools for snubbing her. She is revealing to them that their brazen rejection of her offer to become wise warrants their present shame.

■ **28** Woman Wisdom alerts these fools that they will not find any way of escaping punishment. When misfortune strikes, **they will call *out* to her**, but she **will not answer.** Even if they *search diligently* for *her*, they **will not find *her.*** The opportunity for their entering into alliance with Woman Wisdom has passed. In the Law Yahweh states that he will be found by those who seek him (Deut 4:29). This promise, however, does not mean that God may be found at any time a person chooses to seek him (see Hos 5:6; Amos 8:12).

■ **29-31** Their inability to find Woman Wisdom is grounded in their *hating* **knowledge** as expressed in their **not *choosing* to fear Yahweh.** She brings again to their attention that instead of *accepting* her **advice** they *have* spurned *her* **rebuke** (see Prov 1:25). Thereby Woman Wisdom makes it very clear that their

57

punishment resides in their own decision. They would not respond even to the urgent note in *her* rebuke. They judged her call to be too demanding.

Woman Wisdom makes it clear that they have brought this ill-fate on themselves with an analogy from nature. As a result of rejecting her advice **they will eat the fruit** produced by **their ways** and **their schemes** (*mô'ăṣôt*). They have exercised lordship over their own lives rather than submit to Wisdom's lordship.

■ **32** Woman Wisdom concludes by describing the two opposing fates that all humans face. (1) **The waywardness of the simple will kill them**. Waywardness (*mĕšûbâ*) stands for a disposition of contrariness or deviance. Fox (2000, 103) describes it as "the tendency to turn away . . . from right behavior." **The complacency** or indecisiveness **of fools** [*kĕsîlîm*] **will destroy them**. Those who keep putting off making the decision to pursue wisdom drift deeper and deeper into foolish practices. *Hardened* **fools** indulge in luxuries afforded by their self-centered, unjust practices. Their enjoying these indulgences makes them complacent. That complacency ends up destroying them.

■ **33** *Woman Wisdom* concludes on a high note. (2) She declares that those who **listen** to **her** [i.e., *hear* and thus heed her call] **will live in safety**. They are secure because she will construct a wall of protection about them (see Job 1:10). They will have opportunities to enjoy life without being tormented by *the dread* (*paḥad*) of suffering a tragic loss like that which awaits fools (Prov 1:26-27).

The Hebrew word for *dread* or **fear** (*paḥad* [v 33*b*]) is a different Hebrew word than the one used in the phrase **the fear of Yahweh** (*yir'at yhwh*). This difference needs to be noted given that these two terms, translated the same in the NIV, stand at the head (v 7) and at the base (v 33) of this chapter. Proper fear (*yir'â*), that is, reverence of God produces a spiritual confidence that enables a person to grow in wisdom. But *dread* (*paḥad*) is debilitating anxiety at being overcome by a catastrophe. It can cause a person deep depression on realizing that one must face the hard consequences of life alone. That is, these two types of fear are at the opposite ends of a spectrum: devotion to God in contrast to ominous fright.

FROM THE TEXT

Every youth is faced with deciding on which life path to take. The choice is critical. It often determines one's course throughout life. That is the reason that the sage begins the instructions in Prov 1—9 by describing in detail the two major options before youths. One is an invitation to join a gang. The other is to accept the call of Woman Wisdom. The sage warns of the dangers that attend joining a gang. Similarly, Woman Wisdom gives a stern warning by describing the ill consequences that befall those who delay too long in accepting her call.

The sage's guidance is very significant for contemporary youths. Today many of them are sorely distressed by feelings of loneliness, insignificance, and inadequacy. These feelings make them prone to accept the opportunity of becoming a gang member. This is especially true for those who have never received recognition for a special talent or who have never been encouraged to consider their potential for achieving. The many benefits that attend joining a gang are very attractive to them. They will gain a sense of belonging. They get to engage in exciting activities. Then they will have something to brag about. Also they share in a common purse. This will give them access to more money than ever imagined. However, they will develop a lifestyle that will prevent them from becoming honorable citizens. But, given these enticements, a youth is not likely to give much consideration to the negative impact on one's moral character that comes from belonging to a gang. Neither does a youth consider being culpable for the crimes the gang commits.

Other youths, especially those from the middle and upper classes, will be encouraged to pursue advanced education in order that they may find employment at a good-paying job. Nevertheless, along that path they too will be enticed by the call of Woman Folly. She will seek to convince them that since they are special, they have many entitlements. They will come to believe that they are entitled to receive good grades regardless of how hard they study. When it is time to join the work force, they will feel entitled to a high salary, even if they are deficient at reading, writing, and mathematics. Folly has persuaded them that their inherent rights trump their achievements.

As a result of the sense of entitlement, they show little respect to those in authority. They are not inclined to follow directions. Convinced that the world owes them, they are confident that no one can deny them. However, orienting one's life according to this perspective is as foolish as joining a gang.

Youths are offered another choice. Woman Wisdom goes about calling out to all regardless of class, nationality, race, or gender. She invites all to accompany her on the path of understanding. Those who take this path must make a firm commitment to the pursuit of wisdom. That commitment includes submitting to the disciplines and rebukes that accompany Wisdom's instructions.

Those who travel the path of wisdom will gain intellectual acumen and acquire virtues. Their achievement is guaranteed because Wisdom endows them with her spirit. Spending time with her makes them competent, reliable, and conscientious. Those who develop these qualities will be sought after by employers. They will receive a good starting wage. Over time they will increase in competence at their task or profession. Consequently, they will earn sufficient income to support a vibrant family that fears Yahweh.

2. Instruction: Wisdom Gives Understanding and Protection (2:1-22)

BEHIND THE TEXT

This instruction serves as an index to key topics discussed in the instructions found in Section I (Murphy 1998, 14). The primary thesis, the pursuit of wisdom leads to a close relationship with Yahweh (2:1-11), is developed in 3:1-26; 4:1-9; 8:1-36; 9:1-6. In ch 2 the sage emphasizes that a youth needs to pursue wisdom diligently as the path taken in life. This theme is explored in 4:10-27. The emphasis on Wisdom's protecting the upright from the lure of a wayward woman (2:16-19) is a recurring theme (5:1-14; 6:20-35; 7:1-23; 9:13-18). These connections between ch 2 and a large amount of the material in Section I indicate its author either structured or at least influenced the ordering of the instructions in Prov 1—9.

OVERVIEW

This instruction consists of two main sections, impetus to pursue wisdom (2:1-11) and wisdom's protecting the upright from wicked men and the wayward woman (vv 12-19), plus a conclusion that motivates the pursuit of wisdom (vv 20-22).

In structuring this instruction, the sage was influenced by the Hebrew alphabet. The twenty-two verses correspond to the number of letters in that alphabet. The first word of the three units in the first section begins with the letter aleph, the first letter of that alphabet. The three units in the second section are headed by a lamed, the letter that heads the second half of that alphabet.

This instruction is tightly knit together by the recurrence of several terms from four semantic domains: wisdom, path, justice, and moral identity. Seven words belonging to the domain of wisdom are used: "insight" (*bînâ* [v 3a]), "understand" (*bîn* [vv 5a, 9a]), "understanding" (*tĕbûnâ* [vv 2b, 3b, 6b, 11b]), "wisdom" (*hākām* [vv 2a, 6a, 10a]), "ingenuity" or "success" (*tûšiyyâ* [v 7a]), "knowledge" (*da'at* [vv 5b, 6b, 10b]), and "discretion" (*mĕzimmâ* [v 11a]). This set of words is dominant in the first section. Three words from the domain of path occur twelve times: "course" (*'orḥôt* [vv 8a, 13a, 15a, 19b, 20b]), "path" (*ma'gāl* [vv 9b, 15b ("ways"), 18b]), and "way" (*derek* [vv 8b, 12a, 13b, 20a]). These words mostly occur in the second section. Five words from the domain of justice occur throughout: "just" (*mišpāṭ* [v 9a]), "right" (*ṣedeq* [v 9a]), "fair" (*mêšārîm* [v 9b]), "straight" (*yĕšārîm* [v 13a]), and "good" (*ṭôb* [v 9b]). In the first and third sections there are eleven words that identify a person morally. Seven are used for the righteous: "upright" (*yāšār* [vv 7a and 21a]), "blameless" (*hôlĕkê tōm* [v 7b]; *tĕmîmîm* [v 21b]), "righteous" (*ṣaddîqîm* [v 20b]), "faithful ones" (*ḥăsîdîm* [v 8b]), "the just" (*mišpaṭ* [v 8a]), and "the good" (*ṭôbîm* [v 20a]). Conversely, four terms are employed for the wicked: "wicked men" (*ra'* [v 12a]), "the wicked" (*rĕšā'îm* [v 22a]), the "devious" (*nĕlôzîm* [v 15b]), and "the unfaithful" (*bôgĕdîm* [v 22b]). In addition, four terms are used six times either for wicked deeds or as descriptors of such deeds: "evil" (*ra'* [v 14]), "perverse" (*tahpûkôt* [vv 12b, 14b]), "dark" (*ḥōšek* [v 13b]), and "crooked" (*'iqqēš* [v 15a]). Terms for the upright occur primarily in the first and third sections while those for wicked/wickedness are concentrated in the second section.

The sage places great emphasis on God's protecting people committed to the pursuit of wisdom. He concludes the first section by asserting that the skills of discretion and understanding given by Wisdom will provide protection (v 11). By structuring the verbs in vv 8 and 11 in a chiastic pattern the sage underscores this affirmation: guards:protects (v 8)::will protect:will guard (v 11). The wording in v 11 prepares for the development of this theme in the second section. Wisdom saves the Godfearer from wicked men (vv 12-15) and the adulterous woman (vv 16-19). The result is reinforced in the conclusion (vv 20-22).

IN THE TEXT

a. Exhortation to Earnestly Seek Wisdom (2:1-11)

OVERVIEW

The sage challenges the son to pursue wisdom with intense determination (vv 1-4). This challenge is motivated by the two benefits that result from that pursuit: understanding the fear of Yahweh (vv 5-8) and understanding justice (vv 9-11). The first benefit is assured because Yahweh gives wisdom (vv 6-7) and protects the way of the faithful (v 8). The second benefit is realized as a result of Wisdom entering the son's heart (v 10*a*), producing skills that guard the son (v 11*b*).

■ **1-4** The sage addresses this instruction to *his* son (see 1:10). In place of the usual command to listen, the sage employs three conditional sentences (vv 1-2, 3, 4). With this style he impresses on the student the necessity of *accepting his words*, identified as **commands** (*miṣwôt*). This word occurs frequently in the Torah for God's commandments. Thus, the sage is identifying these wisdom instructions as authoritative. From another perspective the sage is informing *the* son that he will not gain **wisdom** by reason of his position, lineage, or place of birth. Regardless of his lineage he must accept the sage's instructions and store them in his memory.

The sage identifies three steps *the* son needs to take to gain **wisdom**. (1) He has to *open his* ear to wisdom. "Opening one's ear" is a Hebraic idiom for listening. Since the essential means of instruction in ancient Israel was oral, *the* ear was a key organ in learning. That is why the psalmist says, *You [God] have dug out both ears for me* (40:6 [7 HB]). He is expressing gratefulness to God for equipping him with good hearing so that he may receive and understand all that God is teaching him.

(2) *The* son must *apply* his **heart** (see 4:21) or *mind* to understanding. That means he is to ponder the sage's teachings until he has grasped their meaning. **Understanding** them will guide him in ordering his life according to the sage's teachings. (3) He must **call out** *to* **insight and . . . understanding.** *Calling* out means that he diligently seeks to acquire these aspects of **wisdom**.

The sage amplifies the last exhortation by directing *the* son to **search for** wisdom as ardently as prospectors search **for silver** and **hidden treasure**.

Miners focus all their energies in their search for precious minerals. A vivid description of their efforts is found in Job 28:1-11. That poem describes workers digging shafts deep into the earth to locate these treasures. At times they hang from ropes, swaying dangerously back and forth, as they descend deep into the earth to reach a treasure. Their drive to find these valuable metals and stones overcomes their fear of danger. Also legendary are accounts of the hardships borne by modern prospectors, for example, those who participated in the California Gold Rush of 1848-55. Anyone who desires **wisdom** needs to have a drive comparable to that of these miners.

■ **5-8** By *searching* diligently for **wisdom** *the son* **will understand the fear of Yahweh** and **find the knowledge of God** (see Prov 1:7). That is, he will gain key insights about the nature of his relationship with Yahweh. As his devotion to God increases he will develop a dynamic relationship with God, as conveyed by the phrase **the knowledge of God**.

Fear of Yahweh refers to a person's devotion to God. Out of reverence a person places Yahweh at the center of one's affections. **Knowledge of God** stands for being in a committed relationship with God. That relationship is characterized by loyalty. In this phrase **knowledge** does not refer to information. Rather, it stands for the strong bond between God and those who fear him. It emphasizes the communion between them. From this communion Godfearers develop a sterling character. This is seen in the four descriptors of those who fear God at the end of vv 7-8: **the upright**, *the* **blameless**, **the just**, and God's **faithful ones** (*ḥăsîdîm*). The last epithet stands for loyal members of the covenant.

Yahweh honors the faithful by *giving* **wisdom**. He also shares **knowledge** and **understanding** or *good sense* with them. By having fellowship with God those who fear him gain insights into God's character and values.

God equips the faithful with intellectual skills listed in the prologue (1:2-6). Specifically, God *stores* for them *ingenuity* or *resourcefulness* (*tûšiyyâ* [v 7]; see "*tûšiyyâ*" in Gertz 2006, *TDOT* 15:647-49). Fox (2000, 114) renders this term *mental dexterity*. It is the ability to address complex issues or situations insightfully and honorably. Thus, God provides this ability especially when those who know him are facing difficult situations, huge obstacles, or harsh setbacks. This skill serves as **a shield** for *the* **blameless** and **the just** (vv 7-8), *protecting* their **way**. It enables them to overcome complex challenges in ways of maintaining integrity in their relationships. As a result they enjoy **success**.

■ **9-11** *Fearing Yahweh* and *knowing God* (v 5) provide a person a profound *understanding* of justice. Justice is conveyed by three terms: **right** (*ṣedeq*), **just** (*mišpāṭ*), and **fair** (*mêšārîm*; see 1:3*b*). That is, a person gains insights to make decisions that are morally **right**, legally **just**, and socially **fair**. The upright strive to do all things in justice. As a result, they take **every good path**.

In this phrase **path** (*ma'gāl*) references **lanes** or **byways**. Thus, a wise person applies the standards of justice to every aspect of life, including small matters.

Whenever the son displays a profound grasp of justice in handling a specific matter, he gives evidence that **understanding** and **wisdom** *have entered his* **heart**, the locus of his thinking and acting. The skills of **discretion** and **understanding** that Wisdom gives **will protect** him. They will give him confidence, both in his relationship with God and in leading others. Moreover, the son will discover that knowing God is very **pleasant**. Although the pursuit of **wisdom** is arduous, the resulting relationship with God is energizing and refreshing.

The reasoning in vv 5-11 is circular. Gaining wisdom leads to **knowing God**. God's presence in a person's life develops various intellectual skills, including **knowledge**, **discretion**, and **understanding**. Possession of these skills leads to greater **wisdom**. As Fox says, the sages make "learning proceed both from and toward piety" (2000, 116).

b. Wisdom, the Great Protector (2:12-19)

The sage assures the son that wisdom will protect him, particularly "from the ways of wicked men" (vv 12-15) and from the lure of "the adulterous woman" (vv 16-19).

■ **12-15** *The* **wicked** are characterized as those **whose words are perverse** (*tahpûkôt*). Skilled at twisting words, they are able to motivate many to participate in a grand program that offers amazing benefits. For example, they describe the great returns that a particular investment will make, even though they take on virtually no risk.

These promoters are skilled at motivating people to buy into what they are selling, even against their better judgment. They achieve this by getting people's imaginations to run wild at the prospect of becoming rich. That possibility motivates many to buy into the program. These schemers, lacking the virtues of honesty and integrity, dupe people without regret or shame. Many who buy into such a scheme lose most of what they put into it.

The **wicked**, *having* **left the straight paths**, *are* **walking** down **dark ways** and **paths** that **are crooked**. Everything they say is insincere, even concerning small details, conveyed by the word for **ways** (*ma'gĕlôt* [v 15*b*]; see v 9*b*). They feed on deceit. Nothing they say can be trusted. In fact, they take great **delight** in conning people. They love to play on people's basic desires, such as greed, lust, and pride, in order to cloud their thinking so that the naive will buy into their scheme. The craftier the scheme, the greater their pleasure.

They especially prey on honest, unsophisticated people, for such people are inclined to be very trusting. Persuading such people to buy into their perverse schemes gives them great joy, for they feel like they have proven that their intellectual shrewdness is greater than that of honorable people. As a result of these feelings of power and superiority these promoters become addicted swindlers.

Unlike outlaws who separate from society to form a gang in order to rob and plunder (see 1:10-19), such schemers work within the social system to bilk the unsuspecting. They present themselves as respectable professionals. That is why those seeking wisdom need the special skills of discretion and ingenuity to keep from becoming victims of such schemes.

■ **16-19** Gaining **wisdom** also *saves the son* from the adulterous woman. This woman enamors naive youths through the skillful use of **smooth**, titillating **words**. She charms a youth by inviting him to engage with her in sensuous pleasure. She arouses his libido to such a pitch that passion threatens to overpower his reason. In contrast to the speech of "wicked men" (2:12), her **words** are not deceptive. She will deliver the pleasures she promises. Nevertheless, her **words** are destructive because they entice a youth into an unwholesome relationship fraught with numerous dangers. Even though his relationship with such a woman lasts for a brief time, the consequences of such a relationship remain throughout his life. He will be quickly devastated on finding out that once she has made him a victim, she has no more use for him. Over time he will recover, but the scars will remain.

The Wayward Woman

Who is **the adulterous woman** (*'iššâ zārâ*) and **the wayward woman** (*nokriyyâ* [2:16; 5:3, 20; 7:5])? Since these terms occur in parallel lines, except for 5:3, both terms describe the same type of woman. There are four primary options as to her identity: (1) an Israelite harlot, alien because of her conduct, (2) a foreigner serving as a harlot in Israel, (3) a foreign woman who primarily promotes worship of a pagan deity, and (4) another man's wife. In Proverbs this woman does not function as a harlot nor as a foreigner promoting a fertility goddess. Therefore, she is another man's wife (Fox 2000, 134-41). She is alien because her marital status makes her off-limits to every other male. Moreover, since she does not adhere to Israelite family mores, she is an "alien to the family structure" (Camp 1991, 27).

A sage frequently and fervently warns the son or student against yielding to the lure of any woman who is off-limits. Entering into a liaison with her is utter folly because of her "socio-sexual deviance." Her activity is destructive to a family's coherence, its property, its honor, and its standing in the community (ibid.). Consequently, the sages portray this woman as a formidable force of wickedness. In their view she is the greatest threat to undoing, in a moment, the results of training a youth over several years.

A naive youth is strongly tempted to yield to *a* wayward *woman's* enticing offer to accompany her to her house. But he needs to recall the sage's frank description of *this woman's* character and past behavior so that he perceives that she cannot be trusted. She **has left the partner of her youth**, thereby *ignoring* the covenant she made before God. Thus, her behavior clearly reveals that she cannot be trusted. The reference to **the covenant *of her* God** suggests that she is an Israelite. Even though Israelite law never refers to marriage as sacred, that human bond is regulated by the sixth commandment: "you shall not commit adultery" (Exod 20:14). The censure of adultery in that foundational code clearly indicates that marital infidelity is a grave offense against God. Committing adultery breaks the covenant (see Mal 2:14).

Having turned from her husband and her God, this woman becomes a conduit to an early death. In fact, **her house**, the place where she seduces men, **leads down to death** (Prov 2:18; 7:26-27; 9:18). **Death** references the realm where the **spirits of the dead** (*rĕpā'îm* [9:18; 21:16]) eke out a weak existence.

Rĕpā'îm, the Spirits of the Dead

Rĕpā'îm occurs in Northwest Semitic languages for the weak, ghostlike apparitions of the deceased. The phantoms of the dead eke out a bleak existence in a dark, dreary realm known as Sheol. Since there is not a good English equivalent for this Semitic word, it is rendered imprecisely with various terms: **ghosts**, **shades**, and **spirits**. The *rĕpā'îm* are weak, powerless shadows of their former selves. Nevertheless, the identity of each person is recognizable. This term is also used for dead kings in two biblical texts (Isa 14:9, possibly Job 26:5) and in some Ugaritic texts (Smith 1992, 674-75).

With these word pictures the sage is teaching **the son** that any who yield to the appeal of **the wayward woman** face doom, because **her house leads** to the realm **of the dead**. The son must realize that whoever enters that realm never **returns**. There is no path leading back to life. That is why one of the names for Sheol is "the place of no return" (Job 10:21; see 16:22).

c. The Preferred Path and Two Alternatives (2:20-22)

OVERVIEW

The use of "ways" and "paths" in v 20 establishes a direct tie to the preceding section of the instruction framed by these terms: "ways" in v 12*a* and "paths" in v 19*b*. The author uses these terms in the same order to assure the students that by seeking wisdom they will avoid the pitfalls described in the preceding section and will truly "walk in the ways of the good."

IN THE TEXT

The conclusion is also structured to echo the conclusion of the first instruction (1:32-33). That is achieved by a chiasm: the simple are destroyed (1:32):those who accept Wisdom's call "live in safety" (1:33)::"the upright . . . live **securely** in the land" (2:21):"the wicked" are "cut off from the land" (2:22). Both conclusions underscore the critical nature of a youth's decision regarding the path to take in life, for the results are either living well, long, and securely or facing an early, often shameful death.

■ **20** The sage concludes by emphasizing the decision that confronts every youth. If the son heeds his words, he will **walk in the *way* of the good**, that is, those who live by the highest moral standards. Keeping to ***this path***, he will escape the ill consequences that befall those who are duped by the wicked or seduced by the adulterous woman.

■ **21-22** The sage motivates the son to take "the *way* of the good" by contrasting the fate of **the upright** with that of **the wicked**. In describing their fates he employs terms embedded in the blessings and curses of the Sinai covenant. Thereby he ties this instruction to the premiere description of Israel's relationship with God.

The covenant emphasizes that God blesses Israel for keeping the covenant. He strengthens her so that she may "live long in the land" (Deut 11:8-9; see 28:1-14). However, if she continually violates the terms of the covenant, God will bring on her harsh discipline in a determined effort to motivate her to repent (Lev 26:14-46; Deut 28:15-57; 30:15-16). If Israel persists in breaking the covenant, God will punish her by uprooting her from the promised land. She will be taken into exile (Lev 26:27-33; Deut 28:58-68; 29:25-28 [24-27 HB]; 30:17-18).

Drawing on wordings in the blessings and curses of the covenant, the sage assures **the upright**, that is, those who conduct their lives ***in integrity*** (*tĕmîmîm*), that they **will live** securely **in the land**, the heritage God has given them (Lev 26:3-13; see Ps 37:3, 9, 11, 22*a*, 29, 34). As a result of God's blessing, they will enjoy prosperity.

However, **the wicked will be cut off** [or **torn**] **from the land**. ***Being* torn from *the land*** is one of the harshest penalties in the covenant. The "cut off" penalty is a punishment prescribed for certain violations of the Law in the law codes. It is prescribed for individuals who commit specific sins (e.g., Lev 20:3, 5, 6, 18). A person subject to this penalty is banished from the community, becoming a wanderer who has to eke out a meager existence in another land. By alluding to these severest penalties, the sage stresses the grave consequences that will befall those who do not follow his authoritative instruction.

By formulating the rewards and the penalties that attend following or rejecting this instruction, the sage is earnestly seeking to motivate the son to "keep to the paths of the righteous" so that he may "live" long "in the land."

FROM THE TEXT

Wisdom equips those who become her followers with intellectual skills, including sound judgment, discretion, shrewdness, perception, and ingenuity. These skills protect them from being waylaid by two powerful forces: (1) the deceptive schemes of evil men and (2) the inducements to engage in sensuous encounters. Since the upright escape these dangers, they live a long, abundant life. Throughout life they take delight in the pleasantness that attends communing with God. Thus, they find that their life with God is truly blessed. (See Prov 3:13-18.)

3. Instruction: Trusting and Praising God = Being Blessed (3:1-35)

OVERVIEW

This chapter contains a medley of sayings including instructions, exhortations, prohibitions, and praise of wisdom. Even though it lacks a defined order, it is one of the best known and most highly prized chapters in Proverbs. This is due to the grandeur of many of its sayings. The chapter will be discussed in three sections: trusting Yahweh (vv 1-12), exalting wisdom (vv 13-20), and treating neighbors with civility (vv 21-35).

Prominence is given to Yahweh in each section. His name appears nine times (vv 5, 7, 9, 11, 12, 19, 26, 32, 33). The general term "God" occurs in v 4. Several exhortations encourage the son to have a dynamic relationship with Yahweh. Yahweh is to be trusted (v 5), feared (v 7), and honored (v 9), but never despised (v 11). He expresses his care for those who trust him through discipline (v 12). Yahweh is exalted for creating the world in wisdom (vv 19-20). The last section gives guidance on using sound judgment to avoid behaviors that cause dissension among neighbors (vv 21-35). It ends with a poem that lauds Yahweh's role in cursing the wicked and blessing the righteous (v 33).

The second section describes the great benefits wisdom offers. The first segment is encased by two beatitudes. A person is declared blessed or fortunate for finding wisdom (vv 13-20). One is so honored because Wisdom endows those who seek her with wonderful benefits such as long life, wealth, honor, and a pleasant life. Her role for humans is so crucial that she is identified as a tree of life. Her value, then, is inestimable. A primary reason wisdom is so important for humans resides in God's having ordered the world in wisdom (vv 19-20). In that role wisdom brings praise to Yahweh.

a. Trusting in Yahweh (3:1-12)

OVERVIEW

This section, which is encased by the sage's addressing it to **my son**, may be described as "a pietistic homily" (Fox 2000, 154). It consists of six exhortations and prohibitions. Each saying has four lines except the second, which has five (vv 3-4). In the first four sayings the lines in each couplet alternate between a prohibition and a command (vv 1, 3, 7) or vice versa (v 5). The fifth saying has a single exhortation (v 9). The last saying consists of two prohibitions (v 11). These instructions encourage the son to trust (v 5), fear (v 7), and honor Yahweh (v 9). Each is supported by a great motivation. It needs to be recognized that only God is able to make the promised outcomes a reality in human lives (Waltke 2004, 239).

These instructions are built on the close tie between pursuing wisdom and trusting in Yahweh. At the center are the exhortations to trust and fear Yahweh (vv 3-6, 7-8). Genuine trust means that even persons who have some wisdom do not lean on their own understanding (v 5) nor do they consider themselves wise (v 7). To emphasize this teaching the key verbs in vv 5 and 7 stand in chiastic order: trust in Yahweh:lean not on::be not wise:fear Yahweh. These exhortations encapsulate the motto that the fear of Yahweh is the foundation of wisdom (1:7; 9:10).

The promises that attend trusting Yahweh are grand: long life and prosperity (3:2), favor and a good reputation (v 4), straight paths, that is, success (v 6), health, emotional and physical (v 8), and abundant harvests (v 10). The last saying, however, speaks of God's discipline (v 12). Concluding this section it adds the dimension that even unpleasant instruction through discipline yields great benefits and is evidence of Yahweh's love.

IN THE TEXT

■ **1-2** The parent or the sage begins by directly addressing the apprentice as **my son.** At the outset he challenges **the son not *to* forget** his **teaching** (see 1:8). To accomplish this goal the son must **keep *the* commands in** his **heart,** the center of his will. The verbs **do not forget** and **keep** address the son's will (Fox 2000, 142).

A primary way that the son ***keeps the* commands** is by memorizing the sage's **teaching.** By committing them to memory, ***the* son** will be able to meditate on them at any time of the day or night. Times of reflection embed the precepts deep in his mind. As a result, they become an integral part of his thinking, enabling him to follow them instinctively.

The sage offers two motivations for keeping these commands. The first is a long **life,** conveyed by two phrases: ***length of days*** and ***years of living*** (3:2a; see 4:10). The second is ***well-being*** (šālôm). The Hebrew šālôm has a wide range of senses. It includes tranquillity, confidence, well-being, contentment, harmony, and prosperity.

■ **3-4** The son is challenged **never** to **let *loyal* love** (ḥesed) and ***truth*** or **faithfulness** ('emet) **leave** him. Wisdom nurtures these qualities in the son's life. Since these virtues are rooted in the will, a person must continually exercise them. They do not operate on automatic pilot.

To achieve this goal the son is instructed to **bind** these qualities about his **neck.** They will adorn him like a beautiful necklace. Also he is to **write them on the tablet of *his* heart.** This metaphor means that the student is to store these virtues deep in his mind, the center of his will (see Jer 31:33-34a). There they will guide his thinking, speaking, and acting throughout the day. They assess his attitudes and thoughts, bringing them into alignment with God's standard as taught in the Law and in wisdom instruction. A person whose character is molded by these virtues ***wins*** favor . . . **in the sight of God and**

humans. That is, the son gains a stellar reputation. People entrust this kind of person with key leadership roles.

The directive to **bind** (Prov 3:3) *"the* teaching" and *"the* commands" (v 1) **around *the* neck** recalls a similar instruction in Deuteronomy (6:8; 11:18). The Israelites are to bind the Law on their hands and forehead. In that way they serve as external reminders so that the people keep the Law throughout the day in their work and in their relationships. Humans need external reminders to keep fresh before them the most important values.

This instruction seeks to prevent these virtues from slowly and unsuspectingly dissipating under the pressures of life and wandering desires. To counter that human proclivity **loyal love and faithfulness** must become an integral part of a person's outer and inner life as conveyed by reference to their being placed **around *the* neck** and **in *the* heart.** Such love transcends emotion, for emotions tend to be unstable. This love is maintained by a focused commitment to God, a person, or a value.

Loyal Love or *Ḥesed*

Ḥesed, a distinctive Hebrew term, has no obvious English equivalent. As a result English versions translate it with a variety of words. Some versions use different English words for *ḥesed*. Examples of the primary renderings in major English translations include "steadfast love" (NRSV, NJPS), "kindness" (NIV), "love" (NIV, REB), "lovingkindness" (NASB), "faithfulness, goodness" (NJPS), and "mercy" (KJV, NIV a few times).

Ḥesed is also unusual in that it occurs solely as a noun. Most Hebrew roots yield both a verb and a noun. This anomaly indicates that *ḥesed* describes a trait, the blending of **kindness** and **loyalty.** Several times it is coupled with **and truth** (*we'ĕmet*). That phrase characterizes *ḥesed* as **genuine, authentic, faithful** (Exod 34:6; Prov 3:3; 14:22; 16:6; 20:28).

Ḥesed describes the filial bond between those in a committed relationship. The commitment is a decision of the will. Since *ḥesed* is rooted in a person's decision rather than in one's emotions, it stands for loyalty more than love. A *ḥesed* relationship may exist between those on equal standing as family members (Gen 20:13; 47:29), friends (1 Sam 20:8), tribes, or nations. It may also be established between those who are on different levels socially, such as king-people, empire-state, God-Israel.

The parties expect that all their interactions will be characterized by *ḥesed*. A party shows *ḥesed* by helping the other deal with difficult, demanding situations, losses, and enemies. The party in need can depend on receiving that help. Often, but not always, the relationship between the parties is formalized by a covenant.

Ḥesed is a key descriptive term for God. In fact, God refers to himself as abounding in genuine *ḥesed* (Exod 34:6; Ps 108:4 [5 HB]). His display of *ḥesed* inspires people to praise him exuberantly (e.g., Pss 31:7-21 [8-22 HB]; 32:10; 57:3 [4 HB]; 59:10 [11 HB]; 94:18; 143:12). They describe his *ḥesed* as reliable (Pss 33:5; 119:64), "great" (Ps 86:13), full of grace and compassion (Exod 34:6), infinite (Ps

103:11), and eternal (Ps 103:17). It never wavers or fails (Isa 54:10; Ps 103:17). A favorite hymnic refrain is "the *ḥesed* of Yahweh endures forever" (see Ps 136).

Given the frailty of human nature and the fact that *ḥesed* is a decision of the will, those who fear God must be diligent in nurturing this virtue. Otherwise it will wither and disappear (Isa 40:7). Such was the case with Israel. After years of living in the promised land, she ceased showing God *ḥesed*. As a result, the people became engaged in all kinds of wicked behaviors, including theft, fraud, and murder (Hos 4:1-2).

God responded by withdrawing his *ḥesed* (Jer 16:5). Nevertheless, God did not give up on Israel. Through the prophets God continued to plead with Israel to rekindle her *ḥesed* (Hos 6:6; 10:12). It is in light of Israel's experience that the sage exhorts the son **never to let** *ḥesed* **leave** him. This virtue is essential for a dynamic relationship with God and fellow humans.

■ **5-6** The son is charged to trust **Yahweh** with all **his** heart and not to **rely** on **his** own understanding. A person demonstrates complete **trust** in God by seeking his direction in every matter.

The human mind constantly entertains numerous thoughts. It tends to focus on one of them. That leads to considering ways of acting on that thought. Aspects of implementing a thought often have elements that are at odds with acting wisely or in accord with what God values. Therefore, instead of acting quickly on a possible plan, the son needs to seek God's guidance. In so doing he shows that he truly ***acknowledges Yahweh***.

Yahweh responds to those who **trust** him by ***making their* paths straight** (*yiššar*). In Isa 40:3-4 this verb describes making a highway level by lowering the hills and filling in the valleys. Here God straightens out the way of those who trust him in order to keep them from veering from the path of wisdom.

■ **7-8** This instruction reinforces the preceding one. A person who grows in wisdom becomes very knowledgeable about a particular subject or highly skilled at a trade. Excelling brings one high acclaim. On receiving recognition a person must guard against ***becoming* wise in *one's* own *sight***. A major danger of considering oneself very wise is that one begins to think that one can fulfill any desire at any time. Such arrogance leads even a wise person to act foolishly (Prov 26:12; see Isa 5:21; Jer 9:23-24).

The best antidote for a prideful attitude is ***fearing Yahweh*** and ***shunning*** evil. This combination of phrases in the Wisdom literature characterizes a person as truly devout. God uses it twice in boasting about Job's unblemished character to the Satan (Job 1:8; 2:3; see 1:1). ***Fearing Yahweh*** and ***shunning*** evil promote physical and emotional health as conveyed by the parallel terms **body** (lit. ***navel***) and **bones** (see Prov 15:30; Isa 58:11; 66:14). For the Israelites strong bones were the essence of a healthy body.

■ **9-10** The person who fears Yahweh ***honors*** him in the use of **wealth** and resources. Thereby a person recognizes Yahweh's lordship over all one's possessions. In ancient Israel a person specifically honored Yahweh's lordship by presenting **the firstfruits of all . . . crops** at the sanctuary (Exod 23:19; 34:22, 26; Num 15:17-21; 18:13-14). The first of the crops and the herds belonged to Yahweh as Israel's sovereign. The liturgy for presenting the firstfruits stands in Deut 26:1-11. In offering the firstfruits a family recognizes Yahweh's lordship and praises him as the giver of the harvest. God, in turn, releases the rest of the harvest for a family to use at its discretion.

This command is supported by a marvelous promise. Yahweh promises to bless those who honor his lordship with such a bountiful harvest that *their* **barns will be filled to overflowing** and *their* **vats will brim over with new wine**. Such abundance leads to a large, prosperous family. In this tangible way God continues to honor the promise he made to Abraham that his offspring would become as numerous as the stars (Gen 15:5; 22:15-18).

Reference to Liturgical Practices in Proverbs

There is a noticeable absence of references to the temple, sacrifices, festivals, and other acts of worship in Proverbs. This is the only reference that directs making a specific offering.

Nevertheless, this lack of references is not to be interpreted as a chasm between the cult and the wisdom school. This is evident in Solomon's role in both the cult and the wisdom tradition. After becoming king, he made a pilgrimage to Gibeon to make sacrifices. There he waited for God to reveal himself. God appeared, inviting him to make any request. Solomon responded by asking for wisdom in order to rule the people wisely and justly. God granted his request. As a result, Solomon became legendary for his great wisdom. Solomon then built the beautiful temple to honor Yahweh, placing worship at the center of Israel's national life. To inaugurate worship at the temple, Solomon offered the dedicatory prayer (1 Kgs 8:22-53).

Further evidence of the wise recognizing the vital role of worship is seen in wisdom texts from other Middle Eastern countries. For example, in Merikare, an Egyptian wisdom text, a king advises his son to be generous in making offerings and attending the festivals at the temple (63-67; see Any 4:2-5; 7:12-15). In Amenemope, a later Egyptian text (see 22:17—24:22), there are several sayings that promote piety (e.g., 3:1-3; 6:14; 8:13-14, 19-20; 10:12-15; 25:16-21; 26:13-14). Without neglecting or despising the cult, the wise emphasized developing character over performing religious rituals.

■ **11-12** The sage makes a significant shift in approach. To make sure of having the student's attention, the sage again addresses him directly: **my son**. He enjoins him not to **despise** or *belittle Yahweh's* **discipline**. Sometimes, but certainly not always, a setback or misfortune is an expression of *Yahweh's* **discipline**. Sometimes a person who *trusts Yahweh* is taken aback when unexpectedly confronted by a hardship. Since that experience appears to fly in the face of the preceding promises, a person is prone to become discouraged. Some may even be prone to despise Yahweh.

The sage takes up this topic to address another dimension of life. He wants to keep the son from forsaking the way of wisdom when he faces a major loss or a serious illness. The son must not take a major difficulty as evidence that he is failing to follow the preceding exhortations. Such trouble is **a discipline** or *a rebuke* that Yahweh has brought about for his instruction. Despite the agony *a rebuke* produces, the son must avoid ***despising*** or ***resenting the discipline*** by realizing that it is evidence of **Yahweh's love**.

Wesley (1975, 1835) describes ***despising*** as "making light of it, or not being duly affected with it, or by accounting it an unnecessary thing." Rather, the son is to realize that **Yahweh** is relating to him **as a father**. He is seeking to bring about a greater depth in the son's understanding or to enhance a particular virtue in the son's character.

It is natural for a person to resent *a rebuke*, rather than to seek to learn from it. But despising a setback only increases the agony of the learning experience. Later the son will regret despising discipline (5:23). When beset by a difficulty, he needs to continue to trust Yahweh, realizing that Yahweh is working for his highest good.

Fox (2000, 153) points out that the juxtaposing of the promises with guidance on dealing with discipline is evidence that the sages did not have a mechanical or oversimplified view of retribution. They recognized exceptions to their teaching that good benefits follow the pursuit of wisdom and observance of the Law or instruction. Here the sage is seeking to guide the son to deal with setbacks with a proper attitude. Specifically, he must rely more on God than on his own interpretation of life's experiences.

FROM THE TEXT

Wisdom inspires one to trust Yahweh completely. A wise person places doing God's will over relying on one's own ambitions and understanding. One who is wise seeks to acknowledge God in everything undertaken. Trust in Yahweh leads to honoring him by giving the first or best to him.

God's favor is expressed in many ways. A person gains honor in the community. God directs that person's life. As part of that direction God disciplines along the way so that a person does not develop a detrimental attitude, stray from the way, and become arrogant.

God seeks to have a relationship characterized by loyalty and authentic kindness with those who fear him. These qualities lead to a long life. God blesses their work so that it yields abundantly. Thereby a person gains sufficient income to support the family. God's favor at times brings about discipline in order to develop or refine traits of character so that a person becomes more like God.

It is important to keep in mind that these principles are addressed to an individual seeking wisdom. It assumes an era with a stable government that is led by a wise ruler. These promises are not to be taken as an insurance policy for a guaranteed future.

In times of widespread upheavals in society, such as wars, recessions, and natural disasters, other proverbs (e.g., vv 25-36) encourage the wise to draw on their resourcefulness for dealing with these complex, threatening situations in ways that preserve their lives and work to bring solace and relief to those who are suffering intensely.

b. Exalting Wisdom (3:13-20)

OVERVIEW

This section has two segments: (1) the benefits wisdom bestows (vv 13-18) and (2) a poem exalting Yahweh for creating the world in wisdom (vv 19-20). For humans, wisdom possesses the highest value. Nothing on earth equals the benefits she offers: long life, riches, honor (v 16), pleasant ways, peace (v 17), and good fortune (vv 13, 18). Humans may experience her gifts because God established the world order in wisdom (vv 19-20). Wisdom's role in creation heaps praise on Yahweh.

The first segment is encased by an inclusio that consists of two terms from the root *'šr*. It opens with the noun *'ašrê*, blessed, *fortunate, honored*, and closes with the verb *mě'uššār*, be blessed, *be deemed fortunate*.

A Beatitude

In the OT Hebrew *'ašrê* identifies a statement as a beatitude or makarism. Usually it stands at the beginning of a saying, but a few times at the end (14:21; 16:20; 29:18). *'Ašrê*, often translated **blessed**, needs to be clearly distinguished from the verb "bless" (*bārak*). The noun describes an attainment or a condition one has attained or received. The verb stands for imparting favor, energy, or protection to a person or group, especially by God.

In the OT beatitudes appear most frequently in the Psalms (e.g., Pss 1:1; 40:4 [5 HB]). Proverbs has eight beatitudes (3:13; 8:32, 34; 14:21; 16:20; 20:7; 28:14; 29:18). Jesus adopted this form in his teaching. His most noteworthy beatitudes head the Sermon on the Mount (Matt 5:3-11; Luke 6:20-22). Others appear in his teachings (e.g., Matt 11:6; 13:16; 16:17; 24:46; several in Luke; John 13:17; 20:29). A few appear elsewhere in the NT (e.g., Rom 14:22; 1 Cor 7:40; Jas 1:12, 25; 1 Pet 3:14; 4:14).

Since there is no clear English equivalent for *'ašrê*, various terms are used for it in English translations, as "blessed," "fortunate," "happy," or "favored." However, each has a limitation. **Blessed** is too sanctimonious, "happy" is too superficial, and "fortunate" implies that the benefit described is the result of luck. *'Ašrê* is essentially a word of congratulations that honors a person (Hanson 1996).

A person is honored for a variety of reasons: a virtue such as wisdom (Prov 3:13), a particular disposition such as fearing Yahweh (Ps 128:1), a pattern of behavior such as being generous to the poor (Prov 14:21), an achievement such as keeping wisdom's ways (8:32), a victory (Deut 33:29), a special relationship or standing (1 Kgs 10:8), a special benefit such as having many children (Ps 127:5), a spiritual reality such as having one's sins forgiven (Ps 32:1-2) or a favorable standing with God (Ps 33:12).

A beatitude also honors a person for a particular trait. One who is blessed has a deep, enduring joy and a profound sense of accomplishment. The beatitude gives a person confidence spiritually. Thereby it fans one's zeal for God. A beatitude also brings praise to God because he is the source behind the trait or accomplishment for which a person is being honored (Ps 144:15).

IN THE TEXT

■ **13-17** *A person* who *finds* wisdom or *gains* understanding *is* blessed. A person is considered *fortunate*, blessed ('ašrê), or *honored* in finding wisdom. Wisdom provides a person greater *profit* than can be made in trading **silver** and **gold. She is more precious than rubies.** Wisdom is priceless, so priceless that no stockpile of gold, silver, jewels, gems, or crystal has sufficient value for purchasing wisdom (Job 28:15-19). In fact, **nothing** a person *desires may* **compare with her.** This claim is clearly supported by the nature of the benefits she provides: **long life** . . . **riches and honor.** Those who find her will discover that **her ways are pleasant** *and peaceful.*

■ **18** Wisdom is identified as **a tree of life** (Prov 11:30; 13:12; 15:4). **Those** who *embrace* her gain access to the source of life that takes the place of the tree of life from which humans were excluded because the first humans disobeyed God's command (Gen 3:22-24). Now through wisdom God has provided people a new way to access life, that is, by embracing **wisdom.** That means that they must focus their deepest affection on her. In return, they will *become* **blessed** or *considered fortunate* for the quality of life she bestows on them. Being recognized as fortunate means that they will be highly respected in the community.

A tree of life may reference life that transcends death, but that position is neither stated directly nor clearly articulated elsewhere in Proverbs. It is only hinted at a few times. The imagery of this tree provides an inkling. That belief, however, will not become a central tenet of biblical faith until Jesus' teaching and his victory over death.

FROM THE TEXT

It is important that those who pursue wisdom grasp the great values she gives. This is especially critical for those who live in materialistic cultures, because her benefits (such as discernment and resourcefulness) are intangible. Nevertheless, they far outweigh the worth of any portfolio.

In the pursuit of wisdom people come to the realization that the primary goal in life is not to accumulate things in which they can take pride. Rather, the goal is to develop the virtues, skills, and abilities that wisdom provides.

These make people resourceful adults and lead to their being honored in their community. They also give people confidence of God's approval and the assurance that they are traveling the road of wisdom.

Although wisdom's gifts have the highest value, they do not shelter those who embrace her from encountering setbacks and obstacles, even gigantic ones. Those who embrace wisdom will continue to have hills to climb and foes to withstand. Wisdom equips them with insights and resourcefulness to cope with and surmount these obstacles.

IN THE TEXT

■ **19-20** This brief poem praises **Yahweh** for establishing **the earth** on firm **foundations** and for **setting the heavens in place** *through* **wisdom** and **understanding** (see 8:22-31). And **by his knowledge the watery depths were divided**. God also provided **clouds** to bring **the dew**. **Understanding** (*tĕbûnâ*) is the skillful application of **knowledge**. **Knowledge** includes the information and the skill for doing a task well (see Exod 31:6; 36:1; 38:23). Through **wisdom** God established the earth with an environment that sustains all kinds of life forms throughout the various seasons. God empowered those life forms to reproduce abundantly in order that they might fill the earth. Consequently, the earth has become a marvelous menagerie and botanical garden (see 8:22-31). Wisdom also gave God **understanding** to embed various cycles in nature that support the continual renewal of nature.

In the Genesis account of creation on day two God made an expanse or plate, that is, the sky, to separate the waters of the deep into the upper and lower waters or deep. The expanse is held securely in place by the mountains on the horizon and by pillars (Job 26:11). Part of **the watery depths** is stored behind this expanse (Gen 1:6-7). From these upper waters come the rain and **the dew**.

Next God gathered the water beneath the sky so that dry land appeared (Gen 1:9-13). The lower waters of **the depths** feed the seas. The Israelites also considered **the depths** to exist beneath the dry land. Its waters burst through the ground in gushing springs and filling wells. Thereby **the depths** provide water for farmers and shepherds especially during the dry season that lasts from the end of April into October or November. Also dew is a significant source of moisture during the dry season.

The mention of **the dew** highlights a distinctive weather phenomenon in Palestine. Clouds from the Mediterranean drift inland and hover over the hills during the early morning from late spring into the first part of summer. Some clouds even reach into the desert regions. The rising sun makes these clouds quickly disappear. They leave behind dew, often heavy. **The dew** nourishes the vegetation, especially vines, during the hot, dry summer. It provides farmers in the hill country, especially if they use terracing, an abundant harvest of grapes in the fall (see the blessing in Gen 27:28).

In these ways **Yahweh** provides water from **the watery depths** above and below the earth in order that all kinds of plants and animals may flourish throughout the year. These patterns in nature bear witness also to **wisdom**.

c. God-given Confidence and a Series of Prohibitions as a Guide to Harmony with Neighbors (3:21-35)

BEHIND THE TEXT

This section has three segments. In the first the benefits of sound judgment and discernment are specified (vv 21-26). In the second is a collection of five prohibitions denouncing behaviors that threaten neighborly relationships (vv 27-32). Whybray (1994a, 69) posits that the emphasis on the two traits attending wisdom serves as an introduction to the prohibitions. The third segment consists of three sayings regarding Yahweh's cursing the wicked and blessing the righteous (vv 33-35). The results that attend adhering to the prohibitions or failing to do so serve as motivations for observing the prohibitions.

IN THE TEXT

(1) Benefits of Sound Judgment and Discernment (3:21-26)

■ **21-24** Again addressing *the* son, the teacher exhorts him to **preserve** two virtues wisdom provides: **sound judgment** [*tûšiyyâ*] **and discretion** or *discernment* (*mĕzimmâ*). He is **not** to **let** *them* out of *his* sight. In other words, the youth must not let the routines of daily living lead to neglecting these virtues. Since the exercise of these qualities requires deep reflection, he must guard against making important decisions quickly.

Nurturing these mental skills promotes a wholesome **life**. They will adorn him with a gracious demeanor similar to the way a beautiful pendant adorns one's neck (see 1:9; 3:3). Also these qualities will enable him to **go on** *his* way in full stride without *stumbling* over obstacles along the path. At night when *he lies* down, he **will not be afraid** of facing ill consequences from his actions or decisions of that day. *His* sleep will be sound and refreshing.

■ **25-26** By keeping these skills fresh, the son will never **fear** having to face **sudden disaster** (*paḥad*). The **disaster** in view is destruction from *a fierce storm* (*šô'â*). *A* disaster is one of God's means for punishing **the wicked** (1:26-27). By maintaining trust in God, the son will never face God's punishment. By contrast, the wicked, mindful that one day they will face their comeuppance, are anxious about being hit by *a* disaster.

Because the son places his confidence in **Yahweh**, he has the assurance that Yahweh **will keep** *his* **foot from being** *caught in a snare*. The sage recognizes that life's path is lined with all sorts of traps. One who trusts in Yahweh's guidance, however, will escape **being snared**. Confidence in God's protection provides a person courage to take risks in obeying and serving God and in helping people.

(2) Being a Good Neighbor (3:27-32)

■ **27-32** A group of five prohibitions denounces behaviors that cause disharmony with neighbors or acquaintances. The first two stress the harm that results from failing to do **good**, especially when one possesses the resources to meet a neighbor's need (vv 27-28). The other three identify ruinous behaviors that must be avoided: *plotting evil* against *a* neighbor (v 29), pursuing litigation against a person *without grounds* (v 30), and *envying* the violent (vv 31-32). These prohibitions emphasize that by treating people, especially those in one's community, in a cruel, underhanded manner a person shows lack of "sound judgment and *discernment*" (v 21).

It is prudent to build strong relationships with one's *neighbors*. A neighbor (*rēaʿ*) references a person with whom one has a good relationship rather than a person who lives in proximity (Fox 2000, 165-66). A wise person never treats a neighbor thoughtlessly or cruelly. Whenever a neighbor asks to borrow something, a caring person does not dismiss the request with a flimsy excuse: **"Come back tomorrow and I'll give it to you."** Responding to a neighbor's serious request in a flippant manner is dishonoring. It is most offensive when a person actually has the means to meet the request.

A person *should never* plot harm against *a* neighbor or a friend who lives *trustingly nearby*. There is never a valid reason to devise a vile plan to harm a reliable **neighbor**. Two examples of actions that will destroy a neighbor's standing in the community are spreading malicious rumors and making unfounded accusations (Whybray 1994a, 72).

Furthermore, a person should never *enter into a legal dispute with* another for no reason, that is, not having incurred any harm (*rāʿâ*). Rather than seeking to restrict a neighbor who has an irritating habit, a person needs to discover some way to bear whatever irritation that neighbor causes.

A person who is striving to be wise *must* not envy *a* violent *person*, one who relishes treating others cruelly. Warnings against **envy** appear in other proverbs (14:30; 23:17; 24:1, 19; 27:4), suggesting that envy was a real temptation among the learned. It appears that they were tempted to envy those who had become rich or who received public honor undeservedly (see Pss 37; 73). A person tempted to envy another needs to be aware of the curious reality that envy often leads an upright person to take on characteristics of the one envied, especially the traits that are deeply despised in the one envied. Hence the command: **do not . . . choose any of their ways**.

Whenever one becomes exceedingly distressed at the possessions and recognition a violent person receives, it is crucial to remember that *Yahweh* detests *a devious person* (→ sidebar "Yahweh Detests or Abomination to Yahweh" at end of 6:19). It is even more important to remember that Yahweh takes the upright into his confidence. God's acceptance far outweighs becoming out of sorts at *a* violent *person's* apparent good fortune.

(3) Yahweh's Response to the Wise and to Fools (3:33-35)

■ **33-35** Three sayings, each cast in opposing parallelism, emphasize God's active role in the **households** of the wicked and **the righteous.** *Household* references an extended family living in proximity along with their flocks, fields, and possessions. *Yahweh's* **curse** *lies* on the *household* of the wicked. As a result they face setback after setback, incurring significant losses. But God **blesses the *household*** of the righteous. As a result of his blessing, that household prospers.

Yahweh responds to people's demeanors in kind (see Ps 18:25-26). Yahweh *scoffs* at *scoffers.* Conversely, Yahweh **shows favor to the humble,** that is, those whose confidence is placed in him rather than in their possessions. **Favor** means they receive recognition and respect in the community (see Prov 3:4).

A brief proverb states the principle that underlies Yahweh's activity described in v 34. **The wise inherit honor. Inherit** is a strong word. It conveys that their **honor** is inalienable (Waltke 2004, 273). This is certainly a result of Yahweh's blessing as expressed in the two preceding verses. **Fools,** however, **get only shame.** This proverb is formulated to place stress on the opposing rewards, **honor** (*kābôd*) and **shame** (*qālôn*). These terms are chosen because they have two long vowels, emphasizing the social standing. Also they stand in a chiastic pattern as the first and last words.

FROM THE TEXT

The virtues of sound judgment and discernment given by wisdom enable people who fear God to live confidently. They are able to walk the path of life unafraid of stumbling. Their sleep is peaceful. They do not have a gnawing fear that something untoward will befall them.

Furthermore, those who fear God strive for good relations with neighbors and those with whom they work and associate. They shun temptations to make life difficult for a person who annoys them. Since they are thoughtful in relating to others, Yahweh blesses their homes. Their lifestyle brings them honor.

This group of sayings communicates that God is actively involved in the daily lives of all households. That is, God relates to or works with communities. While Western thought and morality is strongly individualistic, every family member is impacted by the character and fate of the family unit. When one member is ill or does wrong, all members bear that burden in some measure. Conversely, all family members share in the success and honor accorded any of its members. In this light it is important to consider that God blesses family units, and he also lets a family that lives disgracefully receive shame. God honors and shames individuals also.

4. Instruction: My Son, Get Wisdom (4:1-27)

OVERVIEW

The sage presents an instruction having three sections. Each begins with the father addressing his son(s) to listen (vv 1a, 10a, 20b). He emphasizes that by following his teaching they will stay on the straight path throughout their lives.

The sage uses several terms for teaching and path. For teaching there is "instruction" (vv 1a, 13a), "learning" (v 2a), "teaching" (v 2b), "my words" (vv 4, 5, 20b), and "my commands" (v 4). For path he uses "way" (derek [vv 11a, 14b, 15, 19, 26b]) and "path" (two Hebrew terms: ma'gāl [vv 11b, 26a] and 'ōraḥ [vv 14a, 18]).

A unique feature of this instruction is the father's sharing the counsel he had received from his father (vv 1-9). The grandfather personifies Wisdom (vv 4-9), as is often the case in Section I (e.g., 1:20-33; 8:3-36; 9:1-8), to stress that Wisdom will protect the son and bring him honor (4:6, 8-9). The father then provides his own counsel for traveling the way of wisdom. He adds an admonition: avoid the way of the wicked (vv 14-17), supporting it by contrasting the ways of the righteous and the wicked (vv 18-19).

In the third section (vv 20-27) the father enjoins the son to store his teaching in his heart, for it is the source of life and health. He emphasizes the importance of guarding one's heart, keeping one's lips from speaking corrupting words, and focusing one's eyes on the goal ahead. By heeding his instruction the son will never deviate from the straight path.

The father especially emphasizes the importance of controlling the heart or mind, the center of one's thoughts, desires, and actions. Managing the heart well leads to good health (v 22) and upright behavior (v 23), because the heart directs the members of the body: eyes (vv 21a, 25), gaze (lit. **eyelids** [v 25b]), ears (v 20b), mouth (v 24), lips (v 24b), and feet (vv 26, 27).

IN THE TEXT

a. The Highest Goal: Acquiring Wisdom (4:1-9)

■ **1-2** A *father* exhorts his **sons** or students to **listen** to his **instruction** in order to **gain understanding** (bînâ). Assuring them that he *is giving* them **sound learning** (leqaḥ), he admonishes them: **do not forsake my teaching** (tôrâ). The term for **teaching** is often translated *law* outside of Proverbs. Here it refers to the core of the *father's* teaching. That corpus provides guidance on proper behavior in all kinds of dealings, especially in the presence of the king and nobility. He includes guidance on proper etiquette and stresses the importance of maintaining integrity in all dealings. These topics are commonly stressed in the instructions of sages, including Egyptian sages such as Any (see 22:17—24:22).

■ **3-4** To inspire his sons the sage recounts the teaching he received from his father. He also expresses the importance of being **cherished by *his* mother**. By including her the sage calls attention to the vital role she had in his education (see 1:8). The father mentions these details as evidence that his teaching is in accord with that of the honored sages. Therefore, it may be trusted.

In sharing his father's instruction, he gains his children's full attention. They relish hearing about their parents' lives when they were young. Sharing these stories also strengthens the bond between the generations. He especially notes that his **father** exhorted him to **take hold of *his* words with all *his* heart.** By storing them in his mind, he ***will* keep *his* commands** and **live** long.

■ **5** The grandfather stressed the importance of **_acquiring_ wisdom** and **understanding.** *Acquire* (*qānâ*; see 8:22) means "buy, purchase, obtain." The son must pay the price, either in the cost of education or in expending great effort, for learning. The grandfather added, **Do not forget my words or turn away from them.** Should the son **forget** an essential principle, he will not act circumspectly in a pressured situation.

The terms **forget** and **turn . . . from** show that the grandfather was aware that humans are prone to modify, adapt, or alter the instructions of an authority figure. He sought to counter this tendency with this prohibition. He does not want his son to change his counsel or to select only certain principles to follow.

■ **6** At this point the grandfather speaks of ***Wisdom*** as an honorable woman. She will be present with the son as a strong spiritual force. In personifying wisdom he increases the son's interest in his teaching. The grandfather says forcefully: **Do not forsake wisdom. Forsake** means willfully turning away from her guidance. Rather, the son is to have a personal relationship with ***Wisdom*** (see 1:20-33). He is to **love her.** She, in turn, **will watch over *him*. *Watching* over** indicates that at times in his life she will give him special guidance for dealing with difficult, even threatening situations.

■ **7** The grandfather repeats his core exhortation. The first step in becoming wise is to **get** [or ***purchase*** (*qānâ*)] **wisdom** and **understanding,** no matter the **cost.** The son is not to hold anything back in the pursuit of **wisdom,** either because of the cost or the energy that needs to be expended in gaining **wisdom.** Nothing that can be gained on earth compares in value to ***Wisdom***, for she was the first being that God brought into existence (8:22-31).

■ **8-9** Again speaking of Wisdom as a woman, the grandfather enjoins the son to bond closely with her by ***cherishing*** and ***embracing*** her. She, in turn, **will honor** him. **Honor** is the highest reward in ancient Middle Eastern cultures. One way that Wisdom honors the son is by endowing him with intellectual skills as prudence and discretion. In drawing on these skills to devise plans that promote the good of the community, he will win public accolades like **a garland** or **a glorious crown** (see 1 Chr 20:2; Jer 13:18; Ezek 23:42). The son will proudly wear these symbols of honor. The grandfather is encouraging his son by describing the acclaim he will receive as a result of his ***acquiring*** and ***cherishing*** wisdom. Today communities continue to honor those who have performed outstanding service to the community with medals, plaques, or flowers.

b. The Two Paths (4:10-19)

■ **10-13** The sage begins the next segment with **listen, my son, accept *my words***. He motivates this exhortation with the promise: **the years of your life will be many**. He reassures *his* son that he **is guiding** him **in the way of wisdom**, described as **straight paths** or *trails* (ma'gāl [v 11]). With this metaphor he is assuring *his* son that the details of his instruction are accurate and thus reliable. Heeding the sage's teaching *the* son will keep to the **straight *path*** and his progress **will not be hampered**. In fact, *he **may*** run without fear of *stumbling*, for this *path* is free from major obstacles.

In order that this will be **the son's** experience he must **hold on to** and **guard** the sage's **instruction** (mûsār). The sage uses personal pronouns to underscore the promises he is making to *his* son. He underscores the necessity of following his **instruction** by exhorting him: **hold on to *it*, do not let it go,** and **guard it well**. The reason: **it is your life**.

■ **14-17** To make sure that the son follows his instruction the sage adds several prohibitions. He enjoins him **not *to* set foot on the path of the wicked**. He reinforces this injunction with three short prohibitions: **avoid it, do not travel on it,** and **turn from it**, adding **go on your way**. The son is not even to take one step on the way that the wicked travel because of the possibility of being influenced by their corrupt demeanor. This injunction indicates that while walking along the straight path a person, at times, comes close to or may even cross **the path of the wicked**. Whenever that is the case, the son must not pause and ponder its character, lest he be drawn to take a step on it to look at some intriguing feature on that way. If he should do so, he may never return to the way of wisdom.

As motivation for these injunctions the father describes the character of **the wicked** traveling the crooked path. They are so keen on harming people that **they cannot rest** or **sleep *until*** they make someone stumble. They take special delight in causing the righteous to fall, usually by creating a situation that traps an upright person into doing something wrong. This desire is so ingrained in their character that they are described as those who **eat the bread of wickedness and drink the wine of violence**. As Fox (2000, 181) says, "Their characters (are) warped to the core." Thus, it is not prudent for the son even to step on their path. In so doing he places himself in danger of becoming one of their victims.

■ **18-19** The sage concludes this segment with two general sayings that contrast **the path of the righteous** and **the way of the wicked**. **The path** that **the righteous** travel is well lit. Its light becomes **brighter** and brighter as one travels along **the path** similar to the **sun's shining ever brighter** as it rises.

The way of the wicked, by contrast, is beset by **deep darkness**. Consequently, **the wicked** have no awareness of where they are on that path or of the obstacles that lie before them. They often **stumble**, but they have no idea over what. Even before death they are plagued by a profound sense of lostness.

c. A Focused Life (4:20-27)

■ **20-22** As a prelude to the crucial importance of staying on "the way of wisdom" (v 11), the sage exhorts *his* son *to* pay attention to his words. He earnestly desires that *his* son keep his words ever present in his thinking by planting them *in his* heart. The sage supports this exhortation by emphasizing two great benefits that attend *keeping his* words. (1) *His* words . . . are life to those who grasp them. That is, following his teaching leads to a long, blessed life. (2) *His* words promote health throughout *the* body. Good health is essential for having a joyous, long life.

■ **23-24** Here the sage takes up two new topics: *guarding the* heart (vv 23-24) and focusing one's sight on the premier goal, acquiring wisdom (v 25). It is essential that *the* son guard *his* heart because everything he says and does flows from it. Since Hebrew lacks a specific word for mind, it uses heart for the activities we associate with the mind. The heart is the locus of a person's thinking and vital feelings, such as love, delight, and anger. In the heart a person ponders ideas in the context of one's feelings, desires, ambitions, and attitudes and decides on a course of action. Thus, the heart is the locus of a person's will. Consequently, a person striving for wisdom must diligently guard *the* heart.

In this context the sage emphasizes the body members that *the* heart controls: *ears,* "eyes" (v 25), mouth, lips, *eyelids,* and "feet" (v 26). Through the ears and the eyes the heart receives sights, impressions, and ideas. Responding to this information, the *mind* expresses one's thoughts, feelings, and desires through these organs. The most immediate responses are made in words (*the* lips) and action ("*the* feet"). Thus, it is critical that *the son* guard *his* heart to avoid speaking or acting in a way that will make him vulnerable to breaking a commitment, incurring harm, or damaging a relationship.

Above all it is crucial that the son controls *his* mouth or *his* lips, the organs that express his thoughts and feelings verbally. He needs to keep *his* mouth free from speaking perversity and *his* lips from uttering corrupt or demeaning talk. By controlling his speech, the son's words will be genuine, not duplicitous. He will become respected as a person who speaks judiciously and holds confidence well.

■ **25** The son must keep *his* eyes *looking* straight ahead. While traveling life's path, he is not to be looking all around. By glancing here and there he is likely to lose focus and unwittingly deviate from moving toward the supreme goal, attaining wisdom (see 6:12-19).

The metaphor of keeping one's eyes focused straight ahead derives from farming. To plough a straight furrow, essential for cultivating and harvesting, a farmer focuses on a fixed point in the distance. Jesus employed this imagery: "No one who puts a hand to the plow and looks back is fit for service in the kingdom of God" (Luke 9:62). Thus, it is essential that the son keep *his* eyes focused on wisdom so that he may live honorably and reach the supreme goal.

■ **26-27** The son must also **give careful thought to** [lit. *make level* or *straight*] **the paths** on which he is traveling. Then all *his* **ways** [i.e., all his goals and the projects he engages in] *will be established*. That will be his experience because he works diligently and deals honorably in all relationships.

It is also important that as he travels along the son *examine the* **ways**, particularly **the** *byways* (*ma'gāl*), his **feet** are taking. Then he will not deviate from the true way by obliviously turning either **to the right or the left**. By never setting **foot** on the **evil** path, he walks confidently forward. In other words, by keeping his eyes focused "straight ahead" (v 25), the son never cuts corners or compromises his integrity.

The exhortations in this instruction give the son clear guidance for ordering his life discreetly and honorably. The son who guards what enters the heart and carefully evaluates what the heart prompts him to say, to gaze at, and to do, lives wisely and righteously.

FROM THE TEXT

The acquisition of wisdom is the highest goal in life. To reach this goal a person must follow diligently the instructions that have been passed down through the great sages.

This goal is realizable because Wisdom embraces one who maintains focus on the primary goal while traveling through life. Wisdom provides guidance and protection. At critical junctions she prods one's conscience to prevent straying from the true path.

While traveling along, a person has the assurance of being on the right path, because it is well lit. In fact, the lighting becomes continually brighter as one proceeds. This imagery means that one's understanding of God's ways becomes continually clearer—more expansive and more comprehensive. One's growth in understanding moral and spiritual issues increases one's joy in engaging wisdom.

While walking on the straight way, one must guard the heart, that is, one's thinking, to prevent compromising one's character in regard to attitude, speech, or action. As part of guarding the heart, it is important to manage all one's bodily organs so that none of them compels one to deviate from the honorable course. It is critical to control one's speech and the inner self that is at the core of self-control (Murphy 1998, 29). Also it is important to keep one's eyes fixed on the goal of developing a blameless upright character. As one matures, one gains a strong sense of place in the community by helping others, thereby honoring God.

5. Instruction: Shun the Adulterous Woman; Take Delight in Your Wife (5:1-23)

OVERVIEW

This instruction has four sections. The first two and the last two are tightly connected. The sage begins with a vivid description of the dreadful results that attend connecting with an adulterous woman (vv 1-6). Given these perils the sage exhorts his son to stay far away from her house (vv 7-14). In the third section he emphasizes that the proper way to satisfy one's libido is with one's wife (vv 15-20). The sage undergirds his teaching with two great truths (vv 21-23): (1) Yahweh examines all the ways a person takes (v 21), and (2) wrongful deeds trap the wicked, leading to an early death (vv 22-23). In this instruction the sage skillfully uses evocative imagery that has various shades of meaning to engage the son's imagination (Alter 1985, 181-84).

The instruction is tightly knit by the intertwining of several words: "my son(s)" (vv 1, 7, 20), "the adulterous woman" or "another man's wife" (*zārâ* [vv 3*a*, 20*a*]), "strangers" (*zārîm* [vv 10*a*, 17*b*]), "another" (*nokrî* [v 10*b*]), "a wayward woman" (*nokriyyâ* [v 20*b*]), "the end" of life (vv 4, 11), *tāmak* (rendered "lead straight to" [v 5*b*] and "hold . . . fast" [v 22*b*]), "discipline" (vv 12, 23), *pallēs* (rendered **gives thought** [v 6*a*] and **examine** [v 21*b*]).

Words from two domains occur throughout. The dominant domain is parts of the body: "ear" (vv 1, 13), "lips" (vv 2, 3), eyes (rendered "full view" [v 21]), palate (rendered "speech" [v 3]), voice (v 13 NRSV; omitted by NIV), "heart" (v 12), and "feet" (v 5). The domain way has four terms: "way" (*'oraḥ* [v 6*a*]), "paths" (*ma'gĕlôt* [vv 6*b*, 21*b*]), *derek* (rendered "path" [v 8*a*] and "ways" [v 21*a*]), and "streets" (*ḥûṣâ* [v 16*a*]). The root *mût* occurs both as a noun ("death" [v 5]) and a verb ("die" [v 23]).

The sage's thesis is that the true antidote for the allure of a wayward woman is a vibrant marital relationship. That relationship is deeper, more enduring, and far safer. This assertion is underscored by two poignant metaphors. The adulterous woman is a pit leading to Sheol, while a wife is a well of refreshing water (Murphy 1998, 33).

Since making love with one's wife takes place inside one's household, the lovers enjoy pure, unadulterated pleasure in safety. But since consorting with an adulteress takes place outside one's dwelling, one faces various dangers, even the potential of losing one's wealth to strangers and death if discovered by the husband.

IN THE TEXT

a. The Consequences of Consorting with an Adulterous Woman (5:1-14)

■ **1-2** In typical style the sage addresses *the* son, exhorting him to **pay attention to** *his* wisdom (see 2:2; 4:20). This time the sage refers uniquely to his teaching as **my wisdom** and *my* **understanding**. With these lofty phrases he underscores the importance of his guidance on moral fidelity. *The* son *will* **maintain discretion** (*mĕzimmâ*; see 1:4*b*) in all his relationships by heeding this counsel. As Fox says (2000, 191), "[Discretion] provides a shield against the wiles of wicked people." This skill will guide his speaking so that he *preserves*

knowledge, namely, speaking insightfully and truthfully in all situations. The goal for a wise person is "harmony of thought and speech" (ibid.). Maintaining that harmony a person produces a virtuous character.

■ **3-6** The sage counsels the son in dealing with the sweet, enticing appeal he will receive from **the adulterous woman.** With the term **lips** the sage ties a primary weapon of **the adulterous woman** to his opening exhortation for the son to control his lips (v 2*b*). Her **lips . . . drip honey**, a highly desired sweet in ancient Israel (see Song 4:11). And **her speech is smoother than oil.** Her charming words will mesmerize him. They will so overpower him that he will forget his convictions and join her.

The sage describes the disastrous consequences that result from yielding to her enticement by focusing on **the end** of the affair. After the son has had a brief euphoric experience with her, he will discover that **she is bitter as gall.** That is, he will come to experience deep, lasting regret for having connected with her. The **bitter** taste left in his mouth, the opposite of her honeyed words, will linger for a long time. He will feel as though he has been pierced by a **sharp . . . double-edged sword.** Morally wounded, he will discover that **her steps lead straight to the grave.**

Too late the son will realize that an adulterous woman **gives no thought to the way to life,** the key gift of Wisdom (3:16-18). Focusing solely on herself and her power over men, she fails to find value in **life** that transcends wanton pleasure. Living only for momentary conquests, she *wanders* aimlessly through life, unaware that there are higher values. She feels no concern for those she has afflicted with deep regrets. Such a woman is completely clueless of the honor that attends living wisely.

■ **7-11** With an appeal to *his* **sons** to **listen to** *him*, the sage signals a shift in topic. Given the critical importance of this counsel, he makes three exhortations: (1) **do not turn aside from** my teaching, (2) *make your way* far from where the adulteress walks, and (3) **do not go near the door of her house.** The wording of the last exhortation alludes to Woman Folly's sitting on her doorstep, inviting those who pass by to join her company (9:14-17). **Door** may also carry a double meaning: entrance to **her house** and to her body. The sage is providing a sound principle. The best way to avoid being solicited by an adulterous woman is to stay away from the places where she lurks.

The sage backs up these exhortations with solid reasons. As a result of coupling with an adulterous woman the son *will* lose his **honor** and thus his standing in the community. He may also lose *his* **dignity** (*hôd*). The precise meaning of the Hebrew *hôd* is uncertain. Two likely meanings are *wealth* and sexual *vigor*.

Strangers who observe his disgraceful behavior will seek to control him. These antagonists are not identified other than as **others, cruel,** and **strangers.** Possibly these men sponsor the adulterous. In any case their goal is to take advantage of *the son's* vulnerability as a result of having joined with this woman to gain control of his **wealth**. The sage does not state how they exercise their power over him. Having gained control of his **wealth**, they spend it freely, most likely in wild partying.

Apparently this man is eventually sold into slavery, possibly to pay off the debts these **cruel** people have incurred in his name. As a result he must **toil** for **another**, *enriching* that person's **house**, rather than his own. Another possible explanation is that these **strangers** blackmail him.

In any case, having been consigned to hard labor, *his* **flesh and body are spent**. No longer carrying himself with confidence, he is bent over, walking with a limp. Because his whole body aches, he *groans*. In his later years he will regret deeply that he "hated discipline" (v 12). The suffering that now plagues him may be from sexually transmitted diseases. In any case his life ends in bitter agony and disappointment.

■ **12-14** Too late the son will admit that his stubborn attitude has led him to *spurn* his *teacher's reproofs*. He has come to realize that the sage was being stern with him primarily to get through his belligerent attitude. But, being a youth, he refused to *hear*, that is, **obey** *the voice of his* teachers. As a result he is **in serious trouble in the** community's **assembly**. That phrase means that **the assembly** was holding him accountable for his deviant behavior. As a result, he experiences the worst punishment in an ancient community: humiliation.

b. Taking Delight in One's Wife (5:15-23)

■ **15-17** Without any linguistic signal the sage suddenly shifts subjects. He instructs the son in the proper way of satisfying his libido, a way that is truly honorable.

The sage exhorts the son: **drink water** heartily . . . **from your own well**, that is, your wife. The son needs to keep in mind that she is a deep **well**, offering cool, sweet, *flowing* water. *Drinking* water drawn from a deep **well** is most refreshing, especially on a hot day. *Drinking* is a double entendre. Besides its basic meaning, it stands for vigorous lovemaking (see Song 4:15). When he *drinks* deeply of her love, he will experience satisfying sexual pleasure—pleasure free from negative consequences. Wesley comments, "Content thyself with those delights which God alloweth thee in the sober use of the marriage bed . . . That there may be excess in the marriage bed is manifest" (1975, 1839).

The sage is telling the son that rather than placing himself in danger of dishonor and grave losses by connecting with an adulteress, he will be far more invigorated by making love with his wife. Not only will he strengthen the bond between them, but also she will give him a healthy family.

To enjoy deep pleasure with his wife the son must discipline his sexual expression. The sage drives this point home with a bold rhetorical question: **Should your springs**, that is, seed, **overflow in the streets** or **in the public squares?** That is, should he wander through the town searching for a woman with whom he might connect for a night of intense pleasure? Certainly not! Rather, he must take pride in his virility by never **sharing** his seed **with strangers**, that is, particularly other men's wives (similarly Whybray 1994a, 90). Children born from those unions will not belong to him, but to the husbands of their mothers. In antiquity children were treasured; they were valuable assets that increased a family's strength.

Because his seed holds the potential for new life, he needs to preserve it solely for his wife. If he heeds this counsel, his children will grow up as vibrant contributors to his household, bringing him honor and increasing his wealth. In contrast to the wayward woman who seduces a man and then casts him away, the true wife imparts vigor, joy, and life to her man. "She protects her man, guides him, and converses with him" (Clifford 1999, 71).

■ **18-20** The sage pronounces a blessing on the son: **May your fountain** [i.e., your wife] **be blessed.** This blessing empowers her to give him a large, healthy family. The sage adds another blessing: **may you rejoice in the wife of your youth.** He is praying that the son's affection for his **wife** never wavers. Throughout life he will continue to cherish her as **a loving doe, a graceful deer** as he did when he began courting her.

Speaking more directly, the sage enjoins the son to **satisfy** his libido: he says **be satiated** by her breasts (**nipples**) and be **always** intoxicated with her love. A well-fed person is never driven to violate a society's mores in order to satisfy hunger.

The sage underscores this instruction with a double rhetorical question: **Why, my son, be intoxicated with another man's wife? Why embrace the bosom of a wayward woman?** The obvious answer for one striving to be wise is "Never, never!" Thereby he affirms that no **wayward woman** is able to provide him the deep sexual satisfaction that his wife can.

■ **21-23** The sage reinforces the principles in this frank instruction by emphasizing two sobering truths. (1) *The eyes of Yahweh* are ever vigilant, *examining* (*pallēs*) all the **paths** a person takes. Nothing escapes his attention. Yahweh is not only aware of what a person is doing but also aware of a person's motives and desires, including those that have the potential of leading to deviant behavior. The son should never even imagine that he might conceal a tryst from Yahweh's observation. The sage makes this assertion poignant with the verb **examine**. It emphasizes that Yahweh not only sees but also scrutinizes his every activity. Earlier he used a homonym to describe the adulteress as refusing to go *straight on* the way of life (v 6). Why, then, would a youth who is taking the path to wisdom connect with a woman who does not value him, the course he is taking, or honor? If reflecting on this question does not bring the youth to his senses, he needs to realize that Yahweh is fully aware of any dalliance. That awareness hopefully will bring a youth leaning to have such an encounter to his senses.

(2) Evil deeds committed by **the wicked ensnare them**. That is, every *sin* has **cords** attached. These **cords** bind the doer to the consequences of a wrongful deed. There is no way to commit a sin and not be held account- able eventually. Usually when doing something wrong a person is confident of getting away with it. For example, a man thinks that God will not care if he yields to a beautiful woman's appeal, especially just one time. But such a thought is most deceptive. It blinds him from the strings that are attached to such a sinful act. In time these strings will wrap around him, binding him to the consequences of that sin.

Once a wrong is committed it may be addressed, but it can never be un- done. The outcome for those who *lack* the **discipline** to control their libido is certain. **They will die,** *having been* **led astray by their own great folly.** In this conclusion the sage identifies adultery as *a sin* and *a great folly*.

FROM THE TEXT

This instruction describes "the life-confirming pleasures of conjugal love against the scheming embrace of deadly lust" (Alter 1985, 184). The manner in which a person satisfies the sexual drive leads either to a vibrant life of honor filled with love or to a tragic, agonizing fate. Those who satisfy their lust in multiple sexual experiences gain a sense of power. But that sense, being illusory, does not last. Over time they become entwined in a web of complex relationships that hold them hostage to their indiscretions. Many are plagued with various physical and emotional woes. Some lose their wealth. Most have to endure the reproaches of relatives and friends. Some experience loss of standing in the community. A few lose their jobs.

Jealousy is likely to take root in one or more of the sexual partners. That jealousy may propel a person to act violently, inflicting grave harm, even death, to one or more of those involved in entangled relationships (see 6:32-35).

Conversely, a couple who nourishes their love grows together through- out life. By caring for each other, they engage freely in passionate love. As the years pass their commitment to each other increases, becoming impregnable. At the end of their lives their vibrant marriage is free from the doldrums of deep regrets and a gnawing sense of having wasted one's life.

This instruction against having multiple sexual liaisons is addressed to males, because the setting of wisdom instructions was the training of young men to serve in the government and in business. An integral part of that train- ing dealt with relating to women, especially aggressive women who sought to satisfy their libido by seducing men, similar to Potiphar's wife's attempt to get Joseph to lay with her (Gen 39:6c-18). Yet it is easily imagined that in a patri- archal family mothers gave their daughters instructions on appropriate sexual behavior in order to preserve a clan's integrity (see Prov 1:8; 6:20). However, given the character of ancient Israelite society, these instructions have not been preserved. But that does not mean they did not exist, especially orally.

6. Epigrams and Instruction against Adultery (6:1-35)

OVERVIEW

This chapter has two distinct segments. The first is a collection of four sapiential maxims (vv 1-19): (1) the urgent necessity of gaining release from being the guarantor of another person's loan (vv 1-5), (2) disparagement of laziness (vv 6-11), (3) the traits of a villain (vv 12-15), and (4) a numerical saying that lists human characteristics God hates (vv 16-19). The second segment is an extended instruction against adultery (vv 20-35).

The first four maxims are connected by several words for parts of the body: "eyes" (vv 4, 13, 17), "eyelids" (v 4), "mouth" (vv 2 [2x], 12), "tongue" (v 17), "hands" (*kap* [vv 1, 3]; *yād* [vv 5, 10, 17]), "fingers" (v 13), "heart" (vv 14, 18), and "feet" (vv 13, 18). The first and second epigrams are further connected by the terms "sleep" and "slumber."

IN THE TEXT

a. A Sapiential Collection (6:1-19)

(1) Freeing Oneself from Serving as Security for Another's Loan (6:1-5)

■ **1-3** In typical fashion the father begins with **my son**. In place of a call to attention, he addresses the need for **the son** to take immediate steps to free himself from a bad obligation. He **has trapped** himself by swearing to serve **as security** for a loan taken out by **a stranger** (*zār*). **Stranger** references a friend or **a** neighbor (11:15; 17:18; 20:16; 22:26-27; 27:13). The statement that **the son has** fallen into **the** neighbor's hands (v 3) identifies **the** neighbor as the lender. **Shaking** hands in antiquity was binding similar to co-signing a loan.

The sage wants **the son** to realize that in taking on this obligation he has placed himself and his family at risk. If the borrower fails to repay the loan, he will be obligated to pay it in full. Should that time come, he may lack the resources to meet the obligation. In such a case he faces the possibility of losing everything he has accumulated, for his possessions will be taken to cover the loan.

In becoming **security** for that loan **the** son has put himself in his **neighbor's power** until the loan is repaid. Given the great risk **the** son has assumed, the sage instructs him: **Go** immediately, **humble yourself** before that neighbor, **pestering** (*rāhab*) him for release from the obligation. That is, **the** son is to keep troubling him until he gives in to the request. **The son must not give** the lender **any** rest until he is released from the obligation. The approach recommended is similar to the approach taken by a widow in one of Jesus' parables. She kept pestering a judge for justice until he granted her petition (Luke 18:1-8).

■ **4-5** The sage underscores the urgency and the need for persistence in winning release from this obligation with two sayings. (1) The son is not to **sleep** until the release is granted. That is, he is to focus all his efforts on *freeing himself* from this commitment. (2) The son must spend all his energy and ingenuity on *freeing himself* just like the determined efforts of **a gazelle** caught by *a* **hunter** or **a bird** held in *a fowler's* snare to get free.

Even though a person's word was binding in ancient Israel, the wise recognized that sometimes a person makes a commitment that is unrealistic or carries a price that is too high. A person who gets into such a bind needs to own up to the blunder and seek diligently to gain release from that obligation.

FROM THE TEXT

A youth who loves to talk may make a commitment that carries the possibility of damaging the youth's economic standing for years. A compassionate youth is very vulnerable to getting into such a bind, especially on hearing a person speak about a pressing obligation. On the spur of the moment the youth promises more than can reasonably be delivered. A youth who makes an unrealistic promise needs to seek release immediately from such an obligation.

There are situations, however, when a trustworthy person needs a co-signer for a loan. Anyone who is thinking about co-signing a loan needs to take counsel with a financial adviser or those who are well acquainted with the borrower before taking on that obligation. Wesley (1975, 1840) says "suretyship in some cases may be not only lawful, but an act of justice and charity."

IN THE TEXT

(2) Disparaging Laziness (6:6-11)

■ **6-8** With a brief parable the sage seeks to motivate a lazy person to make a radical change. *A* **sluggard** needs to stop *sleeping* and get to work. But an idler has an ingrained resistance to working. One proverb pictures a lazy person as loving sleep so much that he spends the whole day tossing about on his bed like a door on its hinges (26:14). Unless there is an attitude change, *a* **sluggard** will self-destruct (see 10:4, 26; 15:19; 20:4; 21:25; 22:13; 24:30-34; 26:13-16). The sage's concern is that such behavior endangers not only *the sluggard's* well-being but also the community's.

To get the idler's attention the sage addresses him directly: **you sluggard** (ʿāṣēl). He then seeks to motivate him with the challenge: **consider *the* ways of the ant.** By pondering the persistent diligence of such a small creature, hopefully the **sluggard** will come to realize the importance of working diligently to meet future needs.

The ant is as diligent as it is small. Even though it lacks **an overseer** for assigning the amount of food that it needs to gather for the winter, *an* **ant** busily **gathers its food** throughout the **summer**. It never takes a vacation or shortens its workday. It does not stop gathering even when a large amount of food has been stored.

The sage stresses the diligence of this small creature to instruct a youth who, though having far greater ability to think and plan than **an** ant, wastes every day in idleness. By pointing to the diligence of this small insect the sage hopes to motivate him to work diligently. This saying, constructed as an analogy from nature, has the traits of those that fit the description of Solomon's wisdom in 1 Kgs 4:33 (Heb 5:13).

■ **9** Wanting to grab the dolt's attention, the sage addresses him again, **You sluggard**. The intended audience, though, is the son or anyone pondering this teaching. The sage is endeavoring to turn youths away from falling into such a worthless lifestyle. He proceeds by putting to *the* **sluggard** a double rhetorical question: **How long will you lie there . . . ? When will you get up from your sleep?** These probing questions disclose the sage's distress at *the sluggard's* indolence and also serve to rebuke the sleepyhead (Fox 2000, 217).

■ **10-11** In place of **the** *sluggard's* answer, the sage quotes a lyrical saying: **A little sleep, a little slumber, a little folding of the hands to** *sleep*. The repetitive sounds (very prominent in the Hebrew text) imitate the sluggard's snoring in order to embarrass him. By **folding** *his* **hands** the sluggard gestures his resolve to stay in bed. The sage challenges his determination by describing the harsh consequences that will suddenly overtake him. **Poverty** and **scarcity** will attack him **like an armed man. The sluggard** is placing himself in danger of starving to death during the coming winter.

The sage may be confronting the sluggard so harshly because the setting is harvesttime, the most critical time of the year for farmers (Clifford 1999, 76). The loss of any part of the harvest decreases a community's food supply, making life harder for everyone. (See Prov 10:5.)

FROM THE TEXT

Many employees today, at all levels of a business, are inclined to waste time rather than stay focused on their tasks. They take extended coffee breaks, long lunches, and frequent trips to the restroom. Some even find a place to take a siesta. Those who behave in this way soothe their conscience by believing that they deserve a break.

Other employees like to walk about the building or the campus. While walking, some become engaged in long conversations, interrupting the work of others. Those who are inclined to engage in this type of behavior need to ponder the ways of the ant. They may come to recognize that they need to be focusing diligently on their own tasks. The way they approach their work honors both their employer and God (Col 3:17). Diligent workers tend to be more resourceful in coping with unexpected complications. Lackadaisical workers, however, are often stumped when confronted by challenges.

(3) Traits of a Villain (6:12-15)

■ **12-14** This epigram lists the obnoxious traits of **a troublemaker** or **a villain** (see Prov 16:27-30). Its goal is to censure these behaviors as characteristics of repugnant characters (Fox 2009, 219). **A troublemaker** (*'ādām bĕliyyaʿal*) is employed in the OT for people who engage in revolting behaviors: sexual perverts (Judg 19:22), scoundrels who lead people into idolatry (Deut 13:13 [14 HB]), priests who commit sacrilege (1 Sam 2:12), malcontents (1 Sam 10:27), and perjurers (1 Kgs 21:13). Such people have intolerable traits. They **go** about with corrupt **mouths**, that is, speaking either out of the corner of **the** mouth or with a contorted **mouth**. Their manner of speaking is in accord with their intent to mislead, deceive, or denigrate. They have nervous mannerisms: **squinting with the eyes, scraping** with **the** feet, or **motioning** with **the** fingers. Most people find such mannerisms to be very annoying. Some, taking them as signs of disapproval, become very irritated. Since **perversity** lodges in **their hearts**, they **constantly plot** evil and **are** always **stirring** up conflict. Because the thinking of **troublemakers** is perverted, their behaviors are morally corrupt.

■ **15** As a consequence of their malicious behaviors and vile deeds, **troublemakers** will face a terrible fate. **Disaster will overtake them** in an instant. Unexpectedly they will incur fatal injuries.

(4) A Numerical Saying Listing Negative Human Traits (6:16-19)

■ **16-19** This epigram is a numerical saying (see the overview at 30:15-33). The first line of a numerical saying states a characteristic that is common to a certain number of items. The second line, structured as affirming, raises that number by one and adds a second characteristic that is common to all members of the list. In this saying **six** is paralleled by **seven**. This list has two categories. First, it lists **five** ways that people employ parts of the body to dishonor others: their **eyes, tongue, hands, heart**, or **feet**. God considers such misuses of the body members **detestable**. Second, the list identifies two types of people God **hates**.

This epigram is similar to the preceding one in associating repulsive thoughts and behaviors with parts of the body. Whereas the behaviors in the preceding epigram are mostly gestures, in this epigram people use a body member to commit aggravating sins. These vile deeds are condemned strongly by the phrase **detestable to *Yahweh.***

(1) **Haughty eyes**. A person walks about with the eyes tilted upward, conveying "I am the greatest" (Job 21:22; Ps 101:3; Isa 2:11-18; 10:33). An arrogant bearing arouses contempt in others. It also blinds a person to one's own hubris.

(2) **A lying tongue**. Lies are destructive. Lying destroys trust (see Prov 12:17, 19; 14:5; 19:5, 9; 21:6; 26:28). Servants and officials who give faulty

information to a supervisor prevent that person from developing sound strategies to deal with problems.

(3) **Hands that shed innocent blood**. Suddenly and for no apparent reason, this kind of person strikes an **innocent** bystander so hard that blood begins to flow. The person struck may die from that blow (see 1:11-14). Such violent behavior arouses fear and hatred in the community.

(4) **A heart that devises wicked *plans***. Such a *mind* loves to concoct intricate, malicious **schemes**, especially for advancing one's own interests at the expense of others. That kind of *mind* takes pleasure in watching people becoming distressed.

(5) **Feet that are quick to rush into *doing wrong***. This kind of person jumps at a chance of getting involved in wicked activities.

(6) **A false witness who *blows* out** [*pûaḥ*; DCH 6:665; Fox 2000, 223-24] **lies** (12:17; 14:5, 25; 19:5, 9). Such **a witness** enjoys presenting a fabricated description of something that took place in order to lead the court to render a judgment against an innocent person. The verb *blows* pictures this witness speaking excitedly and loudly, as a myriad of faulty details pours out of his mouth. The witness speaks in this manner, believing that it will persuade people that his account is accurate. Such a witness mocks the judicial system.

(7) **A person who stirs up conflict in the community**. A malcontent enjoys instigating disputes, thereby setting people at odds. Lies and slander are key means for arousing animosity.

In God's view these demeanors, actions, and types of people are **detestable**. They behave in ways that are totally opposite to his character. This epigram, then, encourages people to emulate God's attitude toward such obnoxious behaviors.

"Yahweh Detests or Abomination to Yahweh"

The Hebrew *tôʿēbâ* (**detestable** [NIV, REB], "abomination" [NJPS, NRSV]) condemns a behavior or an act as very offensive, highly repulsive, or extremely loathsome. Such behaviors or attitudes grate against a community's sensitivities, religious beliefs, or moral standards. Engaging in any of these practices threatens a community's solidarity.

The phrase "***Yahweh* detests**" or *abomination to Yahweh* expresses even stronger condemnation of a particular practice. This phrase occurs eight times in Deuteronomy (e.g., 18:9, 12; 23:18) and eleven times in Proverbs (3:32; 11:1, 20; 12:22; 15:8, 9, 26; 16:5; 17:15; 20:10, 23). It stands in 6:16*b*, but in place of God's name is **to him** (*napšô*).

This phrase censures practices that Yahweh considers to be contrary to his holy character. In committing such an offense a person's behavior is an affront to God. Practices so condemned in the Law include idolatry (Deut 7:25; 27:15), sacrificing blemished animals (Deut 17:1), and sacrificing children (Deut 12:31).

In Proverbs Yahweh detests "dishonest scales" (Prov 11:1; see 20:10, 23), "perverse" hearts (minds) (11:20; see 15:26), "lying" (12:22), "the sacrifice of the wicked" (15:8; see 21:27), "the way of the wicked" (15:9), "the proud of heart" (16:5), and perversions of justice (17:15). Also reprehensible are the prayers of a person who brazenly refuses instruction (28:9).

Other proverbs describe what a particular group detests. "The righteous detest the dishonest; the wicked detest the upright" (29:27); "people detest a mocker" (24:9); "kings detest wrongdoing" (16:12); "fools detest turning from evil" (13:19); Wisdom's "lips detests wickedness" (8:7).

b. The Dangers of Adultery (6:20-35)

■ **20** The sage signals a change in subject by exhorting *the* son, **keep your father's command and do not forsake your mother's teaching** (see 1:8). The reference to both parents underscores the importance of this **teaching** on adultery. The reference to *the* **mother's teaching** is vital, for an act of adultery threatens the clan's solidarity. The sage is thereby recognizing that both parents play an essential role in raising their children to adhere to Israel's sexual mores.

■ **21-24** Because parental instructions on this subject are so vital, the sage enjoins the son to **bind them . . . on** *his* **heart.** By committing them to memory they will be vividly present in his thoughts, especially on those occasions when he finds himself in a tempting situation. The sage goes on to enjoin him to wear them about *his* **neck** (see 1:9; 3:3). That is, he is to wear a pendant that reminds him of their *teachings*.

Throughout his life their *teachings* will serve as a reliable **guide. When** he *sleeps*, **they will watch over** him. **When** he *awakes*, **they will** *converse* with him, guiding him to proper conduct in the presence of another's wife. They will function as **a light** illuminating his path throughout life.

Should he ever deviate from that path, their words will function as *reproof* and **instruction**, keeping him on **the way to life.** In other words, when he finds himself in an ominous situation, these words will prick his conscience, alerting him to the danger of being led astray by **the smooth talk of a wayward woman.** If he heeds that *reproof,* he will reject that woman's appeal and avoid getting involved in a devastating, life-threatening affair.

It is valuable to note that in the Hebrew text the terms **command** (vv 20*a*, 23*a*) and **teaching** (vv 20*b*, 23*a*) are feminine along with the suffix on the verb in v 22*c*. With these feminine forms the sage is skillfully personalizing the parents' **instruction**. Their **instruction** is being visualized as being with the son like a faithful woman. She *watches* over *him* day and night and *converses* with him on awakening (v 22; Yoder 2009, 78; Fox 2000, 229).

At opportune moments she will engage him in conversation, keeping him from departing from the straight path. In this manner the sage is saying that the parents' *teachings* offer him companionship that is far more enriching than the pleasure offered by another man's **wife.**

■ **25** The sage forthrightly commands: **Do not lust in your heart after her beauty.** The way a seductress adorns herself exalts her sensuous appeal. Gesturing invitingly with her highlighted eyes, she seeks to capture a man's attention. Whenever a man becomes enamored of a woman's beauty, desire may so overpower him that his inner moral restraints are vanquished. Unless he comes quickly to his senses and harnesses his **lust**, he will become her prey.

■ **26-29** The sage motivates his exhortation by describing the dreadful consequences that attend yielding to the lure of **another man's wife**. She **preys on his** very life. In fact, **no one who touches her will go unpunished**. In joining her he is likely to pay with his life.

To get this point across the sage boldly contrasts the high cost of such a tryst with the low cost of hiring a prostitute—an act that the son would shun even though it would only cost the price of **a loaf of bread**. In making this comparison the sage is no more condoning hiring **a prostitute** than he is encouraging theft in the coming analogy of stealing bread (v 30). His point is that if the son would not think of paying for **a prostitute**, why would he consider succumbing to the lure of a married woman, especially given the much higher price he likely will have to pay?

The sage supports the grave danger that accompanies joining with a married woman by using two vivid analogies. They are structured as rhetorical questions to impress on the youth that he cannot escape terrible consequences. **Can a man scoop fire into his lap without his clothes being burned?** Is it possible for **a man** to **walk on hot coals without his feet being scorched?** The wording of the second question ties into the sage's desire for the son to "**be guided on** the way to life" by heeding **the teachings** of his parents (vv 22-23).

Both of these rhetorical questions demand the exclamation: "Of course not!" Incidentally, the ancient Israelites must never have seen entertainers amaze crowds by walking on hot coals.

Most rhetorical questions are left unanswered. Here the sage provides an answer, for he does not want the son to miss the point. If the son **sleeps with another man's wife**, he will face harsh, long-lasting consequences. By not stating specific consequences, the sage lets the youth imagine all kinds of appalling troubles.

■ **30-31** The sage proceeds by focusing on the consequences that attend committing adultery. He begins with an analogy. When a starving **thief** is caught stealing to **satisfy his hunger**, he has to pay a heavy penalty. This is his fate even though **people** are not inclined to **despise** such **a thief**. Nevertheless, he must pay **sevenfold** the cost of what was stolen. While there are laws in the covenant code in Exodus that prescribe restitution for a theft at a multiple of the value of the object (see Exod 22:1, 4, 7, 9 [21:37; 22:3, 6, 8 HB]), none stipulate a **sevenfold** penalty. Thus, the sage is using a hyperbole. However, in this example the sage describes the punishment as even more onerous. The fine is not reduced even if it **costs the thief** all **the wealth of his house**. Certainly **a thief** who was unable to afford food would not be able to pay such a high penalty. A possible reason that the penalty is so high is that there were other ways for a hungry person to get food rather than by stealing, such as gleaning in a field.

In any case the sage is using **sevenfold** as a hyperbole to underscore the extreme cost of committing adultery. Assuredly, the sage's using **a thief** as an analogy for the lure of a married woman is sound, for both men are driven to break the Law in order to satisfy a strong physical desire. The central point is that if a small theft incurs a steep, unbearable penalty, the penalty for committing **adultery** will be even higher.

■ **32-33** The sage specifies more harsh consequences that result from committing **adultery.** Through such a foolish act a person **destroys himself,** socially and morally. He will face **blows and disgrace,** most likely from her husband, who is *furious* at him for being with his wife (Prov 6:34). When he is beating on the culprit, he will show no lenience. The adulterer faces even greater social punishment in that **his shame will never be wiped away.** Small communities, especially in antiquity, have long memories.

■ **34-35** The sage reiterates that an adulterer's indiscretion ignites *the* husband's fury, propelling him to *take* revenge without *showing* any mercy. Should that fool try to dampen *the* husband's fury by offering **compensation** or **a bribe** (*kōper*), he will refuse any offer, no matter how **great it is.** *Kōper* is a term used in the sacrificial legislation for sacrifices that achieve forgiveness for wrongdoing.

When God accepts such a sacrifice, his anger is soothed and he grants forgiveness. However, there is nothing that will calm an offended husband's fury. In fact, the offended husband is likely to become angrier, taking the offer as an insult. He may view it as payment for the services of his wife. This possibility is conveyed by the term **bribe,** a term that implies the offer is illegitimate.

This instruction against adultery ends on a solemn note, thereby underscoring the seriousness of committing such a transgression. All who have been offended by that act carry lasting resentment against the adulterer.

FROM THE TEXT

Given the current individualistic, hedonistic culture of the West, the general populace expresses little concern with acts of adultery. In fact, such acts are viewed as normative, that is, the activity of two consenting adults. Those who commit adultery today have little fear of serious consequences.

Nevertheless, sexual intercourse is a very private matter that has profound social consequences. Some who commit adultery do encounter harsh consequences. That act has the potential of inflaming relatives of either party. Sometimes one of the offended parties becomes so irate that he inflicts great harm on the offender, even murder. A few even become so irate that they go on a shooting spree, wounding or killing people at random. Thus, it remains critical even today to be mindful of the potential terrible consequences that may attend an act of adultery.

From another perspective those who fear God need to be aware that there is a deep connection between faithfulness to God and faithfulness to one's spouse. The way one treats a spouse is parallel to the essential character of one's relationship with God. This reality behooves a person to be faithful to one's spouse. In so doing a person honors God.

Moreover, those who are key leaders of a congregation, ministerial or laity, must be vigilant in withstanding the allure of a person who is intent on corrupting a faithful person by enticing the person to engage in sexual exploits.

Leaders who commit sexual indiscretions, above all adultery, send shock waves throughout a congregation. Their infidelity causes great confusion in those they have inspired to believe in Jesus. Some become so disheartened that they become unsure of the viability of having faith in God. Others become so disgusted at such behavior that they turn their back on the church. A congregation may suffer a split. Should that happen, it usually takes years for that church to become healthy again.

This teaching encourages all who fear God to quench the fire of lust before it leads to committing adultery. When facing a woman's appeal, Joseph's response in that situation offers a great model. Because he feared God, he pulled himself away from Potiphar's wife and fled. Fleeing is often the best way to escape the temptation to engage in sexual misconduct. It is essential to keep in mind that the pleasures of a few moments never come close to outweighing the shame and regret of a lifetime.

The sage's teaching is frank and forceful. But Jesus' teaching on lusting after another is even stronger. He says that a person who looks on a woman lustfully has already committed adultery with her in his heart (Matt 5:28). His standard is the highest. In following Jesus a Godfearer will strive to keep from feeding lust. Nevertheless, all believers need to remember that Jesus was willing to forgive the woman taken in adultery (John 8:2-11). Jesus forgave her, removing the guilt of her sin and setting her free from the bondage of that sin.

7. Instruction: A Portrait of Seduction (7:1-27)

OVERVIEW

This instruction has a chiastic structure A-B-A'. The core teaching (Prov 7:6-23) is framed by exhortations to listen carefully and to be diligent in keeping this counsel (vv 1-5, 24-27). At the center is a vivid picture of an adulterous woman seducing a youth. The sage's goal is to keep his son or student from falling to the skillful wiles of such a woman, for succumbing to her carries severe consequences.

a. Exhortation to Keep the Sage's Words (7:1-5)

■ **1-5** In typical fashion the sage begins with **my son** and an exhortation to **keep, store up,** and **guard his words** so that he *may* **live** well. He desires that *the* **son** value his **teachings as the apple** [*pupil*] **of** *his* eye. If he prizes them highly, he will gladly **write them on the tablet of** *his* heart, that is, memorize them (see 3:3). He is also to **bind them on** *his* **fingers.** This directive encourages the son to wear a symbol representing the commands as a continual reminder to follow them.

The sage goes on to urge *the* **son** to identify **wisdom** as *his* **sister** and **insight** as his **relative.** By personifying **wisdom** and **insight** as close *relatives,* the sage wants *the* **son** to become so enamored with **wisdom** that she will always be present with him as a guide. She will watch over him, *keeping* him from yielding to the **seductive words** of **the wayward woman.** *Wisdom's* guidance will alert *the* **son** to realize that the seductress's promises are hollow and that the pleasures she offers are fleeting.

b. A Portrait of Seduction (7:6-23)

■ **6-9** The sage gives a vivid description of an adulterous woman seeking for a companion. He recounts what he saw taking place one early evening as he *looked out* **the window of** *his* **house.** A **lattice** that covered **the window** concealed him from the view of those moving about in the streets below. He noticed **a youth who** *lacked judgment* **going down the street . . . in the direction of** *the wayward woman's* **house.**

Since it was **twilight, . . . the day was fading.** Likely this youth was returning home from working all day in the fields located outside the city's walls. He was unaware that a woman was observing him. Since it was getting **dark,** others passing by would not pay any attention to the encounter that was about to take place.

■ **10-20** *A woman,* **dressed like a prostitute,** *came out to meet him.* From her haunt she had been looking for a man she could entice to spend the evening with her. The sage, having watched her walking the streets on other occasions, knew that **she** *was loud* and **defiant** (see 9:13). **Her feet never** *stayed* **at home.** Her brazen demeanor indicates that she relished breaking the behavioral standards for a married woman. Often she spent an evening looking for a companion. In light of her mannerisms and dress, the sage knew that she was approaching this **young** *man* **with crafty intent.**

The sage is describing to his son a seductress's tactics in detail in order that on an occasion when a woman approaches him and begins bragging about her activities of the day, he will be alert to her real intent. This woman is not a harlot. Rather, she is a bold, defiant, rich woman who habitually seeks to satisfy her libido with men she is able to charm. She leads a double life likely because her husband is often away on long business trips.

This evening she noticed *this* youth approaching *the* corner where she *was lurking*. Leaving her haunt, she went up to him, **grabbed** his arm, **and kissed him**. With **a brazen face** she addressed him: **Today I** *have* **fulfilled my vows**. With this assertion she was telling him that she had gone to the temple earlier that day and presented **fellowship** or *peace offerings*. She made these *offerings* to **fulfill** her **vows**. By mentioning that she had gone to the temple and offered these sacrifices, she was presenting herself to him as a very religious person, one who kept her word. She was also letting him know that she was rich, for she had made *offerings*. Most people could only afford sacrificing one animal, but she was rich enough to present *offerings*.

More importantly for *the* youth is her mentioning the *offerings.* She is letting him know that she has a large supply of meat at her house on which they could feast for hours—a rare treat in antiquity save for the rich. This fact would be very appealing to *a* youth, especially one who was hungry after having worked hard all day. The adulteress was offering him a key incentive for continuing to listen to her.

The Fellowship Offering

In the sacrificial legislation *a* **fellowship offering** was presented for any of three purposes: praising God, fulfilling a vow, or engaging in a spontaneous act of worship (see Lev 7:12, 16). The animal was brought to the main altar located near the entrance to the temple and slain. The priest splashed its blood against the altar. The internal organs, the kidneys, liver, and fat, were burnt on the altar (Lev 3:3-5). Most of the meat was then returned to the presenter, providing the basis for a grand feast with family members. Meat from this type of offering presented in fulfillment of a vow could be eaten for up to two days after the sacrifice was made (Lev 7:16-18).

This woman had presented these offerings to *fulfill* her **vows**. She says nothing about the nature of her **vows**. Many explanations have been proposed, but none have gained wide acceptance. If *this* youth were to focus on her religious zeal, he would deem her worthy of trust. Also he would be aware that she had an abundance of delicious meat, a luxury in antiquity, at her house. If he accompanied her, he would dine sumptuously.

She continued, **I came out to meet you**. She added, **I looked** *eagerly* **for you and have found you!** In the Hebrew text the pronoun **you** is stressed; she uses it three times in Prov 7:15. She was continuing to boost his ego and arouse his excitement. His thoughts of spending an evening with her were beginning to erode his moral resistance against joining a wayward woman.

She proceeds to describe the elaborate preparations she has made for them to spend a delightful evening together. She *has* **covered** *her couch* with quilts made of exquisite *multicolored Egyptian* linens (*DCH* 5:477). These quilts were soft and warm. She *has* perfumed *her* bed with all kinds of expensive spices: **myrrh, aloes and cinnamon** (see Song 1:13; 3:6; 4:6, 11, 14-16; 5:5, 13). These spices were imported from Arabia and the Far East. Their aroma was making her house pleasant, providing a sensual atmosphere for lovemaking.

Having reached the critical moment of decision, she invites him to join her for an evening of sexual indulgence. She says, **Come, let's drink deeply of love till morning; let's enjoy ourselves with love**. The term **love** is plural, and the verb **let's enjoy ourselves** stands in the reflexive stem. Using these words with this sense, she is stimulating his erotic imagination. They will delight each other throughout the night.

Perceiving that this **youth** might be hesitating to accept her offer of an evening of sensual pleasure because she is married, she proceeds to assure him that he need not fear their being discovered by her **husband**. She says, **My husband is not at home; he has gone on a long journey**. To assure *the* youth that her **husband** is indeed gone for several days, she adds, **He took his purse filled with money**, that is, a bag full of gold and silver coins. This fact indicated that he planned to be away for several days. The earliest time he would return would be at **full moon**.

In antiquity traveling a long distance was safer when a **full moon** brightened the landscape. Moreover, since their conversation was taking place on a dark evening, it was the time of the new moon (Fox 2000, 248). That meant her **husband** would not return for a couple of weeks.

■ **21-23** *Her* **persuasive words** and **smooth talk** convinced the youth to accompany her. After all, she was offering him an abundance of rich food and exotic pleasure free of charge. If he were to go to a professional prostitute, he would have to pay a goodly sum.

Suddenly the youth **followed** her. Whenever a youth suddenly decides to engage in a wrongful deed, it is very unlikely that he will change course before having completed that deed. No doubt the youth walked slightly behind her as she led the way to her house, oblivious to the danger he was getting into.

To stress that danger the sage describes the outcome of his joining her with three graphic metaphors. His *following* her was **like an ox going to the slaughter** or **like a deer stepping into a noose**. *The* **noose** holds it *until* the hunter comes and shoots **an arrow** that **pierces** *its* **liver**. Or he was **like a bird darting** about **a snare**, *unaware* that at the very moment it stepped on it, the snare would take *its* life. Like these clueless animals the youth was too naive to realize the disastrous fate that awaited him at her house.

c. Exhortation against Yielding to a Wayward Woman (7:24-27)

■ **24-27** Having completed the portrait of seduction, the sage appeals to *his* sons to **listen** *attentively* to *his* **words**. He earnestly pleads, **Do not let your heart turn to her ways**. *Do not* **stray into her paths**.

100

The sage motivates his pleas by describing the horrible fate of those who have followed a wayward woman. *She has brought down many victims.* Among **her slain are *numerous powerful*** men. With this straightforward description the sage is telling *his* sons that they are not sufficiently skilled or strong to escape the punishments that follow carousing with such a woman. In fact, **her house is a highway to the grave** or *Sheol*, vividly referenced as **the chambers of death**. That is, in Sheol there are rooms where the deceased eke out a meager existence.

FROM THE TEXT

This forthright, detailed instruction against spending a night with an adulterous woman warns a youth seeking wisdom to resist a seductively dressed, outgoing, bold, rich woman. Such a woman is highly skilled at seduction. She boosts a man's ego and arouses his libido to such a pitch that he will find it virtually impossible to resist accompanying her for an evening of pleasure. Her skills at captivating his interest are so wily that she is able to overcome a man's moral resolve against frolicking with a married woman. Thus, it is best that a young man not begin to converse with such a woman.

Similarly, a woman must not let her guard down when a man engages her in sensual talk. This especially includes a man who has a reputation for being spiritual. If such a male begins to speak with her in intimate, sexual ways, she must resist her inclination to trust him because she believes him to be a godly person. Given his high standing in the community of faith, she may believe that he is offering her counsel rather than seeking to lower her defenses so that he may satisfy his sensual longings with her. This kind of man uses spirituality to lower her resistance to becoming involved in an affair.

Outside of marriage two people of different genders may have a deep intellectual or spiritual working association as long as they avoid all sensual overtones. Once sexual innuendos enter their rapport, their libido is likely to dominate the relationship, leading them to engage in unacceptable behaviors.

Their getting involved sexually will lead to disastrous consequences for both parties. When a woman and a man mix sensual pleasure with spiritual conversation or activities, they confuse their moral bearing. They delude themselves into sanctifying sensual acts as spiritual expressions. Becoming convinced that God has made them for each other, they will break their commitments to their spouses. In so doing they will inflict deep hurt on their spouses, children, parents, and siblings. They will lose the trust of relatives and close friends. Many times the consequences may prove irreparable.

In today's permissive culture all who fear the Lord must take this instruction to heart. By storing it deep within them, it will serve as a warning whenever a friendly conversation with a person of the opposite gender starts to turn in a direction that is likely to lead to intimate contact. If one of those conversing does not forthrightly see the danger and change the direction their relationship is heading, the outcome will produce devastating consequences, possibly the death of their marriages and their relationship with God.

8. Wisdom's Exaltation (8:1-36)

OVERVIEW

This instruction lauds Wisdom for her special relationship with God and for endowing Israel's leaders with the skills to govern justly and prudently. She is highly exalted as the first entity God brought into being. Since she observed God's making the world, her knowledge and insight are supreme. On earth she walks throughout the city, energetically calling out, inviting all to accept her invitation to become wise.

This portrait of Wisdom is strategically placed. It serves as a bold contrast to the preceding instruction that describes a wayward woman's seducing a youth (ch 7). Whereas the adulteress waits until the shadows of the day grow long before entering the streets to search for a companion, Wisdom walks throughout the city during the day, calling out to anyone who will listen (Murphy 1998, 49). The adulteress offers intense pleasure for a night while Wisdom offers to empower those who accept her call with keen intellectual skills and a long, honorable life.

IN THE TEXT

a. Wisdom's Role on Earth (8:1-21)

■ **1-3** A third party, possibly a sage, introduces **Wisdom** with two rhetorical questions whereby Wisdom invites people to join her. These questions shift the student's focus away from the portrait of the seductress to the role of Woman Wisdom. As she **calls** out she moves throughout the city so that all hear her call. **She takes a stand** at the **highest point along the way**, the location of government offices, temples, and markets. Eventually she arrives at **the city's gate**, where people gather to converse, traveling merchants display their wares, and cases are tried. There she stops and **cries out loudly.** At this location visitors entering the city have the opportunity to respond to her calling.

■ **4-5** From here on Wisdom is the speaker. She **calls out** to all people (*'îšîm*). She makes no distinction as to class, profession, or social standing. She specifically addresses **the** simple (*pĕtāyîm*; i.e., malleable youths) and **fools** (*kĕsîlîm*; i.e., adults set in their ways; see 1:22). The last two terms function as a merism for everyone. She invites **the** simple to **gain prudence** or **cunning** (*'ormâ*; see 1:4a) and **fools an understanding heart**. Her addressing **fools** (*kĕsîlîm*) suggests that she holds out hope that even hardened fools may accept her invitation and change their ways.

■ **6-9** She motivates people to **listen** to her invitation by assuring them that she has **trustworthy things to say.** She adds that her words are **right, true,** and **just.** They are reliable and morally sound. To strengthen her claim she asserts that *her* lips detest wickedness. **Detest** is a very strong Hebrew word for *disgust* (→ sidebar "Yahweh Detests or Abomination to Yahweh" at 6:16-19). She assures those listening that **none of *her words* is** **crooked or perverse.** Given the context of the preceding chapter, she is stressing that her words are unlike those of the adulteress (1:10-19; 5:1-14; 7:14-21). She supports these assertions by stating affirmatively that **they are upright to those who have *attained* knowledge.**

■ **10-11** Boldly **Wisdom** exhorts those listening to **choose *her* instruction** (*mûsār*; → sidebar "Reference to Liturgical Practices in Proverbs" at 3:9-10) and **knowledge** over the pursuit of material wealth as represented by **silver** and **choice gold.** She adds that **wisdom is *better* than rubies.** In fact, the value of all jewels and precious metals, even including the British crown jewels, *cannot be compared with wisdom.*

FROM THE TEXT

Wisdom invites everyone to gain prudence by seeking it diligently. Those who take up the search must prize honesty. Making that decision in today's materialistic world is very difficult for many. Middle-aged adults, in particular, have a hard time perceiving that the course of prudence is the pursuit of instruction and knowledge over the acquisition of wealth. Wisdom challenges that errant perspective by describing the skills and virtues they will gain by following her. These skills are more valuable than any amount of wealth. In fact, they are more valuable than anything humans desire. Her presence with a person is the highest value in life.

IN THE TEXT

■ **12-14** Wisdom describes her own character. She makes several self-declarations: **I *am* wisdom; I . . . dwell with prudence** (*ʿormâ*), that is, the skill of developing strategies to live righteously and to escape pitfalls (compare 1:4a). She adds **I possess knowledge and discretion** (*mĕzimmôt*; compare 1:4b). With these skills she knows what is best for every person. In v 14 she asserts: **counsel and sound judgment** [*ʿēṣâ wĕtûiyyâ*] **are mine. I have insight** [*bînâ*; see 1:2b], **I have power** (*gĕbûrâ* [v 14b]). The ancients believed that only God had these skills (Job 12:13).

This recounting of her character in Prov 8:12 and 14 encloses her declaration of things she hates. This declaration is headed by the principle: **to fear Yahweh is to hate evil.** On this foundation she declares: **I hate pride and arrogance, evil behavior and perverse speech.** Because of her virtues she does not countenance self-centered, egotistical behavior. Sinners, however, prize these attitudes. They use them to control and harm others.

But Wisdom resists vices and distortions of truth with all her strength. This is especially the case with speech. God gave humans the ability to use words for sharing ideas, encouraging one another, and expressing needs. But **perverse speech** demeans a person, inflicting deep, painful wounds.

■ **15-16** Wisdom boasts that she bestows intellectual abilities on **kings, rulers, princes**, and **nobles**. She enables them to rule judiciously and mercifully (Fox 2000, 273). When a nation is ruled by a wise king, there is peace and prosperity. The first years of Solomon's reign illustrate the way wisdom equips a king to promote a nation's welfare.

Wisdom equips **rulers** to **issue decrees** that promote justice. That is no easy task. **Decrees** need to be worded carefully in order to address an issue precisely. Obscure decrees are difficult, even impossible, to enforce. Decrees formulated imprecisely produce effects that are often contrary to the intent of rulers. Not long after such decrees become law they must be altered or repealed.

■ **17** Wisdom makes another affirmation: she loves **those who love** her. **Those who seek *Wisdom*** find her and develop *a* love for her. She returns that **love** by letting herself *be found*. Similarly, Yahweh tells Israel that if they will seek him with their whole heart, they will find him (Jer 29:13; see Deut 4:29). Wisdom's way of relating with people is counter to that of the wayward woman. The adulteress spends great effort in searching for a partner (Prov 7:10-23), whereas humans must **seek** Wisdom to **find** her. That is, Wisdom calls out to them, but they, in turn, must diligently **seek** her.

■ **18** Wisdom emphasizes that she has marvelous resources to offer those who seek her: **riches and honor, enduring wealth and *righteousness*.** Even though the MT reads ***righteousness*** (*sĕdāqâ*), many versions render it **prosperity** without sound reason (Whybray 1994a, 126). In fact, ***righteousness*** serves as an excellent parallel to **honor**. The combination of these two terms confirms that the **riches** she bestows have been acquired in integrity. As Whybray (1994a, 127) says, "[In Proverbs] prosperity and moral righteousness are inseparable." Wisdom blesses those who follow her with wealth, enabling them to support a family and increase in number. She empowers her followers to live morally and to become honored.

The skills Wisdom gives enable officials to govern in ways that inspire the people's confidence in the government. When the state has an abundance of resources, the people feel secure, confident that their nation is able to deal with a sudden disaster and to withstand an enemy. As the population grows, so does the state's income. This leads to an era of peace and prosperity.

■ **19** Wisdom declares that her **fruit** (i.e., the virtues, the skills, and the rewards she gives) ***excels* fine gold** and **choice silver** (notice that these terms for these metals stand in chiastic pattern with those in v 10). It is important for youths to keep in mind that the benefits Wisdom promises are received as a by-product of pursuing her. Those who seek Wisdom must never make acquiring these benefits the primary reason for seeking her. If they ever do, they will become self-deceived. Also they need to realize that these benefits accrue over time; they are not received instantaneously.

■ **20-21** Wisdom makes another declaration: **I walk in the way of righteousness**. In this context this declaration means that she distributes her gifts in fairness, free from favoritism. There is no untruth in anything she says, does, or gives. Out of integrity she **bestows wealth on those who love** her and **fills their treasuries**. The **wealth** she gives is likened to an **inheritance** or an endowment. It is given as a financial basis for a clan or a people to build a heritage (see 13:22*a*).

This kind of wealth has staying power, because it is not gained quickly. Wealth gained quickly, such as by avarice (23:4), by oppressive measures (28:8*a*), or by hoarding (28:22), disappears quickly (23:5; 28:8*b*). Moreover, it is important to note that the term **love** encloses the sayings in 8:17-21 (Murphy 1998, 51). Wisdom's sharing her resources is clear evidence of her **love**. She wants her devotees to follow her example.

b. Wisdom's Origin and Presence at the Creation (8:22-31)

OVERVIEW

This passage in which Wisdom recounts her origin is the theological summit of Proverbs. Ten or eleven phrases in the first five verses reference a time before creation (vv 22-26). At the outset Wisdom honors Yahweh by beginning the account with his name. In Hebrew the grammar is unusual; usually a Hebrew sentence starts with a verb. Furthermore, the last word in this poem is **humans**. The location of these two terms, "Yahweh" and "humans," form a merism. It emphasizes that Yahweh's goal in creating was to provide humans a habitat. The bridge between humans and Yahweh is Wisdom.

IN THE TEXT

The poem has three segments: Wisdom's origin (vv 22-26), Wisdom's presence at creation (vv 27-29), and Wisdom's exuberant joy at watching God create (vv 30-31).

■ **22-26** In the first four couplets Wisdom recounts her origin (vv 22-25). She stresses that she came into being as the very **first of** God's **works** by using nine parallel statements that establish her origin as prior to the existence of matter: **the first of his way** (v 22*a*), **before his deeds of old** (v 22*b*), **ages ago** (v 23*a*), **at the very beginning**, **before** the **earth** (v 23*b*), **when there were no ... depths**—that is, a time before the **watery** deep mentioned in Gen 1:2 (Prov 8:24*a*). This last phrase is underscored by the parallel phrase, **when there were no springs** (v 24*b*).

Since the ancients believed that the **deep**, also referred to as **depths** or **watery mass**, existed beneath the seas and the dry land, they thought it fed the springs and wells. The next two phrases, **before the mountains** and **before the hills**, refer to the oldest land masses. Verse 26*a* adds: **before he made the dry land** or its fields or any **soil** (‘oprôt, DCH 6:515). These phrases refer to a time before there was dry ground (see Gen 1:9). The cumulative effect of these ten or eleven phrases is that Yahweh **brought . . . forth** Wisdom before matter existed.

In the first four lines Wisdom recounts her origin. She says that **Yahweh brought** her **forth** (*qānâ*). The Hebrew *qānâ* usually means to **purchase, acquire** (see Prov 4:5*a*), hence **possess**. When Eve bore a son, she said that she had acquired (*qānâ*), that is, birthed, a man (Gen 4:1). Thus, **possess** is used for natural generation.

Since some Hebrew dictionaries also offer the gloss **create** (e.g., Gen 14:19, 22), there are English translations that read "create." This rendering receives support from the LXX, which translates the Hebrew with "create." But the usual Hebrew word for create is *bārā'* (Gen 1:1). Investigating the OT texts in which *qānâ* might mean "create," Fox (2000, 280) concludes that in fewer than six of these texts it may have that sense. In his judgment it clearly means "create" in only two texts: Ps 139:13 and Deut 32:6. These details favor the meaning **acquire** in this text. It is functioning as a metaphor for "being birthed."

In Prov 8:23*a* Wisdom speaks of her origin as **being poured out, being fashioned** or **woven** (*nissēk*, DCH 5:699-70). The precise meaning of this term is uncertain. If it means **be woven**, it may be a metaphor for an infant's growing in the womb. This possibility is supported by the use of a word for weaving to describe the growth of an embryo in Ps 139:13 and Job 10:10-11. In Prov 8:24*a* and 25*b* Wisdom describes her origin with birth language: **I was given birth** (*hôlal*). *Hôlal* connotes the writhing pain of giving birth. This term receives emphasis by being positioned as an inclusio (vv 24*a* and 25*b*).

Wisdom, therefore, speaks of God's bringing her forth similar to a woman's giving birth, for half of the verbs used reference natural birth (vv 24*a*, 25*b*) and the two parallel terms in vv 22-23 do not oppose this sense. **Birth** is, therefore, clearly preferred to "create." This distinction is important, for that which comes into existence by birth differs significantly from that which is created. What is created stands apart from its maker. The maker determines its shape and the material out of which it is made. But that which **is birthed** has the same essence as the begetter.

Therefore, before God did anything as Creator, he **gave birth** to Wisdom. Thus, there is an inherent identity between them. She "has an organic connection with God's very nature and being" (Waltke 2004, 409).

This description of Wisdom's origin stands in stark contrast to the myths of origin recited by Israel's neighbors. In some of them the deity Wisdom played a key role at the origin of the world. But the god(dess) Wisdom was quite distinct from the first god(s) and had a role distinct from that of the ruling god, often the storm god. The god of power ruled but often acted capriciously.

The god(dess) of wisdom had superior insight but lacked the power to implement those insights directly. For example, the Babylonian god of wisdom was Ea or Enki. He was also the god of divination and magic. Having extraordinary insight into matters, he gave counsel to the ruling god(s). He did not execute his plans. That was accomplished by the god of power, Enlil. For example, when the host of lower gods rebelled against the pantheon, Enlil sought counsel from Ea.

Ea advised Enlil to have humans created and assign them the menial tasks that the rebellious gods performed. Enlil executed the plan. The rebellion ended. This story brings out the vast difference between the roles of the deity wisdom in the myths of Israel's neighbors from those of Wisdom in ancient Israel. Moreover, in Mesopotamian myths of creation conflict was central to the plot, but in this poem as in Gen 1 there is no hint of any conflict as Yahweh created. In both accounts there is harmony between God and what God creates.

Yahweh **begot Wisdom**. This metaphor means that Wisdom is fully like Yahweh. Of all things created, only Wisdom's essence is like Yahweh's. Thus, in Israelite thought Wisdom and Yahweh are one. Her role was to be present with Yahweh as he brought the world into existence. Her presence served to guarantee that everything was made precisely according to blueprints.

As a result, the world supports a vast variety of life forms, and all of creation is intelligible. This means that when humans study God's works, they gain knowledge. They also gain insights into the heavenly or spiritual world from such study. This is possible because God designed many aspects of this world to correspond to patterns in heaven. This is attested in Jesus' teachings. He frequently supported spiritual truths with analogies drawn from nature.

Furthermore, Wisdom's presence with Yahweh as he brought the world into existence means that the natural order is intelligible, though some processes in nature may be beyond human intelligence to explain.

■ **27-29** It is not the intent of this text to address the order of Yahweh's making the world. It makes reference to specific elements Yahweh created to establish that Wisdom's origin was before any of these basic elements of the created order existed. The central teaching is that Wisdom was present observing the process of creation. Nothing indicates that she did any of the creating. Yahweh is the Creator.

Given the emphasis on her origin before Yahweh began to create, she must have participated in some way, but the text gives no specific clues. Possibly, since speech is a major function of both Wisdom and Yahweh, she was Yahweh's dialogue partner about the design of various aspects of the creation.

Yahweh set the heavens in place. He then **drew a circle,** that is, **the horizon,** over the deep. **The horizon** functions as a boundary between the lower and upper waters. This picture is in accord with the description of God's activity on day two of creation (Gen 1:6-7). After making an expanse or plate, he divided the waters, placing part of them above the heavenly expanse or sky. The other part lay beneath the sea and the dry land.

Yahweh provided ways for **waters** from these two **deeps** to nourish the landmass. However, in this account no reference is made to the dry land's appearing, perhaps because of the reference to fields and dust, or **soil** in Prov

8:26. **Yahweh established the clouds** (Fox 2000, 285) for transporting **water** from the upper **deep** to pour out on the earth (see Job 36:27-29; 38:25-27). Below Yahweh **fixed securely the fountains of the deep.** This wording means that for the "watery depths" (Prov 8:24) beneath the earth he made channels for its water to fill wells and bubble forth in springs.

Yahweh **gave the sea** *a* **boundary** so that its mighty **waters would not overstep his command.** Since the ancients viewed the **sea** as a force, they often employed this term as a metaphor for the spiritual force that was hostile to God. Thus, this text stresses that at the beginning God curtailed the **sea's** power with *a* **boundary. Waters** from these two great reservoirs will never cover the earth except at God's command (Gen 7:11). Also God made **the earth** secure by setting it on **foundations** that **he marked out.** It may quake and shake, but it will not crumble.

■ **30-31** While Yahweh was creating, Wisdom was **daily** at his side . . . re-joicing. She expresses her glee with two words: **filled with delight** (*šaʿăšûʿîm*) and **rejoicing** (*mĕśaḥeqet*). The Hebrew word translated **filled with delight** is an onomatopoetic word. Joy is heard in its pronunciation. This joyful note is strengthened by a chiastic arrangement of these words: **filled with delight:re-joicing::rejoicing:filled with delight** (Prov 8:30b-31).

Wisdom asserts that as God created, she was present as *'āmôn*. This He-brew term has resisted explanation. Suggestions for its meaning are numerous. Four options that have received the most support are **craftsman** or **artisan** (*'āmôn*), **child** or **ward** (*'āmûn*), **growing up** (taking *'āmôn* as an infinitive ab-solute used adverbially [Fox 2000, 287]), and **constantly, faithfully** (taking *'āmôn* as an infinitive absolute of *'mn*, **be firm, faithful**; Waltke 2004, 420; Plöger 1984, 95).

If she functioned as a **craftsman**, she assisted in the work of creation. That Wisdom has the skills of an **artisan** is confirmed by the mansion of seven pillars that she built (9:1). But there is not the slightest hint in this poem that she did any creating. Further, there is virtually no linguistic support for this Hebrew term meaning **artisan.**

The second option, **child** or **ward** under Yahweh's care, coincides with her recent birth and her joyful dancing as she watched God creating. Besides lacking solid linguistic support for this sense, Wisdom at the end of the poem functions as an adult. The third and fourth options fit the context better. **Growing up** corresponds to her speaking in the verses following the poem as an adult. **Constantly,** however, fits with the parallel phrases: **day after day** and **in his presence.** Thus, it is accepted.

Yahweh created the world as a marvelous habitat that supports a host of plants and animals. The wonders of the creation provide humans joy, amaze-ment, and wonder. The earth is truly a majestic botanical garden and a gigantic zoo. Wisdom's rejoicing exuberantly as God created foreshadowed the great pleasure the created order provides humans.

Wisdom

Wisdom is personified as a dynamic woman. As the bearer of God's presence in society, she walks throughout the city, inviting all to acquire wisdom (esp 1:20-27; 8:1-11, 32-36; 9:1-6). To authenticate her authority as God's representative, she recounts her origin using metaphors of a woman's giving birth (8:22-31). Her unique origin establishes that her wisdom is identical to God's. She is "intrinsic to [God's] own identity" (Bauckham 2008, 17).

As God's representative she makes promises to those who become her followers that only God can fulfill: health, wealth, and long life (3:16-18, 22; 4:22; 8:18, 21, 35). Also her presence in their lives endows them with knowledge, insight, sound judgment, prudence, discretion, shrewdness, and strategic planning (2:2, 6, 7, 10-11; 3:21; 5:2; 8:12, 14). Gaining these conceptual skills, they manage their households well, teach their children in the fear of Yahweh, gain keen insights into justice, and serve the community as prudent leaders. Also her presence develops within them godly virtues.

Wisdom takes great delight in forming a deep relationship with humans (8:17a, 31b). Addressing them as her sons, that is, students, she pronounces those who keep her ways blessed (v 32). They are blessed because they find life through her and receive Yahweh's favor (v 35). She also bestows on them honor (4:8-9; 8:18b). Thus, those who seek her find their deepest spiritual longings fulfilled.

In order to understand Wisdom's roles it is helpful to note that they are similar to those of God's Spirit in the prophetic tradition. That similarity is expressed in authentication of Joshua as Moses' successor: a man "filled with the spirit of wisdom" (Deut 34:9; see Dan 5:14).

In the OT the Spirit came on the prophets, communicating God's word to them and then inspiring them to proclaim it (Ezek 11:5-12; Mic 3:8). In the same vein Wisdom declares that she pours out her thoughts (lit. *spirit* [1:23]) on those who accept her invitation to join her. God's Spirit also came on Israel's key leaders (e.g., Saul [1 Sam 11:6] and David [1 Sam 16:13]). The Spirit empowered them to lead the people in defeating their enemies and in building a strong nation. Likewise, Wisdom says, "By me kings reign and rulers issue decrees that are just" (Prov 8:15).

From this perspective Isaiah describes Israel's ideal king as having wisdom, understanding, counsel, might, knowledge, and the fear of Yahweh because God's Spirit will rest on him (Isa 11:2-3a). Isaiah adds that the Spirit will equip him with the discernment to render just judgments in all matters (11:3b-4; see 8:14a, 20).

In the OT the primary difference in the accounts of God's Spirit and Wisdom is the people they empowered. The Spirit came on only a few, those God selected for a task or a role (e.g., 1 Sam 16:6-13; Mic 3:8). By contrast, Wisdom invites everyone to seek her (Prov 1:20-23; 8:4-11; 9:4-6). Similarly, the sages entreat those under them to seek or acquire wisdom (e.g., 2:3-5; 4:5-8; 7:4; 8:5, 10, 17b, 35). Thus, Wisdom as the bearer of God's presence is available to all. Unfortunately, the OT does not address the relationship of the Spirit and Wisdom within God's identity. Further insight has to wait for God's revelation in Jesus.

A frequently asked question is why is Wisdom personified as a woman? The basic reason is that the Hebrew word for wisdom is feminine (all Hebrew words are either masculine or feminine). Capitalizing on this fact, the sages personify Wisdom to make their instructions more attractive and understandable, especially for youths. By presenting Wisdom as a woman, they are able to gain a deeper appreciation of the values that attend committing their lives to her. She will guide their course through life (2:20), provide protection (2:10-19; 7:4-5), and endow them with special skills (8:12, 14). Personification provides a basis for their students understanding the intensity of their exhortations to pursue Wisdom (2:3-5; 4:3-7). By getting them to realize that Wisdom is indeed present with them, the students are emboldened to spurn the allures of Woman Folly.

In personifying Wisdom the sages drew on traits commonly associated with women: expressing compassion, desiring long-term relationships characterized by love, being protective, being a gracious hostess, providing counsel, even displaying spite at being rejected (1:24-31; Camp 1985, 90-109; Fox 2000, 338-39). To have them visualize the deep, enduring joys that attend a faithful relationship with Wisdom, they used metaphors from the values and pleasures of marriage (Camp 1985, 99-103; 4:6-9; 7:4; 8:34-35; see 3:13-18, 21-22; 4:6).

Another key advantage that attends their personification of Wisdom is that her authority resides in her relationship with God, not in a political base. Her authority, thus, is spiritual, intellectual, and moral, not political. Her counsel is grounded in truth and reason, not in power politics (8:6-9, 12). For the NT connection of Wisdom with Jesus, see the Introduction.

c. Wisdom's Blessings (8:32-36)

■ **32-34** Leaving the account of her origin, Wisdom as teacher addresses her children: **my children, listen to me**. She encourages them with a beatitude: **blessed are those who keep my ways** (→ sidebar "A Beatitude" in overview for 3:13-20).

Wisdom enjoins her followers to **listen to *her* instruction** in order that they *may* be wise. In *becoming* wise they will receive the skills she distributes to those who follow her. It is important, though, that none presume on her kindness by *disregarding* her **instruction** (*mûsār*). Possibly she is emphasizing *the discipline* (*mûsār*) that ordinarily attends instruction (Fox 2000, 290). In that case she does not want her **children** to become disheartened by either a rebuke or a punishment that is integral to their learning. They need to realize that their discomfort will be mild compared to the learning gained.

Wisdom pronounces another blessing. **Those who *heed*** her words are **blessed**. Rejoicing in her role in their lives, her devotees long to hear her speak. Like a lover waiting near the beloved's dwelling in hopes of seeing her, they *watch* **daily at *her* doors**. Their **waiting** is evidence of their deep longing to grow in wisdom.

■ **35-36 (v 35b = 12:2a; 18:22b)** Wisdom concludes with a blessing and a curse. She declares that **those who find *her* find life** (see 3:2, 16; 9:11). Even more importantly, they **receive *Yahweh's* favor** (see 18:22). Conversely, those who *offend* [*ḥôṭē*] **Wisdom harm themselves**. That *ḥôṭē* refers to doing something offensive to **Wisdom** is supported by the fact that their behavior intimates they **hate *her***. She alerts them to the consequences of such hatred; it means that they **love death**. This last line serves as a grave warning. Any who are considering turning away from **Wisdom** must realize that the cost of doing so is far too high.

FROM THE TEXT

Coming to understand Wisdom's role in creation enhances the worldview of those who fear Yahweh. On the one hand, her presence at creation confirms that there is nothing inherently evil in the created order. It also means that every dimension of the created order has the potential of bringing joy and insight to humans. The world is a huge theater with continuous new productions, providing humans delightful entertainment. No wonder Isaiah describes the hills as singing and the trees as clapping their hands (55:12). Wonders that are found throughout creation refresh the human spirit.

Since Yahweh made everything in wisdom, the study of nature provides insights into the ways people act and relate to each other. Throughout the centuries these insights have been preserved in proverbs, sayings, and wisdom instructions (see 1 Kgs 4:33). After several millennia humans have learned to study nature by the scientific method. This method has led to an explosion of knowledge that continues to grow. The fact that nature provides such a wealth of knowledge supports the assertion of this text that it has been created in wisdom.

The study of God's revelation leads also to moral and spiritual knowledge. Wisdom is the bridge between the knowledge gained from natural science and that gained from revelation. To be wise and not just knowledgeable, humans need to draw on both of these sources. According to Murphy (1990, 138-39), Wisdom is more than "the self-revelation of creation as von Rad says (1972, 147-48, 163-64), she is the revelation of God."

Although the destructive powers in nature are not directly addressed in this text, God's placing boundaries in the created order affirms that no natural force, even the most destructive, has the power to threaten God's rule. These forces may wreak havoc in parts of the world, but they are unable to wipe out humans from the face of the earth or bring the cosmos to an end.

9. Two Invitations to Dine (9:1-18)

OVERVIEW

Proverbs 9 has three distinct units with twelve lines each. The first and the last units are vignettes of invitations to dine: one from Woman Wisdom (9:1-6) and one from Woman Folly (vv 13-18). The center unit is a collection of proverbs on three topics: a scoffer, a wise person, and the fear of Yahweh (vv 7-12).

Based on the similarity of the material in this chapter to that in ch 1, this chapter is designed to conclude Section I. This is confirmed by its structure. The core theme of the middle unit forms an inclusio with the motto in 1:7, namely, the fear of Yahweh as the beginning of wisdom. Further, the two vignettes of Woman Wisdom and Woman Folly stand in a chiastic relationship to the two calls in ch 1: made by sinners (1:10-19) and by Woman Wisdom (1:20-33).

The two vignettes are structured as opposing. In the first Woman Wisdom prepares a grand banquet (9:1-6), sending out servants to deliver formal invitations to youths. In the second Woman Folly sits at the door of her dwelling, calling out to passersby to join her in drinking stolen water and eating bread in secret (vv 13-18).

The central unit (vv 7-12) addresses three topics, each receiving four lines. The lines are placed in a chiastic pattern: three lines about a scoffer (vv 7-8a) followed by three lines about a wise person (vv 8b-9). Then four lines are given to the fear of Yahweh (vv 10-11). The concluding couplet establishes the chiasm: a line pertaining to a wise person (v 12a) and a line about a scoffer (v 12b).

This central unit is also structured chiastically in relationship to the two vignettes. The outer ring about a scoffer (vv 7-8a, 12b) evaluates the vignette on Woman Folly (vv 13-18). The middle ring on wisdom (vv 8b-9, 12a) validates the invitation of Woman Wisdom (vv 1-6). The two couplets at the center emphasize the fear of Yahweh as the foundation of wisdom, the motto of Section I.

The pattern of this description is as follows:

A	A-
Wisdom's Invitation to a Banquet	Folly's Calling to Share Pleasure
Orientation: Wisdom's grand house (v 1)	Folly's mannerisms (v 13)
Preparation: Preparing a meal (v 2)	Sitting at her door (v 14)
Invitation: Sent formally and calling (v 3)	Calling out randomly (v 15)
Addressees: The simple (v 4)	The simple (v 16)
Fare: Food and wine (v 5)	Stolen water and bread (v 17)
Outcome: Life and understanding (v 6)	Death (v 18)

B

A Scoffer, a Wise Person, and the Fear of Yahweh

A- Correcting a scoffer leads to insult, abuse, and hatred (vv 7a-8a).

    A Correcting a wise person leads to love, wisdom, and learning (vv 8b-9).

        B The fear of Yahweh leads to wisdom and understanding (vv 10-11).

    A The value of being a wise person (v 12a). Wisdom rewards the one who is wise.

A- The ill consequence of being a scoffer (v 12b). A scoffer suffers alone.

a. Woman Wisdom's Invitation to a Grand Banquet (9:1-6)

■ **1-6** At the heights of the city **Woman Wisdom** has **built** a grand **house** with **seven pillars**. Her mansion, suitable for royalty, attests to her skill at architecture (see 14:1*a*; 24:3). It is evidence of her wisdom. Because her house is securely established, it will endure (Whybray 1994a, 144; Prov 7:14).

Woman Wisdom oversees the preparation of a sumptuous meal centered around **meat** from freshly slaughtered lambs and cattle with **mixed . . . wine**. In organizing the banquet she displays her talents of planning and hospitality. Certainly the dining area and the banquet table have been tastefully decorated (see Esth 1:6-7). In addition, the grandeur of the banquet attests to her wealth, a gift she promises those who follow her (Prov 3:16*b*; 8:18).

Following proper etiquette, Woman Wisdom sends out her maids to deliver invitations to those who are invited, namely the **simple**. Not wanting to exclude anyone, Woman Wisdom herself also **calls from the** *heights* **of the city** to the **simple**. She appeals to their desire to **leave** *their* **simple ways and . . . walk in the way of insight**. The wording in the Hebrew is unclear as to whether the quote of her calling is the content of the invitation delivered by the maids or her own call made in addition to the formal invitations. The view that she herself extends an oral invitation is accepted. That is in accord with the description of her walking through the city calling out as found in 1:20-21 and 8:1-5.

It is important to note that no qualifications are required of the invitees. They do not have to attain a certain level of knowledge to attend the banquet. Furthermore, it is to be understood that she regularly invites the simple to her mansion so that they may gain wisdom.

She exhorts those who are going to accept her invitation to **leave** *their* **simple ways** so that they *may* **walk** *forward* [*'išrû*] **in the way of insight**. To attract those invited she makes a grand promise. Those who leave *their* **simple ways** *will gain life*. In learning the rudiments of wisdom, they will have a happier, longer life. Gaining **insight** will provide a deeper meaning to their lives. Thus, those who come to dine with Woman Wisdom will receive much more than a delicious dinner.

b. Characteristics of a Scoffer, a Wise Person, and the Fear of Yahweh (9:7-12)

■ **7-8a** These three lines underscore the harsh consequences that befall any who seek to *correct a scoffer*, referenced as **a wicked** *person*. *A scoffer* is likely to heap **insults** on anyone who offers correction. Cynicism shields *a scoffer* from being open to accepting a *rebuke*. In fact, *a scoffer* is so calloused that

PROVERBS

9:1-8a

such a person is inclined to insult anyone who offers a word of guidance, even one for his best interest.

One who **reprimands a wicked** person is likely to **incur harm** (*mûm, DCH* 5:175), that is, an injury caused by a blow. In this context the term may reference emotional **scars** produced by a torrent of bitter words hurled at the person who is offering to help *a wicked person*. Or this term may stand for an ugly scar left by a blow from the scoffer.

In light of these potential consequences, the next proverb counsels: **do not rebuke scoffers**, for they **hate** anyone who rebukes them. **Hate** expresses their deep resentment toward anyone who encourages them to change their ways. Clearly, instructing *a scoffer* is fraught with risk.

■ **8b-9** The next three lines characterize **the wise**. Internally they are structured as affirming. But they are opposing in relationship to the preceding three lines. **The wise**, identified as **the righteous**, learn quickly. They respond well to all modes of instruction, being conveyed by three verbs: **rebuke** (*hôkah*), **instruct** (*tēn lě*, lit. *give to*), and **inform** (*hôda'*).

One who seeks wisdom is very receptive to any kind of instruction. Whenever such a person *is rebuked*, the response is very different from a scoffer's. That student *loves* rather than *hates* the teacher. A person who wants to be wise and is aware of the benefits of instruction is very open to any kind of guidance that *increases* learning.

Among the most endearing rewards a teacher experiences is praise from former students, particularly those whom the teacher had to deal with firmly in order to overcome an obstinate attitude or a detrimental behavioral pattern. Positive learning experiences energize a student to travel the path to greater wisdom.

■ **10** The next four lines, standing at the center of the chiasm, are the focal point of this chapter and of Section I. Each of the two couplets is structured as affirming. In the Hebrew the first couplet is also structured chiastically: **the beginning of wisdom:the fear of Yahweh::knowledge of the Holy One:understanding** (see 1:7). **The fear of Yahweh**, standing at the center, is the focal point.

Knowledge has a wide range of nuances. In many contexts as here it conveys far more than factual knowledge. It stands for the godly traits a person gains from fellowship with **the Holy One**. That is, knowing God means that God's presence actively transforms a person's character. That transformation leads to a deep appreciation of God's word or instruction plus the confidence to share what is being learned with others.

Yahweh is identified as **the Holy One**. In Hebrew the term **Holy One** is a plural substantive adjective. The plural carries superlative force. Holiness is God's very essence. In other words, **holy** is Yahweh's defining quality. All other persons or objects described as holy have that quality solely because they are either in God's presence or are dedicated to God. No person or object ever becomes intrinsically holy. God's holy presence in a person's life empowers a person to live righteously. God's presence also **adds** years to one's **life**. The values and disciplines that attend living righteously promote good health.

Fear or **reverence** is the proper human response to **Yahweh, the Holy One**. Rather than causing a person to cower and hide, **the fear of Yahweh** inspires one to grow in wisdom and reach out to others. **The fear of Yahweh** overcomes the twin evils of pride and cynicism, core traits of a foolish person. This is because God, rather than the self, is at the focus of a person's identity. Devotion to God lifts a person's life above the mundane, transitory character of all things earthly.

■ **11** Standing uniquely at the beginning of the sentence, the first person pronoun *me* is the object of the preposition **through**. There is no obvious antecedent. The only possible one is Woman Wisdom. If that identification is correct, Woman Wisdom is the one making the promise of *living many days*. This promise also is underscored by standing at the chiastic center of this chapter. It adds a powerful incentive for accepting Woman Wisdom's invitation to dine (vv 4-5).

■ **12** This couplet, in opposing style, concludes the central unit. The first line reads literally: **if you are wise,** *you are wise for yourself*. A person who subjects the self to learning from the discipline of wisdom discovers that the pursuit of wisdom is self-rewarding and self-authenticating. This is true even when those disciplines cause a lot of hardship. But the results are worth the effort. By increasing in wisdom a person allows the image of God, the essence of being human, to flourish (Gen 1:26). In the pursuit of wisdom a person becomes like God. Thus, one fulfills Jesus' command to be complete as God is complete (see Matt 5:48).

The second line, which concludes the frame of the middle unit, connects with the topic of the first three lines (Prov 9:7-8*a*). It states *a scoffer's* fate. *A scoffer* heaps suffering *on the self* by denying the spiritual dimension of his essence. A self-centered lifestyle centered on the pursuit of pleasure makes a person a hardened cynic. As a result, a sense of darkness settles over one's inner being. *A scoffer* comes to believe that life has no value. Feelings of worthlessness cause *a scoffer* great *suffering*.

c. The Call of Woman Folly (9:13-18)

■ **13-18** This vignette recounts Woman Folly's inviting the **simple** to join her in engaging in exciting indulgences. Rather than conducting herself in an elegant, dignified manner, *Woman Folly* is characterized as *loud, undisciplined,* and *lacking in knowledge*. Both her demeanor and her speech reveal that she truly is a woman of foolishness. Being *gullible*, she is *devoid of any depth of character* (*pĕtayyût*; Fox 2000, 301). Self-confident, she never puts forth any effort to learn. But since she lacks resourcefulness and discipline, she has no mansion. She also lacks the skill to prepare a delicious meal.

Woman Folly calls out to *the* simple to join her. The manner of her inviting differs drastically from that of Woman Wisdom. She merely **sits at the**

115

door of her house, . . . **calling out to those who pass by**. To reach additional youths she goes and takes **a seat at the highest point of the city**, where most residents of the city pass by during the day.

The Foolish Woman

The Hebrew *'ēšet kĕsîlût* stands for *a foolish woman* (Fox 2000, 300). However, given that she is portrayed as the counterpart to Woman Wisdom, she is referenced as Woman Folly in this discussion.

Woman Folly calls to those who **are going** straight **on their way**. The phrase **going** straight implies that these youths are following their fathers' instructions (4:25-26). It indicates that they are intent on going to a set destination. However, **Woman Folly** seeks to turn them aside from the **straight . . . way**. She "wants to exploit the failings that Wisdom would remedy" (Fox 2000, 302). She appeals to the wild longings that stir deep within youths. To catch their attention she calls out more loudly.

Woman Folly's basic invitation is identical to Woman Wisdom's: **Let all who are simple come to my house**. She entices them by declaring **stolen water is sweet; bread eaten in secret is delicious**. To offset the fact that her fare is meager, she emphasizes that **the** water is **stolen** and that **bread** eaten in **secret is pleasant**. In so doing she is offering **the simple** the chance to experience great excitement by participating in immoral behavior. The use of **water** may refer to engaging in illicit sexual pleasure.

In transgressing a custom or breaking a law, humans experience a surge of power, even a sense of invincibility. They feel that they are above the law. In drinking **stolen water** and **eating** food . . . in secret these youths will be shaking their fists at the social order. And in sharing together that which is illicit these youths will gain a strong sense of bonding.

It is important to point out that Woman Folly is not making false or deceptive promises. Those who accept her call will experience these feelings. However, the cost will be high. They will engage in immoral behaviors and start down the road of folly. Lacking the ability to discern that the titillating pleasures offered are fleeting and unsatisfying, several youths are drawn to her invitation.

This vignette concludes with the frightful consequences that attend the acceptance of Woman Folly's call. Those who join her will in time discover that **the dead** are in her dwelling. They will find out that **her guests** end up **in the depths** of **Sheol** or **the grave**, that is, the abode of the dead. In Mesopotamian literature this realm is known as the Land of No Return. That name clearly conveys that there is no way for any human to escape this realm. Unfortunately, the naive who accept her call have little awareness that they are taking the fast track to an early death. Those who join Woman Folly have no future.

FROM THE TEXT

The two vignettes capture the essence of the teachings of Section I. These pictures bring into sharp focus the decision that every youth faces. One has the opportunity to pursue wisdom by accepting the invitation of Woman Wisdom. Or one may choose to yield to the seductive call of Woman Folly. The choice a youth makes often determines that one's destiny in life. Thus, the decision is often the most important one a youth makes. It is a choice to pursue wisdom and receive life or to join folly and find an early death. The way of wisdom leads to gaining wisdom and a noble character. These gains bring one honor. But the way of folly leads to experiencing deep shame.

Adolescence is an exciting time for youths. The decisions before them are wide open. While traveling through this stage of life, a youth needs to listen to the guidance wisdom offers. Also it is important that they be taught about the character of Woman Folly in order to understand the true nature of her call. Then it is hoped that they will realize that her offerings are meager. The most she can offer is thrilling experiences that cannot be sustained over a long life span. Those who follow her never develop an honorable character. In time a youth will come to understand that her call leads to death, both spiritually and physically.

This instruction is designed to motivate youths to make the right choice. Given the drive for independence that surfaces in an adolescent, parents must teach their children about these two choices. Then they have to trust God's guiding their sons and daughters to accept the call of Woman Wisdom. Parents of youths who follow Woman Wisdom will experience many joys as they watch their children grow into wise adults.

II. PROVERBS OF SOLOMON: 10:1—22:16

BEHIND THE TEXT

Section II, the largest section of Proverbs, has the title Proverbs of Solomon. Solomon likely directed court sages to compile an anthology of Israelite proverbs. The resulting collection provided sages a superb document for teaching their sons as well as becoming a grand addition to Israel's literary heritage. In the centuries from Solomon to Hezekiah, Israelite scribes made copies of the collection, possibly inserting additional proverbs.

There are two parts to Section II: Part 1 (10:1—15:33) and Part 2 (16:1—22:16). The significant differences in the character and content of the two parts indicates that they existed as independent collections before being combined.

In Part 1 the majority of the proverbs are structured as opposing (156). Two antithetical pairs are dominant, "righteous"/"wicked" (26) and "wise"/"fool" (13). However, these opposing pairs are scarce in Part 2. The pair "righteous"/"wicked" is attested only in 18:5 and 21:15 and the pair "wise"/"fool" only in 21:20. Another major contrast between the two parts is the greater number of proverbs in Part 2 that are structured as advancing (94 in contrast to 11 in Part 1) and as affirming (51 in contrast to 12). Part 2 is also distinct from Part 1 in having several clusters of proverbs on a specific topic. Its opening chapter, ch 16, consists of four clusters: God's directing a person's path (vv 1-9), the king (vv 10-15), virtues (vv 16-24), and characterizations of people (vv 27-32). Moreover, Part 2 has more Yahweh sayings than Part 1, thirty-two compared to twenty, and more on the king, twelve in contrast to two. It is likely, however, that ten of the Yahweh sayings in Part 1, the one in 10:3 and nine in 14:26—15:33, along with the two sayings about the king (14:28, 35) are editorial insertions as will be described below.

Furthermore, for centuries scholars have viewed Section II to be a random collection of proverbs. Recent studies, however, have uncovered various principles that account for the juxtaposing of several proverbs in this collection. These studies indicate that the collection is the product of skilled editing. The extent of the editing, however, remains uncertain.

An amazing fact loans further support to the view that Section II was skillfully edited: the number of its proverbs, 375, corresponds to the numerical value of Solomon's name. That name has this value because every Hebrew consonant also has a numerical value. Solomon (šělōmōh) equals 375 since š = 300, l = 30, m = 40, h = 5.

When the two parts were joined, scribes inserted nine Yahweh sayings (14:26, 27; 15:3, 8, 11, 16, 25, 29, 33) and two on the king (14:28, 35) at the end of Part 1 (14:26—15:33) to provide a lead into Part 2. This position is supported by the fact that in Part 1 outside of 10:1—11:1 there are only three Yahweh sayings before 14:26 and none on the king. It is also possible that these editors added the five Yahweh sayings at the beginning of Part 1 (10:3—11:1) in order to establish a tie with the Yahweh sayings in Section I and to provide a frame for Part 1.

Additional evidence of editorial activity in Part 1 is the location of proverbs based on the word pair "righteous"/"wicked." There are twenty-two at the opening (10:1—12:26) and four at the end (14:32—15:29). The placement of these proverbs enhances the frame of Part 1. This possibility gains support from the fact that the word pair "righteous"/"wicked" diminishes in 11:14—13:25 and is infrequent in Part 2. Also a few proverbs have been placed together to form a chiastic pattern.

These ways of linking proverbs not only serve to facilitate memorization but also impact the meaning of both proverbs (Murphy 1998, 67). Goldingay (1994, 79) adds, "Surface links between things are parables of deeper links.

They suggest that a collection of proverbs is not merely a compilation of random observations but a compendium of insights from a coherent world and throwing light on a coherent world."

The impact of these links and patterns on the proverbs juxtaposed will be noted in the commentary. The word pair "wise"/"fool," four in 10:1—12:15 and five in 14:24—15:33, enhance this frame. As with the other possible insertions, only four proverbs with this pair stand in the core of Part 1 and only one in Part 2 (21:20) and that one is structured differently.

Additional evidence that Section II is not a random collection is the fact that many proverbs have been juxtaposed on the basis of a variety of features: common theme, nodal terms, opposing pairs, key words with similar sounds, alliteration, and word plays.

A. Proverbs 10:1-32

OVERVIEW

All the proverbs in this chapter are structured as opposing except for two: one as advancing (v 22) and one as an analogy (v 26). In twelve of these proverbs "the righteous" or "the blameless" are contrasted with "the wicked" (vv 3, 6, 7, 11, 16, 20, 24, 25, 28, 29 ["those who do evil"], 30, and 32). "The wise" are contrasted with "a fool" in five proverbs (vv 1, 5 ["prudent"/"disgraceful"], 8, 14, 23). The opposing pair "wealth"/"poverty" is present in two proverbs (vv 4, 15; see v 16). Also seven proverbs are structured chiastically (vv 4, 6, 11, 15, 17, 20, 31). Several proverbs are linked in a variety of ways: key terms, themes, and a play on sound. These links will be described in the comments.

The first five proverbs serve as an introduction to Section II. They stand in a chiastic pattern. The proverbs that form the outer frame contrast a wise son with a foolish son (vv 1, 5). In the inner circle (vv 2, 4) the contrast between ill-gotten treasures and righteousness are echoed in the contrast between poverty from laziness and wealth earned by hard work. At the center (v 3) is the assertion that Yahweh satisfies the hunger of the righteous but thwarts the cravings of the wicked.

The proverb following this cluster (v 6) describes the honor of the righteous in contrast to the demise of the wicked. It serves as a capstone to the cluster (Fox 2009, 514-15). This theme is reinforced by six proverbs about the rewards of "the righteous" in contrast to the ills that befall "the wicked" that conclude the chapter (vv 27-32). The structure of the opening to Section II establishes a link with Section I, especially in emphasizing the parent-child relationship, fearing Yahweh, and the righteous having a long life.

A prominent theme of the proverbs in this chapter is the benefits of the righteous in contrast to the woes of the wicked. The righteous are rewarded by wealth (vv 4b, 15a, 22a) and a long life (vv 2b, 3a, 6a, 7a, 16a, 17a, 27a, 30a). They walk "securely" (v 9a), being protected like a "fortified city" (v 15a), by wealth gained from hard work (vv 4b, 5a), and by Yahweh's blessing (v 22).

When beset by troubles they stand steadfast because they live righteously and Yahweh is their refuge (vv 2*b*, 9*a*, 15*a*, 25*b*, 29*a*, 30*a*).

By contrast, the wicked experience numerous woes: loss of reputation (v 7*b*), failed hopes (v 28*b*), expulsion from the land (v 30*b*), and ruin (vv 14*b*, 29*b*). Many of them are cut off in the prime of life (vv 16*b*, 21*b*, 27*b*). Their treasures, having been gained by wickedness, do not last (v 2*a*).

Moreover, three proverbs mention Yahweh (vv 3, 22, 29). He cares for and blesses the righteous (vv 3, 22). Fearing Yahweh adds years to one's life (v 27*a*). Speech is another significant theme. It is often referenced by the instruments of speech: mouth (vv 6*b*, 11*a*, 14*b*, 31*a*, 32*b*), lips (vv 8*b*, 10*b*, 13*a*, 18*a*, 19*b*, 21*a*, 32*a*), or the tongue (vv 20*a*, 31*b*). Since sin is not missing in an abundance of words (v 19*a*), the prudent restrain their lips (v 19*b*). Conversely, words spoken by the righteous bear the fruit of wisdom (v 31*a*). Their words are "a fountain of life" (v 11*a*).

IN THE TEXT

Opposing: A Wise Child / A Foolish Child (Line *a* = 15:20*a*) (10:1)

■ I The demeanor of children has a great impact on the parents. Distress caused by **a foolish son** is underscored by its impact on **his mother**.

Opposing: Ill-Gotten Treasure / Value of Righteousness (10:2)

■ 2 The transitory **value** of **ill-gotten treasures** is contrasted with the enduring value that attends **righteousness**. The wicked acquire wealth without any concern for ethical standards. As a result, their wealth has **no lasting value**. But those who are upright in all their dealings find that **righteousness delivers from death**. In other OT texts the phrase **delivers from death** describes escaping life–threatening situations (Josh 2:13; Ps 33:18-19; Clifford 1999, 112). Because of God's protective role in their lives, the righteous live to an honorable old age. Reading the first line in light of the second, this proverb implies that wealth gained unjustly does not help a person escape a life-threatening situation.

Opposing: The Righteous / The Wicked (10:3)

■ 3 Yahweh responds to **the craving of the wicked** and **the righteous** according to their character. **Yahweh does not let the righteous go hungry, but he thwarts** (*hādap*) the **desires** of the wicked. The Hebrew *hādap* stands for very forceful action; for example, Yahweh's driving Israel's enemies out from the promised land (Deut 6:19; 9:4; Josh 23:5).

Opposing: Hands of the Lazy / Hands of the Diligent (10:4)

■ 4 This proverb is structured as a chiasm in the Hebrew text: being poor:**lazy hands::diligent hands:bring wealth** (similar Prov 31:19-20). God's design for keeping people from going hungry is for them to work diligently. Since those who have **lazy hands** live counter to God's design, they are likely to face **poverty**. But this proverb should not be read inside out to contend that the poor are locked into poverty primarily because they are lazy. Several proverbs identify other causes of poverty, such as having one's wealth suddenly wiped out by a tragic misfortune.

Conversely, **diligent hands bring wealth**. **Wealth** in this setting stands for sufficient income for daily food and basic shelter, not mega riches. When the **diligent** face setbacks, they strive diligently to address them and continue to provide for their families' basic needs.

Opposing: Harvesting Crops / Sleeping during Harvest (10:5)

■ **5** The principle of working diligently, praised in the preceding proverb, is followed by the behavior of **a prudent son** at harvesttime, the season that demands intense work for a farm family. That **son** works diligently. He brings in *the* crops from the field. He then winnows the grain and mills it into flour. A family who has **a prudent son** is very fortunate.

But *a son* who sleeps *heavily* (*rādam*) during harvest is a *disgrace*. That son is too self-centered to discipline himself to be engaged in working for the family's well-being. Because of his laziness some of the harvest is likely lost. His behavior heaps shame on his parents, especially in a farming community.

Opposing: Blessings on the Righteous / The Wicked Experience Violence (Line *b* = v 11*b*) (10:6)

■ **6** The next two proverbs are connected by the term **blessings** and the opposing pair **righteous/wicked** (Murphy 1998, 73). In Hebrew the first proverb is structured as a chiasm: **blessings:head of the righteous::mouth of the wicked**:*covers*:violence. God generously bestows **blessings** *on* **the head of the righteous** (see Gen 49:26). But **the wicked** *cover up* their deeds of **violence** (see NIV mg.; RSV) with sly words. *Cover up* has this sense in other proverbs (e.g., Prov 10:11, 12, 18; 11:13; Fox 2009, 524). Whereas God is the source of **blessings** that provide **the righteous** honor, **the wicked** heap on themselves disgrace and ignominy by speaking deceptively.

Opposing: The Memory of the Righteous / The Name of the Wicked (10:7)

■ **7** Believing that the *memory* of the righteous is *a blessing*, the ancients placed great value on memorializing the name of **the righteous** (see 22:1). One method was telling stories of the ways God led them. These stories not only served as a memorial to the upright but also encouraged the pursuit of righteousness. **The righteous** are also honored by having their **names . . . used in blessings**. By contrast, **the name of the wicked** *rots*. That is, their memory soon perishes like their decaying body.

Opposing: The Wise Heed Commands / A Fool Comes to Ruin (Line *b* = v 10*b*) (10:8)

■ **8** **The wise in heart** embrace the **commands** of their teachers and God. By memorizing the **commands**, **the wise** find guidance throughout life, above all in making wise choices. By contrast, the major trait of a **fool** is speaking con-

PROVERBS

10:5-8

tinuously. That one's constant **chattering** prevents the fool from listening and learning. Much speaking leads a **fool** into uttering outrageous, even hurtful words (Eccl 10:12b-14a). As a result a **fool comes to ruin** (*lābaṭ*; unfortunately, the precise meaning of this Hebrew word is not known).

Opposing: A Person of Integrity / One on a Crooked Path (10:9)

■ **9** A person who **walks in integrity** [*battōm*] **walks securely** or *confidently* (*beṭaḥ*). Alliteration underscores the force of this line. A person of **integrity** has no fear of being confronted for wrongdoing. By contrast, anyone who **takes crooked paths**, that is, constantly misbehaving or taking advantage of people by deception, is anxious of *being* **found out**. That person's anxiety is well-founded because in God's providence a schemer *is* eventually *discovered*.

At the outset of the twenty-first century numerous American politicans, including those who presented themselves as scrupulously moral, have been exposed. These leaders took crooked paths, often at the expense of the public, to enrich themselves. When a politican's shady behavior is disclosed, any wrongdoing is vigorously denied. Nevertheless, an investigation into the charges frequently finds several wrongs have been committed. As a result, that official loses both office and face. (See Prov 11:20; 17:20; 22:5; 28:6, 18.)

Opposing: One Who Winks / A Chattering Fool (Line *b* = v 8*b*) (10:10)

■ **10** A person who **winks** *inflicts pain* (see 16:30). In every culture certain facial expressions communicate a variety of attitudes, as awareness, affection, or insult. In some cultures a person winks to signal the possession of special knowledge about a matter. Or with a wink a person may signal that a scheme is in the process of being carried out. At other times a person winks to express agreement on a matter. Some people, however, wink deceptively. A person who sees that gesture takes it as a positive signal but is being led into a trap that will cause **grief**. Unfortunately, the meaning conveyed by winking in ancient Israel is unknown. Out of thin air the NIV inserts the word **maliciously** in an attempt to interpret the gesture.

The sentence **a chattering fool comes to ruin** is repeated from v 8*b*. In that verse the line implies that a **fool** rebels against the commands of God or a teacher. In this proverb **chattering** and *winking* are annoying traits that characterize **a fool**. Because *chattering* produces greater harm than *winking*, the consequence is more severe—**ruin**.

Opposing: Speech: Gives Life / Covers Up Wrongdoing (Line *b* = v 6*b*) (10:11)

■ **11** In the Hebrew text this verse is structured chiastically: **a fountain of life:the mouth of the righteous::the mouth of the wicked:*covers*:violence**. The chiasm highlights the contrast between **the *speech* of the righteous** and **the *speech* of the wicked**. Because **the *words* of the righteous** are insightful and uplifting, they function like **a fountain of life** (13:14; 14:27; 16:22). They inspire people to live uprightly as they lead them to have a blessed life.

Conversely, words spoken by **the wicked** *conceal* violence. Thus, their words promote distrust and discord in the community. Although line *b* repeats v 6*b*, it has a different sense since it follows a line with a very different meaning (Goldingay 1994, 79-80). (See 13:14; 14:27; 16:22; Ps 36:9 [10 HB].)

Opposing: Hatred / Love (10:12)

■ **12** **Hatred**, whether expressed through words, deeds, or attitudes, **stirs up conflict** in families, clans, and communities as well as among tribes, races, and nationalities. Those who hate relish causing skirmishes among various groups. Conversely, **love** is a powerfully healing force, because it **covers** or overcomes **all** kinds of **wrongs** (*pĕšāʿîm*). Its warmth melts **hatred** inflicted by **wrongs**. It enables those who are hurting to put aside disagreements and move toward reconciliation. (See Jas 5:20; 1 Pet 4:8.)

Opposing: Wisdom Visible in Speech / Discipline for the Simple (Line *b* = 19:29*b*; 26:3*b*) (10:13)

■ **13** Two terms that represent speech, **lips** and "mouth," and two forms of the Hebrew word **wisdom** (*ḥokmâ, ḥăkāmîm*) connect the next two proverbs. In this proverb there is an unusual antithetical pair: **lips::back**.

Wisdom is found *in the speech* of the discerning. People enjoy listening to the wise talk, for their words provide insights. But **the back of one who has no sense**, that is, the simple, is struck by **a rod**. In an effort to motivate a dolt, a teacher delivers a blow to his **back**. Given the character of the parallelism, it is likely that **a rod . . . for the back** is a metaphor for a stiff rebuke addressed to a dull learner or one who is misbehaving during instruction (Fox 2009, 518).

Opposing: Wise / Fool (10:14)

■ **14** The word **ruin** connects the next two proverbs. **The wise store up knowledge**, guarding it like a treasure. One way that **the wise** *stored* wisdom was by formulating their insights into memorable sayings or short essays.

The mouth [i.e., *the speech*] of a **fool** is undisciplined, filled with imaginative expression and partial truths. Consequently, his words *invite* or lead to his **ruin**. A *fool's* words are comparable to a building that has a faulty foundation. In time that building collapses, becoming *a ruin*.

Opposing: Wealth Provides Protection / Poverty Leads to Ruin (Line *a* = 18:11*a*) (10:15)

■ **15** This proverb is descriptive not prescriptive of patterns in society. It is structured as a chiasm in the Hebrew: the wealth of **the rich:fortified city::the ruin of the poor:poverty**. **The wealth of the rich is their fortified city.** Wealth enables them to take measures for self-protection. For example, they have the funds to build a secure dwelling and hire guards.

Poverty, however, **is the ruin of the poor.** Trapped in **poverty, the poor** lack the means for acquiring the tools or the training to rise above their low standing. Since they lack sufficient food, shelter, and medicines, their lives are much harder.

Certainly having some wealth is valuable (see 13:8*a*; 14:20*b*; 19:4*a*; 22:7*a*). Nevertheless, several proverbs caution the rich against trusting in their wealth. The only secure fortress is Yahweh (18:10-11).

Opposing: Wages of the Righteous / The Earnings of the Wicked (10:16)

■ **16** Income, or **wages,** is essential to support life. However, more critical to a person's well-being is the way those **wages** are used. **The righteous** spend their **wages** on activities that nourish their lives and promote the good of the community. But **the wicked** use their **earnings** to indulge in all kinds of *sinful activities*, activities that over time cause them distress and shorten their lives. Wesley (1975, 1848) says that "the fruit of all their labor tends to sin, and serves only for fuel to men's pride and luxury." (See Rom 6:23.)

Opposing: Discipline Heeded / Reproof Ignored (10:17)

■ **17** This proverb has a chiastic pattern in the Hebrew text: **way to life:heeds discipline::ignores correction:leads . . . astray**. *One who* heeds discipline, that is, by changing behavior in response to *a discipline,* continues on **the way to life**, that is, a rich, full, long life. But *one who* ignores *reproof* leads others astray. A person who does not learn from an appropriate *rebuke* not only departs from **the way to life** but also influences others *to go* astray.

Opposing: Conceals Hatred / Spreads Slander (10:18)

■ **18** The next four proverbs address the power of speech. A person **conceals hatred** of another by **lying**. While appearing friendly, that one so despises the other that he is prone to let that person down when facing a difficult situation. A more harmful way of expressing hatred is *spreading* **slander** about the person hated, thereby undercutting that one's standing in the community. Whoever stoops so low **is a fool** (*kĕsîl*), a person characterized by stupidity and self-indulgence (Fox 2000, 41). Wesley (1975, 1848) points out that this proverb "condemns two opposite vices, secret hatred, and manifest slander." (See 16:27-28; 27:6*b*.)

Opposing: Multiplied Words / Restrained Speech (10:19)

■ **19** Some people talk on and on even after having run out of something to say. Speaking so much leads them to embellish what they say. The danger inherent in **multiplying words** is that in many words *a* **sin** or *an offense* [*pešaʿ*] **is not** *lacking*. *Offense* in wisdom texts references *affronts* to others (Fox 2009, 521).

By contrast, **the prudent** [*maśkîl*] *restrain their lips* or, as Americans say, **hold their tongues** (see Eccl 5:2, 6; 6:11). They speak reflectively, precisely, and honestly, refraining from making prejudicial statements or gross exaggerations.

Opposing: Tongue of the Righteous / Heart of the Wicked (10:20)

■ **20** A word that represents speech, **tongue** or "lips," stands in contrast to a word for thought, **the heart** or *mind* (*lēb*), in the next two proverbs. The lead proverb is structured chiastically in the Hebrew text: **choice silver:the tongue of the righteous::the heart of the wicked:little value**.

This proverb sharply contrasts **the tongue** and **the heart** or ***mind***. Normally the higher value is given to the ***mind***. But in regard to **the wicked** the value of these organs is inverted. That is because their minds are so occupied with impure, sensuous, harmful thoughts that they are unable to entertain ideas that benefit others. Their minds have such **little value** that it is far less than ***the speech*** of the righteous, being as valuable as **choice silver**. People enjoy listening to **the righteous** because their words engage their thinking and provide insights into important issues.

Opposing: The Speech of the Righteous / The Stupidity of Fools (10:21)

■ **21** The lips [i.e., ***the speech***] of the righteous nourish or ***shepherd*** many. Through their skillful use of words **the righteous** offer insights that enrich people's lives. For example, their counsel helps farmers and shepherds increase the production of their fields and herds. In another interpretation their words ***provide nourishment*** for people's minds. But **fools**, because of their shallow thinking, **die** before reaching old age. They are ignorant of ways to nurture their physical and emotional well-being.

Advancing: Blessing of Yahweh / Freedom from Trouble (10:22)

■ **22** ***Yahweh's*** blessing on a person or a community **brings wealth, without painful toil**. That is, when people work hard, God blesses their work. They receive a reasonable reward or a good harvest without having to bear excessive pain (ʿeṣeb) like what God prescribed for Adam and Eve for their disobedience (Gen 3:16-17). In other words, God blesses those who labor honestly and hard, providing sufficient support of their families. God keeps them in good health and protects them from harm. This proverb adds to the saying in Prov 10:4b that to prosper God must bless the work (see 21:5; 28:20). Another way to read the second line is that excessive hard work does not add to the income that God has blessed (Fox 2000, 523).

Yahweh blessing Abraham is a sound example of this principle. Abraham's flocks and herds increased greatly at various stages of his journey: on his departure from Egypt (Gen 12:16), on his separation from Lot (Gen 13:14-17), and on his separation from Abimelek (Gen 20:14-15). He became sufficiently rich that he was able to buy the cave of Machpelah as a burial place for Sarah, his wife (Gen 23:16).

Nevertheless, when Abraham had the opportunity to increase his wealth by keeping the spoils he had taken from the kings of the East he had defeated, he refused to keep any of them for himself because he did not want others to claim that some earthly ruler had made him rich (Gen 14:21-24). Because Abraham viewed his wealth to come from God's blessing, he did not yearn to continually add to his wealth.

Another way of reading the second line is that those who endure great pain in an effort to gain riches add nothing to their wealth in the long run. In other words, excessive, strenuous work adds little to the abundance God gives a diligent worker (Murphy 1998, 75; Fox 2009, 522-23). Read in this way the proverb encourages hard work and discourages compulsion to engage in excessive work. (See Eccl 4:6-8.)

Opposing: Finding Pleasure in Wicked Schemes / Delighting in Wisdom (10:23)

■ **23** A **fool gets pleasure** from engaging **in wicked schemes** (*zimmâ*) (see Ezek 16:27, 43, 58). The term **wicked schemes** or **vices** (*zimmâ*) stands for horrific acts such as murder (Hos 6:9) and accepting a bribe (Ps 26:10). This term condemns strongly perverted sexual acts (Judg 20:5-6; Ezek 16:23-29, 58; see Lev 18:17; 19:29; 20:14; Job 31:9-12). Only a depraved person gets exuberant joy from committing such acts. Their **pleasure**, however, is like "the crackling of thorns under the pot" (Eccl 7:6). The thorns make a lot of noise but generate no lasting heat. But **a person of understanding** [*'îš tĕbûnâ*] **delights in wisdom**. Gaining **wisdom** gives that person enduring satisfaction.

Opposing: Dread of the Wicked / Desire of the Righteous (10:24)

■ **24** *Fear* and **desire** are strong motivators. Even though **the wicked** enjoy engaging in schemes that harm others (Prov 10:23), they **dread** the consequences that may attend their wayward schemes. This deep, gnawing fear robs them of the joys of daily living. In God's providence what they **dread will overtake them**. Conversely, **what the righteous desire will be granted**, for their **desire** comes from a heart that fears Yahweh.

Opposing: A Storm Sweeps Away the Wicked / The Righteous Stand Firm (10:25)

■ **25** When *a tempest* (*sûpâ*) strikes a community, it leaves behind a wide path of destruction. After such a powerful storm **the wicked** cannot be found. **The storm** has carried them away. *Tempest* is an analogy for hard times that beset a community. **The wicked**, being unable to handle the difficult conditions, disappear. But **the righteous stand firm**, for they have *an enduring foundation*.

This wording recalls Jesus' parable regarding the fate of two houses built on different foundations. A wise person built a house on bedrock. During a fierce storm that house stood. A fool, however, built his house on sand. When it was hit by that storm, it fell with a loud crash (Matt 7:24-27). (See Prov 12:7.)

Analogy: Lazy Compared to an Annoyance (10:26)

■ **26** The ancients, lacking means for communicating with people at a distance, employed messengers to deliver a communiqué. Often the message was delivered orally. Sometimes messengers transported money or received valuable items to be returned to the sender. Since it took a courier days, even weeks to deliver a message, it was crucial that one employ a reliable person.

A messenger who turned out to be *a* **sluggard** would cause the sender great distress. That distress is compared to the irritating sensation of **vinegar to the teeth** or **smoke** in **the eyes**. (See 13:17; 26:6.) The taste of **vinegar**, cheap wine, set one's **teeth** on edge, and **smoke** causes the eyes to burn sharply.

Opposing: A Long Life for the Righteous / A Short Life for the Wicked (10:27)

■ **27** In that **the fear of** *Yahweh* provides life with a depth of meaning, it **adds** years to one's **life**. But **the wicked**, troubled by their bad deeds and a deep sense of life's futility, have their **years . . . cut short**. (See 1:7.)

Opposing: Expectation of the Righteous / Hope of the Wicked (10:28)

■ **28** Both **the righteous** and **the wicked** have *hope*, but their **hopes** produce markedly different outcomes (see v 24). The *expectation* **of the righteous** fills them with **joy**. Over time their **joy** is realized because God's blessing exceeds their dreams. But **the hopes of the wicked**, being founded on their own efforts to achieve them, **come to nothing**. Consequently, they experience keen disappointments throughout life. (See 11:7, 23; 24:14.)

Opposing: The Way of Yahweh: Refuge for the Righteous / Ruin for Evildoers (10:29)

■ **29** The way of *Yahweh*, that is, the way Yahweh prescribes for humans to follow, is experienced as a refuge by **the blameless** (*tōm*). When facing adversities **the blameless** escape harm because they are traveling on that **way**. But for **those who do evil** *Yahweh's* **way** is their **ruin**. Hosea draws on this saying to conclude his prophecy: the ways of Yahweh are straight; the righteous walk in them, but the rebellious stumble in them (14:9*b* [10*b* HB]).

Opposing: Righteous / Wicked (10:30)

■ **30** In the next three proverbs **the righteous** (*ṣaddîq*) are contrasted with **the wicked** (*rĕšāʿîm* [vv 30*b*, 32*b*], whose speech is **perverse** [*tahpûkôt*] [vv 31*b*, 32*b*]).

The righteous, being grounded on Yahweh (see v 25*b*), **will never be toppled**. That is, nothing will so overpower them that they fail to enjoy God's promises of a long life and an inheritance. However, **the wicked will not remain in the land. Land** is functioning as a metaphor for the inheritance God gives those who follow him (see 2:21-22).

This saying reflects the assurance Moses gave the Israelites in his farewell address: they will live long in the promised land if they keep the commandments (e.g., Deut 30:15-16, 19-20). Moses also warned them that they would not remain long in the land if their affection turns from Yahweh to other gods (Deut 30:17-18).

Opposing: Speech of the Righteous / A Perverse Tongue (10:31)

■ **31** Key terms bind the next two proverbs. A part of the body associated with speech begins each line. These words are placed in a chiastic pattern: **mouth:tongue::"lips":"mouth."** Also the term **perverse** (*tahpûkôt*) stands in the second line of both sayings. This saying emphasizes the tie between **wisdom**, *righteousness*, and *speech*.

Words spoken by **the righteous *bear* the fruit of wisdom** (see 12:14; 13:2; 18:20; Ps 92:12-15 [13-16 HB]). In other words, **the righteous**, being truly wise, speak fruit-bearing truths.

But **a perverse tongue will be *cut out***, that is, **silenced**. Here the penalty for doing wrong is enforced against a person's offending organ. This penalty may also be a metaphor from horticulture. **A perverse tongue will be *cut off*** just as an unproductive branch is pruned from a vine (see John 15:6*a*). Given that the tongue may be used to inflict grave harm, even death (see Jas 3:6-10), the harshness of the penalty accentuates the harm that the tongue may cause.

The Meaning of "Cut Off"

Some peoples of the ancient Middle East had laws that prescribed physical mutilation for specific offenses (see middle Assyrian laws). Israelite law did not condone such penalties. There is, however, a metaphorical reference to such punishment in Ps 12:3 [4 HB]. Likewise, the wording in this saying is metaphorical. It is similar to Jesus' prescribing the gouging out of an eye or cutting off of a hand should one of these members of the body cause a person to stumble (Matt 5:29-30). Another interpretation takes the tongue as a synecdoche for a person. The penalty, then, is expulsion from the land as in Prov 10:25*a*, 30*b* (Yoder 2009, 129).

Opposing: Speech: Righteous / Wicked (10:32)

■ **32** **The righteous**, being skilled (*yādaʿ*) at speaking in ways that ***find* favor**, address issues insightfully and graciously. ***Finding*** [*yādaʿ*] **favor** (*rāṣôn*) means being honored by a high authority, God or the king (Clifford 1999, 118). But often **the wicked** vent their negative attitudes and frustrations through an outpouring of **perverse**, hurtful words. Their words produce distress, conflict, and unbelief.

B. Proverbs 11:1-31

OVERVIEW

The dominant structure of the proverbs in this chapter is opposing. In addition four are constructed as affirming (vv 7, 25, 29, 30) and one as an analogy (v 22). Several times a key word serves to connect two or three successive proverbs: "righteousness" (vv 4-6, 8-9), "wicked" and "city" (vv 10-11), "blessing" (vv 25-26), and "righteous" (vv 30-31). Five proverbs standing near the end deal with being generous or adventuresome (vv 24*a*, 25, 26*b*, 28*b*, 30).

Yahweh's name occurs twice, both times with the Yahweh detests statement (vv 1, 20).

The righteous are contrasted with the wicked in sixteen proverbs (vv 3, 5, 6, 8, 9, 10, 11, 16, 17, 18, 19, 20, 21, 23, 27, 31). The terms "righteous" and "righteousness" along with several synonyms ("upright," "kind," "blameless," "trustworthy") are prominent in this chapter. Given the opposing structure of these proverbs, there are also numerous synonyms for "the wicked": "unfaithful," "cruel," "ungodly," "whoever pursues evil," "sinner," "those whose hearts are perverse," and "a gossip." The concluding proverb captures this contrast in a traditional retribution formula: both the righteous and the ungodly experience their appropriate fate on earth (v 31).

Two other prominent themes in this chapter are speech (vv 9, 11, 12, 13, 26) and wealth (vv 4, 16, 18, 24, 26, 28). A person's speech can destroy a friend (v 9) or a city (v 11b). Thus, it is essential to keep entrusted information confidential (v 13).

Blessings of the people are heaped on a distributor who foregoes profit to help those who lack food. Respect carries greater value than wealth (v 16), and a greedy person who seeks a higher profit at the expense of human suffering is cursed (v 26). A person is never to trust in wealth (v 28a). It is important to remember that wealth has no value in the day of judgment (v 4).

Women are the topic of two proverbs: a kindhearted woman is respected above cruel men (v 16), but a beautiful woman without discretion lacks honor (v 22). In three proverbs deception is denounced (vv 1, 18, 20).

Two proverbs employ sharp irony. One line reads: "the hope of the wicked [brings] wrath" (v 23b). That is certainly not what they hoped for. Irony is strongly felt in comparing "a beautiful woman who [lacks] discretion" to "a gold ring in a pig's snout" (v 22).

IN THE TEXT

Opposing: Deceptive Scales / True Weights (11:1)

■ **1** Yahweh applauds that which is true, reliable, and genuine. Thus, the use of *rigged* scales *is detestable to Yahweh*. Conversely, **accurate weights find favor with him** (see Lev 19:35-36; Deut 25:13-15). The Hebrew term for **weights** is *a full stone*. This phrase indicates that some merchants shaved their weights, usually shaped stones, to make them lighter. Their weights were not reliable.

Bartering was the basis of buying and selling. After a merchant and a buyer agreed on a price, the merchant measured out the commodity or item bought. The buyer paid with small pieces of bronze or silver bullion that were weighed by the merchant. Consequently, a merchant could cheat a buyer twice: (1) he could use a smaller measure to give the buyer less than he had bargained for, and (2) he could collect more in payment either by weighing the buyer's bullion against a heavier weight or by using scales that were not in balance (see Prov 16:11; 20:10, 23). References in Amos 8:5 and Hos 12:7 suggest that cheating in the marketplace was fairly common.

Unfortunately, cheating continues today in multiple forms, such as over-billing customers, billing for services not rendered, selling a product without disclosing all the deals in a contract, or providing goods of lesser quality than the customers thought they were purchasing.

Ancient Practice of Buying and Selling

In antiquity merchants displayed goods for sale inside a city's main gate. In a cloth bag they had a collection of weights (16:11). These weights had different shapes. Some were dome-shaped. Others were shaped as frogs, bulls, and lions (King and Stager 2001, 196-97). The weight's value was often inscribed on it.

When a buyer agreed to a price, the merchant measured the quantity of the item purchased with a dry measure. Next he set up a portable scale consisting of two trays suspended from each end of a bar with a ring in the center for hanging the scale. In one tray he put the buyer's bullion, usually irregular pieces of bronze or silver, and in the other tray he placed a weight. The standard for the weights was set by the king as attested by the reference to **the king's stone** in 2 Sam 14:26. Nevertheless, deceitful merchants altered their weights and measures.

The use of minted silver coins began in the sixth century BC in Lydia, a country in southwestern Turkey. These coins of varying weights had their values stamped on them. In the fifth century BC the Persians promoted the use of minted currency throughout their vast empire. Authentic coins bore the emperor's name or image. The shift to a monetary system slowly spread throughout the Mediterranean world.

The use of coins in Palestine appears to have begun under the Persians in the fourth century BC. Minted coins became common. A common silver coin weighed a shekel. That coin eventually took on the name of its weight. The Hasmoneans were the first Jews to mint coins in the latter part of the second century BC (Kletter 2009, *NIBD* V:831-41; Bilkes 2009, "Weights and Measures," *NIBD* IV:130-37).

Opposing: Pride / Humility (11:2)

■ **2** Various character traits yield specific outcomes. Pride *develops, and* disgrace *follows*. The similar sound of the key terms, *zādôn* (**pride**) and *qālôn* (**disgrace**), captures their interconnectedness. **Pride** is blinding. It prevents self-reflection and self-criticism. A proud person is prone to act presumptuously. It is only a matter of time until that kind of person makes a grave blunder and suffers disrepute. On the other hand, those who have a *contrite disposition* seek to learn from their experiences. Such reflection yields significant insights.

Opposing: Upright / Treacherous (11:3)

■ **3** The **upright** are contrasted with **the unfaithful** or *the treacherous* (*bôgĕdîm*). **Integrity**, a reliable moral compass, **guides** the upright throughout

132

life. It is a reliable guide during chaotic times. But **duplicity**, a characteristic of *the treacherous, destroys* them.

Opposing: Wealth / Righteousness (Line *b* = 10:2*b*) (11:4)

■ **4** The term **righteousness** (*ṣĕdāqâ*) serves as a connecting thread for the next three proverbs. **Wealth** has no value on **the day of wrath** (Ezek 7:19). It will not provide escape from the horrors of that day. **A day of wrath** was a most ominous time. It could be caused by a natural disaster or by an attack from a dreaded enemy. The people viewed such a day as Yahweh's execution of judgment against those who have persistently transgressed the Law. Yahweh was holding his people accountable for failing to keep the covenant (see Zeph 1:18). Throughout her history Israel faced several days of wrath. The most devastating one was when the Babylonians captured Jerusalem and destroyed the temple. This proverb, being generic, references any such day of calamity.

In **the day of wrath** only **righteousness** has value. It **delivers from death**. That is, God will make it possible for the righteous to escape death that reigns supreme during such a chaotic time of judgment. While certainly some, even many, righteous die during such a time, God keeps a core of them alive. From these survivors he builds a community of those who serve him.

Opposing: Righteous / Wicked (11:5)

■ **5** The righteousness of the *innocent* [*tāmîm*] makes **the way** they travel **straight** (see 3:6). Free from sharp curves and snares, that way leads to a genuine, honorable life. But **the wicked are brought down by their own wickedness**. That is, wicked deeds committed by evil people unleash forces that lead to their downfall. (See Phil 2:12-13.)

Opposing: Righteous / Treacherous (11:6)

■ **6** The first line is similar to that of the preceding proverb, save that **the upright** stands in place of *the innocent* and **delivers** replaces **makes . . . straight**. In the second line **the unfaithful** or *the treacherous* (*bōgĕdîm*) stands in place of **the wicked**.

Those who deal treacherously [see Prov 11:3*b*] **are trapped by evil desires** (*hawwâ*). For the Hebrew *hawwâ* there are various glosses, including *desire*, *passion*, *wickedness*, *ruin*, and *evil word* (*DCH* 2:502-3). This fact allows for various ways of understanding the character of the trap. It may be a bad desire, speaking evil words, or being caught in a disaster. These options are intentional. It allows the proverb to address multiple situations. In all the options **evil desires** prod the *treacherous* to act in ways that set a trap that captures them.

Affirming: Hope Perishes at Death (11:7)

■ **7** When *a person dies*, so also do the **hopes** based on the person's **promise** of using personal **power** or *wealth* (*'ônîm*) to help a group of people or a community. Because of those promises the people were filled with enthusiasm.

However, with that person's untimely death their enthusiasm *dies*. This proverb warns against putting trust in **mortals** rather than God. Hopes often end in keen disappointment.

An Unclear Saying (Prov 11:7)

The verb *'ābad* (**dies, *perishes*, comes to nothing**) standing in both lines receives stress. In the Hebrew text line A has an extra word, likely **wicked** (not translated by the NIV), for this line is longer than any other in ch 11. A scribe may have placed this noun in the margin to explain why the people's hope dies with this person's death. A later scribe included the term in the text. Then the proverb says whatever **a wicked *person*** expects personal **power** or ***wealth*** (*'ônîm*) will accomplish **comes to nothing**. Given the emphasis on wealth in the preceding proverbs, it is the preferred sense of this term here. The revised reading provides a sound reason as to why **hopes** attached to **mortals comes to nothing**.

Opposing: Righteous / Wicked (11:8)

■ **8 The righteous person is rescued from trouble.** This assertion assumes that Yahweh watches over the righteous. When such a person encounters **trouble**, Yahweh brings deliverance. That **trouble . . . falls on the wicked.** Besides stressing the protection Yahweh gives the righteous, this saying warns the wicked against aggressively attacking the righteous by asserting that they will suffer harm like they planned against the righteous.

This principle was evident in Daniel's experience. His foes devised a scheme to have him put to death by having him thrown into a lions' den for violating the law prohibiting making petitions to a god other than the king (Dan 6). When they found Daniel praying to Yahweh, they had him thrown into that den. Yahweh, however, delivered Daniel by shutting the lions' mouths. The king became so angry at those who had tricked him into punishing his trusted servant that he had them thrown into that lions' den. They were immediately devoured, suffering the fate they had designed for Daniel.

This plot, that is, that of a villain's being wiped out by the device or the plan he had designed to eliminate the hero, continues today as a plot in cartoons and movies such as *Spiderman* (see Lennox 1998, 103). Both Ecclesiastes and Job demonstrate that retribution works infrequently. Nevertheless, at times Yahweh does see that retribution is exacted, even in kind. (See Prov 26:27.)

Opposing: The Godless Destroy a Neighbor / The Righteous Escape (11:9)

■ **9 The godless,** aware of the power of words, defame **their neighbors with their mouths.** Their negative gossip undercuts a person's standing in the community, at times causing a person significant loss, such as their position of leadership or, if a merchant, the loss of customers, jeopardizing the business.

Through knowledge, however, **the righteous escape. Knowledge** means that they practice the teachings of sages and are aware of the values Yahweh affirms. That **knowledge** enables them to live virtuously and perceptively, thereby *escaping* plots designed to harm them.

Opposing: Reasons for Joy in a City: Righteous Prosper / Wicked Destroyed (11:10)

■ **10** The next two proverbs laud the rejoicing of city dwellers. The first saying identifies two situations that bring joy to a community. **When the righteous prosper, the city rejoices.** This is the outcome because the citizens recognize that **the righteous** contribute to the stability, security, and well-being of the city. **When the wicked perish,** they also celebrate with loud **shouts of joy.** Watching the demise of the wicked brings them great relief as they anticipate the end of conflicts and corrupt practices in their city (see v 11*b*).

Opposing: City: Exalted / Destroyed (11:11)

■ **11** The different impact **of the upright** and **of the wicked** on a city is asserted. The wording of the first line echoes v 10*a*. However, different terms are used: **upright** in place of "righteous" and **is exalted** (*rûm*) in place of "rejoices" (*'ālaṣ*). The thesis is that **the upright** promote a city's prosperity. The second line, reiterating v 9*a*, uses **wicked** in place of "godless." It declares that words spoken by the wicked *destroy* a city.

Opposing: Speech: Belittling a Neighbor / Remaining Silent (11:12)

■ **12** The next two proverbs concern speech. In the first one the subjects are sharply contrasted: *a person* who lacks *understanding* versus *a person* of *great* understanding (*tĕbûnôt*). The Hebrew term **understanding**, being in the plural, describes a person as adept in understanding. But *a person who lacks judgment* foolishly **derides** *a* neighbor. For example, when that kind of person sees a neighbor do something unusual or ridiculous, such as making a strange addition to his dwelling or wearing something odd, the person says something belittling to that neighbor. The ridiculing remarks, even if meant in jest, show that the person fails to realize the value of maintaining a strong relationship with that neighbor and is certainly unmindful of the difficulty of reestablishing a good relationship with the one who has been embarrassed. But *a person* with a depth of **understanding** *keeps silent*, suppressing the urge to make a sarcastic quip at a neighbor. By **holding** *the* **tongue** the person maintains good relationships with others.

Opposing: Gossiping / Keeping Confidence (Line *a* = 20:19*a*) (11:13)

■ **13** It is critically important to be diligent in keeping **confidence. A gossip** (*rākîl*), however, goes about *revealing secrets. Going about* (*hālak*), standing with *rākîl*, describes a person whose manner is to wander from place to place spreading rumors and distorted tales. Having little concern for the privacy of others, a talebearer delights in spreading confidential information or rumors, as the case may be. The harm caused increases with each retelling, for the details grow more salacious. No wonder such behavior is denounced in the Law

135

(Lev 19:16a). However, **a trustworthy person** (lit. one with a disposition to be reliable) is careful to keep confidential any known personal information. (See Prov 20:19; 25:9.)

Opposing: Lack of Guidance / Many Advisers (Line *b* = 24:6*b*) (11:14)

■ **14** A community, be it a clan, a tribe, a city, or **a nation,** needs leaders who take counsel for developing policies and programs to deal wisely with matters facing the community. When a leader or a governing council fails to take proper **guidance, a nation falls**. That is, the community endures hardships due to the lack of sound planning.

On the other hand, a city or a nation experiences **victory** or *success* in dealing with difficult situations through the counsel of **many advisers**. Since **guidance** stands in the plural, it conveys that much careful deliberation is taken in developing a plan to deal with a particular situation. It is assumed that *the* **advisers** work together, challenging and affirming each other's ideas, in order to develop a viable plan that addresses all aspects of the situation (see Eccl 9:14-15). Taking careful counsel is critical for a military action to lead to **victory**.

Opposing: Putting up Surety / Refusing to Put up Surety (11:15)

■ **15** Numerous proverbs like this one counsel against putting up security for a loan given to a stranger (see Prov 6:1-5; 17:18). This proverb warns that **whoever puts up security**, either money or property, *on behalf of* a stranger **will surely suffer** *loss*. The nature of the loss is not specified.

In providing security for a stranger, a generous person faces three risks. One risk is the likelihood that the loan will not be repaid, for a borrower who needs to have another put up security has few if any resources. Thus, if the venture for which the funds are borrowed fails, that borrower lacks the means to repay the loan.

The second risk for the person who puts up the security resides in not being able to hold the borrower accountable since that person is **a stranger**. The third risk is that a person who needs another to put up security is taking little, if any, personal risk. Thus, the borrower's resolution to make the project sponsored by the loan succeed is significantly diminished. The borrower is more likely to take greater risks with the borrowed funds.

For these reasons a shrewd person **refuses to shake hands in pledge**. This metaphor stands for entering into a firm commitment. A person who never puts up security for another avoids putting his own property at risk, a risk that could greatly harm that person's family.

Opposing: Kindhearted Woman / Ruthless Men (11:16)

■ **16** The next two proverbs are connected by contrasting the *gracious* and *kind* woman with uncaring persons, **ruthless men** (*'ārîṣîm*) and "the cruel" (*'akzārî*).

Both lines in the first proverb are anchored by the verb *take hold*, gain (*tāmak*). People *respect* **a** *gracious* **woman** and enjoy her company. But ruth-

less men are hated because they use strong-arm tactics to **gain . . . wealth**. In so doing they refuse to recognize God as their Lord (Pss 54:3; 86:14). Men who use such tactics receive no **respect**.

Opposing: Kind / Cruel (11:17)

■ **17** *Loyal* or kind *persons* **benefit themselves** by treating others thoughtfully. A person's attitude toward the self is very influential in the way that person relates to others. This truth is heard in the command to love one's neighbor as oneself (Lev 19:18*b*). By caring for the self a person nurtures one's own physical and emotional well-being. That person has the strength and the disposition to show respect and to display kindness to others.

By contrast, **the cruel bring ruin on themselves** (lit. *their own flesh*). *Flesh* may reference either *their own bodies* (*šĕʾēr*) or *their family* (Fox 2009, 538). Cruel thoughts prod this type of a person to disregard caring for one's own body or family members. Possibly both senses of *flesh* are intended (so Fox). The parallelism, however, indicates that *their own flesh* is the primary focus of this line.

The values applauded in these two proverbs are **kindness** rather than physical strength, **respect** rather than **wealth**, and a *gracious* woman rather than **ruthless** men, the **kind** rather than **the cruel**.

Opposing: Wages: Wicked / Righteous (11:18)

■ **18** The character of the **wages** earned by **a wicked person** is contrasted with those of **one who sows righteousness**. Often the work done by **a wicked person** is faulty because such a person is more concerned with the appearance of the job rather than its structural integrity. Over time his work is likely to fail, possibly inflicting harm on someone. Consequently, the **wages** that worker earned are **deceptive** or *dishonest*. In other words, that laborer received more than the value of the work done. But **one who sows righteousness** [i.e., performs a task in a skilled and honorable manner] **reaps a sure reward.** In the United States one would say the person earns "an honest day's wage."

Opposing: Life for the Righteous / Death for the Wicked (11:19)

■ **19** The introductory word *kēn* (*thus, so* [truly]) signals that this proverb draws on inference from the principle set out in the preceding saying (Fox 2009, 538). The tie between these two proverbs is confirmed by the chiastic relationship of their subjects (ibid.): "a wicked person":"one who sows righteousness"::**the righteous**: *a pursuer of* **evil**.

The ultimate wages of **the righteous** is **life**, but *a pursuer of* **evil** is rewarded with **death**. Although the pursuit of righteousness is arduous and at times costly, that pursuit rewards one with both a high quality of life and a long life. "Pursuit of" is implied in the first line by its presence in the second line. *A pursuer of* **evil**, however, incurs hardships, that is, multiple troubles and physical ailments or injuries. These difficulties lead to an early **death**.

A few interpreters see in this wording a hint that a righteous person's life does not end at death, but that theme is not developed in Proverbs. (See 10:16; 12:28; 21:21.)

Opposing: A Person with a Perverted Heart / The Blameless (11:20)

■ **20** Yahweh responds to people according to their inner character. This principle echoes Yahweh's words to Samuel, "the LORD looks at the heart" not on "the outward appearance" (1 Sam 16:7). God evaluates a person on the basis of that person's temperament, thoughts, and convictions.

In particular **Yahweh** detests those who have **perverted mind** or foul disposition. But **he delights in those whose ways are blameless**. The term **way** is singular, indicating a person's entire manner of conduct. The fact that the terms **perverted** and **blameless** are plural conveys that the thoughts of the wicked person are completely perverted, but the conduct of the upright is fully **blameless**.

Opposing: Evil Fate / Escape (Line *a* = 16:5*b*) (11:21)

■ **21** This proverb is introduced with **be sure of this** (lit. **hand to hand**). This sense may have arisen from the practice of clasping hands to confirm an agreement. This phrase guarantees the assertion being made: **the wicked will not go unpunished**, that is, will not escape being held accountable by either the community or God.

Indeed, the wicked will not escape being held accountable for hostile attitudes (e.g., 16:5), such as gleefulness at another's misfortune (e.g., 17:5), arrogance (16:5), or greed (e.g., 28:20; Fox 2009, 539). But **the seed** or children of **the** righteous **will escape**, that is, will not suffer an ill-fate. This saying affirms that by living righteously parents benefit their children. Spiritual qualities handed on from one generation to the next become stronger in each successive generation.

Analogy: A Beautiful Woman without Discretion (11:22)

■ **22** In hearing this proverb it is helpful to remember that many in the Orient wear nose rings. The analogy **like a gold ring in a pig's snout** immediately catches one's attention because of the sharp contrast made between a valuable object, a gold ring, and its setting, the **snout** of **a pig**. Furthermore, pigs were repugnant to the ancient Hebrews. This analogy vividly brings out the reality that the worth of a highly valued object may be greatly diminished by being used in an uncomely way.

It is also surprising that this analogy is applied to a beautiful woman lacking discretion. While her beauty attracts many admirers, it is not sufficient to compensate for her lack of discernment. Clearly, character and prudence have far greater worth than a person's appearance.

This proverb motivates a woman not to focus her efforts on her appearance at the expense of gaining wisdom. It also informs a young man that a prudent bride will bring him far more honor than marrying a beautiful woman who lacks discretion.

Opposing: Desire of Righteous / Hope of Wicked (11:23)

■ **23** Each line of this proverb is a verbless clause. This style prods hearers to ponder various verbs that bring out the connection between the elements juxtaposed in each line. **The desire of the righteous** is far more productive than **the hope of the wicked**. That is, the deep longing **of the righteous** leads to results that are **surely beneficial**. This principle is heard in the beatitude that "those who hunger and thirst [after] righteousness" are blessed (Matt 5:6).

The righteous receive good results in pursuing their **desires** because those desires flow out of an upright heart. Often they arise from God's promptings. But **the hope of the wicked** leads to **wrath**. It is not that the wicked hope for wrath but that what they hope for will cause them to experience fury either from the people they harm or from God. This is their fate, because they enjoy causing people heavy losses and suffering. The fury aroused by the wicked was very visible in the outcries of people throughout the world at those who drove planes filled with unwitting passengers into two skyscrapers in New York City in 2001. (See 10:24, 28.)

Opposing: Generosity / Stinginess (11:24)

■ **24** The next three proverbs laud generosity over stinginess. Generosity is on center stage by virtue of standing at the beginning (v 24a) and the end (v 26b) and in the center (v 25) of this small cluster of proverbs. It is accentuated further by being contrasted with stinginess in vv 24b and 26a. Moreover, the principle presented in the first line (v 24a) is illustrated by reference to the benefits of being generous in v 25. Next both principles set out in v 24 are illustrated in the saying in v 26.

Life is full of paradoxes. The paradox brought out in this proverb is that a person who **gives freely** and without a definitive goal experiences increase. Since the verb **gives freely** lacks an object, the first line sets out a principle that is applicable to a variety of situations. A frequent, and possible, interpretation of this line is that those who give generously, even impulsively, to the poor are blessed with increased wealth.

Because this proverb calls attention to an anomaly, it cannot be viewed as establishing a principle that anyone who gives to the poor will have an increase in wealth. The outcome is a windfall. For example, a merchant who invests in a new enterprise over piling up profits in time sees an increase in income. Certainly it is implied that in such cases God is behind the increase.

In the second line another type of person **holds back funds** or **saves them out of sincerity** (*miyyōšer*; DCH 4:341; rather than **unduly**). This kind of person is genuinely cautious with his resources. But surprisingly, this person's timid approach leads to a decrease in his net worth as conveyed by the phrase **surely comes to poverty**. **Surely** serves to stress the contrast between the **good**

11:23-24

outcome that attends **the desire of the righteous** with ***the want*** that those who ***hold back*** too much experience.

This particular saying is not intended to discourage financial prudence, but it seeks to alert a person to the potential downside risk that accompanies being overly cautious. Clearly, the application of this principle in v 26a shows that either hoarding or being resistant to sharing assets with others because it appears to be wasteful is disparaged. (See Deut 15:1-11; Matt 13:12; Mark 4:25; Luke 19:26.)

Affirming: Wealth / Refreshing (11:25)

■ **25** Generosity leads to abundance (see Prov 11:24a). A person who brings blessings to others by sharing liberally **prospers** (lit. ***becomes fat***). In ancient societies (e.g., Job 15:27), and today in many third world countries, "being fat" is a metaphor for being well-to-do. This is the case given that only the well-to-do could afford rich food and thereby put on weight.

The positive imagery of fatness in the ancient Middle East is evident in Pharaoh's dream of the fat cows and the lean cows, representing years of abundance and of want respectively. This principle is reinforced in the second line: **whoever refreshes** [*marweh*] **others will be refreshed**. The root *rāwâ*, rendered **refreshes**, is literally ***water abundantly, saturate,*** and metaphorically **satiate** (*DCH* 7:426-27). A person who strives to bring relief or refreshment to others will find relief in times of need (see Luke 6:38).

Opposing: Selfish / Generous (11:26)

■ **26** Both sides of the principle set out in Prov 11:24 are illustrated in this picture. During times when the food supply is limited, such as is often the case in Palestine due to the erratic nature of seasonal rainfall, many farmers or distributors hoard grain in anticipation of getting a higher price as conditions worsen—a practice considered shrewd by the law of supply and demand. Their behavior, however, so angers the **people** that they **curse** such persons. Such anger often leads to riots.

But the people ***bless a distributor*** (*mašbîr*), that is, a merchandiser or a government official (Fox 2009, 544), **who is willing to sell** grain during such a time. Out of compassion for the people threatened with hunger, that distributor foregoes making a huge profit. During a terrible seven-year famine in Egypt, Joseph, manager of the granary, was highly esteemed for providing the people food throughout the famine (Gen 41:57; 45:16-20; 47:25; 50:7-9).

Opposing: Searching: Good / Evil (11:27)

■ **27** The themes in Prov 11:24-26 are capsulated in a statement of principle. **Whoever *pursues* good** seeks ***the* favor** of God and the community. That person's focus on receiving honor by helping others is reiterated as a principle. However, **evil** [*ra'*] **comes to one who searches for it** by being selfish or miserly. It is important to note that in the negative sequence evil is the aggressor.

140

Opposing: Fall of Those Who Trust in Wealth / Flourishing of the Righteous (11:28)

■ **28** Being an instrument that facilitates commerce and exchange, wealth is viewed as beneficial in Proverbs. The acquisition of wealth is one way God lets those who pursue wisdom prosper (e.g., 8:11-20). However, wealth carries an inherent temptation—namely, to put one's trust in that wealth rather than in Yahweh (see Deut 6).

But wealth is not a deity or a spiritual force, though many people devote themselves to it as though it were. Wealth is a dead, lifeless object that is not worthy of being made the foundation of one's trust. Consequently, whoever comes to **trust in . . . riches will fall.** Either that person's riches evaporate into thin air or they come to have no value before the kind of trouble that threatens that person's life.

The righteous, however, **will thrive like a green leaf. A green leaf** is a frequent metaphor for the vigor, stability, and prosperity of the righteous. In Ps 1:3 the righteous are pictured as a tree planted by streams of water. Continually nourished, they flourish, bringing forth fruit in season. A tree that puts down deep roots stands against powerful storms (see Jer 17:8). The righteous, then, must always view wealth as a by-product of fearing God, not as its goal. (See Prov 10:2; 11:4.)

Affirming: A Troubler of a Family / A Fool Becomes a Servant (11:29)

■ **29** In antiquity a noble man worked diligently to provide his family an inheritance, for an inheritance was the basis for his children and grandchildren to support a large family. But a person, possibly a son (Fox 2009, 544), who is so foolish as to **bring *trouble* on *his*** family receives an unwelcome inheritance: **wind** (*rûaḥ*). A powerful **wind** drives everything away, leaving nothing for one's descendants to inherit. Furthermore, ***a* fool,** possibly the child who brings trouble on the household, becomes ***a* servant to the wise,** having been sold into servitude for the debts incurred. Bad behavior has turned an inheritance into a debtor's obligation.

Affirming: Fruit of the Righteous (11:30)

■ **30** **The fruit of the righteous is a tree of life. Tree of life** is a metaphor for "supporting a long life," for fruit does not become a tree. Righteous behavior empowers a patriarch to sustain the family. Thus, living a righteous life, because it promotes the continuation of a family, is comparable to eating from the tree of life (see 3:18).

The second line is difficult to render into English. The NIV reads **and the one who is wise saves lives,** but the Hebrew idiom is literally ***one who takes lives.*** Although this idiom usually means ***kill*** (1:19; Ps 31:13 [14 HB]; Ezek 33:6), the word **wise** quickly discounts its having that meaning in this context. Moreover, the wise are characterized as nourishing other persons as expressed in the first line. The Hebrew *lāqaḥ* may mean ***take out*** of danger, *receive* (Ps 49:17 [18 HB]); the line then means that **the** wise have power **to nourish** or guide **people** (Clifford 1999, 127; Fox 2009, 454).

Opposing: Reward: Righteous / Wicked (11:31)

■ **31** This proverb is built on the argument that if A is true then B is assuredly true (see Job 15:15-16; 25:5-6). The first premise is that **the righteous receive their due on earth**, that is, *in this life*. If that is the case, it is even more certain that *the wicked* and **the sinner** will receive their due *in this life*. *In this life*, found in the first line, is implied in the second line. This proverb encourages those who pursue righteousness to wait patiently for their reward as it also warns the wicked that they will surely be punished for their evil deeds.

This certainty of retribution is challenged in Ecclesiastes (e.g., 8:14) and Job (see Job's argument against retribution in ch 21). According to the NT, both the righteous and the wicked will receive their rightful rewards, sometimes in this life, but assuredly in the final judgment. (See Sir 11:21; 1 Pet 4:18.)

C. Proverbs 12:1-28

OVERVIEW

All the proverbs in this chapter are structured as opposing except for two, one in affirming style (12:14) and one a better-than saying (v 9). Yahweh is the subject of two sayings. He bestows favor on the truthful (v 2*a*, 22*b*) but condemns an evildoer (v 2*b*) and false speech (v 22*a*). The primary opposing pair is the righteous, the upright, or the good in contrast to the wicked or evildoers (eleven proverbs; vv 2, 3 [wickedness], 5, 6, 7, 10, 12, 13, 20 [plotting evil:promoting peace], 21, 26). "The house of the righteous" endures (v 7*b*). "The wise listen to advice" (v 15*b*) and "escape trouble" (v 13*b*). They are on the path to a long life (v 28), but the wicked are overthrown and disappear (v 7*a*).

Another contrast is between a noble wife who brings honor to her husband and a disgraceful wife who is like a cancer (v 4). Truth and lies are contrasted in three proverbs (vv 17, 19, 22). Also three proverbs contrast the fool with the wise or the prudent (vv 15, 16, 23), and three state the benefits of diligent work in contrast to the ill consequences that befall the lazy or daydreamers (vv 11, 24, 27).

A major topic is speech (eight proverbs, vv 6, 13, 14, 17, 18, 19, 22, 25). Interestingly three parts of the face are used to represent speech: lips (vv 13 [HB], 19, 22), mouth (vv 6 [HB], 14 [HB]), and tongue (vv 18, 19). A rare theme in Scripture is the humanitarian way that the righteous treat animals (v 10*a*).

IN THE TEXT

Opposing: Loving Discipline / Hating Reproof (12:1)

■ **1** Learning requires discipline, whether a student receives a physical blow as in the days of old or a rebuke as is the usual method today. **Whoever loves** discipline [i.e., love in the sense of openness to learn from discipline] **loves** the acquisition of **knowledge**. To gain knowledge there must be a passion to study hard and to learn from the various kinds of corrections offered by an instructor. Students who respond well to corrections and comments make good progress in becoming well educated. But ***one*** who hates [i.e., despises] ***reproof*** or **correction is stupid**. There is little hope that this kind of person will become skilled in a particular field of knowledge.

Opposing: Yahweh's Favor / Yahweh's Condemnation (Line *a* = 8:35*b*; 18:22*b*) (12:2)

■ **2** A good ***person*** [i.e., one who is living in accord with the principles of wisdom] ***obtains*** favor from **Yahweh**. The good person's work succeeds as a result of Yahweh's blessing. But **Yahweh** condemns a person given to ***craftiness*** or scheming in order to become wealthy at the expense of others. The second line is similar to 8:35*b*, except the latter lacks the word **good**.

Opposing: Instability of the Wicked / Stability of the Righteous (12:3)

■ **3** This proverb shows how a community responds to the righteous in contrast to the wicked. A person given to **wickedness . . . *cannot* be established** in a community, for that one is a constant threat to harm people or their property. Citizens look down on such a person, hoping the wicked one will move elsewhere. But **the righteous,** like a stalwart tree, put down deep ***roots***, enabling them to stand firmly before the strong gusts of adversity. A tree's lush appearance and its sturdiness often serve as a metaphor for the righteous (Ps 1:4-6). This image reoccurs in several proverbs in order to drive this important principle deep into the thinking of the young.

Opposing: Honorable Wife / Shameful Wife (12:4)

■ **4** A wife contributes significantly to her husband's standing in the community and especially to the strength of her household. **A wife of noble character** [*'ēšet ḥayil*; i.e., a resourceful person with an outstanding character] **is her husband's crown.** The Hebrew *'ēšet ḥayil* is the feminine counterpart of *gibbôr ḥayil*, a mighty man of valor.

The latter term is used for gifted leaders who guided Israel in settling in Canaan (e.g., Judg 6:12; 11:1). This descriptor is applied to Ruth for her loyalty to Naomi, her mother-in-law, and her determination to follow the levirate law (Ruth 3:11). A noble wife is like a diadem, a jewel of great beauty, in bringing her husband honor and dignity (see Prov 31:10-31). Her value to the family is beyond measure.

A disgraceful wife is comparable to ***rottenness* in *the* bones**. The deterioration of a person's skeletal structure takes place slowly, but persistently, robbing a person of physical and emotional strength; this picture is similar to the effects of cancer. "Bones" in Hebrew thought stands for one's emotional strength. A disgraceful wife causes her husband extensive grief and loss of standing in the community.

Opposing: Thoughts of the Righteous / Thoughts of the Wicked (12:5)

■ **5** The next three proverbs contrast the wicked and the righteous. **The plans** or **strategies of the righteous are just**. There is no distortion in them. But **the skillful planning** [*taḥbūlôt*] **of the wicked is deceitful**. They use their intelligence to formulate plans that are ingeniously lined with deceit in order to dupe others to buy into their schemes.

At the outset of the twenty-first century this trait is well attested in all areas of Western society, especially in politics and the financial markets. Besides being a descriptive proverb, it serves as an exhortation to practice just planning and to shun deceitful strategizing (Fox 2009, 549).

Opposing: Speech of the Wicked / Words of the Upright (12:6)

■ **6** The wicked take pleasure in using powerful **rhetoric** to arouse people into a mob that strikes out against leaders and employers causing blood to run in the streets. But **the speech of the upright** serves to **rescue** people from trouble. Their words enlighten people to overcome obstacles as snares set within the words of the wicked. (See 10:2*b*; 11:6*a*, 8*a*, 9*b*; 12:21.)

Opposing: The Downfall of the Wicked / The House of the Righteous (12:7)

■ **7** When **the wicked are overthrown**, presumably by some disaster or in battle, they **are no more**, for they lack the resources to overcome defeat and reconstruct their lives. By contrast, **the house of the righteous stands firm**. **House** includes all the persons, animals, and artifacts that belong to a family. Since the righteous build their houses on solid ground, they stand firm even when pounded by a torrential storm (see 10:25; Ps 37:10, 11; Matt 7:24-25).

Opposing: Speech of the Skilled / Thought of the Perverse (12:8)

■ **8** A person is praised for **offering sound insight**. But one who has **a warped mind is despised**. The citizens of a town, on realizing the inadequacy of the planning and the speech of a person whose thinking is twisted, dismiss his presentation. Lasting honor goes to a person who is skilled in wisdom.

Better-than: A Commoner over One Who Pretends to Be a Noble (12:9)

■ **9** This saying recommends that a commoner who has a servant accept his standing in a community, though it is lower than he desires. Having a servant indicates that though this person has low standing, he has some financial resources. Some interpreters wonder how a commoner could have a servant, but in primitive cultures the basic chores of daily life, such as getting and preparing food, going to a well for water, taking care of animals, was so time consuming that even a family of limited means needed the help of a servant.

A plebeian needs to realize that it is far better to have the resources of a servant **than pretend to be a person of high standing**, by putting on airs as by the way one dresses, but in reality lack **bread**, the most basic food. The ridiculous picture painted by this proverb underscores the buffoonery that attends pretending to be rich or a prominent person.

For some interpreters a commoner's having a servant is puzzling, if not impossible. In addition, the phrase "who has a servant" does not match the parallel "bread." Clearly, a servant is much more costly than bread (Fox 2009, 550). Based on the reading in the LXX, Syriac Version, and the Vulgate, "and serves himself" (see Sir 10:27), some emend the text. Fox (2009, 550-51) recommends reading the consonants of "has a servant" as *wa'ăbûr* "and produce" (agricultural).

The proverb, then, lauds a person who successfully gets produce from the land. Life for this person is better than for one who pretends to have high standing. Since emendations always make sense of a difficult text, they are to be accepted with much caution.

Opposing: Manner of Treating Animals: Righteous / Wicked (12:10)

■ **10** This proverb reflects a nascent humanitarian perspective as it highlights the considerate manner of **the righteous** in ***caring*** for **their animals**. For example, they do not overwork an animal, realizing that it is a great asset and can significantly increase the family's food supply. But **the wicked**, imaging that they treat their animals kindly, in reality **are cruel** to them. The literal Hebrew ***cruel mercies*** is a vivid oxymoron.

This proverb lauds the humanitarian treatment of animals. Such counsel, though infrequent in the OT, is clearly present in a few commands, such as not muzzling an ox while it is threshing the grain (Deut 25:4). It is also seen in the prohibition not to sacrifice an animal and its offspring on the same day (Lev 22:28; for other examples of concern for animals see Exod 22:29-30; 23:19; Lev 22:27; Deut 14:21*b*; 22:10; 25:4).

Opposing: Worker / Dreamer (=28:19) (12:11)

■ **11** This saying contrasts the value of doing purposeful work to engaging in worthless pursuits. Both types of people are busy, but the outcomes from their activities are drastically different. Those who diligently **work their land** are rewarded with a harvest that is sufficient to meet the family's **food** needs. But **those who chase *empty pursuits lack*** good **sense**. The result is they disgrace their families by failing to provide for them sufficiently, a great disgrace in an honor-based society. (See Prov 10:4, 5, 26.)

Opposing: Desire of the Wicked / The Root of the Righteous (12:12)

■ **12** The owning of possessions never satisfies humans, not even the wicked. Besides coveting the goods of others, **the wicked** covet **the stronghold of evildoers**, their secure hiding place for their treasures and themselves (see Waltke 2004, 529). In contrast to the wicked **the root of the righteous endures**.

Root symbolizes their nourishing patiently the unseen aspects of their lives, those that support their values. After several seasons they produce an abundance of fruit, that is, they make solid contributions to the community. Their deep roots anchor them to withstand the tempests of life.

Opposing: Transgression of Lips / Righteous Escape Trouble (12:13)

■ **13** In committing a transgression through speech, *an evil person* sets a snare to defraud another but is caught in that snare. However, *a righteous person escapes* trouble, that is, harm from the various kinds of traps set by evildoers.

Affirming: Fruit of Speech / Reward of Work (12:14)

■ **14** The words of those who speak truthfully, using good rhetorical skills, bear delicious **fruit**, that is, a life **filled with good things**. In other words, they receive an honorarium and honor, a **reward** that is comparable to the products produced by **the work of their hands.**

Opposing: Fools / Prudent (12:15)

■ **15** The term **fool** (*ĕwîl*) connects the next two proverbs. This proverb points out that one way to identify fools is to evaluate the path they are treading. Fools are very confident that **the way** they are taking is **right**. They never take counsel—implied from the wording of the second line. So when someone offers them guidance for taking a better course, they reject that input without giving it due consideration. **The wise**, on the other hand, not only **listen to advice**, they seek it out. They are never offended at being given suggestions to improve their way of life. They consider the input and act on it.

Accurate perception of one's own deeds and lifestyle is difficult for many. They find it hard to recognize their own faults. Thus, all humans need people to provide insight into the manner of their behavior in order to reinforce good traits and to correct harmful ones.

That even the best need counselors is very visible in professional sports, for each team has many coaches to guide the pros to do better. These coaches help athletes to get out of bad habits so they can perform up to expectations.

If the best athletes need constant guidance in order to perform up to their potential in the sport at which they excel, how much more do ordinary humans need guidance from the wise and the faithful in matters of morals and spiritual disciplines in order to excel in righteousness and wisdom?

Opposing: Annoyance at Vexation / Insult Overlooked (12:16)

■ **16** **Fools**, being easily irritated, *display* their annoyance. Thus, they have a hard time maintaining a conversation with any who have a different perspective. But *the astute* (*ārûm*), having good self-control, are able to **overlook an insult**. They are sufficiently secure in their own knowledge that words of contempt hurled at them do not quickly upset them, prodding them to respond in an irritated manner. Thereby they keep open the possibility of having vital conversation with the person who has affronted them.

Opposing: Witnesses: Reliable / False (12:17)

■ **17** The following three proverbs are connected by contrasting truthful, helpful speech with lying, harmful words. This proverb teaches that one who *testifies truthfully, declares* or establishes that which is **right**. But a *lying* witness speaks *deceitfully*. Both "testify" and "witness" indicate that this saying has a legal setting. Truthful witnesses are essential for justice to be established, for false testimony thwarts justice and threatens the stability of the community (see 14:5, 25; 19:5, 9, 28; 21:28; 24:28; 25:18).

Opposing: Speech: Rash Words / Wise Words (12:18)

■ **18** An impetuous speaker recklessly pours out an abundance of words without giving much thought to what is being said, often using words so sharp that they **pierce like swords**. These words deeply wound the hearers; these emotional wounds take a very long time to heal. Conversely, **the tongue** [i.e., the speech] **of the wise brings healing**. Words matter. They wound and they heal. In order to speak healing words, the tongue must be well trained. This is the picture in the description of God's servant in Isa 50; he has diligently gained a "taught" tongue in order to sustain those who are weary (v 4).

Opposing: Truthful Speech Is Enduring / Lies Last for a Moment (12:19)

■ **19** The effect of **truthful lips** is contrasted with that of **a lying tongue**. Words spoken by a truthful person **endure forever**. They offer insight into reality and God's ways. Many sayings of the wise, such as those of Abraham Lincoln, are repeated throughout the generations, offering guidance on crucial issues of morality and life. **But a lying tongue lasts only a moment.** Falsehood collapses under the weight of someone trying to build something on it. This proverb is a chiasm: **truthful lips:endure:forever::only a moment:lying tongue**.

Opposing: Devisers of Evil / Counselors of Peace (12:20)

■ **20** Deceit characterizes the ***thoughts*** **of those who plot evil**. The term **plot** is literally ***plough***, suggesting that such plotting takes great effort. The term **joy** in the second line implies that those whose thoughts are evil are unhappy (see Fox 2009, 556-57). Conversely, those who give counsel that ***promotes harmony*** or **peace** have lasting **joy** as a by-product. That is because they observe the beneficial impact of their efforts. This proverb is chiastic: **deceit:** *plotters of* evil::***promoters of*** peace: joy.

Opposing: Wicked / Righteous (12:21)

■ **21** **No harm overtakes the righteous.** This is a hard saying, for many righteous people go through severe trials (see Prov 24:16; 25:26). The interpretation depends on what is meant by **no harm** (*ʾāwen*). Since *ʾāwen* references ***wickedness***, the **harm** in view is the kind that befalls those who do wrong. The righteous experience troubles, but not the harsh results that attend doing wicked deeds. **The wicked**, however, receive **their fill of trouble** or ***setbacks*** (*rāʿ*).

Read in light of the first line, the second line says that trouble over-whelms the wicked, bringing them down. In light of the second line, the first one says that no harm so overcomes the righteous that they have to forsake righteousness. The first line is in accord with Paul's saying that nothing can separate believers from the love of Christ, whether they be things on earth or under the earth (Rom 8:35-39).

Opposing: False Speech / Reliable Deeds (12:22)

■ **22** This proverb contrasts Yahweh's reaction to liars versus those **who are trustworthy**. It is very easy to lie, but **Yahweh detests lying lips** so intently because lies distort truth and lead people astray. Rather, Yahweh **delights in** those **who are trustworthy**, literally *acting faithfully*. Their deeds as well as their speech are genuine. By their acts and words truth-tellers bring Yahweh honor. Such people live up to their being made in God's image.

Opposing: Astute / Fools (12:23)

■ **23** *An astute person* [ʾārûm] *conceals* knowledge. This kind of person does not put his knowledge on display for self-acclaim. In any given situation he avoids speaking long and in detail about a subject and in sharing confidential information. He shares only the information that is needed to address a spe-cific situation.

But **a fool's heart *proclaims* folly.** Seeking to impress others with how much they know, fools talk long and loud about any topic. But the more they speak the more they display their folly. They lack any sense of the proper time to speak or of the proper amount of information to give.

Opposing: Diligent Person / Slothful (12:24)

■ **24** The fate of the diligent is contrasted sharply with that of the lazy. *The* **hands** *of the* **diligent**, hands being a metaphor for a person's skill at a particu-lar task, calls attention to the quality products produced by diligent workers. Since the diligent do excellent work, they receive advancements. They are ap-pointed to **rule** or *manage* other workers.

The ideal model of a diligent worker who comes to rule is Joseph in Egypt. Serving a large landowner well led to his being made head manager of the household (Gen 39:6). When false charges led to Joseph's imprison-ment, he continued to work diligently and rose to become the supervisor of the prison. Later during the threat of a national crisis, Pharaoh appointed him as special assistant to manage farm production and storage in order that Egypt could survive a dreadful famine.

Those who are lazy, however, are conscripted for slave labor or corvée to do hard work. Deuteronomy 20:11-16 has regulations for putting citizens of a captured city into forced labor. Solomon had so many building projects that he organized Canaanites into labor gangs to get the work done (1 Kgs 9:15, 20-21); later he put Israelites into labor gangs (1 Kgs 5:13-16).

This practice was a primary reason that northern Israelites challenged Rehoboam, Solomon's successor, to lighten their workload. Because he did not heed their request, northern Israel separated from Judah. These texts illustrate the contemptible nature of **forced labor**, the fate of the lazy. (See Prov 10:4.)

Opposing: Anxiety Brings One Low / A Good Word Brings Cheer (12:25)

■ **25** Anxiety [i.e., great apprehension about possible troubles] **weighs** heavily on a person, rendering that person very despondent. Anxiety curtails greatly a person's productivity. Some causes of anxiety mentioned in the OT include suffering during a natural disaster such as a famine (Jer 42:16), living in a city under siege (Ezek 4:16), beset by the threat of violence (Jer 38:19), and facing the consequences of doing wrong (Ps 38:18; Diamond 1997, *d'g*, *NIDOTTE* 1:906-7). But a *pleasant* or kind [*ṭôb*] **word** extended to a person troubled by uncertainties **cheers** *the person* up. This proverb underscores the power of a proper word spoken at the right time. (See Prov 15:13, 30; 17:22*a*.)

Opposing: Righteous / Wicked (12:26)

■ **26** The Hebrew of the first line is unclear. Thus, English translations have widely different readings. The second line is clear: **the way of the wicked leads them astray**. The wicked are disposed to take a pleasure-laden path that appears to be easy, thinking that it leads to a desirable destination. However, being deceived by their wickedness, they will eventually discover that the path they are on leads to an abysmal end, a destiny that is appropriate for their having committed immoral deeds.

Since this saying is structured as opposing, the first line makes a contrasting statement. It likely describes **the righteous** giving sound direction (see NJPS; Longman 2006, 279) or providing help to **their friends** or neighbors (see NRSV).

Opposing: Slothful Person / The Diligent (12:27)

■ **27** There are some textual problems in this verse. What is clear is that the behavior of **the lazy** is contrasted with that of **the diligent** and also that **game** taken in hunting parallels **riches**. A possible reading of the first line is that **a lazy *person*** fails to **roast** *the* game that has been caught; **game** may be a metaphor for "spoil" taken by some scheme (Fox 2009, 559). The scheme worked, but the schemer did not—unless the line means this lazy person has taken no game and thus has no food (see RSV). However, **the diligent**, realizing the value of *wealth*, prize it (based on some textual emendations).

Opposing: Life / Death (12:28)

■ **28** In the way of righteousness there is life, but another **path** leads to *death*. Why doesn't everyone take the path of righteousness? Two reasons are prominent: first, the path of righteousness is narrow, requiring hardiness to tread that way without straying. The other reason is that the entrance to the broad path, leading to death, is lined with fancy billboards promising great rewards for those who take that route. These advertisements entice people to expect great rewards for little effort. So many are enticed into taking that path over the way of righteousness (compare Matt 7:13-14).

The Meaning of the Second Line of Prov 12:28

The Hebrew of the second line is difficult. It reads literally **way**, **path**, **not death**. Some translations take "not death" to refer to **immortality** (compare Waltke 2004, 544-45). But the two lines expressed opposing ideas. This reading has little support in the Hebrew text for *'al* ("not") standing before the noun *māwet* ("death") negates it. When it is attached to a noun, a jussive is implied: **let there be no death** (Prov 8:10; 17:12; 27:2; Fox 2009, 560). So it is better to read the consonants as *'el māwet* ("to death" [RSV], but "there is no death" [NRSV]).

Following the term **way** [*nĕtîbâ*], **path** is a tautology. Likely the latter word has resulted from a misspelling. Determining the original word is only a guess. One suggestion is to read *tô'ēbâ* ("abomination, detestable") as the opposite of righteousness (Murphy 1998, 88, with some support from the LXX). This leads to the reading: **the detestable way leads to death**. Little weight can be placed on this reconstruction.

In addition, it is never directly asserted in Proverbs that humans have immorality, a blessed existence in an ideal land after death. This point is significant given the frequent references to life and the tree of life in Proverbs. Moreover, nothing is gained in finding support for a theological concept, especially from a disturbed text, that is not clearly taught in the OT. Biblical faith does teach that believers have immortality, but this is gained by being resurrected (Dan 12:2, and possibly Isa 26:19; Pss 49:15; 73:23-25).

This belief explains why Enoch and Elijah were translated to the heavenly realm. Since Daniel, one of the wisest men, spoke of resurrection, it is possible that some wisdom sayings point to a life after death. So such a belief should not be ruled out on the basis that this belief is not definitively presented in several texts. But this disturbed verse offers little if any evidence for such a view. It is not until after the resurrection of Jesus that eternal life by physical resurrection became an established doctrine of biblical faith.

D. Proverbs 13:1-25

OVERVIEW

The proverbs in this chapter are encased by the first two and last sayings having similar themes: discipline accepted and rejected (vv 1-2, 24) and the righteous enjoying good things contrasted with the wicked craving violence, but going hungry (vv 2, 25). All the proverbs in this chapter are formulated as opposing except for two structured as advancing (vv 14, 23). Four contrasting pairs are dominant: the righteous and the wicked or sinner (six sayings: vv 5, 6, 9, 21, 22 ["good":"sinner"], 25), the wise and fools (two sayings: vv 16 ["prudent"], 20), the rich and the poor (two sayings: vv 7, 8; see v 22), and the lazy and the diligent (one saying: v 4). The name of Yahweh does not occur, and there are no references to women.

Three topics are prominent. Wisdom is the focus of six proverbs (vv 10b, 13b, 14, 15a, 16a, 20a). It is "a fountain of life, turning [one] from the snares of death" (v 14). One gains wisdom through fellowshipping with the wise (v 20a). Instruction or discipline stands in four proverbs (vv 1, 13, 18, 24).

Wealth and poverty are considered in seven proverbs (vv 4, 7, 8, 11, 22, 23, 25). Wealth accumulated slowly is lasting, but money gained dishonestly quickly vanishes (v 11). To provide a legacy for one's family it is important to pass on an inheritance (v 22a). Two other themes are speech (vv 2, 3, [16]) and hope (vv 12, 19).

IN THE TEXT

Opposing: A Wise Child / A Mocker (13:1)

■ **I** This saying gives the primary reason for why in one family a child becomes **a wise son** while in another family a son becomes **a mocker**. One **son** becomes **wise** because he continually **heeds his father's instruction** (i.e., *discipline* [*mûsār*; see 4:1-9]). In antiquity discipline included physical punishment. Since that son stores his father's teaching in his heart (4:3), as he grows up, he draws on it daily for guidance. At a young age people admire him for the way he conducts himself. When he becomes an adult, the community honors him as a leader. However, the outcome is vastly different for a son who constantly mocks even at a young age. Refusing to heed his father's instruction, he becomes proud and develops a spiteful attitude. A **mocker** is described as **arrogant** and behaving with **insolent fury** (21:24). In a desperate effort to correct his son's demeanor, the father addresses him with **rebukes** (13:1). But the son, chaffing at those stern words of guidance, refuses to **respond** to them by changing his behavior. Because he becomes a hardened **mocker**, the community *detests* him (see 24:9).

Opposing: Results of Good Speech / Appetite for Violence (13:2)

■ **2** The proverbs in vv 2-4 are connected in the Hebrew by *nepeš* (**appetite,** "lives," "desires" [vv 2b, 3a, 4a, 4b]) and *pî* (**lips** [vv 2a, 3a]) as the relationship between speaking and craving is explored. **From the fruit of their lips** [i.e., speaking judiciously, wisely, and encouragingly] **people enjoy good things** (see 12:14; 18:20, 21). Disciplined speech produces words that are as delicious as fruit.

But *the treacherous* have an **appetite for violence**, that is, the wanton destruction of property and life. They relish turning society upside down. It was because of widespread violence on the earth that God became compelled to judge the human race with the catastrophic deluge (Gen 6:9-13).

Opposing: Speech (13:3)

■ **3** Those who, like a sentinel, **guard** the words coming from **their *mouths* preserve their lives** (*nepeš*). They are well aware that those who **speak rashly** (lit. ***opens wide his lips*) *face* ruin,** as conveyed by the poignant expression in the Hebrew ***destruction to him***.

A person who has a wide open mouth spews out whatever enters the mind. Unreflective babbling frequently leads to saying something that the speaker soon deeply regrets. But the regret may come too late; misspoken words often produce ruinous results that cannot be easily corrected.

Opposing: Lazy / Diligent (Similar to 13:25) (13:4)

■ **4** *A lazy person's* **appetite is never filled.** He is just too lethargic to take the effort to meet any of his desires. But the **desires of the diligent** drive them to take great efforts to satisfy their desire richly (lit. ***become fat***). Becoming fat in antiquity and in many current third world cultures is a metonym for success and wealth. In Proverbs this term also conveys that one is "refreshed" (11:25).

Opposing: Righteous / Wicked (13:5)

■ **5** The next two proverbs are connected by words from the roots *ṣdq* (**right**) and *ršʿ* (**wicked**), arranged in parallel position: **righteous** (*ṣaddîq*):**wicked** (*rāšāʿ*)::"righteousness" (*ṣĕdāqâ*):"wickedness" (*rišâ*). In this proverb the subjects stand at the center, mirroring each other for emphasis. **The righteous hate *anything* false.** But **the wicked *cause* a stench** by some base action. Wicked behavior is as revolting as a nasty, pungent odor. It ***brings* on** the doer deep **shame.**

Opposing: Righteousness / Wickedness (13:6)

■ **6** Righteousness and wickedness are personified as dynamic forces. **Righteousness guards *the way*** taken by **the person of integrity,** while **wickedness overthrows the sinner.** Read in light of the first line, wicked behavior has the power of ***subverting*** the course that a sinner is following (Waltke 2004, 546 n. 14, 556). That course has pitfalls and obstacles that trip up and eventually destroy the sinner. (See 11:5.)

Opposing: Poor / Rich (13:7)

■ **7** Two different ways of reading this proverb are possible. One way is to take it as a riddle: ***a person becomes rich and* has nothing** while **another *person becomes poor,*** yet **has great wealth.** The riddle emphasizes that a person who becomes rich spends money freely and then is suddenly surprised when nothing is left. But another person who is poor in material goods **has great wealth.** One is led to ponder what is meant by **wealth** in the second line. Could it be rich in family or friends? If it is friends, they stand with the poor person, seeing that physical needs are met.

The second way of reading this proverb is that ***a* person pretends to be rich, yet has nothing.** That is, a person lives as though he is very wealthy even though he has little. **Another** kind of person **pretends to be poor** though he **has**

152

great wealth (*hôn*). Numerous well-to-do people live below their means, for they know that money is transitory and not the real basis of their worth. This proverb serves to alert students to the fact that there is often a vast distance between a person's public appearance and one's actual financial standing.

Opposing: Rich / Poor (13:8)

■ **8** The value of a person's life far exceeds one's wealth. A rich person who gets into an oppressive situation, such as being taken hostage, may stay alive by paying *a* **ransom** (*kōper*) from personal **riches**. Since the sense of the Hebrew in the second line is not clear, it is variously translated. On the basis that in the Hebrew text the last word (**rebuke** [*gĕ'ārâ*]) is parallel to the first word (**ransom** [*kōper*]), which in some contexts has the sense of **bribe**, **rebuke** in this context may have the sense of **threat**, a meaning it has in Isa 30:17 (Yoder 2009, 152). The line may be rendered: **the poor *do not* respond to *threats***. That is, they are not so tied to their possessions that they cower before those who threaten to confiscate something they own. Amos describes a time in Israel when the powerful exacted bribes from the righteous, that is, solid members of the community who had possessions (5:12). They also deprived the poor of justice, possibly using threats to keep them from going to court for redress.

This proverb brings out that wealth is not always a blessing. It also shows that the poor have less cares about material goods than the rich.

Opposing: Light of Righteous / Wicked (Line *b* = 24:20*b*) (13:9)

■ **9** **The light of the righteous** is contrasted to **the lamp of the wicked**. **Light** and **lamp** are metaphors for one's life force and one's influence. **The light of the righteous shines brightly** in bringing encouragement to others and in promoting right behavior. But **the lamp of the wicked is snuffed out.** Having harmed others, their lives are cut short, presumably by God. (See Job 18:5-6; Prov 20:20.)

Opposing: Presumption / Counsel (13:10)

■ **10** Usually wherever **there is strife, there is pride**. Those who are brazenly *proud* get entangled in **strife** in whatever they do. Overly self-confident, they shun counsel. As a result while working on a project all kinds of quarrels break out diverting attention from the details of the project. Since too much energy is spent on arguing, rather than on doing the job well, the work is either poor in quality or never finished. By contrast, whatever the wise take on has a favorable outcome, because they continually *take counsel*.

Opposing: Wealth (13:11)

■ **11** People today dream of getting rich quickly, often as a result of a windfall, such as winning the lottery. Others turn to dishonest means. But money obtained easily is spent carelessly. In a short span of time it **dwindles** to nothing (see 20:21; 28:20, 22). But one who **gathers money**, regardless of the amount, *by his own hands* through hard work, that is, **little by little**, sees it gradually accumulate. That enables that one to develop the skills for managing the money judiciously so that it continues to increase and benefit the family.

An Alternative Reading of the Hebrew Text (Prov 13:11)

The MT of the first line reads **wealth will become smaller than a vapor**. Since this wording conveys the opposite of what usually happens to the wise, some interpreters postulate that there is a textual problem. Clifford (1999, 135-36) and Murphy (1998, 94 n. 11a), with support of the LXX read *mĕbōhāl* ("acquire hastily") for the MT *mēhebel* (**from a vapor**), explaining that the present Hebrew text arose from an error of metathesis. The verb is understood as a metaphor for wealth gained dishonestly (so NIV). In support of this reading is the occurrence of *bāhal* in 28:22, and possibly 20:21. In addition, this reading provides good opposing parallelism.

On the other hand, the new reading is questionable because in Proverbs wealth is usually a benefit of wisdom, and Proverbs has a rich lexical field for deceptive practices. Waltke (2004, 561) and Plöger (1984, 160), therefore, follow the MT and take *hebel* as a metaphor for schemes designed to get money quickly. Since the MT yields an intelligible meaning, it is followed.

Opposing: Hope: Frustrated / Realized (13:12)

■ **12** Hope plays a vital role in a person's life. It keeps one energized to reach a goal. But **hope deferred makes the heart sick**, that is, discouraged and depressed. Such negative emotions drain one's inner resources for coping with daily issues. **A longing fulfilled**, however, so energizes a person that it is comparable to **a tree of life** (see 3:18; 11:30; 15:4). The energy received from realizing a dream brings joy, empowers one to take on bigger tasks, and lengthens one's life.

Opposing: Command: Despised / Respected (13:13)

■ **13** There are two ways to respond to a word of instruction from a wise teacher. One may despise that word, but the person *will suffer harm*, that is, experience ruin (*ḥābal* II). The line does not specify the nature of the harm since it depends on the nature of the instruction rejected. But one who **respects a command** [i.e., follows it] **is rewarded**. "Reward" is a general term; the nature of the reward depends on the nature of the command feared.

Advancing: Instruction of Wisdom (= 14:27 except for the first two words) (13:14)

■ **14** Cool, clean water from a fountain is very refreshing. Similarly, **the teaching of the wise is a fountain of life**. Their teaching guides students to a refreshing, long life. It also guides them to escape **the snares of death** that lie hidden along life's path. As the opposite of "the tree of life" (Gen 2:9), **the snares of death** is an appropriate metaphor for the deadly perils that attend the way of folly (see Waltke 2004, 565). This proverb's force is carried by numerous "m" sounds (Fox 2009, 567): *tôrat ḥākām mĕqôr ḥayyîm lāsûr mimmōqĕšê māwet*.

154

For the ancient Israelites one snare was the attraction of the polytheistic religions around them. Their fertility rituals attracted Israelites. Today all kinds of enticements and ideologies are snares on the path to life. Among those snares are the lures to excessive drinking, overeating, viewing erotic pictures, driving at excessive speeds, and driving while engaged in another activity. The teaching of the wise seeks to prevent youths from being trapped by any of these snares.

Opposing: Good Sense / Way of the Treacherous (13:15)

■ **15** Exercising **good judgment**, such as displaying grace in a difficult situation, **wins favor** in the community. Conversely, **the way** or *manner of the treacherous* **leads to their destruction**. The last word in the Hebrew text does not fit the flow of the sentence. The reading of the NIV is based on the LXX and Syriac versions (also Fox 2009, 567; Waltke 2004, 548 n. 29).

Opposing: Prudent / Fool (13:16)

■ **16** The **prudent** [*'ārûm*] **act with knowledge**. They seek to understand a matter and then respond to it thoughtfully. For example, a prudent person who receives a package containing unassembled parts takes a measured approach by reading the instructions before beginning to put the object together. Prudence leads to significant accomplishments. By contrast, **fools *go about exposing*** **their folly**. Acting on impulse, a fool usually starts a project without making plans. In a short time the fool gets frustrated, often quitting that project and soon starting another. Over time a host of partially finished projects bear witness to the fool's folly.

Opposing: Bad Messenger / Faithful One (13:17)

■ **17** Since ancient leaders and merchants relied heavily on messengers as the means of communication, they needed to be very discerning in hiring a messenger, for **a wicked messenger falls into trouble**. **Falls** suggests that while on a journey the messenger is unwittingly caught by some scheme. Possibly someone tricks the messenger and gets hold of the message; as a result confidential information is compromised, leading to significant loss for the sender. Or, if the message is oral, someone might finagle confidential information out of the messenger.

Another possibility is that the messenger becomes prey to a person who pressures the messenger to falsify the message. On the other hand, a ***reliable*** or **trustworthy envoy** (Fox 2009, 568), one who succeeds in delivering the message, **brings healing**. The messenger's efforts refresh both the sender and the receiver and strengthen the bond between them.

Opposing: Shame / Honor (13:18)

■ **18** The structure of this saying in the Hebrew is chiastic. The consequences stand at the extremities and the actors in the center. ***One who spurns*** [*pôrēa'*] **discipline comes to poverty and shame**. *Pôrēa'* characterizes a person as one who ***casts off social restraint***. It is used for the carousing of the Israelites around the golden calf while Moses was with God on Mount Sinai (Exod 32:25; see Prov 29:18).

Poverty and shame, the results of such behavior, stand first in the Hebrew for emphasis. Also they are juxtaposed to the subject without a verb, leaving it up to the one reflecting on the proverb to supply a verb. On the other hand, one who characteristically **heeds correction is honored**. "Honor," the highest reward in ancient society, is highlighted by being placed at the end of the line.

Opposing: Desire Fulfilled / Loathing of Fools (13:19)

■ **19** The realization of **a longing** fills a person with very pleasant feelings, that is, a sense of satisfaction and approval (Ps 104:34; Mal 3:4). **Fools**, however, have an inverted value system. Being so perverted, they **detest turning from evil**. Wisdom is as repugnant to them as folly is to Yahweh. Moral reform for a fool is almost impossible.

Opposing: Influence of Companions (13:20)

■ **20** A person takes on the characteristics of one's closest associates. Attitudes, values, and ambitions are caught more than taught. Thus, one *who keeps company* with the wise *becomes* wise. The idea is stressed by the subject and the verb being from the same root, *ḥăkāmîm weḥkām*. Conversely, **a companion of fools** not only takes on foolish traits but also **suffers harm**. In the second line the play on the sound of *rōʿeh* (*consorts with*) and *yērôaʿ* (*gets into trouble*) serves to stress the connection between one's character and the consequences. (See Prov 14:7; 22:25; 26:4.)

Two Readings of the First Line of Prov 13:20

For the first line there are two readings. One is based on the consonantal text that goes back to OT times. The other reading is based on the oral reading preserved by the Masoretes, centuries later. The interpretation above is based on the oral tradition. In the written tradition the verbs are imperatives: *accompany the wise and become wise* (Fox 2009, 569). Either reading offers a strong proverb.

Opposing: Sinners / Righteous (13:21)

■ **21** The next two proverbs, which contrast the fate of sinners with that of the righteous, are connected chiastically by the first and last words of each proverb *ḥaṭṭāʾîm:ṭôb::ṭôb:ḥôtēʾ* (**sinner:good::"good":"sinner"**). **Trouble** [*rāʿâ*] **pursues the sinner. Pursues** conveys that the consequences are sure to come and that without delay. Sinners cannot escape evil's pursuit.

On the other hand, **the righteous are rewarded with good things** (*ṭôb*). **Good** applies to all dimensions of life, including marriage, raising children, and the produce of the land and the flocks. The implied subject of the verb **rewarded** is Yahweh.

Opposing: Wealth: Good Person / Sinners (13:22)

■ **22** By handling one's assets such as land and flocks prudently, **a good person**, that is, a wise and righteous person, accumulates wealth to be passed on as **an inheritance** to the children and grandchildren. That parent promotes the growth and stability of the clan by providing a financial base for future generations.

A sinner's wealth, however, **is stored up for the righteous**. By consuming whatever he gains, a sinner has little concern for leaving an inheritance for building a strong lineage. As a result of being completely unmindful of providing for posterity, whatever wealth he leaves goes to others, usually the stable members of a community, **the righteous** (see Job 27:13-17; Prov 28:8).

This text along with Job 27:13-17 reflects a belief that wealth accumulated by the wicked accrues over time to the upright. In other words, the righteous come to acquire what the wicked leave, not through shrewd business deals, but by being dependable, industrious members of the community and, then, as a result of God's redirecting that wealth.

Advancing: Land of Poor / Loss of Land (13:23)

■ **23** This proverb makes a bold assertion: when **the poor** work their *fallow ground*, it **produces food**. But a powerful person, seeing an abundant crop growing in the field of a poor person, takes unjust steps to gain control of that harvest. The term **injustice** hints that this person twists the legal system to confiscate that poor person's harvest. One way that the rich might gain control of the harvest would be to force the poor farmer to repay a loan before a crop was harvested. But the proverb does not state the nature of the **injustice** that sweeps . . . away the harvest.

Another Reading of Prov 13:23

Another way to render this proverb is offered by Fox (2009, 570). "The great man devours the tillage of the poor, and some people are swept away without justice." Fox reads *rāb* ("great man, chief") for the MT *rob* ("much") and *ʾōkel* as the verb "devours" rather than as the noun "food." He takes *yēš* in its usual sense ("there is") and *nispeh* ("swept away") with people, not property, as the subject, because other occurrences of this verb have people, not property, as the subject. The emphasis, then, is that some are poor because the rich use the legal system to get control of their tillage.

Either reading of the Hebrew is possible. In favor of the alternative reading is the tension between being poor and having an abundant harvest, for such a harvest would lift the poor farmer out of poverty. The lack of a specific subject for "is swept away" hinders the choice between these alternative readings.

Opposing: Children: Lack of Discipline / Careful to Discipline (13:24)

■ **24** Two types of parents are considered. One type is aloof, rarely disciplining a child, by *sparing* **the rod**, the primary means of administering discipline in antiquity. The term **discipline** may be understood as any type of "discipline" used appropriately to guide a child.

Instead of showing parental love, a parent who refrains from disciplining a child actually ***shows hatred*** for that child. The parent does not care enough for the child to turn the child from wrongdoing. Another type of parent, who truly **loves** the child, ***is diligent*** in applying appropriate **discipline** in a timely manner. The parent does so in such a way that the child is aware of the parent's love, possibly because the parent explains clearly the reason for the discipline.

Moreover, by disciplining a child properly and consistently, a parent seldom, if ever, has to use great force. A little discipline administered at the onset of a problem is often sufficient to correct a child's improper behavior. Thus, it is important to correct a child's errant behavior before it becomes habitual. (See 3:12; 19:25; 22:15; 23:13-14; 26:3; 29:15.)

Opposing: Well-fed / Hungry (13:25)

■ **25** The righteous have sufficient food ***to satisfy their appetite***. This assertion is based on two facts: (1) the righteous have the motivation to work hard and skillfully, and (2) they have God's favor. Enjoying good harvests and breeding seasons, they have sufficient food to ***satisfy*** all members of the family. But **the stomach of the wicked goes hungry**. Their lack of food is the result of their failure to work diligently and honestly. (See 10:3; 11:25; 21:5.)

E. Proverbs 14:1-35

OVERVIEW

In this chapter five proverbs are structured as advancing (vv 7, 12, 17, 26, 27), two as affirming (vv 13, 19), and the other twenty-eight as opposing. The predominant subjects of the opposing proverbs are as follows: in seven the wise or prudent are contrasted to fools or the naive (vv 1, 3, 8, 16, 18, 24, 33), and in four the upright or good are contrasted to the wicked or devious (vv 11, [14], 19, 22, 32). "Fear of *Yahweh*" occurs three times (vv 2, 26, 27). This phrase connects vv 26 and 27. The other catchword (*'aḥărît*; "the end") connects vv 12 and 13.

The most far-reaching theological principle comes in the proverb that assigns intrinsic worth to the poor based on God's being "their Maker" (v 31). Those who help the poor are "blessed" (v 21b) because such action "honors God" (v 31b). Conversely, a person who "oppresses the poor" reproaches God (v 31a). This line of reasoning attributes intrinsic worth to all humans. Over many centuries this idea became the basis for developing democratic forms of government. It eventually led to the renunciation of slavery. For the first time in Section II the king is a topic (vv 28, 35).

A distinguishing feature of this chapter is several proverbs that characterize types of people: those who are "good" (vv 14b, 22b), the "patient" (v 29a), "an honest witness" (vv 5a, 25a), "a false witness" (vv 5b, 25b), the "quick-tempered" (vv 17a, 29b), "the faithless" (v 14a), a schemer (vv 17b, 22a), an oppressor (v 31a), and "the poor" (vv 20, 21, 31). Another distinguishing feature is several proverbs pertaining to emotions: anger (vv 16b, 17a, 29b, 35b), "envy" or jealousy (v 30b), "grief" (v 13), "bitterness" (v 10a), "joy" (vv 10b, 13b), patience (v 29a), and "peace" (v 30a).

IN THE TEXT

Opposing: Woman: Wise / Foolish (14:1)

■ **1** The way **the wise woman** manages **her house** is contrasted with that of **the foolish *woman*. The wise woman builds her house.** The term **wise woman** in Hebrew, being plural, has superlative force. This exceedingly wise woman is diligently at work feeding and clothing her family as well as doing multiple chores (see 31:10-31). Honoring her husband, she raises her children in the fear of Yahweh.

But **the foolish *woman***, preoccupied with herself, that is, making sure that she is properly groomed and well-dressed, **with her own hands . . . tears** her house **down**, that is, by her selfish actions. Her self-centered demeanor produces rancor among family members. Over time the house becomes dysfunctional.

Opposing: Fearing Yahweh / Despising Yahweh (14:2)

■ **2** Two walks of life are contrasted. **Whoever fears *Yahweh* walks uprightly.** That is, one's conduct corresponds to one's commitment to Yahweh. But the **ways** of a person **who *despises* [*bôzeh*] *Yahweh* are devious** (*nālôz*). The second line receives stress by a play on the sound of the first and last words: *nĕlôz* and *bôzēhû*. The character of a person's daily life shows whether that person **fears *Yahweh*** or ***despises*** him.

Opposing: Speech: A Fool / The Wise (14:3)

■ **3** The speech of a fool differs greatly from that of **the wise. A fool's mouth lashes out with pride.** A fool is proud of the ability to harm others by speech. His words are a rod of **pride**, and out of **pride** the fool ridicules others with harsh words. By contrast, **the wise** use speech to **protect *themselves*.** Their words, free from sarcastic jabs, encourage others: thus the wise are highly respected. Indeed, their words turn discouragement into resolution, sadness into possibility. (See 11:9b.)

Opposing: Lack of Oxen / The Value of an Ox (14:4)

■ **4** A farmer who has **an ox** is able to bring in **abundant harvests**. This strong animal assists greatly in the heavy work of farming, such as drawing a plow, pulling a loaded cart, and turning the large wheel of a mill. But a farmer who does not have **an ox** has ***an* empty *trough***. Though the farmer is spared the cost of feeding such a large animal, **harvests** are much smaller. But a smaller harvest is more costly than keeping an ox. This proverb teaches that some ways of economizing are counterproductive. The structure is chiastic: **no oxen:empty stall** [manger]::**abundant harvests:strength of an ox**. The words at the pivot of the chiasm—*bār* (**empty**) and *rōb* (**abundant**)—emphasize the contrast (Clifford 1999, 143).

Opposing: Contrasting Witnesses: Reliable / False (14:5)

■ **5** Truth spoken by *a reliable* witness is contrasted with **lies *breathed*** out by **a false witness**. Since *a reliable* witness never distorts details, that person's testimony promotes justice. In antiquity the testimony of an eyewitness to an incident was critical, for communities had no police or forensic units to investigate a crime. By contrast, **a false witness *breathes*** out lies, obstructing justice.

This proverb is structured chiastically. It begins with *a reliable* witness and ends with **a false witness**; in the center, the focus of the saying, stand the verbs: **does not *lie*** and ***breathes*** out lies. (See 14:25; 19:5; 21:28a.)

Opposing: Mocker Seeks Wisdom / Knowledge Comes to the Discerning (14:6)

■ **6** Some people have a proclivity for grasping the meaning of a topic quickly. But others have difficulty in understanding certain subjects. *A* **mocker** (*lēṣ*) or insolent person **seeks wisdom *but* finds none**. Conversely, **knowledge comes easily to the discerning**. A person who learns quickly makes good progress. Still, a gifted person must work hard to excel at a subject.

Advancing: Avoiding a Fool (14:7)

■ **7** A student who wishes to become wise is exhorted to **stay away from a fool**. Since **a fool** is not a viable source of **knowledge**, it is not prudent to spend time conversing with an empty head. Besides wasting time, there is the danger that one may pick up a fool's distorted attitudes.

Opposing: The Prudent / Fools (14:8)

■ **8** The temperament of **the prudent** (*ʿārûm*) is contrasted with that of **fools**. **The prudent**, being wise, carefully evaluate **their ways**. Thereby they gain valuable insights into life. These insights lead them in pursuing a deeper understanding of life in relationship to Yahweh. But **the folly of fools** [*kĕsîlîm*] **is deception**. Blinded by folly, fools believe that their twisted view of reality is right-on. As a result, they are unable to discern truth from error.

Opposing: Fools and Guilt / The Upright (14:9)

■ **9** Fools mock [*lēṣ*] at making amends or ***reparation*** (*ʾāšām*). The sacrificial laws prescribe the presentation of a guilt offering for a breach of faith against God or for an offense that caused a person loss that could be compensated (Lev 5:14—6:7). By despising this powerful sacrifice **fools** expose their disdain for taking responsibility for a misdeed against another's property or for behaving in a way that is an affront to God.

But goodwill is found among the upright. The upright work at maintaining strong relationships among members of the community. If any of them harms another, that one takes responsibility for personal actions, making compensation for all losses and offering the appropriate sacrifice at the central altar. Since the Hebrew of this verse is awkward, especially in the first line, the translations in English versions vary widely.

Opposing: Emotions of the Heart: Sorrow / Joy (14:10)

■ **10** *The* heart knows *bitter sorrows* and *joys*. Emotions produced by past experiences reside deep in a person's *soul* or *psyche* (*nepeš*); ancient Hebrew locates these emotions in the **heart**. Lingering sorrows have the potential of making a person very bitter. Conversely, people love talking about the *joys* of life. Most *joys*, however, are so personal that another is unable to fully share the joy. According to this proverb everyone has deep feelings of **joy** and **bitterness** known only to God.

Opposing: Wicked / Upright (14:11)

■ **11** The house of the wicked is contrasted with **the tent of the upright. House** and **tent** are synecdoches for a family's entire habitat—children, flocks, and land. This proverb surprisingly reverses the usual metaphors of **the upright** living in a sturdy structure and **the wicked** in a transitory one. It thereby addresses a situation in which **the wicked** are more prosperous and stable than the righteous. Nevertheless, whenever that is the case, God's favor is on **the upright**, for their **tent . . . will flourish** (lit. *blossom*). But **the house of the wicked** [the locus of their security] **will be destroyed.** From another perspective, this proverb shows that it is not possible to discern God's favor on a person by the grandeur of that one's dwelling. (See 11:28; Pss 72:7; 92:12-14 [13-15 HB].)

Advancing: Road to Death (= 16:25) (14:12)

■ **12** At times in life's journey a person comes on a fork in the path being taken. One must decide which path to take. One of the ways usually appears more appealing. It looks *straight*, that is, level and easy to traverse. The traveler, envisaging that it leads to a grand destination, is inclined to take that **way**. Unfortunately, at the entrance there are few indicators that it is the path *leading* to death. **Death** means either a shortened life span or life's final destiny. This proverb underscores the importance of evaluating carefully the options when coming upon a fork in one's path in order not to take the wrong **way**.

Jesus said, "Wide is the gate and broad is the road that leads to destruction" (Matt 7:13). When confronted with such a critical choice, a person needs great discernment seasoned with the fear of Yahweh to avoid taking a seemingly right **way.** Fortunately Wisdom offers that guidance to those whose ears are open to her voice.

Affirming: Sorrow (14:13)

■ **13** In the Hebrew text the term **end** (*'aḥărît*) connects this proverb with the preceding one. It stands as the first word of the second line in both proverbs. In addition, this proverb is connected to the following by words having the sound *ûg*: *tûgâ* (**grief**) in v 13*b* and *sûg* (**turn aside** = "faithless") in v 14*a*.

People are prone to disguise their true feelings. Some conceal *an aching heart* with laughter. People may seem to be having a *joyful* time but inwardly they are sad. This saying alerts the naive against assuming that those who appear cheery have no sorrow.

Opposing: Retribution for the Faithless / For the Good (14:14)

■ **14** This proverb asserts that every person, both **the faithless** (lit. *turncoats* [*sûg lēb*]), and **the good, will be fully repaid** [lit. *sated*] **for their ways.** *Sated* conveys that all receive in full measure the rewards that attend the character of their deeds.

Opposing: The Simple / The Prudent (14:15)

■ **15** Humans vary widely in degrees of gullibility. **The simple** (*petî*) are inclined to **believe** completely whatever they hear. But a naive disposition often proves costly. For example, such a person is easy prey for all types of schemes that lead to suffering financial loss.

By contrast, **the prudent** or *discerning* [*ārûm*] **give thought to their steps.** Before agreeing to a proposal, they carefully investigate what is involved in order to make an appropriate response. Usually they take counsel to gain a greater perspective on what has been set before them, because they respond to exaggerated claims with skepticism. This approach prevents them from getting caught in deceptive schemes.

Opposing: The Wise / A Fool (14:16)

■ **16** The temperament of **the wise** is contrasted with that of **a fool. The wise fear *Yahweh* and *turn away from*** evil as did Job (Job 1:1). They eschew all enticements to engage in shady or ungodly activities. For example, if someone encourages *a* wise *person* to cut corners in order to increase profits, *a* wise *person* rejects outright such a proposal.

But **a fool is *stubborn* [*mitʿabbēr*] and yet feels secure** or *confident.* The Hebrew root *ʿbr* has several homonyms, *be headstrong, be* hotheaded (*DCH* 6:242), *be negligent* (*DCH* 6:242-43), or *butts in* (Fox 2009, 578-79). Since all of these glosses fit **a fool,** it is difficult to know which is the most accurate reading. The first and last options function better as antonyms to *turn away* in the preceding line. Stubborn, argumentative, and not inclined to accept counsel, **a fool** gets involved in entangling situations, often suffering significant loss. Overconfidence is a hindrance to a fool's success.

Advancing: An Angry Person / A Schemer (14:17)

■ **17** **A quick-tempered person** is contrasted with *a schemer.* The Hebrew idiom for **quick-tempered** is *short nostrils.* Volatile anger drives a person to act foolishly, for anger overrides a person's reason. Nevertheless, this type of person is tolerated, as implied by the wording in the next line. But *a schemer* (*'îš mĕzimmôt*) cunningly **devises** a harmful plot and then calmly carries it out. As a result the schemer **is hated** by all because the **schemes** are so cunning that no one is able to escape being cheated.

Opposing: The Simple / The Prudent (14:18)

■ **18** The simple (*pĕtā'îm*), failing to accept the call of Wisdom, **inherit folly** (*'iwwelet*). By contrast, **the prudent** (*'ărûmîm*) develop keen insights and **are crowned with knowledge** (*dā'at*). The metaphor **are crowned** indicates that they receive high public acclaim for their knowledgeable, insightful leadership.

Affirming: The Fate of the Wicked (14:19)

■ **19** **Evildoers** scoff at **the good**, that is, the upright who eschew deceit. Nevertheless, a time is coming when they **will bow *before* the good**. This takes place when they receive proper judgment **at the gates** of a city inhabited by **the righteous** (Isa 2:9, 11, 17; 5:15). **Gates** stands for the main entrance into a walled city (Fox 2009, 580). Inside the **gates** people sat about conversing, merchants displayed their wares, and the elders ruled on disputes. In a city inhabited by the upright, the court in **the gates** was known for rendering justice. At this location **the wicked** will be tried and receive just punishment. This saying offers the hope to all who are oppressed by **evildoers** that one day those who have bullied them will be humbled. (See Prov 24:7.)

Opposing: The Poor Shunned / The Rich with Many Friends (14:20)

■ **20** This saying offers a description of a common pattern in society. **The poor are *disliked* even by their neighbors.** People with resources feel self-conscious around the poor. This feeling leads them to despise the poor, especially when the poor ask for a handout. As Fox (2009, 580) notes, the poor, feeling entitled to alms, can be very brash at begging. Consequently, people *shun* **the poor.** They rationalize their contempt with the belief that the poor live in poverty because of laziness or lack of intelligence. This rationale, though, indicates that they are unmindful of the numerous forces and circumstances that reduce people to poverty. Some of these forces are so powerful that they make most people destitute. This saying seeks to arouse greater compassion for the poor.

The rich, by contrast, **have many friends.** People hover around them, hoping to win favors and share in their good fortune. But they are not genuine **friends.** Whenever a rich person has to deal with loss, these friends are never around to help. This proverb teaches that true friendship requires a stronger foundation than wealth or notoriety. (See 19:4; Eccl 9:16*b*; Sir 13:19-23.)

Opposing: Despising / Being Kind (14:21)

■ **21** It is a sin to despise one's neighbor (*ḥôṭē'*). Such an attitude demeans *a* neighbor, since it fails to recognize another as bearing God's image. **But blessed** [i.e., fortunate (*'ašrē*); → sidebar "A Beatitude" in overview for 3:13-20] **is the person who is kind to the needy** (*'ănāyîm*). **The needy** are often shunned (v 20a). But they need to be encouraged. Encouraging them by acts of kindness—such as providing food, clothing, and various types of assistance— helps them cope with their situation.

This proverb encourages behavior that will counter the description found in the first line of the preceding proverb.

Opposing: Devising Evil / Devising Kindness (14:22)

■ **22** Formulated as a negative rhetorical question, this proverb makes a strong assertion (Waltke 2004, 581 n. 38). The question brings out the contrast between the destiny of **those who *devise* evil** (*ḥôrĕšê rāʿ*) and that of **those who *devise* good** or **beneficial** [*ḥôrĕšê ṭôb*] **plans**. The Hebrew *ḥāraš* basically means "plow" and carries the secondary meanings of "plan, devise." This term indicates that the Israelites recognized the energy that goes into planning. The verb translated **plot** in the first line and **plan** in the second line is the same Hebrew word. The variation in these glosses is unfortunate given that the English glosses carry very different connotations, scheming versus astute planning.

The results of diligent planning, whether done for an honorable purpose or a corrupt purpose, depend on what is planned. **Those who *plan* evil** or ***harm* go astray**, that is, they stagger about helplessly (Fox 2009, 581). However, **those who plan *doing* good find love** [*ḥesed*] **and faithfulness**. They are highly respected, for they embody characteristics like those of Yahweh (e.g., Exod 34:6).

Opposing: Hard Work / Mere Talk (14:23)

■ **23** This descriptive proverb contrasts the results of **hard work** with **mere talk**. **All hard work** [*ʿeṣeb*] **produces a profit**. The Hebrew *ʿeṣeb* comes from the same root as ***pain***, especially ***the pain*** that afflicts the labor of men in the field and of women in giving birth (Gen 3:16, 17). Those who endure such pain will enjoy good returns. Their labor usually produces more than they need. That excess supports others. But those who are given to **talk** spend so much time ***talking*** that they never get around to initiating any of their grand plans and dreams. No wonder they end up in **poverty**.

Opposing: Wealth / Folly (14:24)

■ **24** **The wise** get to wear ***the* crown of wealth** (see Prov 3:16; 8:18). **Crown** represents honor and authority. It is a visible indication of God's favor (Clifford 1999, 146). Over time **the wise** acquire **wealth** because of their skill at planning and working diligently. Wealth means having adequate resources to raise a family well, not mega wealth. Wealth must never become the basis of a person's trust (10:15; 11:28).

Since **fools** (*ʾiwwelet*) continually engage in **folly**, the return they get is **folly** (*ʾiwwelet*). The nature of folly is comparable to the habit of smoking. The smoker gets a pleasurable sensation from smoking, but the cigarette soon turns to ash, and the pleasurable sensation is gone. Similarly, acting foolishly provides *a fool* pleasure, but it is short-lived. In fact, folly robs fools of life's deep joys.

Opposing: Truthful Witness / False Witness (14:25)

■ **25** To have a stable, just community citizens must bear witness to any wrongful activity (see v 5). A person who bears witness to a foul act **saves lives**. This is especially the case when a **witness** describes accurately an incident for which a person is being falsely accused. **But a false witness *breathes out* [*pûah*] *lies*.** If that witness's testimony is believed, those lied about will be condemned and punished, as implied by the opposing phrase **saves lives** in the first line. (See 6:19; 12:17; 14:5; 19:5, 9.)

Advancing: Fear of Yahweh / Shelter for Children (14:26)

■ **26** *The fear of Yahweh* connects the next two proverbs. **Whoever fears Yahweh has a secure fortress.** Worshippers of *Yahweh* have security by reason of that relationship. They may live free from being anxious that something ominous may overtake them. Moreover, *Yahweh is* **a refuge for their children**. Parents devoted to God provide **for their children** confidence that difficult situations can be handled well because Yahweh is their source of strength. A family with a solid sense of security is more productive. And **their children** are freer to enjoy life as they mature. (See Jer 17:7-8.)

Advancing: Fear of Yahweh / Avoiding the Snares of Death (14:27)

■ **27** **The fear of *Yahweh*** is a vibrant, refreshing force in the lives of the devout. That **fear** is like **a fountain** or ***spring***, the source of clear, fresh water that refreshes **life** (13:14; 16:22). In a land with little rainfall, this metaphor is powerful. This saying is also suggestive of the support that fearing Yahweh provides a person's psyche.

The intellectual empowerment that comes from ***fearing Yahweh*** keeps a person from being trapped by **the snares of death** that are hidden on the paths taken in life. Being caught in one of these **snares** may lead to an early **death** (see 13:14).

Opposing: A King's Glory / A Prince's Ruin (14:28)

■ **28** This is the first of many proverbs in Sections II and IV that pertain to ***the king***. Its goal is to have ***the king*** realize that the foundation of his **glory** (*hădārâ*) is **a large population**. The basis of **a king's** power and honor is the people. Therefore, the greater the nation's population, the greater the king's acclaim because all the achievements of the people contribute to his fame.

A king, however, is inclined to assume that his **glory** is based on having a mighty army and great displays of wealth, such as building magnificent edifices and putting on lavish festivals (see Esth 1:3-8). Such displays, however, are not the basis of his power. That basis is his people. A ruler who is ignorant of this truth conscripts thousands of the nation's youths into the army and exacts high taxes from the citizens for elaborate building projects, thereby making life harder for most families under his rule. These approaches are likely to lead to a decrease in the nation's population and wealth. As a result, **a prince**, possibly the king's successor, **is ruined** or overthrown. The term **prince** (*rāzôn*) is a rare Hebrew word for a high official without designating the office. It usually stands parallel to "king" or "judge."

In modern history a premier example of a powerful ruler who elevated personal glory far above caring for his people, especially in the latter years of his reign, is Napoleon. After becoming the emperor of France, he elevated members of his extended family and friends to high offices and bestowed on them wealth and power, regardless of their administrative skills. For his extensive military campaigns he recruited vast numbers of French youths and extorted large sums from the wealthy. Over the years his military campaigns incurred numerous casualties. He responded by conscripting youths from countries under his control. Showing little concern for the number of casualties his army was suffering, he continued going to war. Over time his country became impoverished. Severely oppressed, the populace came to despise his rule. Napoleon was deposed and exiled.

Opposing: Patient / Quick-tempered (14:29)

■ **29** In Hebrew the phrases for **patient** and **great understanding** are juxtaposed without a verb. This style conveys that these traits foster each other. *A* patient *person*, by persevering at hard, tedious tasks, gains substantial **understanding**. Having greater **understanding**, that person deals insightfully with complex matters. However, *a* quick-tempered person is prone to frequent **displays** *of* **folly**. Unable to manage his *temper*, he fails to act judiciously in dealing with situations.

In the Hebrew the contrast between these emotions is vividly expressed by two metaphors: *long nosed* for **patient** and *short of spirit* for **quick-tempered**.

Opposing: Tranquil Mind / Passion (14:30)

■ **30** A *healthy* heart [or *mind* (*lēb marpē'*)] **gives life to the body.** The Hebrew *marpē'* may come from one of two homonyms: (1) *marpē'* I—*healing, remedy = a healthy mind* or (2) II—*calm = calm mind*. It is possible that both senses are in play in this saying. **A** *healthy mind*, being *calm*, provides a person with a sense of well-being, empowering one to enjoy life and take genuine delight in the achievements of others.

Envy (*qin'â*), however, is a vicious emotion. It eats away at one's innermost feelings, conveyed by the term **bones**. Envy motivates a person to imagine bold plans for punishing one who is believed to be enjoying something, such as great recognition, which the envier is thoroughly convinced is rightly his. Envy prevents a person from taking any delight in another's accomplishments or honors. It **rots the bones**, one's moral fabric. It robs that person of any sense of well-being.

Though envy is well understood today by psychologists and theologians, people in general fail to realize that it is a deadly emotion. It feeds on a person's firm belief of having been cheated out of a possession, an award, or a position that is rightly one's own. Envy gnaws away deep inside a person until it explodes, driving that person to commit a violent act against the person envied.

Opposing: Oppressing the Poor / Being Kind to the Needy (14:31)

■ **31** Two ways of reacting to **the poor** or **the needy** (*'ebyôn*) are contrasted. In the OT this term for **poor** (*dāl*) references peasant farmers since they often lack economic resources. Despite working diligently, they have meager incomes. Although they lack status, they are not destitute. The Hebrew word for **needy** usually references day laborers. They are dependent on the wages earned each day to sustain their families. Consequently, they are very vulnerable to oppression, mostly by the powerful (Domeris 1997, 1:228). That is, the powerful take advantage of **the needy** to enhance their personal wealth.

This proverb scathingly condemns such harsh treatment of **the needy. Whoever oppresses the poor shows contempt for their Maker.** This moral principle rests on the theological premise that all persons, including **the poor,** are made in God's image (Gen 1:27). Consequently, the manner in which one person **oppresses** another, regardless of that person's socioeconomic status, is in reality how that person is treating God. Living by this principle, Job swore that he never failed to listen to the complaint of any of his servants because the one who made him is the one who made the servant (Job 31:13-15). Before God, masters and servants are on the same plane.

The conviction that all humans have equal footing before God is the foundation of the belief that the gospel is for everyone. Belief in this maxim emboldened leaders such as Abraham Lincoln, Desmond Tutu, and Martin Luther King Jr. to work untiringly for the elimination of slavery, apartheid, and segregation.

Conversely, **whoever is kind to the needy** by acknowledging them and by helping them to deal with economic and legal challenges **honors God.**

This proverb provides insight into the reason that Jesus, God's Son, was born to peasants, worked as a common laborer, ministered to the poor and needy, healed the sick, and called everyday laborers to be his disciples. Jesus *honored* his Father in the way he related to **the poor** and **the needy.** (See Prov 17:5; 19:17.)

Opposing: The Wicked / The Righteous (14:32)

■ **32** The Hebrew of this saying is very difficult to unravel. A possible way to read the first line is **when calamity comes, the wicked are brought down.** One use of the verb rendered **brought down** is for *pushing over* a wall (Ps 62:3 [4 HB]). The verb, then, is a metaphor for a crushing fate that befalls **the wicked,** resulting in their **death.** That fate is implied by the reference to **death** in the second line.

Even in death the righteous seek refuge in God. Whenever they face a natural disaster or a time of social unrest, **the righteous seek** a place of **refuge** to escape **death**, which is taking place all about them. Surviving that dreadful situation, they attribute their fortune to **God**; that is why some translators add **in God** at the end, a term not present in the Hebrew text.

A few interpreters, however, translate the second line as **even in death the righteous *have a* refuge**. Read in this way the line says that **the righteous *find a* refuge *with* God in *their* death** (Longman 2006, 308). This reading may be possible. While the belief that **the righteous** have an afterlife ***with*** God is clearly the teaching of the NT, it is only hinted at in a few OT texts. A vague reference to this great truth in a proverb having Hebrew words with uncertain meanings does not offer reliable support for that belief.

Another way to treat the term *bĕmôtô* (**in *his* death**) is to read *bĕtummô* (***in his integrity***) with support of the LXX and the Syriac Version. Then the line reads **the righteous *find* refuge in *his integrity***. If this reconstruction is accurate, the present Hebrew text resulted from an accidental inversion of two letters in this phrase, a common handwriting error (Murphy 1998, 102 n. 32a). ***In his integrity*** functions well as a parallel to ***in his evildoing*** (rendered in NIV **when calamity comes**). The reconstructed reading is fully opposing (see 10:2*b*; 11:4*b*).

Having a Refuge in Death

Waltke (2004, 582-83, n. 52-53) offers another solution. He interprets **in *his* death** as referring to the process of dying and the verb *ḥôseh* as ***taking refuge in*** Yahweh—Yahweh being the implied object of the preposition. He gives the translation "but the righteous takes refuge in the Lord in his dying." This reading is in accord with other proverbs. However, it is very speculative.

Opposing: Wisdom: In the Discerning / Known among Fools (14:33)

■ **33** Wisdom, personified as in Section I, **reposes in the heart of the discerning** (*nābôn*). **Reposes** conveys that **wisdom** takes up residency **in the *hearts*** of those who have good sense (Waltke 2004, 610).

In the second line the MT reads **among fools [wisdom] lets herself be known**. Waltke (2004, 608, 610-11) understands this line to say that **wisdom** manifests herself to all people, including **fools**. This view is in accord with **Wisdom** walking through the streets of a city, calling out both to the naive and to fools (1:20-23; 8:1-11, esp. v 5*b*). However, because **fools** resist her call, she does not ***repose*** in their ***hearts***.

Another option is to read the second line as saying that it is **the discerning** who ***make wisdom*** known ***to*** **fools**, either by offering a rebuke or by being a model of living wisely (Fox 2009, 587). However, in Section I, Wisdom is never pictured as having an emissary. Other interpreters, following the LXX and the Syriac Version, read ***not*** before the verb **be known** (Plöger 1984, 167-68; see

NIV mg.). It appears that these versions adjusted a difficult text. The first option is preferred since it is in accord with the picture of Wisdom in Section I.

Opposing: Righteousness / Sin (14:34)

■ **34** When relationships and commercial transactions in **a nation** are characterized by **righteousness**, that **nation** *is exalted* or prosperous. The citizens, confident of receiving fair treatment, are friendly and productive. That **nation** becomes widely known for its people's sterling character.

Sin, however, *is a disgrace* [ḥesed] *to* **any people**, because **sin** is a cancer that eats away at a community's moral base. It encourages the practice of deceit in all matters. Deceit produces mistrust even among neighbors. Mistrust leads to conflicts. As conflicts between groups increase, that nation's stability is threatened. If the increasing dissidence is not corrected, the nation will crumble. However, before it falls, the people often revolt against the rulers, putting new leaders in power. This social pattern has been seen frequently in recent history.

Special Meaning of Ḥesed

The Hebrew *ḥesed* usually connotes **kindness** and **loyalty**, traits that characterize strong, committed relationships. Like many Semitic terms, *ḥesed* also has an opposite meaning: **insult, reproach, disgrace** (see Lev 20:17). The negative sense is also attested in Prov 25:10. This linguistic phenomenon is similar to "awe" and "awful" in English.

Opposing: King's Favor / King's Wrath (14:35)

■ **35** A king responds to a **servant** by expressing *favor* or fury. When **a king delights in a wise servant**, he elevates the servant to a position of greater responsibility. Conversely, he punishes a **servant** who **arouses his fury** by *bringing shame* on the palace or the nation. One way a **servant** causes the **king** shame is by bungling an assignment or by lying about a matter. Unique to Section I, this proverb prepares for the one in 15:1 about a gentle answer (Fox 2009, 588).

A story that illustrates this saying is recorded in Esther. A Jew named Mordecai had the Persian king warned of a plot to overthrow the throne (Esth 2:21-23). The king, however, forgot about the matter. Sometime later he remembered Mordecai's good deed and rewarded him by appointing him to one of the highest positions in the government (Esth 6:1-11, 8:1-2, 15). The king honored Mordecai by giving him blue and white royal garments and a purple robe of fine linen. He honored Mordecai so highly because he recognized that his reign depended on reliable, loyal officials.

Conversely, *the king's* fury ('ebrâ) falls on a **servant** who *brings shame* on the nation or the crown. That was the experience of Haman, the Persian king's friend and Mordecai's arch foe. Haman became so angry at Mordecai whenever he noticed that Mordecai would not kneel in homage to him as he entered the king's gate. One day when the Persian king learned of Haman's plan to kill all Jews in his empire, he became so furious at Haman that he ordered him to be hung on the very gallows Haman had made for Mordecai (Esth 7:10). (See Prov 16:13-14; Ps 101:6-8.)

F. Proverbs 15:1-33

OVERVIEW

As is typical in the second section of the book of Proverbs, the majority of aphorisms in this chapter (twenty-two) are structured as opposing, while six are affirming (vv 10, 11, 12, 23, 30, 33) and three advancing (vv 3, 24, 31). The wise are contrasted with fools in six proverbs (vv 2, 5, 7, 14, 20, 21), and the righteous with the wicked in four (vv 6, 8, 28, 29). There are also two better-than sayings (vv 16, 17). Several proverbs are connected by catchwords. The Hebrew *śāmaḥ* ("bring joy") connects three proverbs (vv 20, 21, 23). The root *šm'* (*hear, report*) binds the sayings in vv 29-32. The synonyms *discipline* (*mûsār*) and *reproof* (*tôkaḥat*) are interchanged chiastically in vv 31-33: *reproof* (v 31), "discipline"/*reproof* (v 32), *discipline* (v 33).

Distinctive to this last chapter of the first part of Section II is the frequent use of the name of Yahweh, appearing in nine proverbs (vv 3, 8, 9, 11, 16, 25, 26, 29, 33). Yahweh observes all that takes place on earth (vv 3, 11*b*) as well as in the dark realm of the dead (v 11*a*). He protects the property of a widow but "tears down the house of the proud" (v 25). He loves those who pursue righteousness (v 26) and is pleased with their prayers (v 8*b*, see v 29*b*). The phrase "fear of **Yahweh**" appears twice (vv 16, 33), and the **Yahweh detests** formula is applied to the wicked three times: their sacrifices (v 8*a*), their way (v 9*a*), and their thoughts (v 26*a*). This is the only reference to sacrifice in Section II.

A frequent topic is the well-being of one's household, parents being a topic in vv 5*a* and 20 and the household or the family in three proverbs (vv 6, 25*a*, 27). The value of discipline is heard in five proverbs (vv 5, 10, 12, 31, 32). Another key topic is speech, appearing in nine sayings (vv 1, 2, 4, 7, 14, 18, 23, 28, 31). The tongue may bring healing or joy (vv 1, 4*a*, 23), and it conveys knowledge (vv 2*a*, 7*a*, 31). Yet words can arouse anger or crush one's spirit (vv 1*b*, 4*b*, 18). The wise ponder before giving an answer, but fools pour out folly (vv 2*b*, 7*a*).

An unusual chain of catchwords knits together the proverbs in vv 13-17. *Heart* or *mind* (*lēb*) stands at the head of vv 13 and 14. The second line of v 15 is prefaced by *ṭôb* (*good*). Then *good* begins the next two proverbs (vv 16, 17), making them better-than statements. The four proverbs in vv 15-18 address social turmoil.

Opposing: Speech: Gentle / Hurtful (15:1)

■ 1 The first two proverbs treat the effects of speech by drawing attention to the good results of **a gentle answer** in contrast to the effect of **harsh *words*. A gentle answer turns away wrath** (*ḥēmâ*), calming a volatile situation. Yet ***hurtful speech*** [lit. *a painful word* (*ʿeṣeb*)] **inflames** anger. The Hebrew term *ʿeṣeb* references harsh pain and vexation from strenuous work. On the other hand, the skillful use of soothing words is an effective way of dealing with an angry overseer or a troubled person (Eccl 10:4; Prov 25:15). Those who master the skill of using words effectively become powerful leaders.

Opposing: Speech: The Wise / Fools (15:2)

■ 2 The character of the ***speech*** of the wise is contrasted with that of ***fools***. Words spoken by **the wise** set forth **knowledge** that is ***good*** or ***beneficial***. People, therefore, find pleasure and gain insight from listening to a wise person making a presentation on a vital topic. But **the mouth of the fool gushes folly** like a spring—"plentifully, continually, and vehemently" (Wesley 1975, 1858). A fool speaks loudly and at length without saying anything of substance.

Advancing: God Is Watching (15:3)

■ 3 ***Yahweh's eyes*** are **everywhere** as he observes all that is taking place on earth. Like a watchman he attentively observes the activities of both ***evildoers*** and ***the doers of*** good (see 5:21; 15:11). Thus, everyone needs to behave with the awareness that no one can do anything that escapes God's attention (see Ps 11:4-6).

Opposing: Speech: Tongue Heals / Or Breaks the Spirit (15:4)

■ 4 The tongue, a small member of the body, is so powerful that it can bring healing or inflict great pain. ***A healing*** tongue [*marpēh lāšôn*] **is a tree of life**. It has life-giving or life-restoring power (see Eph 4:25). *Marpēh*, the word for **soothing** or ***healing***, also connotes "balm." Thus, this phrase may be rendered ***the tongue's balm*** (Fox 2009, 589-90). However, **a perverse tongue**, one that speaks twisted or dishonest (*selep*) words, **crushes** a person's **spirit**. Any who trust untrue claims or false promises, especially those made by a person believed to be genuine, are very disheartened upon realizing that those words are nothing but lies. A person wounded by twisted words may languish for a long time.

Opposing: Discipline: Despised / Admonition Heeded (15:5)

■ 5 The manner in which a child responds to discipline determines that child's character. A fool ***despises*** a parent's discipline. Such a response puts that child on the path of folly. Even though a parent guides a child carefully and caringly, that child may refuse to heed such guidance. Thus, the destiny of that child is not the **parent's** fault. However, a child who **heeds *reproof*** (*tôkaḥat*), a term for strong verbal discipline, becomes ***astute***. Reproof teaches a child to figure out ingenious ways for maneuvering through complex situations that will be faced in life (Fox 2009, 590).

Opposing: Treasure / Trouble (15:6)

■ **6** **The house of the righteous contains great treasure**, for a righteous person masterfully builds an estate and collects beautiful artifacts. That treasure remains in the family throughout several generations, providing distinction and a heritage. **But the income of the wicked brings ruin** or ***trouble***. The nature of the trouble is not specified. Perhaps there is discord in the family over how to spend the income. Or the income is not managed well and the family is troubled by a huge debt that requires them to lease the family property until the next Jubilee. Certainly financial woes breed intense conflicts among members of a household.

Opposing: Speech of the Wise / Thoughts of Fools (15:7)

■ **7** The poverty of the thinking of the wicked is underscored. **The wise spread knowledge** through speaking (see Prov 15:2*a*). Whenever they address a group or the community, they offer insight and direction for dealing with issues. But ***the thinking*** of fools is not upright. It is sterile. Since thoughts are the source of insight, fools have no significant ideas to share with the community.

Opposing: Sacrifice of the Wicked / Prayer of the Righteous (Line *a* = 21:27*a*) (15:8)

■ **8** The phrase ***Yahweh*** **detests** and the term **wicked** connect the next two proverbs, which address public worship and daily life respectively (Clifford 1999, 152; → sidebar "Yahweh Detests or Abomination to Yahweh" at 6:16-19). This saying stresses that a person's character carries greater weight with God than the kind of sacrifice one offers.

Yahweh relishes hearing **the prayer of the upright** but **detests** . . . **sacrifice** (*zebah*) offered by **the wicked**. *Zebah* covers all types of sacrifices, but especially offerings of well-being (peace offerings [Lev 3]). After this type of sacrifice was slaughtered at the altar, the fat of the entrails and the two kidneys were burnt on the altar. Some of the meat was given to the priest, and the rest was returned to the presenter for a festive meal with the family or clan.

A feast that was centered around roasted meat was a rare treat for most families in antiquity. That is why the wicked enthusiastically made this kind of sacrifice. Their motive in making these sacrifices was more for their own enjoyment than to honor Yahweh (see Amos 4:4-5; 5:21-22). Consequently, their sacrifices angered Yahweh. But he ***takes pleasure in*** **the prayer of the upright**. Words uttered in genuine worship are more pleasing to God than the presentation of expensive sacrifices. (For the second line see Prov 15:29*a*; 21:27*a*.)

Opposing: Yahweh's Response to the Wicked / And to the Righteous (15:9)

■ **9** **The way** or lifestyle **of the wicked** is ***detestable to Yahweh*** because they behave in ways contrary to his instructions. On the other hand, Yahweh **loves those who pursue righteousness** because they observe his words enthusiastically.

Affirming: Consequences for Haters of Reproof (15:10)

■ **10** There are two ways to read the first line. According to one reading, ***harsh*** or stern [*rā*ʿ] **discipline awaits** a person **who leaves the path**, that is, the straight path to life (NRSV, NIV). This line, then, warns of the punishment that attends leaving the narrow way. But *rā*ʿ, **evil** [rendered **harsh**] never modifies discipline (Longman 2006, 315; Clifford 1999, 152). Since this term is followed by the preposition ***to*** (*lě*), the phrase may mean ***bad in the view of*** the one who forsakes the path. Then this line says: a person, on considering the discipline necessary to continue on the straight path to be too onerous, forsakes that path. Because that person **hates *reproof,*** he will die prematurely.

Affirming: Yahweh Sees into Sheol and into Human Hearts (15:11)

■ **11** This saying employs the argument that if something is true for a major issue, it is certainly true for a minor one. The great truth is that Yahweh sees into the dark regions of ***Sheol*** and ***Abaddon***, often rendered **Death** and **Destruction**, the place where the dead eke out a bare existence. If these dark, dreary, distant places are under God's surveillance, so too are ***the minds of humans***, that is, hidden human thoughts. Thus, God knows everyone's deepest thoughts before they are expressed in words or deeds. Consequently, no one who lives uprightly in public but has a corrupt thought life pleases God. There is no way to hide evil thoughts from God.

Affirming: Mockers Refuse Wisdom (15:12)

■ **12** Mockers (*lēṣ*) or ***scoffers***, being confirmed cynics, are incorrigible. They ***do not love reproof,*** even when offered by a person who has their best interest in view. Neither do they seek out **the wise** for guidance. The implication is that they view any counsel the wise offer as reproof. The tie between these two issues is strengthened by the similarity in the sound of the Hebrew words for ***reproof*** and **wise**: *ḥôkēaḥ* and *ḥăkāmîm* (Fox 2009, 593).

Opposing: Happiness / Depression (15:13)

■ **13** The term **heart** or ***mind*** (*lēb*) connects the next three proverbs. The disposition of a person greatly affects that person's attitude. ***A joyful mind*** or disposition ***produces a*** cheerful ***countenance***. Conversely, ***a mind*** dominated by ***grief*** produces ***a crushed*** spirit, that is, depression. Therefore, it is important to manage one's thoughts to avoid emotional illness. This proverb reveals that the ancients recognized the connection between a person's thoughts and that person's disposition or mood.

Opposing: Wisdom / Folly

■ **14** One's character determines the kind of activities one enjoys. ***The mind of*** **the discerning . . . seeks knowledge.** The verb **seeks** pictures the discerning as aggressively pursuing knowledge. In gaining knowledge they find a deep sense of satisfaction similar to that provided by consuming good food. Knowledge, then, is the nourishment that keeps the mind alert. ***Fools***, however, ***feed*** [rā'â] **on folly.** The verb rā'â pictures them to be like sheep grazing on folly. Their continual feeding makes them obstinate fools.

Opposing: Afflicted / Cheerful (15:15)

■ **15** The next four proverbs concern distressful situations. **All the days of** the afflicted are *hard* (ra'). They find it difficult to enjoy any activity. However, a person who has *a cheerful heart* or disposition experiences life as **a continual feast**, that is, joyful fellowship at a table set with nourishing food. One's disposition determines the way one experiences life more than wealth or title. Does this saying offer further counsel?

The juxtaposition of the two lines, especially given that the saying is structured as a chiasm in the Hebrew—days:*affliction*:*hard*::cheerful heart:feast:*continually*—opens the possibility that it also offers guidance to any who are suffering affliction by encouraging them that they may overcome distress with a cheerful attitude (see 31:6-7; Plöger 1984, 182; Murphy 1998, 113).

Better-than: Few Possessions with Fear of Yahweh / Great Wealth (15:16)

■ **16** The next two proverbs are better-than sayings. Also the term *ṭôb* (**good**) stands in the next three proverbs. **Fearing Yahweh**, even though one has only *a few possessions,* is better than having *a large treasury* and being constantly in **turmoil** (*mĕhûmâ*). *Mĕhûmâ*, with its setting in holy war, references the confusion or panic that erupts when an army is routed. This vivid picture brings out the reality that **great wealth** may become a heavy burden. Reasons for this phenomenon include the need for continual management, the attraction of robbers, and a stream of beggars. Another wearisome burden is the constant fear that it may be suddenly lost. In fact, great wealth may become so burdensome that a person who has only few possessions and trusts Yahweh enjoys life far more than a wealthy person.

Better-than: Little Food with Love than a Feast with Hate (15:17)

■ **17** **A small serving of vegetables** eaten around a table with family members who **love** each other is better than feasting on **a fattened calf** at a table in the company of those who *hate* each other. A fattened calf is one raised on a special diet in a stall. Slaughtered at the ideal stage, it is roasted for a sumptuous meal of tender beef, a meal that only the rich could afford. But the delicacy of the roast beef loses its flavor when eaten at a table so full of tension that the conversation, at best, is about irrelevant matters as all diners keep up their guard. The feast is a charade. Love, not rich food, makes a grand gathering enjoyable.

It is important to prize the most rewarding aspects of life, especially when society prizes the display of power and possessions over committed friendships. For example, in Western society a display of power is living in a high-rise and associating with powerful people at parties renowned for sumptuous food and drink. But such party going is often hollow. Since no one really trusts attendants at the party, a person must carefully guard what is said. The food is so rich that it often upsets the stomach, and the wine may leave one with a terrible hangover.

That is why the wisdom tradition prizes spiritual qualities and genuine fellowship over grandiose feasting. (See 15:17; 16:8; 17:1; Ps 37:16.)

Opposing: Hot Tempered Person / A Patient Person (Line *a* = 29:22*a*) (15:18)

■ **18** Wisdom texts in general, especially those from Egypt, condemn "a hot head." **A hot-tempered person** loves to *stir* up *strife* (see 29:22). No wonder a person who has such a disposition is sternly denounced. *A patient person*, however, takes steps that *calm* **a quarrel**, thereby promoting camaraderie among people. In Egyptian texts this kind of person is referred to as "the silent one" (see 22:24-25).

Opposing: Lazy Person / The Upright (15:19)

■ **19** The condition of **the way** traveled by *a lazy person* is contrasted with that taken by **the upright**. A lazy person's **way** is so overgrown **with thorns** (*ḥēdeq*) that the going is difficult, slow, and painful. *Ḥēdeq* is a shrub or a thorny hedge that is grayish and spiny with numerous branches and large leaves. It has lilac flowers and produces yellow berries (Isa 5:5; Zohary 1982, 164). These shrubs may grow so dense that they block one's path (see Mic 7:4).

The upright, however, take a straight, graded **highway**. This kind of path may be traveled in foul weather as well as in good. The wording gives the hint that the upright work to keep their path clear while the lazy let the path they are taking become so overgrown that it is virtually impassable. With this hint a different dimension is added to the picture about the two paths.

Opposing: Children: Wise / Foolish (Line *a* = 10:1*a*) (15:20)

■ **20** The behavior of children greatly impacts their parents, producing great joy or extensive grief, even though children often do not recognize that effect. **A wise *child* brings joy to *the* father**, but **a foolish *child* despises *the* mother**. While the parents of a wise child are honored indirectly, a foolish child behaves brutishly toward the mother, causing her great shame. The distress such a child causes the entire family is heightened by naming the mother as the one despised. Parents with this kind of child are very disheartened, especially in an honor-based society.

Opposing: Fool / Wise (15:21)

■ **21** Folly brings joy or *delights a person* who has **little** sense (see Prov 15:14*b*; 10:13). That is, a youth who lacks the ability of self-reflection finds more pleasure in pursuing foolish activities than in seeking to overcome folly. But *a person* of **understanding** ['*îš tĕbûnâ*] **keeps a straight course**. That one never deviates from it, neither for pleasure nor for personal gain, because of finding a strong sense of satisfaction in activities that move one forward on that path.

Opposing: Failed Plans / Established Plans (15:22)

■ **22** Every person needs to have counselors to navigate the many challenges that confront one in life. That is why some leaders have an advisory board or an accountability group to help them keep on course. Belonging to a group is important, especially since **plans** or programs entered into without being deliberated over often **fail**. By taking counsel with **many advisers**, a person increases exponentially the possibility of a successful outcome as plans are improved and pitfalls avoided. This assertion is underscored by the variation of key terms between plural and singular, **plans** made without **counsel** (sg. first line), compared to *a plan* (sg. implied by a sg. verb) made with many advisers (Clifford 1999, 154). (See 11:14; 20:18; 24:6.)

Affirming: Joy from an Apt Answer / A Timely Word (15:23)

■ **23** An apt reply spoken in **a timely *manner*** is **very** good. The ability to offer such a word is through training in wisdom. **A person finds joy** in giving an insightful response to an inquiry.

Advancing: Upward to Wisdom / Downward to Sheol (15:24)

■ **24** The prudent (*maśkîl*) take the path that leads **upward**, thereby turning away from the path that *goes downward to Sheol*, the realm of the dead (see the use of the terms **upward** and ***downward*** in Deut 28:43). This proverb encourages the prudent to stay on the upward course in order to have a long, blessed life. This is also the only proverb that describes the two paths of life as upward and downward.

Opposing: House of the Proud Torn Down / Widow's Boundaries Secure (15:25)

■ **25** This proverb highlights Yahweh's compassionate defense of the powerless against the backdrop of his stern punishment of the arrogant for slyly taking land from the weak.

Reading the first line in light of the second line, the proverb offers a snapshot of an ancient scene. Yahweh punishes **the proud** by ***tearing*** down [*nāsaḥ*] **his** house, the basis of his security, for his having confiscated a portion of a widow's property by stealthily moving the boundary stones (see Prov 22:28; 23:10-11). That aggressor is taken by surprise. He did not expect to face punishment for his illegal maneuvering because the widow lacks a defender, that is, a kinsman redeemer, and she has no standing to present her case to the local court.

The severity of God's punishment is carried by the verb *nāsaḥ* (**tears down**), a term that occurs only four times in the OT, always with God as its subject. In Ps 52:5 it describes God's harsh judgment against those who practice deception and gleefully boast of their evildoings (see Prov 2:22). This verb is also used for Israel's ***being driven from*** the promised land, the harshest curse pronounced against Israel for continually breaking the covenant (Deut 28:63).

The egregious nature of **the proud** person's action that warrants such harsh punishment is conveyed by two elements; first, by the stark contrast of the opposing parties, **the proud** person versus a **widow**. Second, it is found in the proud person's actions being an affront to Yahweh, namely confiscating inalienable property, property that was the widow's inheritance under the covenant (Lev 25:23-28; Prov 23:10-11; Isa 5:8-10).

This proverb certainly serves as a warning to the powerful against using their position and wealth to victimize weak members of the community, and it encourages the weak to trust in Yahweh for protection when they are threatened by the arrogant.

Women's Ownership of Property in Ancient Israel

Only rarely did women own property in ancient Israel. A father who had only daughters could leave his land to them (Num 27:1-8). It is also possible that a widow controlled property until her sons became adults (Ruth 4:3). The widow here may own property for a similar reason. Nevertheless, she was susceptible to a powerful landlord encroaching on her land, for she had little access to legal recourse, even though some defended the rights of widows and orphans (see Deut 27:19). Nevertheless, this proverb served to encourage widows by affirming that Yahweh would protect them (Fox 2009, 602). (See Prov 22:28; 23:10.)

Opposing: Pleasant Thoughts / Words of the Wicked (15:26)

■ **26** *Yahweh* **detests the thoughts of the wicked.** The wicked, then, are under his judgment even before they engage in conversation designed to deceive people. But *pleasant* **words are pure in** *Yahweh's* **sight.**

Opposing: Greedy / Hating Bribes (15:27)

■ **27** **A greedy** *person*, one who seeks to accumulate wealth through the use of illicit means such as extortion **brings** *trouble* **to** *his household*. The avarice of such a person is stressed by two forms of the same root occurring together; the subject is the participle *bôṣēaʻ* (*one who engages in extortion*) followed by the object *bāṣaʻ* (*unjust gain*). Anyone who gains wealth by unjust means heaps **ruin** or *trouble* on all the members of the family or clan. According to Wesley, "[He] brings God's curse upon himself and family" (1975, 1859).

But **the one who hates** *gifts*, particularly payoffs or **bribes, will live.** That is, that one will have affirming relationships within the community and a healthy, long life. A person who rejects gifts never becomes obligated to others. Therefore, that person does not have to be vigilant in watching out for someone seeking vengeance against any member of the family.

Opposing: Speech: Pondered / Gushing (15:28)

■ **28** The next two proverbs are connected by the chiastic arrangement of the subjects: **righteous:wicked::wicked:righteous.** These two classes of people respond very differently to an inquiry. **The righteous** *ponder* (*hāgâ*) carefully what they will say before answering, for they want to answer accurately and confidently (Wesley 1975, 1859). **But the mouth of the wicked** instantly **gushes evil**. The words flowing from their mouths are deceptive, even outright lies.

Quick, loquacious answers offered by questionable people often provide a clue that what they are saying cannot be trusted.

Opposing: Yahweh Is Far from the Wicked / He Hears the Righteous (15:29)

■ **29** Yahweh responds to those who make petitions to him according to their character. He maintains a **far** distance **from the wicked**. That is, Yahweh is not inclined to respond favorably to their requests. However, he is close enough to **the righteous** that **he hears** or *attends* to their **prayer**. This proverb describes the usual posture of Yahweh to the wicked, not his response to earnest cries from them in special situations.

Affirming: Seeing / Hearing (15:30)

■ **30** A person rejoices greatly, that is, is encouraged or strengthened (lit. *makes the bones fat*) on seeing the **light in a messenger's eyes** and hearing *a good report*. The idiom "light of the eyes" may refer to a vibrant, enthusiastic expression visible on the face of another, possibly the one who brings a good report (Waltke 2005, 6). In that case the countenance of the speaker fills the one spoken to with **joy**. Such joy affects both one's physical and emotional well-being as conveyed by the use of **bones**. Whenever one's inner spirit is nourished, a person becomes vibrant and resourceful.

Advancing: Hearing a Rebuke / At Home with the Wise (15:31)

■ **31** The following three proverbs emphasize the benefits of discipline. Also the phrase *hearing* or *heeding a rebuke* or correction (*šōmēaʿ tôkaḥat*) (with slight variation in spelling) stands chiastically in the next two proverbs (vv 31*a*:32*b*).

The ear plays a vital role in the process of learning. **An *ear*,** by implication an open, receptive ear, ***hears*,** that is, has regard for and understands the intent of, a **life-giving correction**. The hearer adjusts behavior in light of the rebuke. As a result the hearer *is* **at home among the wise**, that is, welcome to sit in their councils.

Opposing: Ignoring Discipline / Heeding Admonition (15:32)

■ **32** In contrast to a person who learns from a rebuke (v 31), another type *disregards* discipline (*mûsār*), considering it to be either inappropriate or too difficult to follow. Those persons are unaware that because of their attitude they **despise themselves**. Whoever loathes the self has little interest in self-improvement, in taking care of one's health, and in building an honorable reputation. Such a person unwittingly behaves in self-destructive ways (Fox 2009, 604). But one **who heeds correction** or *a rebuke*, by changing behavior in light of that rebuke, **gains understanding.**

Affirming: Discipline / Humility (Line *b* = 18:12*b*) (15:33)

■ **33** The **fear *of Yahweh*** goes hand in hand with **instruction** and thereby leads to *wisdom*. Those who fear Yahweh do not bristle at the discipline necessary to become wise, even when discipline is hard or irritating. By being devoted to Yahweh students become aware that **humility comes before honor**, the highest reward in an honor-based society. In other words, humility keeps students treading the path that leads to wisdom. The acquiring of wisdom brings honor and recognition.

The final verse of this first section of the second collection of proverbs serves to underscore the intrinsic connection between the fear of Yahweh, wisdom, and of honor, themes that encase the first section of the book of Proverbs (1:7; 9:10).

G. Proverbs 16:1-33

OVERVIEW

In this chapter fifteen proverbs are cast in advancing style, eleven in affirming style (vv 4, 6, 11, 13, 15, 17, 18, 20, 26, 27, 30), three in opposing style (vv 2, 22, 28). Righteousness, wisdom, patience, and humility are prized over wealth, injustice, gold, spoils, and aggression. There are four better-than sayings (vv 8, 16, 19, 32). This shows that the distribution of the style of the proverbs assembled in the second subsection of Section II is markedly different from the preference for opposing proverbs in the first subsection. Proverbs structured as advancing or affirming become predominant.

Two other characteristics distinguish the structure of this chapter from those in the first section. First, the chapter is framed by aphorisms about Yahweh's role in directing the outcome of a matter (vv 1, 33). It is the central topic in vv 1-9. There is also a blessing on those who trust in Yahweh (v 20b). Greater emphasis on Yahweh's role in wisdom is attested in that his name appears in eleven proverbs (vv 1, 2, 3, 4, 5, 6, 7, 9, 11, 20, 33).

Second, a few proverbs on the same topic are grouped together. There are four such clusters: the role of Yahweh in peoples' lives (vv 1-9, save v 8), the character of the king (vv 10-15, save v 11), the value of wisdom (vv 20-23), and portraits of bad character (vv 27-30). Such clusters are more common throughout the second section.

The two major topics are Yahweh's role among humans and the role of the king. Yahweh's response to human planning is set out in vv 1-9. Also he establishes honest weights (v 11), and trust in him is the basis for a person's being blessed (v 20). The king, specifically the Davidic king as Yahweh's representative on earth, is responsible to promote justice. Like Yahweh he considers wrongdoing detestable (v 12a), and his favor promotes virtue (v 13). His acceptance encourages the people (v 15).

In addition, there is a cluster of three aphorisms on violent characters, "a scoundrel," "a perverse person," and "a violent person" (vv 27-29). Each of these villains uses fiery speech to promote dissension in the community. These scoundrels use the gestures of winking with the eyes and pursing the lips to communicate their evil intentions with their accomplices (v 30).

The frequent use of Yahweh's name is in accord with the greater interest in divine-human interaction in Section II. Two other topics are speech and arrogance. Arrogance is denounced in three proverbs. It is detestable to Yahweh, for it leads to destruction (vv 5a, 18). Thus, a person is better off living among the poor than sharing spoils with the proud (v 19). Speech is the topic of seven proverbs. Especially powerful are pleasant words. They promote instruction and healing (vv 21, 23, 24). No wonder the king loves to hear such speech (v 13). At times the king's words are received as an oracle (v 10). However, perverse speech is as destructive as a scorching fire (v 27). It creates strife that ruins friendships (v 28).

IN THE TEXT

Advancing: Humans Plans / Yahweh Answers (16:1)

■ **1** Endowed by God with a creative mind, a human makes plans and has big dreams about adventures and grand accomplishments. Indeed, the skill needed for sound planning is in view in this proverb, for the term for **plans** (*ma'ărāk*) describes troops in a battle formation (Gen 14:8; 1 Sam 4:2) and the verb also references a well-constituted argument designed to win a lawsuit (Job 13:18). To accomplish a major task a person must draw up detailed plans. Nevertheless, it is **Yahweh** who determines the outcome, as conveyed by the words **the *reply* of the tongue *comes from Yahweh*.**

When a person initiates a plan to accomplish a major project or presents an argument to win a position, Yahweh is above the scene, directing various circumstances and responses to bring about the desired results. Thus, there is a dialogical interaction between a person's planning and God's response. That is, a tension exists between a human's having the ability as well as the responsibility to plan and Yahweh's establishing his purpose.

The wisdom tradition recognizes this tension, but it never seeks to resolve it. It places high value on humans learning wisdom and their devising astute plans. It teaches that humans must rely on Yahweh's directing the outcome of those plans. Nothing of lasting significance is achieved without his guidance.

Opposing: Human / Yahweh (Line *a* = 21:2a; line *b* = 24:12b) (16:2)

■ **2** Every person views one's own **ways** as **pure**, that is, appropriate, honorable, and pleasing to God. But since a human's self-understanding is clouded, no one is able to make an accurate judgment on the purity of the motivations behind what one does or says. Therefore, it is necessary that **Yahweh assess** the deep **motives** or **moods** (*rûḥôt*) that drive a person's actions. That is, Yahweh scrutinizes a person's inner desires and attitudes in order to identify those that are impure. The wise must pray with the psalmist: "See if there is any offensive way in me, and lead me in the way everlasting" (Ps 139:24).

Advancing: Committing One's Deeds to Yahweh (16:3)

■ **3** A student is exhorted to **commit** *his deeds to Yahweh*. The verb rendered **commit** is literally *roll on*. A person is to entrust all one's doings to Yahweh. Then God will bring about results that promote the building of one's character and advance one's journey on the path to life. By making such a commitment one has the confidence that Yahweh **will establish** the **plans**.

On the one hand, when one commits one's plans to Yahweh, pride is thwarted and that person is in a position to praise Yahweh genuinely for the outcome. On the other hand, if a project does not succeed, the planner is not devastated, believing that Yahweh has permitted the failure. The planner is also confident that Yahweh has a better plan than that which failed. By trusting Yahweh completely, a person overcomes the crippling effect of self-doubt.

Affirming: Yahweh's Sovereignty (16:4)

■ **4** Everything Yahweh does or creates is part of a whole as conveyed by the statement *everything that Yahweh does has an answer to it*. For example, Yahweh makes a tree. That tree generates oxygen, serves as a home for birds, and provides wood for humans. Trees are an integral part of the ecological cycle.

From another perspective this saying asserts that nothing exists or takes place on earth that Yahweh cannot fold into his purpose. The second line illustrates this claim by saying boldly that **even the wicked**, those who act contrary to Yahweh's standards, are not outside of his control, for they will face **a day of disaster**. This assertion is true even though **the wicked** may prosper for a period. **A day of disaster** is coming when God will hold them accountable for their evil deeds.

Advancing: Proud (Line *b* = 11:21*a*) (16:5)

■ **5** **The proud**, those who have an exalted view of their own worth and the superiority of their ideas, *are detested by Yahweh*. Since they have chosen to live according to their own ways rather than by God's, Yahweh will not brook their arrogance as is heard in the assertion **they will not go unpunished**. This assertion is introduced by the phrase *hand to hand*, which is glossed as **be sure of this** or *assuredly* (Fox 2009, 612) to convey that their punishment is certain. In other words, the arrogant are never able to operate outside of Yahweh's lordship.

Affirming: Kindness / Fear of Yahweh (16:6)

■ **6** *Loyal* love and faithfulness are powerful forces that promote good relationships among humans. They are so powerful that they *may atone for*, that is, overcome, **sin**. Sin, being both a harmful act and a selfish act, causes discord among people. That discord arouses anger in those who are harmed. Yet the anger of those who are rightly upset *may be mollified* or atoned by *loyal* love and faithfulness.

These virtues work to remove the sting produced by the harm they have experienced. That is, these virtues achieve results similar to those that attend

181

presenting an atoning sacrifice that brings forgiveness. This saying does not discount making offerings prescribed to atone for sins (Lev 1, 4—5), but it does teach that these high virtues possess spiritual power that counteracts the effects of wrongdoing.

The fear of *Yahweh* is also a mighty force, for it *turns* a person from *doing wrong* or evil (*raʿ*; 3:7*b*). The goal of both lines, then, is to overcome the power of sin that puts people at odds with each other.

The Meaning of "Atone"

The term "atone" means to annul the harmful effects released by a sin. It is especially used for the cleansing power of sacrifices prescribed in Leviticus (e.g., 1:4; 4:20, 26, 31, 35). The manipulation of the blood at the altar from prescribed sacrifices cleanses the altar from the miasma released by the people's sinning and drawn to the horns of the altar.

As a result of making sacrifices that atone, either a person or the people continue to be in a right relationship with Yahweh. This proverb employs this cultic term to stress the great power that love and faithfulness have for mending human relationships damaged by sin.

Advancing: Yahweh's Pleasure / Peace with One's Enemies (16:7)

■ **7** When *Yahweh* takes pleasure in a *person's ways*, he causes their enemies to make peace with them. People please Yahweh by being wise, truthful, reliable, and kind. These virtues also win the respect of their enemies. Under God's influence the enemies come to believe that they are able to **make peace with them**. They come to believe that those whom God blesses will deal with them honestly and without prejudice.

This principle is well-illustrated in the accounts of Abraham and Abimelek, the king of Gerar (Gen 20; 21:22-30). Abraham settled in Gerar. Because of conflict with Abimelek over Sarah, Abraham moved eastward out of his domain. Sometime later Abimelek became impressed by Abraham's prospering as a result of God's blessing. Abimelek and Phicol, his commander, traveled to Abraham. They commended him saying, "God is with you in everything you do" (Gen 21:22*b*). Confident that Abraham would not deal falsely with him or his family, he proposed that they make a covenant of peace. As a result, Abraham stayed at Beersheba for a long time without any further discord with Abimelek.

Better-than: Little with Righteousness (16:8)

■ **8** **Righteousness**, the bedrock on which healthy relationships are built, is essential for good relationships and a successful life. Its value far exceeds all material gains. Consequently, it is **better** to have **little** [i.e., few possessions] **with righteousness** than to have *a large income without justice*. A person who seeks wisdom will never compromise justice, especially to increase wealth. (See Prov 15:16-17.)

Advancing: Humans Plan / Yahweh Determines the Outcome (16:9)

■ **9** This section on Yahweh's role in the lives of those who trust him (vv 1-9) is set off by this inclusio. *A person's mind plans his* course, but *Yahweh determines* or establishes *his step*. The emphasis here falls on Yahweh's directing the course of one's life as the saying reinforces the importance of trusting Yahweh in every activity. Trust promotes humility and confidence in a person (Fox 2009, 613). Clearly, this saying does not negate planning, for it is a plan a devout person designs that Yahweh **establishes**.

Advancing: Order from the King / Justice (16:10)

■ **10** The Israelites, believing that the Davidic king was chosen by Yahweh, consider a legal pronouncement from him as *an inspired judgment* or oracle (*qesem*). The Hebrew *qesem* usually references divination, but magical practices were outlawed in Israel, for they are based on a worldview that is diametrically opposed to the confession that Yahweh is the only God (Deut 18:10). *Qesem*, then, is used in this line metaphorically for inspired decisions rendered by the king.

When facing a difficult case the king may use lots of some kind to guide his decision. The use of lots assumed that God determined the choice that the lots selected (see Prov 18:18; Davies 1980, 552-54). Or it is possible that the king consulted the high priest, requesting that he seek an answer through the Urim and Thummim (Exod 28:30; Longman 2006, 331). In either case, the decision the king makes is accepted as inspired by God. This confidence was underscored by the belief that the king was guided by God's justice (Ps 72:1-2), a belief grounded in God's election of the Davidic line (2 Sam 7:4-17). This belief is the reason for the assertion **his mouth does not betray justice**. It expresses an ideal that unfortunately many kings in ancient Israel betrayed.

Affirming: Just Scales / Weights (16:11)

■ **11** Balanced or **honest scales** are desired by *Yahweh* (Deut 25:13-16). True **weights** carried by a merchant **in *a* bag** are identified as Yahweh's ***work***. That is, a merchant who uses accurate weights is being true to Yahweh's standard. This wording also shows Yahweh's concern for justice even in small matters (see Prov 11:1; 20:10, 23).

Advancing: King against Wrongdoing / And True to Justice (Line *b* = 25:5*b*) (16:12)

■ **12** Kings **detest wrongdoing**, for they are aware that their **throne is** securely **established through righteousness**. In Proverbs a detestable statement usually has Yahweh as a subject, but here the king as God's representative is the subject. That is, the king executes God's will among his people. (See 20:28; 29:14.)

Affirming: King's Delight: Honest Speech / Truth (16:13)

■ **13** Kings *delight* in hearing words from *truthful* lips. They especially *love* (i.e., **value**) a person **who speaks** truthfully or *straightforwardly*, particularly if that person is one who gives advice or reports to them. When officials, messengers, and servants speak to the king in a straightforward, accurate manner, the king is able to make well-informed, just decisions. Furthermore, such officials give the king confidence that his orders are being fully implemented throughout the realm.

Advancing: A King's Wrath / Wise Appease It (16:14)

■ **14** Given that kings were known for being temperamental and that they had absolute power, everyone standing in a king's presence was intimidated. **A king's wrath** is such a terrifying force that it is identified as **a messenger of death**.

This epithet conveys that at any time a king could send out a messenger charged with putting to death any number of persons without fear of being challenged, save that in Israel the king was subject to God, who often spoke to him through a prophet. David was made aware of God's authority when Nathan, the prophet, confronted him for having put Uriah to death (2 Sam 12:1-14). God would not tolerate such selfish abuse of royal power among his people.

The wise, aware of the king's power, seek to **appease** his wrath by showing respect and speaking calmly. Qohelet counsels one at whom the king becomes angry to stay at his post and to be calm, for calmness may put to rest even great errors (Eccl 10:4). (See Prov 19:12; 20:2; 24:21-22.)

Affirming: King: The Source of Life / And Encouragement (Line *b* is similar to 19:12*b*) (16:15)

■ **15** The king promotes the life of the people by maintaining national security and by supporting policies that increase the nation's production. *The light of his countenance*, that is, his gleaming smile, gives **life** to the people. Thus, his smile is likened to **a rain cloud in spring**. In Palestine the spring rains fall gently, bringing the nourishment necessary for the barley and the wheat to ripen, thereby yielding an abundant harvest. Like that gentle rain the king's **favor** motivates the people to be productive, adding to the national wealth.

Better-than: Wisdom's Value above Precious Metals (16:16)

■ **16** The value of acquiring wisdom is stressed. The exhortation: *acquire* wisdom and *understanding*, for the accumulation of them is far more valuable than *fine* gold or silver (see 4:5, 7; 8:10). Whereas silver and gold are static commodities, wisdom is active. It increases with experience. It guides one to a productive life that has far more value than these metals. (See 3:14-15; 8:10-11.)

Affirming: Highway of Upright / Guarding the Way (Line *b* = 19:16*a*) (16:17)

■ **17** The highway (i.e., a road carefully graded so that carts and people may traverse over a smooth, reliable surface) that **the upright** take steers them *away from wrong* or evil (*ra'*). That way is safe from bandits and devoid of hidden potholes or traps. Jesus describes that way as straight and narrow (Matt 7:13-14). Nevertheless, all who travel this highway need to **watch** or **guard** their steps, making sure that they stay on the path and do not inadvertently deviate from it. Thereby they **preserve their lives.**

Affirming: Pride / Haughty Demeanor (Line *a* = 18:12*a*) (16:18)

■ **18** The next two proverbs are connected by the theme of pride. The first supports the value advocated in the second. **Pride** or **a haughty *demeanor*** is very dangerous. It keeps one from noticing small dangers on life's path. Or if a danger is noticed, a proud person usually discounts it, confident of overcoming whatever obstacles there are with minimal effort. That is, a proud person shrugs off warning signs as pride keeps the person from grasping the potential harm. Suddenly a proud person stumbles and ***falls***. The person who persists in being proud will face **destruction.** Destruction (*šeber*) stands for the collapse of something like a wall (Isa 30:13) or the devastation of a nation (Jer 4:20).

This pattern is attested in Western society. Placing the highest value on wealth and glamour, Western society overlooks the corrupt practices of its leaders and celebrities while lauding them as deities. But when their corrupt methods for gaining wealth come to light, these idols often experience a dramatic loss of favor.

Better-than: Lowly / Than the Proud (16:19)

■ **19** It is better to have **a lowly *disposition*** and associate **with the oppressed** than to be haughty and **share plunder with the proud.** The poor and oppressed tend to be kind, very willing to share the little they have. Looking out for each other, they develop solid camaraderie.

By contrast, the proud oppressors boast of the wealth they accumulate as they divide it among themselves. Afterward these plunderers tend to bicker about numerous small things, leading to disharmony and hard feelings. Discord abounds and sometimes leads to their injuring each other.

Therefore, in the search for a good life one needs to associate with those who are unpretentious. True camaraderie takes place among those who have a contrite demeanor.

Affirming: Prospering / Trusting in Yahweh (16:20)

■ **20** The person who **gives heed to *a word*** [i.e., the teaching of the wise] ***finds good things*** or **prospers.** Heeding such instruction reflects ***trusting*** in **Yahweh.** The one who trusts in **Yahweh** is **blessed,** that is, divine favor is at work in that person's life (→ sidebar "A Beatitude" in overview for 3:13-20). Another way to read this proverb is that the second line describes a higher value. One who ***heeds*** **instruction** gains a benefit, while the one who **trusts in Yahweh** experiences good fortune (Fox 2009, 619).

Advancing: The Discerning / Pleasant Speech (16:21)

■ **21** A person who is **wise in *thought*** is known or addressed as **understanding** or **discerning**. **Discerning** may have been a title for addressing renowned sages in ancient Israel, somewhat similar to calling a learned person today "a scholar." Discerning persons were appointed to various councils and were employed as advisers (see Job 29:21-25).

A discerning person has the skill of speaking **graciously** (lit. *sweet of lips*). This ability enables such a person to deliver persuasive speeches that offer the people keen insights into issues facing the community.

Jesus' skill at teaching was the epitome of this ability of a discerning person (see Luke 19:48; John 7:46; Waltke 2005, 29).

Opposing: Insight / Folly (16:22)

■ **22** Prudence [*discretion* or **insight** (*śēkel*)] **is a fountain of life**, a fountain that offers sweet, refreshing water. It energizes its owner to live astutely, to promote good relationships, and to make judicious decisions (see Fox 2009, 620).

The sense of line *b* is not obvious. It seems to say that ***the discipline of fools is folly***. That is, fools increase in the adeptness of folly as they age. Another way to read the second line is **folly brings punishment to fools**. The disposition of fools prevents them from drinking from the fountain of life. For them life is harder, more frustrating, and filled with woe.

Advancing: Guided Speech / Promotes Instruction (16:23)

■ **23** ***The mind of a*** wise ***person*** instructs ***the mouth*** enabling the person to teach ***concepts*** (*leqaḥ*) well. Thereby **instruction** is promoted (see v 21*b*). The wise are aware that the development of good rhetorical skills empowers one to teach persuasively.

Advancing: Pleasant Words (16:24)

■ **24** **Gracious words** are so enjoyable and beneficial that they are comparable to **a honeycomb**. Finding a honeycomb was a fabulous treat for the ancients, who had only a few sweets, mainly dates, figs, and wild honey. For example, when highly famished warriors came across some honey on the battlefield, they devoured it quickly and their strength was revived (1 Sam 14:27-29). Possibly there was honey from domesticated bees in ancient Israel, for beehives have been found at Tel-Rehov. This comparison brings out how pleasant and invigorating are pleasant words. They increase a person's sense of well-being as they bring **healing** to the ***deepest emotions*** (*'eṣem*), as represented by the term **bones**.

Advancing: Road to Death (=14:12) (16:25)

■ **25** (→ 14:12.) Lennox (1998, 167) interprets this saying as continuing the theme of the power of words in the preceding proverbs: "**Right** words are sweet, but sweet words are not always **right**; the cost of failing to know the difference is **death**."

Affirming: Laborer's Appetite / Hunger (16:26)

■ **26** This proverb brings out the main reason people work so hard. It is because they are driven by **an appetite**. As it says in Ecclesiastes: "Everyone's toil is for their mouth, yet their appetite is never satisfied" (6:7). Thus, **laborers**, driven by their **hunger**, toil long and hard, aware that without working they will not be able to purchase food, clothing, and other essentials for their families.

Without a compelling motivation most people fail to act on a matter. They keep putting it off to a more convenient time. But one's appetite is always active, motivating one to work daily to earn enough to buy food. Thus, a constant need like hunger, viewed negatively, has the important role of providing a human with the motivation to sustain life.

Affirming: A Scoundrel and Evil / Fiery Speech (16:27)

■ **27** The next three proverbs (Prov 16:27-29) characterize three types of rascals: **a scoundrel** (v 27), "a perverse person" (v 28), and "a violent person" (v 29). The following proverb (v 30) describes a trait common to these characters.

A scoundrel [*'îš bĕliyya'al*] **plots** [*kōreh*] evil (*rā'â*). The verb *kōreh* (lit. **dig, mine**) conveys a scoundrel's great effort to come up with an intricate scheme to discredit or defraud someone. This verb describes the focused effort of Jeremiah's opponents to discredit him (Jer 18:20-21). Their intricate scheme is likened to digging a pit to capture a wild animal (see Prov 26:27).

A scoundrel's *rhetoric* (lit. **lips**) is so fierce that it is likened to **a scorching fire**. The flames of a wildfire are so hot that they are virtually impossible to put out. Similarly, it is hard to quench a contentious conflict ignited by a scoundrel's cruel rhetoric. The disharmony produced may last for generations.

Opposing: Perverse Person / Use of Gossip (16:28)

■ **28** A perverse person stirs up *dissension* among members of a community in any way imaginable. An effective method for promoting dissension is the spreading of **gossip**, for gossip discredits those spoken about, thereby creating enmity among **close friends**. The character of this kind of person is heard in the English term "backbiter."

Advancing: Violent Person / A Wrong Path (16:29)

■ **29** A violent person entices *a friend* (or a neighbor) to take **a path that is not good. Not good** is a litotes, for *destructive, deadly*. That is, a person who loves to see violence leads a neighbor to do something that people consider to be intolerable, something that person would never normally do. In following this enticement, the neighbor *is led* down a path to strife that will cause great harm, possibly even death.

Affirming: Plotting Perversity / Bent on Evil (16:30)

■ **30** Humans use facial gestures for conveying numerous attitudes, both positive and hostile, and to slyly convey a signal to another person. This proverb describes two facial gestures used as signals by scoundrels like the three rascals described above (vv 27, 28, 29) to promote their schemes. As seen in Prov 6:13, winking with the eye in ancient Israel was a gesture for signaling that something is bad.

In this saying a person signals with a wink that he **is plotting perversity** (*tahpûkôt*). This Hebrew word, being in the plural, stands for a complex plot filled with perverse actions. A person **purses** *his* **lips** possibly as an expression of anticipated satisfaction at *the* evil (*ra'*) he is **bent** on accomplishing.

Advancing: Honor of Old Age / From a Righteous Life (16:31)

■ **31** In ancient Israel a person with **gray hair** was highly respected. Gray hair was viewed as **a crown of splendor** (*'ăṭeret tip'eret*, a phrase heightened by assonance). This glorious crown is found on those who take **the way of righteousness**, for living righteously leads to a long life. The righteous, therefore, are highly honored in old age and are viewed as the wisest.

Better-than: Patience over Might / Self-Control over Capturing a City (16:32)

■ **32** Usually those who have a strong, assertive personality rise to the highest level of leadership. This proverb points out that other qualities also distinguish a person. **A patient person**, described as one *who controls his emotions* or *moods* (*rûaḥ*), which if left unchecked impel one to act without thinking, is better than a *mighty* **warrior** . . . **who** *captures* **a city**. That is, a person who is able to control powerful emotions is more valuable to the community than a person of great strength, for often a warrior foregoes diplomacy, confident that he can achieve a goal quickly by the use of force. But undisciplined use of force against someone often leads to long-term hostilities with neighboring clans or to tyranny at home should that warrior become the ruler.

Advancing: Casting of Lots / God's Decision (16:33)

■ **33** For making a difficult decision, especially one for which there were many options or one for which sufficient information was lacking, the ancients turned to the casting of lots. They believed that Yahweh revealed his will in the decision that the lots disclose. An example in Israel's history is the identification of Achan as the one who had taken banned items from an enemy's tent during the war against Ai (Josh 7:14-21). Also in the selection of the first king the Israelites cast lots to identify that person (1 Sam 10:20-24).

The casting of lots was also used by the early disciples to identify Judas' successor (Acts 1:26). This proverb provides the reason that the disciples in the upper room resorted to this method when there was no obvious person to take Judas' place. (See Prov 18:18.)

H. Proverbs 17:1-28

OVERVIEW

The proverbs in this chapter have the following structures: twelve affirming (vv 4, 5, 6, 17, 18, 19, 20, 21, 25, 26, 27, 28), eight advancing (vv 2,

8, 11, 13, 14, 15, 16, 23), and three opposing (vv 9, 22, 24). Other types of sayings include one better-than saying (v 1), one "how much worse" (v 7), one "more than" (v 10), and two based on an analogy (vv 3, 12; though the NIV renders v 12 as a better-than proverb). The name Yahweh appears only in the "detestable to Yahweh" formula (v 15). A foundational precept is that the poor have inherent value, value that transcends their economic status, because God is their "Maker" (v 5).

Several of the proverbs employ analogies, a characteristic found frequently in the fifth section (chs 25—29): meeting a bear that has lost her cubs (v 12a), letting water out from a reservoir (v 14a), a lucky stone or charm (v 8a), a crucible (v 3a), and a furnace (v 3a). In the same vein is the advice against returning evil for good, for this approach prevents one from getting evil out of the house (v 13).

The two dominant topics are speech in ten proverbs (vv 4, 5, 7, 9, 10, 14, 19, 20, 27, 28) and the fool in eight proverbs (vv 7, 10, 12, 16, 21, 24, 25, 28). Four proverbs concern a household (vv 2, 6, 21, 25). Grandchildren are the crown of the aged (v 6a), and children take pride in their parents (v 6b). However, a stubborn child may need to be placed under the tutorship of an astute servant (v 2), for children who become fools heap grief on their parents (vv 21, 25).

Four proverbs address the ills that result from a perversion of justice (vv 8, 15, 23, 26). The value of love is the topic of two proverbs (vv 9, 17).

IN THE TEXT

Better-than: Little with Peace than Much with Strife (17:1)

■ 1 A meal of meager food, represented by **a dry crust**, eaten with ***tranquility*** is **better** than **a house full of feasting, with strife**. The word for **feasting** is the term for an offering of well-being or a peace offering (Lev 3). A person who presented this kind of sacrifice received back from the priest most of the succulent meat in order to have a festive meal with the family or clan. Thus, the phrase ***sacrifices of strife*** is a startling oxymoron. Instead of being a meal that unites the clan or household, this feast becomes an occasion of strife. As family members gorge on the food, they spar with each other. The tone of the conversation becomes more biting, leading to strife, thereby dampening the festivities. Certainly rapprochement is far more enjoyable and rewarding than rich food.

Advancing: Son Placed under a Wise Servant / Servant Becomes an Heir (17:2)

■ 2 In a wealthy household a parent puts a ***discerning*** servant (*'ebed maśkîl*) in charge of ***a son who acts shamefully***. The servant supervises that son and seeks to correct his behavior in order to save the family from embarrassing situations. That servant's role is so important to the family's honor that he is given *a* **share** *of* the **inheritance** like **one of the family**. Consequently, the errant child's inheritance is diminished. Wayward behavior becomes costly.

Ancient records recount that some well-to-do people made a slave an heir for a variety of reasons, such as to care for them in their old age. Such a transaction usually took place only in extreme situations. This saying functions as a warning to a recalcitrant child of the serious consequences that attend his needing to be placed under a servant's guidance.

Analogy: Testing One's Thought (Line *a* = 27:21*a*) (17:3)

■ **3** *Yahweh* tests peoples' *minds* in order to assess the nature of their thoughts and plans. That is, Yahweh has concern not only with a person's actions but also with one's thoughts and attitudes, for these determine how one will act. Yahweh's testing is comparable to assaying metal. Ore containing precious metal has to be refined in order to bring out the pure, valuable metal. **Silver** was refined in *a* **crucible** and **gold** in *a* **furnace**. Similarly, Yahweh takes measures to refine the thoughts and plans of those who fear him so that they are in accord with the highest virtues taught. (See Job 23:10; Isa 1:25; Jer 9:7; Zech 13:8-9.)

Affirming: Mischievous Gossip (17:4)

■ **4** Just as a lover of music likes to listen to a renowned performer, **a wicked person** relishes listening to words from *iniquitous* lips, finding such thoughts alluring and tantalizing. Similarly, **a liar pays attention to a destructive tongue**. People indulge in activities they like, whether those activities are honorable or dishonorable.

Affirming: Mocking the Poor / Gloating over Disaster (17:5)

■ **5** Mocking the poor and taking pleasure in another's losses are strongly denounced. In *mocking* **the poor**, such as calling attention to their lack of basic possessions, in today's world a house or a newer car, a person *expresses* **contempt** for God, **their Maker**. Such reproaches bring to the surface the shame the poor feel as a result of their poverty. Anyone who is prone to mock a poor person must realize the inherent value of that person based on that person's being made in God's image. That fact implies that whatever is done to another person is being done to God.

Another situation God despises is *gloating* over *a* **disaster**, especially one that has caused widespread destruction. Those who respond to a tragedy in this way *will face punishment*.

Affirming: Honor in the Family: Grandchildren / Parents (17:6)

■ **6** *The* **crown of** *the elderly* is their *grandchildren*. They take pride and have great pleasure in watching them grow and become skilled supporters of the family. On the other hand, **children** *take* **pride** in their **parents**. When children grow up, they come to realize that their station in life comes from the efforts of their parents.

How Much Worse: Excessive Speech / Lying (17:7)

■ **7** That which *is not fitting* or *is* unsuited is presented in the first line, and that which is *even* worse is stated in the second line. It *is not fitting* that a **fool** has the gift of speaking *eloquently*. A fool brazenly employs that skill to intimidate or take advantage of others.

The second line describes an even more deplorable situation: **how much worse** is *a noble person* who has **lying lips**. A public official who resorts to lying undercuts the trust placed in him by both the king and the people. That official undercuts his reputation and is likely to suffer loss of his position.

Advancing: Power of a Bribe / Success (17:8)

■ **8** This proverb describes the way some people view the giving of gifts or bribes (*šōḥad*). Since this Hebrew term carries both meanings, it usually, but not always, has a pejorative sense. It does convey that the gift is made to achieve a highly desired outcome such as gaining a person's agreement to a plan or a request (see 18:16; 1 Kgs 15:18-19; 2 Kgs 16:7-9).

At times a gift is "given in secret" to appease an angry person (Prov 21:14). Those who use gifts in this way view them as functioning like a charm, that is, a magical stone. Thus, **they think success will come at every turn**. Their view, however, borders on folly, for over time they are inclined to turn from trusting Yahweh to direct the outcome (16:1, 9) to trusting in their own skill at achieving their goals.

Moreover, since the line between a gift and a bribe in some cases is very fine, they become vulnerable to crossing that line. Should one of them use a gift to thwart justice, that person "corrupts the heart" (Eccl 7:7*b*; Prov 17:23).

Opposing: Covering an Offense / Repeating a Matter (17:9)

■ **9** Whenever a person sees someone make a mistake or commit a transgression and desires to keep that person's friendship, he **covers over an offense** by keeping it confidential as an expression of **love**. Thereby the friend saves the doer from shame, no doubt hoping that the act of kindness will encourage the offender not to continue to engage in such negative behavior. The continual repetition of offensive behavior **separates close friends**.

More-than: Learning from a Rebuke: A Discerning Person / A Fool (17:10)

■ **10** **A rebuke** makes a lasting impact on **a discerning person**, even more than the impact of **a hundred lashes** on a fool. *A hundred blows* is a hyperbole, for the Law limited punishment to forty blows (Deut 25:2-3). The exaggeration underscores the offensiveness of a fool's behavior and that person's callousness to any attempt at corrective punishment. A fool fails to learn from the blows received. But when *an understanding* person receives **a rebuke**, that one takes it to heart and corrects the behavior that led to the reprimand, never wanting to be rebuked again for the same reason. This saying shows that though the wise are not flawless they diligently work at improving their behavior as they increase in wisdom.

Advancing: Evil Person / Cruel Messenger (17:11)

■ **11** The opening line may be read either as *an evildoer seeks only* rebellion or *a rebel only* seeks evil (compare v 7). The second line is more understandable with the latter rendering. Rebels constantly engage in evil activities, for they love to stir up discord among people. When discord reaches a very high level, rebellion is likely to break out. Therefore, the king or governor *sends a cruel person*, one skilled at harshly subduing rebels.

Analogy: Meeting a Bear Robbed of Cubs / Meeting a Fool (17:12)

■ **12** The lines in this proverb are contrasting. The first line appears to be an analogy of a lesser danger than the one described in the second line. Thus, this proverb traditionally has been translated as a better-than saying.

There are various dangers that a person does not want to chance upon; one of those is coming on **a bear robbed of her cubs**. That bear is ready to charge anyone who crosses her path. However, it is even worse to come across **a fool** (*kĕsîl*) acting in **folly** (*'iwwelet*). The analogy implies that the fool is irate and behaving wildly. Being in such a mood, the fool is likely to strike out at the passerby, inflicting serious harm.

Advancing: Paying Back Evil for Good / Becoming Beset by Evil (17:13)

■ **13** *To return* evil to a person who has treated one *well* is to put oneself and one's house in jeopardy of being continually beset by misfortune (*ra'*). This saying is built on the principle in God's economy that those who harm people who have treated them well initiate a chain of misfortunes that will trouble their households throughout life.

Advancing: Starting a Quarrel / Avoiding a Dispute (17:14)

■ **14** **Starting a quarrel** is fraught with grave danger that is comparable to **breaching a dam**. Given the pressure of the water stored in the dam, a trickle soon grows into a stream. The stream becomes a destructive torrent. Thus, this proverb warns that any expression of fury has the potential of bursting into a quarrel. The quarrel may erupt into a brawl, and the brawl may lead to a riot. Therefore, the sensible course is to **drop *a small* matter** of contention **before a dispute breaks out**.

This proverb underscores the need not to press an issue by the imperative: **drop**. Most volatile issues are not worth bringing up in a discussion because the majority of people are unable to discuss them rationally. In fact, the mere mention of a hot issue may so agitate some that they immediately begin to argue. The course of wisdom is to avoid volatile topics.

Advancing: Injustices / An Abomination to Yahweh (17:15)

■ **15** In *Yahweh's* sight two judicial activities are *detestable*: **acquitting the guilty and condemning the innocent** (see Deut 25:1). (On *detestable*, → sidebar "Yahweh Detests or Abomination to Yahweh" at 6:16-19.) Whenever a king, a judge, or a jury renders a faulty judgment, the basis of the judicial system is undermined, thus threatening a community's solidarity.

Advancing: Money / Purchase (17:16)

■ **16** By pointing out a glaring absurdity this proverb is most humorous. Opening with a **why** question, it seeks to uncover a charade. Why would **fools** take a sum of **money** and go off in search of a teacher or a school with the hope of buying wisdom? Possibly the **fools** are motivated by the high standing of those who have been trained by a notable teacher or in a particular school. Little do they realize that wisdom cannot be purchased. At best the money only lets them become students under the guidance of a master. Being **fools**, they are unwilling to spend long hours in hard study and to endure the disciplines required. Since there is no chance of fools acquiring wisdom, the payment is a waste of money.

Affirming: Friend / Brother (17:17)

■ **17** Both **a friend** and **a brother** play major roles in one's life. **A friend loves at all times**, that is, through all the seasons of life (see Eccl 3:1-8). During a time of hardship a friend offers vital support. A friend is also present to share in times of rejoicing. Similarly, **a brother is born** to help one deal with **adversity** (*ṣārâ*). Ṣārâ, coming from a root that means *narrow*, describes situations that press a person hard. At such a time a brother takes up the challenge to lessen that pressure so that his kin may deal with or overcome the adversity.

Affirming: Surety for a Neighbor (17:18)

■ **18** A naive person (*ḥăsar lēb*), that is, *one lacking in judgment*, is quick to *shake* hands, a gesture that seals *a* pledge. Here a naive person puts up **surety for a neighbor**. But various proverbs warn against taking on surety for another except in a compelling situation (Prov 11:15; 20:16; 22:26-27; 27:13). A present-day example is a person cosigning for a loan in order to help someone with a low credit score make a major purchase.

A person who gives surety for another places one's own holdings at risk. The guarantor must cover the loan if the one receiving it fails to repay the entire amount. Given the number of proverbs against putting up security for another, the practice of serving as another's guarantor must have been frequent among those who worked for the government. Possibly it was fairly common in ancient Israel due to the lack of banks.

Banking did not begin until the fifth century BC in Lydia, a country in the southwestern region of present-day Turkey. It did not become common in Palestine until the second century BC. The first reference to a Hebrew minting coins is Simon Maccabeus in the second century BC (Call 1979, 408). This proverb and similar ones seek to instill caution in taking on financial liability for another person.

Affirming: Loving Strife / Inviting Destruction (17:19)

■ **19** The first line of this proverb may be read either as *whoever loves an offense loves strife* (Fox 2009, 633) or **whoever loves a quarrel loves sin.** Certainly one who loves committing an offense likes to get into conflict, for anyone who is harmed by that offense will seek redress. The other reading offers an admonition to one who takes delight in stirring up a conflict, for that conflict is likely to lead *to an offense* or *a transgression* (*pešaʿ*), an act that incurs God's disfavor. This option is favored by the situation described in the second line.

The second line gives an example of doing something that offends people in the community. A wealthy owner builds **a high gate** or a secure entrance to his house, no doubt to keep intruders out. But vandals view the gate as a challenge tempting them to prove that they can break through it. In their attempts to break in, they destroy part of the gate, even a portion of the house. Thus, the owner's efforts to make the dwelling more secure lead to the gate and house being damaged.

Another reading of the second line understands the word for "entrance, door" as a metaphor for "shooting off one's mouth" (Fox 2009, 634). Read that way the proverb appears to say that haughty speech provokes a hostile response, leading to the speaker's destruction. In either case the second line counsels against displaying superiority in a way that goads some scoundrels to aggressively challenge that display.

Affirming: Twisted Mind (17:20)

■ **20** *A person whose thinking is twisted* does not prosper. *Twisted thinking* means thinking contrary to the standards espoused by the teaching of the wise. Morally it refers to perverse or vile thoughts (see its use in Prov 4:24; 6:12-15). Furthermore, a person who thinks this way is prone to speak deceptively. As a result, the person is sure to *fall* into trouble.

Affirming: Parent of a Fool (17:21)

■ **21** (See 10:1; 13:1; 15:20.) Not all children bring joy to their parents. A parent who **has a fool for a child** (*kĕsîl*) experiences **grief**. The parent of **a hardened fool** (*nābāl*), the worst kind of a fool, has **no joy** in such a son or daughter. A child becomes a hardened fool by rejecting instruction and discipline. Parents who have sought to raise a child well need not add guilt to their grief at a child's foolish behavior. They need to realize that their grief and lack of joy are reasonable reactions of the wise. Parents can only pray that not one of their children becomes a fool. Fox (2009, 634) interprets this proverb as designed to urge a child not to bring grief on the parents by taking the path of folly.

Opposing: Demeanor: Cheerful / Despondent (17:22)

■ **22** A cheerful *outlook* [lit. **heart**] is good medicine (*gēhâ*). The meaning of the Hebrew *gēhâ*, however, is in doubt; suggested glosses include "medicine," "body," and "face" (Fox 2009, 635). A cheerful disposition, evidence of a strong psyche, empowers one to deal well with obstacles that occur along life's path. But a **crushed** or ***despondent* spirit dries up the bones** (*gerem*), that is, one's inner energy. Despondency leads to bad health, both physically and mentally.

Advancing: A Bribe / Justice Perverted (17:23)

■ **23** The giving of bribes is a serious offense. In this picture the wicked person, presumably an official, takes a bribe stealthily from a hidden pocket in the giver's garment. Accepting the gift, the wicked person agrees to decide a case or make a judgment in favor of the giver of the bribe. Bribes, being antithetical to justice, are legislated against in the Pentateuch (see Exod 23:8; Deut 16:19), for by definition a bribe promotes injustice: the innocent are placed in jeopardy of severe punishment and the guilty get off free.

Opposing: Setting One's Face on Wisdom / Eyes Looking to the End of the Earth (17:24)

■ **24** The primary object of one's focus determines one's character and destiny. **Wisdom** is present ***before the face of* a discerning person** so that that person reflects and takes wise counsel. But the **eyes *of a fool*** look far off, **to the ends of the earth**. A fool fails to consider things at hand and focuses on things far beyond reach, such as amassing wealth or traveling to a distant land. Since that one's pipe dreams are way out of reach, the fool ends up floundering about, accomplishing nothing. No one accomplishes great things without focusing on an honorable, realistic goal.

Affirming: Wayward Child (17:25)

■ **25 A foolish son brings grief to his father and *vexation* or bitterness to his mother**, referred to as the one **who bore him**. This proverb echoes the one in v 21. However, it places greater emphasis on the grief that a foolish child causes a family in that both the mother and the father are mentioned. (See Prov 10:1*b*.)

Affirming: Punishing an Innocent Person (17:26)

■ **26** (See 18:5.) The first line of the proverb makes a **not good** statement about a governmental practice. ***Fining* the innocent** or ***righteous* [*ṣaddîq*] is not good**. If that is true, **surely to flog honest officials** for their integrity or candid speech **is not right** (Fox 2009, 637).

A possible scenario is that some officials call attention to abuses taking place in a government office. Their action angers a higher official, who does not want to deal with the corruption, leading to having those who reported the infractions flogged. Or honest officials are flogged for refusing to participate in corrupt practices (Waltke 2005, 63). The moral fabric of the government is undercut. The morale of other officials declines sharply, while corrupt government workers are empowered.

Affirming: Restraining Speech / Being Even-tempered (17:27)

■ **27** *A knowledgeable person* realizes the need to *use* words with restraint. In many situations, such as speaking with a grieving person or in responding to a person who has caused another distress, it is crucial to speak with restraint. Similarly, *a person* of understanding maintains a calm disposition, as conveyed by the phrase *cool spirit or mood* (even-tempered). In conflict situations a person with such a disposition has a way of speaking calmly, thereby soothing those who are troubled.

Affirming: Keeping Silent (17:28)

■ **28** The wisdom school prizes speaking few words so highly that **even fools are thought wise** who **keep silent**. Indeed, if they keep **their** *lips closed*, they will be deemed to be **discerning** (*nābôn*). This is one of the few proverbs that holds out any hope for a fool to act with understanding.

I. Proverbs 18:1-24

OVERVIEW

The distribution of the structures of the proverbs in this chapter are as follows: nine advancing (vv 1, 5, 8, 10, 13, 16, 17, 21, 22), eight affirming (vv 2, 3, 6, 7, 15, 18, 19, 20), and four opposing (vv 12, 14, 23, 24). In addition, three are based on an analogy (vv 4, 9, 11). In the opposing sayings the antithesis of the righteous and the wicked falls to the background as other antitheses emerge: proud and abased (v 12), opponents at law (v 17), and the rich and the poor (v 23; Plöger 1984, 210).

Yahweh appears in two proverbs. Yahweh's name provides security for the righteous (v 10), and his favor is shown in providing a young man with a wife (v 22). Three themes are prominent: speech (ten proverbs; vv 2, 4, 6, 7, 8, 13, 17, 20, 21, 23), fool (four proverbs; vv 2, 6, 7, 13), and disputes (four proverbs; vv 5, 17, 18, 19). The last three proverbs in the chapter describe different kinds of relationships: wife-husband, poor-rich, and unreliable friend-true friend (vv 22-24).

The use of words is given prominence, for words play a critical role in human relations. In fact, the tongue has the power of death and life (v 21); a fool's speech is destructive to a community (vv 2, 13). Moreover, speech reveals one's station in life, whether one is rich or poor, wise or foolish. Since words flow from the heart, they reveal the deepest thoughts of a person (v 4); thus, it is important to listen carefully to what a person says.

IN THE TEXT

Advancing: A Misfit / Defying Sound Judgment (18:1)

■ **1** A person who is estranged (*niprād*; occurring only here in the OT) from the community is *a misfit*, which the NIV renders **an unfriendly person**, but the thrust of the Hebrew root, however, is "to detach." Being a loner and seeking to fulfill personal desires, the person **starts quarrels**, defying **all sound judgment** (*tûšiyyâ*), that is, clear, incisive thinking in practical matters. The precise meaning of this proverb is hindered by the presence of two rare words, **unfriendly person** or *misfit* (*niprād*) and **starts quarrels** (*yitgalla'*).

Affirming: Fool Despises Understanding / Freely Expresses Opinions (18:2)

■ **2** The general truth presented in the first line (**fools find no pleasure in understanding**) is followed by a characteristic trait of fools in the second line (**but delight in *disclosing whatever is on their minds***). Since fools take no delight in listening to what others are sharing, they talk on and on about anything, even their deepest feelings and **opinions**. They freely disclose personal thoughts mindless of the impact on their listener. (See 12:16, 23; 13:16.)

Affirming: Disgrace Follows Wickedness (18:3)

■ **3** Both a wicked act and an insult produce harsh consequences. **When a *wicked person* comes** (i.e., enters a conversation or visits a village) **contempt** or *scorn* follows. When an *insult* (*qālôn* "abuse, contempt, insult" [*DCH* 7:255]) is spoken by a wicked person, it produces **reproach** or *disgrace*, a heavy consequence in an honor-based society. To avoid such a consequence scorners and mockers are to be driven out of a community (22:10). (See 11:2.)

Analogy: Speech like Deep Waters (18:4)

■ **4** Speech that flows from deep within a person's mind may be compared to **deep waters. The fountain of wisdom is a rushing stream**, a continual source of refreshing insight. In a dry land such as Israel a **stream** is greatly prized for its cool water. Similarly, refreshing ideas gush forth from the fountain of wisdom. Thus, people enjoy listening to the wise.

Some writers speak of words flowing onto the paper as they write under inspiration. These words often disclose fascinating insights. From another angle the reality that words disclose a person's deepest thinking plays a critical role in the practice of psychology and psychiatry. In order to help troubled clients, these professionals motivate them to talk extensively so that they express their deep thoughts, attitudes, and prejudices, those inward thoughts that direct a person's feelings and actions. (See Luke 6:45.)

Advancing: Partiality / Perverted Justice (18:5)

■ **5** Those who hear cases are advised **not . . . to be partial to the wicked** or *guilty* (*rāšā'*). Any show of lenience to evildoers, perhaps under fear of reprisal, is **not good**, that is, a serious breach of wisdom (Clifford 1999, 170). It is also not good when **the innocent** [*ṣaddîq*] *are deprived* of justice. In legal texts *ṣaddîq* and *rāšā'* convey *innocent* and *guilty* more than *righteous* and *wicked* (Fox 2009, 658). Any perversion of justice weakens a community's fabric. (See Prov 17:15, 26; also 16:10; 17:23; 19:28.)

Affirming: Consequence of a Fool's Speech (18:6-7)

■ **6-7** The first words of each line, standing in a chiastic relationship, lips:*mouth*::*mouth*:lips, hold these two proverbs together. The careless speaking of fools leads to **strife**, even blows. It is possible to understand the text to mean that fools challenge others to a fight or that their words are so offensive as to incite the hearers to strike them. Consequently, their careless *speaking* is **their undoing**.

This outcome is captured by the vivid metaphor in the next line: **their lips** function as **a snare to their very lives**. Since fools do not reflect on the words that flow out of their mouths, they are unaware that they are setting **a snare** that will capture them.

Advancing: Speech = 26:22 (18:8)

■ **8** People greatly enjoy listening to stories about other people and about events taking place in the community, as evidenced by the numerous daily news programs on TV. A salacious story is very sweet, especially if it is about a prominent person. This human trait attests this proverb: **the words of a gossip** [*nirgān*] **are like choice morsels**, that is, like pieces of candy in Western society. *Nirgān* stands for ***to murmur, complain*** (Deut 1:27; Ps 106:25), suggesting that the content of the whispering is negative.

Whatever is heard as gossip sticks in people's memories and is likely to produce prejudicial thoughts against those talked about. Such thoughts may prompt a person to act in a harmful way toward another regardless of the accuracy of the idle chatter. No wonder gossip is viewed so negatively in the wisdom tradition. (See 11:13; 17:4.)

Analogy: Destroyer—One Who Is Slack at Work (18:9)

■ **9** Shoddy work, that is, work done carelessly, is neither reliable nor aesthetically pleasing. That which has been built poorly may hold a hidden danger. If a worker builds a stairway with weak spots, a person may fall through a step, incurring serious injury. No wonder a careless worker is identified as *a* **brother to one who destroys**, that is, a vandal, a person who loves to tear down or wreck rather than build.

Advancing: Yahweh's Name / Place of Hiding (18:10)

■ **10** The topic of security connects the next two proverbs. Every person or society desires security, especially from wild animals, roaming vandals, and armies, as attested by the huge walls that surrounded ancient towns. **A fortified tower** of a walled city serves as a superb analogy for the secure refuge **Yahweh's** name provides **the righteous**. They **run to it and are safe**. That is why the psalmist prays, "Save me, O God, by your name" (Ps 54:1*a*). In the NT the name of Jesus provides believers security and confidence (e.g., John 14:13-14; 15:16; 16:23-26). Jesus exhorts his followers to live and work under the authority of his name.

Analogy: Protection Offered by Wealth Is like a Fortified City (Line *a* = 10:15*a*) (18:11)

■ **11** **The rich** believe that their **wealth** protects them just as **a *high*** **wall** secures a well-fortified city. Imagining that the **wall** is **too high to scale**, they feel very secure. The relationship of this saying to the preceding one teaches that protection offered by wealth is not nearly as secure as that provided by Yahweh's name (Clifford 1999, 171). This point is underscored by the position of the words *in his imagination* in the place where a parallel to *a rich person* is expected (Fox 2009, 642).

Opposing: Pride / Humility (Line *a* = 16:18*a* and line *b* = 15:33*b*) (18:12)

■ **12** It often happens that things turn out very differently from what one anticipates. For example, a proud person is very confident of continued success but suddenly is surprised by misfortune or experiences *a* **downfall** (*šeber*) that leaves the person in ruins. The reference is to a devastating ruin since the term *šeber* is used for the collapse of Jerusalem before the Babylonian army (Jer 4:20; 6:1; Lam 3:47-48). Conversely, **humility**, often produced by a misfortune or a failure, **comes before honor**.

This saying offers the faithful who have faced a major loss hope for a brighter future as God directs the destinies of humans to correspond to their character. On the other side, this proverb serves as a warning to the arrogant: do not boast about tomorrow.

Advancing: Folly (18:13)

■ **13** **Listening** is hard. It is a skill that must be developed in order to engage in genuine dialogue. Dialogue, in turn, advances wisdom. As one grows older, it is important to continue to practice the discipline of listening. Some adults, however, become so impolite that they start to give *an answer* before another has finished speaking, showing that they are not paying close attention to the speaker. Such behavior is classified as **folly** and **shame** or *an insult*.

Opposing: Enduring Spirit / Broken Spirit (18:14)

■ **14** A person who has a vibrant **spirit** faces illness with energy, courage, and perseverance. These traits quicken one's healing. Little can be done for a person with **a crushed spirit**, for that person lacks the inner strength to fight illness or adversity. This saying calls attention to the reality that an emotional illness may be even more debilitating than a physical illness. In Hebraic thought the body and the spirit function as a unit, not as separate entities.

Affirming: Acquiring Knowledge (Line *a* = 15:14*a*) (18:15)

■ **15** The **heart** or *mind* and **the ears** are the critical organs for learning. The *mind* **of the discerning** is diligent *in acquiring* knowledge (see Prov 2:2). Information and ideas enter the mind through the ears. Thus, **the ears of the wise seek it** [knowledge] **out**. In Mesopotamian thought the ear played a central role in learning.

Advancing: A Gift / Audience before the Great (18:16)

■ **16** This saying addresses the practice of giving gifts rather than making bribes. A gift differs from a bribe in that a gift does not put the recipient under a specific obligation. But accepting a bribe obligates the recipient to do a particular favor for the giver or to influence a person in authority to make decisions in favor of the giver. Whenever a gift/bribe is given to a judge to gain a favorable ruling, justice is thwarted.

On the other hand, in many cultures gift-giving plays a significant role in the way people, especially the upper class, interact. Often the gift-giver is hopeful of maintaining a warm relationship with the recipient. There are occasions in which an appropriate gift **opens _access_** to various activities and institutions in a society, including access to nobility. (See 19:6.)

In daily life the line between a gift and a bribe becomes very thin. This saying stands on the side of a gift. Some people know how to use gifts in order to cut through the red tape of government so that they can get things done (see 21:14). In that light this proverb offers insight into how to get things done in a complex bureaucratic system. While the wise certainly do not condone giving bribes, they do recognize that sometimes a gift opens doors for the benefit of a shrewd person.

Advancing: Cross-Examination in a Trial (18:17)

■ **17** The general tendency of those who hear a lawsuit is to be persuaded by the presentation of **the first** party. The defense's rebuttal brings out deficiencies in the plaintiff's line of argument, thereby casting doubt on the hearers as to the plaintiff's position. This proverb especially serves as guidance to the citizens of towns in ancient Israel who listened to cases tried or debated at the city gate. They should not come to a decision before they have heard the positions of both parties along with any cross-examination.

Affirming: Lots for Settling Disputes / For Separating Opponents (18:18)

■ **18** The next two proverbs are connected by the key term **disputes** (_midyānîm_). When confronted by having to make a difficult decision on a disputed issue among members of the community, the ancients often turned to casting lots to resolve the dispute, for they believed that God revealed the right choice through the lots.

There are a few examples of the use of lots in Israel's history. The Israelites cast lots in the selection of their first king, Saul (1 Sam 10:17-24). Later when God did not answer Saul's inquiry as to whether or not he would have success in battling the Philistines, he turned to casting lots to discover the source of the problem among the Israelite troops (1 Sam 14:36-45). Jonathan, Saul's son, was chosen as the guilty person. Also lots were cast in assigning the tribes' allotment in the promised land (Josh 14:1-2). At the return from Babylonian exile lots were cast to select those who could settle in Jerusalem

(Neh 11:1). However, there is no support for the view that lots were ever used for making judicial decisions (Murphy 1998, 137).

Affirming: Offended Brother / Quarreling (18:19)

■ **19** Both lines employ an analogy for something that will virtually never give way: **a fortified city** and **the barred gates of a *fortress*. A brother** or ***ally* wronged** is likened to **a fortified city.** It is virtually impossible to restore relationship with that person.

Similarly, **disputes** that produce hatred and often injuries make the parties as unyielding as **the barred gates of a *fortress*.** Reconciliation between the parties is virtually impossible. This proverb appears to warn the closest of friends to avoid dealing with a dispute in a way that offends the identity or integrity of any of the parties. Nevertheless, this explanation is tentative since the Hebrew text has many obscure phrases.

Affirming: Satisfying Speech (18:20)

■ **20** The next two proverbs are connected by the word **fruit** (*pĕrî*) plus three facial terms for speech: **mouth** (*pî*), **lips** (*sĕpātayim*), and **tongue** (*lāšôn*). The mouth chews food that ***fills*** or ***satisfies*** [*śāba'*] **the stomach,** providing a feeling of contentment. Similarly, speaking well, referenced by **the fruit of *the* mouth** and ***the produce of the lips*,** creates a sense of contentment in the speaker. That is, a person is able to feel as **satisfied** (*śāba'*) from speaking well as from eating a hearty meal. Truly, speech plays a critical role in a person's sense of well-being. (See Prov 15:23.)

Advancing: Power of Speech / Enjoying Its Fruits (18:21)

■ **21** Speech is so powerful that it can be said that **life and death** are in **the power** of the tongue. Words encourage and inspire people to live uprightly and do great things. At other times speech disheartens people, propelling them to act destructively, harming themselves and leading to an early death. Therefore, **those who love** the power of the tongue, that is, recognize its power, need to learn ways of speaking that help people and promote wisdom. In doing so it may be said that ***they* eat *the* fruit** of the tongue.

Advancing: Finding a Wife / Yahweh's Favor (Line *b* = 8:35*b*; 12:2*a*) (18:22)

■ **22** Finding a wife, described as **good** and as ***receiving* favor from Yahweh,** leads to building a vibrant family. Yahweh blesses the marriage of those who fear him, for he desires strong marriages in which couples work together to raise healthy children who seek wisdom. Given that some marriages are filled with difficulties (21:9, 19; 30:20), this proverb encourages a man to realize his fortune in having a supportive wife and to offer Yahweh praise for having provided her.

There is a strong tendency to add a positive adjective like "good" before **wife** (so LXX). But this proverb reiterates God's evaluation of man's living alone in the garden of Eden—"it is not good for . . . man to be alone" (Gen 2:18)—

without making a judgment on the wife's character. While God promotes marriage, couples need his providential guidance to form a compatible union.

This saying is particularly apropos today given the social complexities in a technological, postmodern world that make establishing solid marriages very difficult. This proverb brings out the value of the synergistic working together of God and a family in finding mates for their sons to form healthy marriages within the cultural conventions of the community. (See Prov 19:14.)

Opposing: Speech: Poor / Rich (18:23)

■ 23 The character of a poor person's speech is quite different from that of a rich person. A poor person, feeling subservient, addresses others politely, often making **entreaties** for mercy. But *a* rich **person**, feeling secure, **answers forcefully**, even **harshly**, thereby intimidating people. This proverb may be viewed as an ethical critique of the rich, encouraging them to abstain from using harsh words in an effort to dominate the poor (Fox 2009, 646).

Opposing: Surface Friends / Loyal Friend (18:24)

■ 24 Every person needs a genuine friend for sharing the joys of life and for facing the numerous challenges that arise. Most people have several casual friends for socializing, that is, those who act friendly, especially at a gathering place or a party. This mode of social interaction is prevalent in current society. It is common to assume that such casual acquaintances are really friends, but in a crisis none of these acquaintances are to be found (see Sir 6:9).

By contrast, a true friend plays a critical role in one's life. This kind of friend . . . sticks closer than a brother, offering help no matter how difficult the problem or the hour of the day. A genuine friend rejoices at one's success; no matter how exceptional the acclaim. There is no jealousy between solid friends. (See Prov 17:17.)

The Meaning of the Verb *Hitrō'ēa'*

The infinitive *lĕhitrō'ēa'*, which occurs in the first line, may be explained from various roots. The two most commonly proposed are *r''* "break," "shatter," "ruin," or a by-form of *r'h II*, **be a friend, socialize with**. The latter fits the context well (Fox 2009, 647; Murphy 1998, 134). If the first option is followed, the line says that **one who has unreliable friends soon comes to ruin**; none of his casual friends comes to help him deal with a threatening situation. The second option yields **there are friends for socializing** (Fox 2009, 646-47). This sense is accepted, for it offers an excellent opposing term to the true friend in the second line.

J. Proverbs 19:1-29

OVERVIEW

Most of the proverbs in this chapter are structured as advancing (thirteen; vv 3, 11, 14, 17, 18, 19, 20, 21, 22, 23, 24, 26, 27) or affirming (nine; vv

5, 6, 7, 8, 9, 13, 15, 28, 29); four are opposing (vv 4, 12, 16, 25). There are two better-than (vv 1, 22*b*), one "not good" saying (v 2), and one structured as "how much worse" (v 10).

Three sayings are formulated as imperatives (vv 18, 20, 27; Plöger 1984, 219). In this collection several words for parts of the body are used: face (v 6*a* HB), lips (v 1*b*), mouth (vv 24*b*, 28*b*), nose (v 11*a* HB), hand (v 24*a*), feet (v 2*b*), back (v 29*b*), and heart (vv 3*b*, 8*a* HB, 21*a*).

Four sayings reference Yahweh (vv 3, 14, 17, 21), and one mentions the fear of Yahweh (v 23). An amazing saying holds that those who aid the poor lend to Yahweh (v 17*a*). The king is the topic of one proverb (v 12). Other topics include the family (four proverbs; vv 13, 18, 26, 27), the poor and/or the rich (seven proverbs; vv 1*a*, 4, 6*b*, 7, 14*a*, 17, 22*b*). The value of wisdom is presented in three proverbs (vv 8, 11, 20) and the importance of justice in three proverbs (vv 5, 28, 29). Laziness is disparaged in two proverbs (vv 15, 24).

IN THE TEXT

Better-than: A Poor Person with Integrity than a Fool with Perverse Speech (19:1)

■ **1** Terms dealing with one's movement (*hālak* [**walk** (v 1*a*)], *'āṣ běraglayim* ["hasty feet" (v 2*b*)], and *derek* [HB; ***way*** (v 3*a*)]) connect the first three proverbs.

A person's character has far greater value than one's portfolio. ***A poor person*** who lives ***in integrity*** is **better** than one who ***twists*** words and is **a fool**. This saying catches our attention, for many proverbs speak of wealth as attending wisdom (e.g., 8:21). But such is not always the case, as is evident in the praise of the sterling character of a poor person, that is, one who fears Yahweh and speaks the truth, in this saying. In God's economy this kind of person has far greater worth than a person who uses twisted speech to gain an advantage over others. (See 10:7; 11:8; 28:1.)

Not Good: Lack of Knowledge / Haste (19:2)

■ **2** In contrast to the preceding proverb stands this **not good** saying. **Desire without knowledge is not good.** In yielding to a desire without considering the consequences, a person is unprepared to deal with troublesome obstacles. It is also ***not good to move in haste and*** **miss the way** of uprightness. A person who is inclined to make choices quickly without reflecting on the consequences often discovers that an ill-advised choice has been made. Correcting such a choice, if possible, requires much time and effort. This proverb is heard in the English saying, "Haste makes waste."

Advancing: Folly Leads to Ruin / Angry at Yahweh (19:3)

■ **3** A person's . . . folly ***perverts*** or ***subverts*** one's way, that is, one's life course. When a person acts perversely and suffers consequences that greatly alter one's

203

lifestyle so much so that the person feels like it is in ruins, that person's ***thoughts rage*** [*zāʿap*] ***against Yahweh***. Such fury is intense, for *zāʿap* is used to describe the raging of the sea (Jonah 1:15) and the roar of a lion (Prov 19:12).

It is very human to avoid ownership of a wrong decision by casting blame on another, particularly God. After disobeying God in the garden of Eden, the man blamed God for giving him the woman and the woman blamed the serpent (Gen 3:12-13). Humans are prone to avoid taking responsibility for the consequences of a stupid action or wrongdoing (see Fox 2009, 649). To overcome this ingrained tendency they must take responsibility for their errors and work to overcome hardships. (See Sir 15:11-20.)

Opposing: Wealth Attracts Friends / A Poor Person Loses Friends (19:4)

■ **4** Humans respond more warmly to the wealthy than to the poor. Wealth is a powerful magnet. It attracts numerous friends, especially those who wish to participate in the generosity of a wealthy person. But poverty separates one from **friends**. Unable to afford the places they frequent, a poor person is ostracized by former friends. This saying encourages the wise to evaluate how they treat friends, especially in regard to their wealth or lack of it.

Affirming: Liars Do Not Escape Punishment (= 19:9) (19:5)

■ **5** A **false witness**, described as someone ***who breathes*** out lies, seeks either to benefit himself or herself or to protect another who has done wrong. Such testimony, though, undercuts the words of a reliable witness and harms an innocent defendant, thereby perverting justice and disrupting community solidarity. Such a witness, expecting to be believed because of a confident posture, **will not go free** or ***unpunished*** in God's providence. This proverb is repeated in Prov 19:9, except that in place of **will not go free** stands "will perish."

Affirming: Currying Favor / Being Friends of the Generous (19:6)

■ **6** Many petitioners ***entreat*** the **favor** or ***face*** of ***a noble***, for a person in power is a resource for helping with the problems the petitioners are facing. Another type of person who attracts numerous friends is ***a giver of gifts***. This proverb instructs students about the way people relate to those in office or to the wealthy as guidance for what to expect when they become officials or wealthy. Standing in the vicinity of the sayings in vv 4 and 7, it also alerts students that they are unlikely to receive help in difficult situations by making such petitions.

Affirming: Poor Shunned (19:7)

■ **7** In the Hebrew this proverb has three lines, though the NIV arranges it into four lines. The first two lines describe **the poor** as ***hated*** and thus **shunned by . . . relatives** and **friends**. The clan perceives that one who is poor is not only nonproductive but that member's situation draws from the clan's income without adding to it. Thus, that person is a source of distress and embarrassment. The clan responds by shunning that person. This saying shows that there are people who become friendless as a result of their station in life. It tempers the affirmation found in Prov 17:17 and 18:24 (see Fox 2009, 651).

The third line is obscure. It literally reads *one pursuing words, not they*. The brevity of the line indicates that some words from the original manuscript have been lost. In addition, the present wording does not connect with the preceding lines. The NIV reconstructs the Hebrew to read: **though the poor pursue them with pleading, they are nowhere to be found.** Another possible reading is offered by Murphy (1998, 140), "Whoever pursues words, they are not (fruitful?)." No reconstruction has won solid support.

Affirming: Get Wisdom / Prosper (19:8)

■ **8** A person who *acquires understanding* loves *himself*. Judicious self-love is important to the ethics espoused in the OT. It is heard in the command to love one's neighbor as oneself (Lev 19:18, 34). A person without a sound sense of self-worth built on a realization of being made in the image of God fails to respect and honor others. Self-love motivates a person to develop one's mind by pursing wisdom. **One who *guards* or cherishes understanding**, through diligent study and speaking astutely, *finds good*, that is, **prospers** or experiences good fortune. To be successful a person needs a sound amount of self-love and a willingness to guard what is understood.

Affirming: Liars Do Not Escape Punishment (= 19:5) (19:9)

■ **9** (→ 19:5.)

Not Fitting—How Much Worse: Fool Living in Luxury / Slave as a Ruler (19:10)

■ **10** The argument here is from the lesser (first line) to the greater (second line). If the first situation is not fitting, the second situation is worse. The ancients had a strong sense that there is a given social order. Any inversion of that order was considered chaotic, an expression of divine judgment.

Nevertheless, peoples like the Egyptians and the Israelites experienced the breakdown of the social order at various times during their long histories. Usually the breakdown was caused by a major crisis, such as a famine or the reign of an incompetent ruler. The Admonitions of Ipuwer is one of several Egyptian texts that lament times of social upheaval. These kinds of laments are also heard in biblical texts (e.g., Job 12:14-25; Eccl 10:5-7; Isa 24:1-3).

This proverb refers to a time of severe upheaval, a time when **a fool *lives* in luxury** and **a slave *rules*** over princes (compare 30:21-22). During a distressful time people despair, being overwhelmed with fear. The lament is heard in the words **it is not fitting.**

Advancing: Patience / Overlooking an Offense (19:11)

■ **11** Two solid traits of a person who has *keen perception* (*śēkel*) are **patience** or *slowness to anger* and *overlooking* an offense, that is, *being forgiving*. It is *honorable* for a sensible person to overlook an offense. Of course, the nature of the offense and the character of the offender must be considered as well as the likelihood that the offender will not persist in doing such offensive behavior. In other words, a sensible person wants to keep from driving a person who has acted offensively into further wrongdoing. It is critical to discern which situations are best handled by overlooking offensive behavior. Appropriately taking this approach brings a person **glory**.

Opposing: King's Rage / King's Favor (Line *a* = 20:2*a*; line *b* is similar to 16:15*b*) (19:12)

■ **12** In a monarchy the king both inspires fear and offers encouragement. **A king's rage** may be so fierce that it is **like the roar of a lion**. The threat of having to face his anger enables a king to maintain control of the people. Anyone the king becomes greatly irritated at faces imminent danger, for the king has absolute power over life and death.

Conversely, the king's **favor** is likened to **dew** falling gently **on the grass**. In Israel, dew is essential for vines and olive trees to flourish in the hill country during the rainless days of the hot summer. Just like dew the king's **favor** nourishes his subjects, motivating them to high achievements. (See Deut 33:28. On the king's wrath see Prov 16:14; 20:2; 24:21-22; Eccl 8:2-4; 10:4; on the king's favor see Prov 16:15.)

Affirming: Foolish Child / Quarrelsome Wife (19:13)

■ **13** A *father* rejoices when his children desire to learn and when his wife provides joyful companionship. However, if a **child** turns out to be *a fool* (*kĕsîl*), it is such a shameful matter that it is classified as **a father's ruin**. That child's behavior heaps disgrace on the household and threatens its stability.

A father also finds very irritating **a wife** who is *contentious* **like the constant dripping of a leaky roof**. The continually repeating sound of a dull thud may make a person so tense that it leads to an outburst of erratic behavior. (For line *a* see 10:1; 17:21, 25; for line *b* see 21:9, 19; 25:24.)

Advancing: An Inheritance / A Prudent Wife (19:14)

■ **14** This proverb connects well with the preceding one by setting out the basis for a strong family. Such a family has sufficient resources, *a house* and **wealth**, provided by *an inheritance*. The son(s) are the recipients of the hard labor of their father and grandfather. Just as important is the son's marriage to **a prudent wife** (see 12:4). Although his parents diligently seek an outstanding wife for him, they are not always sufficiently perceptive to make a wise choice. Thus, they need *Yahweh's* guidance in making that selection.

This saying encourages a youth to honor his parents and to earnestly seek God's leading in the selection of a wife in order to have a solid basis for building his own household.

Affirming: Laziness / A Shiftless Person (19:15)

■ **15** **Laziness brings on deep sleep** (*tardēmâ*), a term for very heavy sleep. Such sleep is not refreshing (Murphy 1998, 184). The picture is that of a lazy person sitting by, watching the work that needs to be done while drifting off to sleep. As a result this kind of person never accomplishes anything. Similarly, **the shiftless** or **slack** (*rěmiyyâ*) **go hungry** due to their failure to stick at a task long enough to gather sufficient food. Clearly, sloth is one of the seven deadly sins.

Opposing: Keeping the Commandments / Despising One's Ways (19:16)

■ **16** By *keeping the* **commandments** a person **keeps** *his own self.* The term *commandment*, being singular in the Hebrew, stands for the instructions of the wise that offer guidance in maintaining a sound relationship with God, with members of the community, and with one's family. That the singular term may have this force is evident from this use in Deuteronomy for the whole Law (e.g., 6:1). But *those who despise* or *show* **contempt for their ways,** that is, their own lifestyles, have little regard for their physical and spiritual health. As a result, they **will die** prematurely.

Advancing: Being Gracious to the Poor / Rewarded by Yahweh (19:17)

■ **17** A person who is **kind to the poor** by giving them aid or a loan, possibly to purchase seed, is actually *making a loan to Yahweh* (see Deut 15:1-11). Since a poor person bears the image of God, the way one treats such a person is the way one relates to God. Yahweh will **reward** a generous person in ways that exceed his generosity. Although the ways are left undefined, this saying encourages generous persons that they will not suffer loss by acting generously out of devotion to God. (See Prov 14:21, 31; 21:13, 26*b*; 22:9.)

Advancing: Discipline a Child Because There Is Hope / Do Not Be a Participant in a Child's Death (19:18)

■ **18** A parent is earnestly exhorted to **discipline** *a child,* because **there is hope** that the child will learn and thus be kept from taking the path that leads to destruction. That is, a parent must be vigilant in discerning when a child needs discipline and then must be diligent in carrying out the discipline in an insightful way, judiciously and compassionately, so that the child will correct wrongful behavior before that behavior becomes deeply ingrained in the child.

This exhortation is underscored by the motive clause **do not be a willing party to** *the child's* **death.** That is, if a parent fails to seek to correct a child's bad behavior, that child will pursue a course that leads to a premature death. An undisciplined child is likely to take up a destructive way of living. Fox (2009, 656) boldly says that "failure [of a parent] as a moral teacher is tantamount to negligent homicide and incurs moral guilt." (See 13:24; 23:24; Deut 21:18-21.)

Advancing: Wrathful Person / Needs Frequent Rescue (19:19)

■ **19** The effort to help change the disposition of **a hot-tempered person** is very challenging. To have success in changing such a person it is important for the person to accept responsibility for bad behavior. That includes having that hothead **pay the penalty** for all damages. Otherwise the helper **will have to** *come to rescue* such a person **again** *and again*, for such a person is prone to become enraged at other times, causing damages to property or even harming a person.

Since this saying stands after the one on being diligent in disciplining a child, it adds the note that a parent needs to be especially diligent in seeking to correct a child who has a volatile temper before the child becomes incorrigible (see Fox 2009, 657).

Advancing: Receive Counsel / Become Wise (19:20)

■ **20** A youth is exhorted *to* **listen** carefully **to advice** and *to* **accept discipline** or *instruction* in order to *become* **wise** over time. A youth needs to realize that learning is a long process, requiring both patience and persistence.

Advancing: Human Thoughts / The Counsel of Yahweh (19:21)

■ **21** A human's planning is subject to *Yahweh's* **purpose**. A person's mind constantly considers ideas and makes plans, such as ways to advance one's standing, increase wealth, or build something. Aware that anything undertaken must overcome obstacles, one's mind ponders ways to address all sorts of contingencies that may be faced in doing a variety of projects. But no human is able to anticipate every problem or setback. One who fears Yahweh rejoices in planning, for he has confidence that it is *Yahweh's* **purpose that** *will be established*. As stated in Prov 16:1, humans are responsible to think and plan and then to trust Yahweh to bring about support for carrying out the plan or adapting the plan to achieve greater outcome.

Advancing: Loyalty Desired / Better-than: Being Poor than a Liar (19:22)

■ **22** The theme of fidelity unites these two lines. Above all humans desire *loyal* love (*ḥesed*; **unfailing love**). A loyal person sticks with a friend through all kinds of situations.

Although the poor are despised, this proverb teaches that there are things far worse than *being* poor. Truly it is **better to be poor than a liar**. A poor person who lives virtuously may be trusted, but a liar can never be trusted. Often a liar comes to believe the lies he tells; over time that one can no longer tell truth from error. A liar will say anything to promote his own advantage no matter how much it harms another. By contrast, a poor person often proves to be dependable, displaying loyalty and love.

Another Reading of Line *a* of Prov 19:22

The NIV margin offers an alternative reading of the first line: **greed is a person's shame**. The alternative reading arises from the fact that some Hebrew words carry opposing meanings somewhat similar to English "awe" and "awful." In the first line two Hebrew words have opposing meanings: *taʾăwâ* (**desire** or **greed** [10:24; 11:23]) and *ḥesed* (**unfailing love** is also used for **shame**, *disgrace* [14:34; Lev 20:17]). The second line leans to favoring the alternative reading. It is better to be **poor** than to use lies to satisfy one's greed. That is, greed may drive a person to act so cunningly and selfishly that the people of the community come to despise the person. But an honest, poor person never has to face the shame that attends being greedy. That reality motivates a poor person never to resort to lying. Thus, a poor person is more likely to maintain personal integrity than a greedy person. This reading provides a more vigorous proverb.

Advancing: Fear of Yahweh / Contentment and Security (19:23)

■ **23** Fear of *Yahweh* promotes **life**. It enables a person to have an authentic life of virtue or a long life filled with joy. This fear provides contentment that enables a person to *sleep well* and confidence that *he will not be visited by evil* or **trouble**. The principle is that since Yahweh protects those who show him reverence, they may live in confidence.

Advancing: Extreme Laziness (19:24)

■ **24** This picture that ridicules a lazy person is most humorous. When eating, a *lazy person* buries his hand in the dish. Amazingly, he is so lethargic that he fails to **bring** his hand **to his mouth**. Usually hunger is the basic motivator that drives a person to work, but hunger fails to motivate the **sluggard** to do even the simplest task of eating from a bowl. The saying is applicable to anyone who begins a project but lacks the determination to bring it to completion (Whybray 1972, 111). (See Prov 26:15.)

Opposing: Mocker / An Understanding Person (19:25)

■ **25** Both lines look at the force of the cause and effect in the development of a person's character. According to the first line, when **a mocker** (*lēṣ*) is reproved by *flogging*, *a* simple *person* (*petî*) who observes the administration of that painful discipline gains insight into how to behave more *astutely* or *cunningly* (*ʿāram*; see 1:4a). Although the mocker is too set in his ways to learn from the punishment, an onlooking youth may learn from that person's being held accountable.

According to the second line, when **the discerning** *are reproved*, they heed the rebuke and **gain knowledge**, that is, a better understanding of the proper way to act in a particular situation.

Advancing: Disrespectful Child / Brings Shame (19:26)

■ **26** Sometimes parents have a selfish or incorrigible child. That child's demeanor is not necessarily the fault of the parents. However, when the parents become elderly, such a self-centered child may take over their finances under the guise of caring for them in their old age with the intent of *robbing his* father and *driving his* mother away from the home. That son's or daughter's only concern is to increase their wealth at their parents' expense. It is even possible that the father is killed by this person since there is no mention of the father's leaving the house. By treating the parents so harshly, a child heaps **shame and disgrace** on the family. (See 20:20; 28:24; 30:11.)

Advancing: Cease Listening to Discipline / The Results (19:27)

■ **27** Astonishingly this saying opens with a command for a lad to **stop listening to instruction**, thereby countering the exhortation in v 20*a*. Perhaps this saying is employing deep irony in order to open the eyes of the disgraceful son described in the preceding verse (Plöger 1984, 227). The second line warns a disrespectful child that in ceasing to listen to instruction he will **stray from the words of knowledge**.

A child who strays from sound knowledge becomes engaged in all kinds of corrupt deeds, such as seeking to turn people from worshipping Yahweh (Deut 13:6-11), participating in sexually deviant behavior (Judg 19:22; 20:13; 1 Sam 2:22), rebelling openly against authority (2 Sam 20:1; 2 Chr 13:7), or condemning the innocent through perjury (1 Kgs 21:8-13).

Another solution to the dilemma of the first line is to emend *cease* (*ḥādal*), but none of the suggestions are compelling. Another option, going back to Rashi, is to exchange the two infinitives and read "cease straying, in order to learn" (see NJPS, NRSV; Fox 2009, 661). This change produces a clear but trite saying.

While the ironic interpretation is not overly compelling, the possibility that this line is intentional irony is supported by the use of irony in the description of the sluggard in Prov 19:24.

Affirming: A Corrupt Witness / Words of the Wicked (19:28)

■ **28** The terms *mock* (*lîṣ*) and **justice** (*mišpāṭ*) connect the next two proverbs. In considering these sayings it needs to be remembered that in antiquity cases were usually decided on the testimony of two or three witnesses. There were no expert witnesses and no police force. Therefore, at a hearing or a trial **a corrupt witness mocks . . . justice**. The reason that these witnesses are so hostile to justice is that they **gulp down *iniquity*** (*ʾāwen*). Their deceit motivates them to thwart justice by committing perjury. They relish confounding the judicial system. This proverb alerts the student to the way some people work to destroy social solidarity. (See 4:17; 13:2.)

Affirming: Penalties for Mockers / Beating for Fools (Line *b* = 10:13*b*; 26:3*b*) (19:29)

■ **29** Various **penalties**, such as **beatings for the *back***, are **prepared for mockers** and **fools**, especially those described in the preceding proverb. If such villains make the courts dysfunctional, they must be severely punished lest a community's social fabric becomes completely dysfunctional.

K. Proverbs 20:1-30

OVERVIEW

In this chapter the dominant poetic pattern is advancing, sixteen proverbs (vv 1, 2, 4, 5, 7, 8, 10, 11, 12, 14, 20, 21, 22, 24, 26, 27); six are opposing (vv 3, 6, 13, 17, 19, 25) and six affirming (vv 16, 18, 23, 28, 29, 30). One proverb is structured as a rhetorical question (v 9) and one as an analogy (v 15). Four proverbs are formulated as an imperative (vv 12, 13*b*, 16, 22*b*) and two as a prohibition (vv 13*a*, 22*a*).

Yahweh appears in six proverbs (vv 10, 12, 22, 23, 24, 27). He has ordered human life so that every age has its glory (v 29). Also he is aware of every person's thoughts, for he searches everyone's mind, which is compared to deep waters (v 5). As a result, everyone who trusts Yahweh is confident that he is directing one's life course. This confidence encourages a person during times when the nature of the circumstances one is facing is far from clear (v 24). Those who trust Yahweh are exhorted not to take vengeance and not to rashly dedicate something as holy in an attempt to move him to act (v 25).

A dominant topic is speech (six proverbs; vv 3, 15, 19, 20, 22, 25). Especially condemned are gossiping (v 19), quarreling (v 3), rash vows (v 25), and cursing one's parents (v 20). Other prominent topics include the king (four proverbs; vv 2, 8, 26, 28) and the family (four proverbs; vv 7, 11, 20, 21). The king is supreme and may take the life of any who anger him (v 2). Loyalty and truth make his throne secure (v 28). He winnows out the wicked to ensure the stability of society (vv 8, 26).

In regard to the family righteous parents bring blessings on their children (v 7). Nevertheless, "small children are known by their actions" as to whether they are pure and upright (v 11). Usually it is not good for a youth to receive an inheritance. Since a youth lacks the skills for managing it, the inheritance often does not last long (v 21).

In addition, merchandizing is considered in four proverbs (vv 10, 14, 17, 23), and knowledge is praised in two. God has given humans eyes and ears so that they may gain knowledge (v 12), which is more valuable than gold, gems, or precious stones (v 15).

IN THE TEXT

Advancing: Wine a Mocker / Intoxication Not Wise (20:1)

■ 1 Those who consume too much **wine** or **beer** *are* led astray. **Wine** mocks even the wise by causing them to engage in foolish, outrageous behaviors. Under its influence some people become boisterous. Saying whatever enters their mind, they embarrass others and themselves. **Beer** is pictured as causing some to become rowdy. Those who *err* by drinking excessively are **not wise**. Rather than controlling their thirst, their thirst controls them.

Strong  Drink

The ancient Israelites had very few drinks available beyond water and milk (primarily goat's milk). They did not have tea or coffee. They knew how to make fermented drinks out of grains and fruits. Wine certainly was the most common drink. It is lauded as God's gift for making the heart joyful (Ps 104:15). A potent liquor was made from dates. Since strong beer or liquor has a higher alcohol content, people need to use good judgment when consuming these beverages. The ancients, however, did not engage in distilling.

Advancing: The King's Wrath / A Life-threatening Danger (Line *a* = 19:12*a*) (20:2)

■ **2** Line *a* is identical to Prov 19:12*a* save that (*'êmâ*) **wrath** or **terror** is used in place of "rage" (*zā'ap*). While in the presence of the king, it is crucial not to arouse his **wrath**, which is as terrorizing as **the roar of a lion**, especially since he has absolute power over the lives of his subjects. Thus, anyone who *infuriates* the king places *one's life* in danger.

Opposing: Avoiding Strife / Fools Are Quick to Quarrel (20:3)

■ **3** The wise seek to **avoid** conflict and to bring tensions with others to a speedy resolution. Whenever a wise person faces a situation that may lead to **strife**, possibly even to a contentious lawsuit, he strives to find common ground for ending that tension. Taking this approach is viewed as an act of **honor**. By contrast, **every fool is quick to quarrel**, for fools enjoy causing strife.

Advancing: Lazy: Not Plowing / No Harvest (20:4)

■ **4** In Palestine the soil is plowed in the late fall for the planting of wheat and barley before the coming of the heavy winter rains. In early spring the lighter rains fall, causing the grains to ripen. They are harvested from mid-April into June. *A lazy person*, however, is so negligent that he *does* not plow in *early winter*. In late spring when the grain in the fields of industrious farmers is becoming golden, the sluggard goes out looking for grain in his field but *there is none*. The ironic twist heard in the fool's attitude is filled with humor. Amazingly a fool, even though he has not tilled the soil or planted the seed, is surprised not to see any grain ripening in his field (see 10:5).

Similarly, in postmodern culture many youths expect significant rewards and high recognition even though they have not done the strenuous preparatory work to master a skill or to learn a profession. Their failure to prepare diligently in their formative years leads to low grades in college and low wages. This proverb warns youths that they must work hard at gaining an education or a trade in order to prosper later in life.

Advancing: Depth of Mind / Draw Out Thoughts (20:5)

■ **5** **Purposes** in a person's *mind* are like **deep waters**. Deep thoughts are beyond the complete grasp of even the thinking person. That is, a person is not fully aware of all the ideas going through one's mind at any given moment. Therefore, *a person* of insight or *understanding* probes the mind to discover the depths of one's thoughts. By probing those deep thoughts a person comes to a better understanding of the self. With a better awareness of the self, a person is less likely to suddenly act in a way that is contrary of the values one espouses.

Without this understanding a person may respond to a particular situation by acting out of character; for example, a person might suddenly become very angry and strike another person. Or on the spur of the moment a person may go off with a new acquaintance for a sensuous weekend. Too often virtuous people suddenly act in very sinful ways, ways that are destructive to the trust built up over decades. In order to live wisely at all times, it is essential to know one's deep thoughts.

Opposing: Self-claimed Loyal / Faithful (20:6)

■ **6** The way some people view themselves may be very different from the way they act. One is known as being loyal (*'iš ḥesed*), somewhat like a person being known as "a scholar" in academic circles. This phrase may have been an epithet for loyal government officials. This title gave them status. As a result many liked to describe themselves as "a loyal person." But over time the epithet became so widely used that it became hollow, leading to the ironic question **a faithful person who can find?** This question underscores how highly leaders value those who are loyal.

Advancing: Integrity of Righteous / Children Are Blessed (20:7)

■ **7** The righteous *conduct* themselves *with integrity*, being true to the virtues espoused by wisdom in all situations. Whenever a person of integrity is made aware of a mistake or of having erred, that one takes full responsibility and makes appropriate corrections. Such conduct brings *blessing* or *happiness* (*'ašrēy*; → sidebar "A Beatitude" in overview for 3:13-20) on **their children.** That is, one's integrity brings honor to the family and paves the way for the children to carry on the family's honorable reputation.

Advancing: King as Judge Winnows Evil (20:8)

■ **8** A king *renders judgment* from the **throne** (16:12; 20:28; 25:5; 29:14). This saying affirms the general belief in ancient Israel that the king, being appointed by God, had special insight into justice. **He winnows out all evil with his** penetrating **eyes.** Winnowing, the process of separating the valuable grain from the worthless chaff, is a grand metaphor for the king's ability to separate evildoers from faithful citizens as he promotes justice in the realm. The king's efforts prevent evil from gaining a foothold in the nation.

Rhetorical Questions: Who Is Free from Sin? (20:9)

■ **9** Here are two questions for self-evaluation. **Who can say, "I have kept my heart pure** [*zikkîtî*]; **I am** *clean* [*ṭāhartî*] **and without sin?"** The implied answer is "No one." This question serves to deflate any who think they are fully righ-

20:6-9

teous. A person must discipline the self to assess accurately one's own behavior, especially those who strive the hardest to live a pure, righteous life, for all come short on some issues. Thus, everyone must petition God for mercy.

The person who has been faithful in heeding the law and making the appropriate atoning sacrifice may say, "My sins are forgiven," not **I am *pure* and without sin**. Self-righteousness must be avoided, for it promotes blinding pride.

Advancing: Diverse Weights / Detestable to God (= 20:23) (20:10)

■ **10** The first line is terse: ***a stone and a stone, a basket and a basket*** (lit. "ephah" [*'êpâ*]; see 11:1; 20:23; Deut 25:13-16). ***Stone*** refers to weights used for measuring the weight of silver or bronze used in payment. A ***basket*** is a dry measurement. The repetition of these two terms suggests that a merchant has two sets of weights and dry measures that are slightly different so that he may increase his profits by giving less than the buyer has purchased and charging him more. Amos condemns the practice of a merchant having a heavy shekel and a small basket (8:5). Yahweh **detests** strongly such a practice of cheating. (See Lev 19:35; Deut 25:13-16; Prov 11:1.)

Advancing: A Youth Is Known by His Deeds (20:11)

■ **11** Responsibility for one's behavior begins at an early age, but Scripture never specifies that age. This proverb says that ***youths***, probably around twelve or thirteen, **are known** [i.e., ***recognized***] **by their actions** whether **their conduct *is* pure and upright**.

Another reading is possible since the verb (*yitnakker*) may mean either ***be known, recognized*** or ***disguise, feign***. If the verb has the latter meaning, the proverb says that even a youth can disguise his behavior, making his actions appear pure and upright, when he is actually rebelling against the standards of wisdom (Clifford 1999, 83-84, and Longman 2006, 379-80). In the latter case this proverb alerts parents and teachers to observe youths carefully in order to assess their commitment to behaving uprightly.

Advancing: Hearing and Seeing / Gifts of Yahweh (20:12)

■ **12** Humans are blessed with **ears for *hearing*** and **eyes for *seeing***—two amazing senses designed by ***Yahweh***. These senses orient humans to their environment as well as serving as the avenues for learning. Humans need to praise Yahweh for these wonderful gifts by using them wisely.

Opposing: Love Not Sleep / Stay Awake (20:13)

■ **13** Sleep is important, especially at night. Nevertheless, some need to heed the prohibition **do not love sleep**. Sleeping during the time when a person is to be working leads to ***poverty***. Thus, the supporting exhortation, ***keep your eyes open***. That is, one needs to keep busy while it is light outside. As a result, one **will have *sufficient* food**. Truly the satisfaction that food gives is far greater than that offered by extra sleep. (See 26:14.)

Advancing: Bargaining / Results in Boasting (20:14)

■ **14** Bartering, a playful contest between the buyer and the seller, is very enjoyable. It was the common way of buying and selling in ancient markets and still is in many cultures. The seller desires to make a profit while the buyer seeks a lower price by continually downgrading the item he wants to buy. He keeps pointing out the flaws in that item, saying, *bad, bad*, meaning the price is far too high. After he gets the price lower and makes the purchase, he goes on his way *boasting* about the bargain he just made. This proverb calls attention to the human tendency to say one thing while really believing another.

Analogy: Value of Knowledgeable Speech (20:15)

■ **15** Humans value **gold**, **rubies**, and precious stones highly. Other jewels are more highly treasured because of their rarity. It is likely that the phrase *a valuable ornament* in the second line suggests that a craftsman has increased a gem's worth by putting it in a setting of gold (Fox 2009, 669). Even more valuable than **a rare jewel** are **lips that speak knowledge**. The phrase **lips *of knowledge*** describes the ability of a wise person to express insights about morals and relationships in an effective way (see 10:20; 25:11-12). This ability is so rare that it carries more value than **a rare jewel**.

Affirming: Giving Surety for a Stranger (20:16)

■ **16** Three homonyms from the root *'rb* connect vv 16, 17, and 19. In v 16 the meaning is *put* up security, in v 17 "sweet," and in v 19 *associate with*. This proverb is formulated as a command, exhorting a person, possibly a leader in the community, to **take** an item **in pledge**, even one's **garment**, from a person who **puts up security for a stranger** so that one might get a loan. But by becoming a guarantor for a stranger he puts the family property at risk. Since he has acted so unwisely, someone needs to take from him *a garment* as security.

It needs to be remembered that in antiquity there were no banks. Therefore a borrower was required to leave something of value with the lender to ensure that the loan would be repaid. If the borrower failed to repay the loan, the lender kept the security.

However, if the borrower was **a stranger**, possibly a resident alien, it was much harder for him to get a loan and the security demanded was high. That is why that person needed a guarantor for the loan. In this case an Israelite agreed to serve as the guarantor, but the borrower did not put up any security. This proverb advises that such a failure be corrected. (See 6:1-2; 11:15; 17:18; 22:27.)

The Identity of the Party Receiving the Loan

In this saying the identity of the party receiving the loan is in doubt. In the first line it is **a stranger** (*zār*; masc. sg.), but in the parallel line it is *foreigners* (*nokrîyyām*). Moreover, the oral reading has *nokrîyyâ* (*a foreign woman*). If the latter reading is correct, the guarantor would likely be helping a prostitute—a theme very alien to proverbs given the wisdom school's zeal for honorable sexual relations. The oral reading may have arisen under the influence of the wording in Prov 27:13, which is virtually identical. However, given the gender roles in antiquity, a general proverb about making a loan would address a transaction between men, not between a man and a woman. The identification of the borrowers as foreigners adds support to this view. Given the fact that both the number and the gender of the parallel terms are different, the written text is the preferred reading (see Fox 2009, 670).

Opposing: Fraud / Wretched Consequences (20:17)

■ **17** Many bad deeds hold within them ill consequences. This reality is illustrated here by the experience of one who **gets** food **fraudulently**. At first the scoundrel enjoys the **sweet *taste*** of that food as he relishes his deceptive skill in getting the food (see Job 20:12-16). But his joy is short-lived. Soon his **mouth** feels like it is **full of gravel. Gravel** is a potent metaphor in that it conveys the sense of something that is very gritty and dry, thus making a person choke. As soon as it enters the mouth, one would spit it out. This is a vivid analogy for guilt.

Affirming: Counsel / Guidance (Line *b* = 24:6*a*) (20:18)

■ **18** Detailed **plans** are carefully drawn up by taking counsel. Counsel improves the quality of the plans. This truth serves as the setting for the exhortation: **wage war *by making strategic plans***. Many battles are won by an army that has a shrewd plan for engaging the battle, rather than by a superior force. (See Prov 11:14.)

Opposing: A Gossip Reveals Secrets / Don't Associate with One (Line *a* is similar to 11:13*a*) (20:19)

■ **19** Some people love to talk. But in much talking ***a gossiper*** is prone to disclose secrets and thereby ***betray*** confidence. This tendency serves as the basis for the command ***do not associate closely*** with a person given to much talking, literally ***one who opens his lips***. Such a person never knows when to be silent. Thus, whoever develops an association with such a person faces the danger of having confidential information spread throughout the community. Usually the sharing of such information proves to be not only humiliating but also devastating.

Advancing: Cursing Parents / Consequence (20:20)

■ **20** Scripture places a high value on revering one's parents as seen in the command to "honor your father and your mother" (Exod 20:12). A child of any age who becomes so irate that he **curses** both **father *and* mother** comes under a heavy penalty (see Exod 21:17; Lev 20:9; Deut 27:16; Prov 30:11). Here the penalty is ***the extinguishing*** in **pitch darkness** the curser's **lamp**, that is, his life force and possibly his posterity. The phrase **pitch darkness** is a potent euphemism for death (Fox 2009, 622; Job 18:5*b*, 6; 21:17; Prov 13:9; 24:20; Isa 43:17).

Advancing: An Early Inheritance / Not Blessed in the End (20:21)

■ 21 The sudden receipt of a large sum of money as from **an inheritance** or today winning the lottery does not always bring a blessing. At first the recipient feels fortunate and is overjoyed. But lacking the skills to manage well a large amount of money and thinking that the funds are endless, the recipient spends them freely, often on frivolous things. Soon all the money is gone. **At the end** the recipient is no longer **blessed**.

Textual Variant of Prov 20:21

In place of the consonantal text *měbōḥelet* (**be gained by greed**) (*DCH* 2:136), the oral reading has *měbōḥelet* (**be gained by haste**) with the support of many MSS and versions. This Hebrew word has a wide range of meanings, **dismay, tremble, be in haste, be gained by haste**. Most interpreters prefer the sense **be gained in haste**, the sense it has in Eccl 5:2[1]; 7:9 and Prov 28:23 (Van Pelt and Kaiser 1997, *NIDOTTE* 1:611; *DCH* 2:97-98).

Advancing: Take Not Vengeance / Wait for Yahweh (20:22)

■ 22 When a person strongly desires retaliation for *a* **wrong** suffered, he often swears, **"I'll pay you back."** Even though one is rightfully angry at having incurred wrong, the wise course, being underscored in the Hebrew by being formulated as a prohibition, is not to utter such an oath but to leave the outcome of the matter to Yahweh. The prohibition is reinforced by the command **wait for Yahweh**. The person wronged needs to place one's confidence in God's enabling to overcome any setback from that wrong rather than in one's own ability to exact vengeance. As noted by Fox (2009, 673), the seeking of revenge displays lack of trust in God's justice (Lev 19:18). (See Prov 17:13; 24:28; 25:21.)

Affirming: False Weights = 20:10 (20:23)

■ 23 **Yahweh's detesting** the use of false **scales** and **weights** is reiterated. The first line is made up of phrases from the proverb in v 10. The first two words are from the second line of that proverb and are followed by the first two words of the first line. Here the formula **detestable to Yahweh** is paralleled by *not good*, a litotes meaning **extremely bad**.

Advancing: God's Direction / Human Understanding (20:24)

■ 24 Since **Yahweh directs** a person's steps, it is difficult for any human at any given time to **understand** or *discern* exactly where one is on the path of life. A human finds that trying to discern where one is on that course is like trying to find one's way through a thick forest with few landmarks. But Yahweh, looking down on a person in the forest, is able to see all that surrounds the person and to lead him through the forest to a good destination.

Those with a deep trust in Yahweh have the confidence that the path that they are traveling is divinely directed and that all things they experience work for each one's ultimate good (see Rom 8:28). As people age, Yahweh's leading becomes clearer to those who fear him as they see a pattern develop in their life experiences. This proverb encourages trusting Yahweh especially during times when one's experiences do not make sense. (See Prov 16:1, 3.)

Opposing: Rash Vows / Reflection (20:25)

■ **25** Making *a vow* is a very serious matter. Vows are sometimes made to seal a major decision, such as entering into a marriage or the ministry. However, most vows are uttered in a desperate attempt to move God to deliver one from an ominous situation. In a moment of desperation a person *rashly declares* something *to be holy* (i.e., *dedicated*) to God. After surviving the danger, the person who made the vow removes the dedicated object from ordinary use and devotes it to God, in antiquity depositing it at the temple. Today a person may promise to give a prized possession, like a car or a watch to the church, if God delivers the person from danger.

Later many face a dilemma when they realize the high value of the object dedicated and that giving it to God may cause the family hardship. They then seek a way to get out of paying the vow. But the OT makes no provisions for presenting a substitute. The classic case was Jephthah's vow to offer whatever met him at his house if God enabled him to return from war. He was chagrined when his daughter was the first to run out to meet him (Judg 11:34-39). He found out how a rash vow becomes a heart-wrenching **trap**.

A person who makes a vow may later suffer great mental anguish, but reneging on the vow incurs God's anger. That is why it says in Deut 23:21-23 and Eccl 5:5 that it is better not to vow than to vow and not pay. Both the Law and the wisdom school strongly discouraged rash vows. The detrimental results of making a rash vow is vividly displayed in Saul's swearing that none of his warriors were to eat any food before evening (1 Sam 14:20-46). Jonathan, Saul's son, being unaware of that oath, ate some wild honey. That evening Saul inquired of God as to whether he should purse the Philistines. But God did not answer him.

Saul was aware that God's silence meant that someone had sinned. Using lots he discovered that Jonathan's eating honey had violated his oath. Saul was prepared to have Jonathan put to death, but the army intervened and saved Jonathan. This account shows that the ill consequences of a rash vow can be annulled by entreating God. Clearly, not all vows should be kept. Anyone who wants out of a vow needs to go through a process to gain release from that vow. Today a person may go before a minister or a board of elders and have them entreat God to be released from what was vowed. The leaders of a community of believers have the authority to release a person from a vow's obligation (see Matt 18:18-19; John 20:22-23).

Advancing: King (20:26)

■ **26** In order to maintain peace throughout the land **a wise king winnows out the wicked** (see Prov 20:8). A king recognizes that the wicked spread fear and cause disharmony among the people, thereby undercutting his authority. After finding them, he has them punished in a manner that is compared to rolling a heavy **wheel** over the grain to crush the husk and recover the seed (see Isa 28:27). Thereby he promotes peace throughout the land.

Advancing: Searching a Person's Inner Being (20:27)

■ **27** God breathed into the nostrils of the first human the breath of life (Gen 2:7). **Breath** (*něšāmâ*), the life force that God gives humans, is identified as **Yahweh's** lamp, a lamp that **searches all the chambers of the belly**, the subconscious mind, where one's deep emotions and attitudes lodge. Possibly the lamp is the conscience.

The ancients located a person's deep attitudes in the belly or the viscera, such as the kidneys and the liver. Since these deep feelings strongly influence the way a person thinks and acts, they must be evaluated by a special lamp so that impure motives and attitudes are cleansed in order that a wise person may act nobly in all situations.

Affirming: Loyalty Guards the King / Secure Throne (20:28)

■ **28** **Loyalty** (*ḥesed*) and **truth** (*'emet*) guard **the** king. Also **his throne is made secure** by **loyalty** or **kindness** (*ḥesed*). When a king's reign, today a president's or a prime minister's term in office, is characterized by **kindness**, his subjects support him enthusiastically and are loyal. Having loyal subjects makes his **throne** far more secure than having numerous guards.

Affirming: Strength of Youth / White Hair of the Aged (20:29)

■ **29** God has structured human life as a journey through various stages of development, each stage or season has its particular **glory**. This interpretation takes the **young** and **the aged** as a merism for everyone. **Youth** find **glory** in **their strength**, which enables them to work hard for a long time and to do a variety of spectacular feats. **The aged** receive **honor** in having **silvery white hair** (see 16:31a). They are respected for their sagacious insights into life.

Unfortunately, white hair is no longer a mark of honor in many cultures of the developed world. Too often the aged are viewed as a liability and are thus deprived of the honor God designed for them.

Affirming: Cleaning Power of Wounds (20:30)

■ **30** Throughout life humans develop emotionally and spiritually. Since bad attitudes and improper emotions are lodged in the chambers of the belly, that is, deep in one's psyche, a person changes very slowly. But **blows** and **wounds** or **beatings** remove (*tamrîq*) bad attitudes and evil craving more quickly. The Hebrew *māraq* means **cleanse** or **polish** an object by intense scouring or by rubbing with an abrasive to remove hardened grime. These metaphors bring out that intense efforts are frequently necessary to bring about a major change in a person's disposition.

L. Proverbs 21:1-31

OVERVIEW

In this chapter twelve proverbs are structured as advancing, nine as opposing, and five as affirming. There are also three better-than sayings (vv 3, 9, 19) and one analogy (v 6). Sayings about Yahweh frame this collection. Yahweh, the supreme ruler, directs the king's thinking (v 1) and also "weighs the heart" of every person to assess the character of each (v 2). All need to be mindful, especially earthly rulers, that no counsel can prevail against God (v 30) and that he directs the outcome of the battle (v 31).

Though sacrifice is seldom mentioned in Proverbs, it is spoken of in two proverbs: righteousness is more highly valued by Yahweh than sacrifice (v 3); the sacrifices of the wicked are contemptible (v 27).

There are eight sayings about the wicked (vv 4, 7, 10, 12, 15*b*, 18, 27, 29). Two contrast the wicked with the righteous (vv 18, 26). The dominant themes are wealth and poverty (vv 6, 13, 14, 17, 20, 26), speech (vv 23, 28), pride (vv 4, 24), the wise or wisdom (vv 11, 20, 22), the mocker (vv 11, 24), a contentious woman (vv 9, 19), and justice (v 15).

IN THE TEXT

Advancing: King's Planning / Yahweh's Direction (21:1)

■ **1** In Israel there was a close tie between the king and Yahweh, for Yahweh had made a covenant with David, adopting him as his son (2 Sam 7:7-16; Ps 2:7). Therefore, **Yahweh guides** the king's thinking to favor **all who please him** like a farmer directs water from an **irrigation canal** to the fields that need water. As a result the fields blossom even in an arid land.

Opposing: Ways: Right in a Person's Eyes / Yahweh Tests Them (Line *a* = 16:2*a*) (21:2)

■ **2** By nature humans are quite self-centered. While quick to find fault with others, they think that their own thoughts and ways are honorable and upright. Nevertheless, given limited human perception and imbedded self-assurance, all people, including the righteous, need to have their ways evaluated. This need is illustrated in the current world in regard to industries and restaurants. They are subject to periodic inspections to make certain that they meet health and public safety standards. The number of establishments that have been fined indicates the need for such inspections.

Yahweh tests the minds (*libbôt*) of humans in order to purify their thoughts. This goal is heard in the psalmist's prayer, "Search me, God, and know my heart; test me and know my anxious thoughts. See if there is any offensive way in me, and lead me in the way everlasting" (Ps 139:23-24).

Better-than: Righteousness than Sacrifice (21:3)

■ **3** This is a better-than saying as conveyed by the preposition *from* (*min*) even though the term *better* (*ṭôb*) is not present. A person doing *righteousness* and *justice* is far **more acceptable to Yahweh** than the presenting of sacrifices at the temple. Humans have a tendency to place greater importance on tangible acts of worship than on developing the virtues that lead to right behavior. But God's values are often the inverse of humans'. This proverb echoes Samuel's words to Saul: "to obey is better than sacrifice" (1 Sam 15:22). (See Prov 15:8; 21:27.)

Advancing: Pride (21:4)

■ **4** **Haughty eyes and a proud heart**, described as **the unplowed field of the wicked**, motivate **the wicked** to commit sinful acts. Those who fail to discipline their eyes and heart become blinded by pride. Their eyes lust after pleasure and wealth. Their heart tells them that they are worthy of getting what they long for even if it involves using deception. Pride blinds people to the consequences of pursing their desires unjustly.

Opposing: Diligence Leads to Surplus / Haste Leads to Want (21:5)

■ **5** **Plans** devised by **the diligent lead to** *abundance*. But *acting hastily*, without careful planning, **leads to** *want*. A project undertaken without careful planning usually ends up costing more. Spur-of-the-moment decisions lead to numerous errors, errors lead to waste, increasing the cost and causing delays in its completion. Sometimes work on such a project becomes so fouled up that it is never completed. Both outcomes are underscored in the Hebrew text by the term **surely** standing before *abundance* and *loss*. (See 10:22; 19:2; also 20:21; 23:4; 28:20.)

Analogy: Fleeting Treasures (21:6)

■ **6** In this proverb a particular activity is described in the first line; in the second line two analogies judge that activity. The first line considers the final results of accumulating **a fortune** by **a lying tongue**. If a liar can convince enough people to buy into a scheme by promising them quick wealth, the peddler of the scheme, even though the promises are lies, accumulates wealth quickly at the expense of the investors.

But such a fortune is **a fleeting vapor** (*hebel*). *Hebel* is the word in Ecclesiastes that is often translated "vanity," that which neither lasts nor provides any sense of satisfaction. Even worse, that fortune becomes **a deadly snare** (based on the LXX). That is, those who accumulate wealth by deception will be held accountable and face severe punishment. The ancients assumed that the ill-gotten treasure itself wanted to be avenged and returned to its rightful owner (see Clifford 1999, 189).

Currently in the media there are numerous appeals for people to take a particular course to become wealthy. In most cases it is the person who promotes the scheme who gets rich. Many who buy into such "opportunities" often discover that they have been duped. They have received only a fleeting vapor.

Lying is so common in the financial global markets that Ric Edelman published a book titled *The Lies about Money*, a work that seeks to expose numerous schemes in the financial markets that are designed to get people's money.

Advancing: Destruction by the Wicked / Reason (21:7)

■ **7** Violence (*šōd*), an act of wanton destruction, done by **the wicked** will come back on them with such force that it **will drag them away** (*gārar*). The verb *gārar* occurs in Hab 1:15 to describe the dragging of a fishing net (Fox 2009, 681). Because **they refuse to do what is right,** they face a harsh fate. Their love for violence motivates them to continually devise harsher ways of afflicting people.

Opposing: Crooked Way / Conduct of Innocent (21:8)

■ **8** The wording of the first line is not clear. If the last word (*wāzār*) modifies **way,** it needs to be vocalized *wĕzār* (**and strange**). Presently this solution is the best offered. It may be read as the NJPS: "The way of a man may be tortuous and strange, though his actions are blameless and proper." According to this reading, a person may engage in strange, contorted behaviors. The term rendered "tortuous" (*hăpakpak*) is a reduplicated form, describing something as very crooked or contorted. Nevertheless, this person's actions or behaviors are **blameless.** They are done without malice. There are too many difficulties with the Hebrew of this proverb to place much weight on this rendering.

Better-than: A Rooftop Dwelling than with a Contentious Wife (= 25:24) (21:9)

■ **9** It is **better to live on a corner on the roof**—the roofs of most houses in the ancient Near East were flat, providing extra living space in small houses—than to live in a **house *shared* with a *contentious wife*.** Because of her noisy, irritating behavior, no resident has a restful place to sit. This woman does not have to be identified as a wife or a relative (Murphy 1998, 159). (See 19:13*b*, 19; 27:15.)

Advancing: Wicked Desire Evil / Their Neighbors Do Not Condone (21:10)

■ **10** *The desire* (*nepeš*) of **the wicked** craves **evil** (*ra'*). They only gain a sense of purpose by planning to do something bad. They long for the thrill and adventure that comes from doing harm (1:10-19). When they are engaged in doing evil, they do not extend **mercy,** not even to **their neighbors.** They take advantage of anyone whenever possible.

Affirming: Naive Take Warning / Gaining Knowledge (21:11)

■ **11** The next two proverbs are connected by forms of the Hiph'il verb *hiśkîl* (**gain insight**). This proverb brings out the importance of learning from observing what happens to others.

Making keen observations enhances one's perception of life, increasing wisdom. **When a mocker is punished, *the naive* take notice.** Observing the harsh consequences of treating people scornfully or with contempt, youths resolve to treat people with respect and kindly. When the **naive pay** attention to the ways of **the wise they *gain* knowledge**. That is, they become more skilled in ways to apply wise precepts in interacting with others. Learning is a long process that the wise recognize must never stop.

Advancing: Righteous Observe House of Wicked / Wicked Come to Ruin (21:12)

■ **12** Interpretation of this proverb is hindered by the precise sense of the subject *righteous person* and the unclear parallel between **the house of the wicked** and **the wicked**. *A righteous person* observes perceptively the character of **the *household*** of the wicked. That one's observations provide insight into the problems that attend wicked behavior, motivating one never to act like the wicked.

One way of reading the second line is that this person notices that the wicked eventually ***are cast down to evil***. This reading is followed in place of the reading that the person **brings the wicked to ruin**, for a righteous person does not have that much power. It is possible, though, to accept the latter reading to mean that a righteous person hastens the ruin of the wicked by cursing them like Eliphaz claims to have done (Job 5:3-4; Fox 2009, 684-85). Or more simply, a righteous person acts in ways that contribute to the demise of the wicked.

Many interpreters (as Murphy [1998, 157], Clifford [1999, 191], and the NIV) take the subject to be **the Righteous One**, that is, God, for God alone consigns or brings the wicked to ruin. But without the article it is doubtful that this Hebrew term serves as an epithet for God. Moreover, there are many proverbs about a righteous person (e.g., Prov 10:3, 6, plus ten more in ch 10). Also God is referenced as the Righteous One only in Isa 24:16. Thus, it is better to identify this term as referring to *a righteous person*.

Advancing: One who Ignores the Cry of the Poor / Cries Not Answered (21:13)

■ **13** The spiritual principle is that God responds to those who fear him in the way that they respond to those in need. Thus, those who ***shut*** **their ears to the cry of the poor** will one day experience an oppressive situation that causes them to **cry out** for help. But their cries will **not be answered**. This principle is found in the prayer Jesus taught his disciples: "forgive us our debts, as we also have forgiven our debtors" (Matt 6:12).

Affirming: Gift / Bribe Pacifies Anger (21:14)

■ **14** In dealing with an angry person, especially if that person is a high official or the king, it is vital to mollify that person's anger. Often **a gift given in secret** achieves that goal. If that official is burning with wrath, one may need to give something of significant value, as indicated by the term **bribe**, to that person in a clandestine manner as conveyed by the phrase **in the cloak** or ***bosom***.

The OT strongly teaches against the use of bribes to influence an official's decision (2 Chr 19:7; see Exod 23:8; Deut 16:19; 27:25; Prov 17:8; Eccl 7:7). But the type of gift applauded in this proverb differs in that there is no intention on the part of the giver to make justice blind (see Prov 17:8; 18:16; 19:6). Rather, the goal of the gift is to soften a person's anger so that the giver may be able to present an idea or a request that will be heard by an angry person. Otherwise it is virtually impossible to get a furious person to hear important information in order to make a fair response.

Opposing: With Justice the Righteous Rejoice / Evildoers Are Dismayed (21:15)

■ **15** When **justice is done** in a community, **the righteous** *rejoice*. The Hebrew term **justice** (*mišpāṭ*), having a wide sense, stands for anything that is done justly, from a merchant's having true weights and measures to a council's planning judiciously to a jury's rendering a proper verdict. Everything done justly **produces joy** to the upright. But when **evildoers** see justice being done, they are filled with **terror**. Because their values are so distorted, they consider justice an act of terror. They take it as a threat to their ability to continue doing evil.

Advancing: Wayward from Wisdom / Ends with Death (21:16)

■ **16** If a person **strays from the path of prudence**, that is, from living a life according to the teachings of the wise, that person is taking the fast path that leads to their **resting with** the weak spirits of those who have died, identified as the *rĕpā'îm* (see 2:18). *Rĕpā'îm* stands for the deceased who eke out an enervated existence in Sheol.

Affirming: Loving Pleasure / Lack of Wealth (21:17)

■ **17** In the Hebrew this saying has a chiastic structure. On the outside are phrases that describe a poor person: **one who suffers want** and one who will **never be rich**. At the center are the actions that lead to this outcome: **whoever loves pleasure** and **whoever loves wine and olive oil**. This proverb emphasizes the high cost of the pursuit of **pleasure**. Pleasure (*śimḥâ*) may also mean *feasting*. In Num 10:10 a day of pleasure is a day of feasting (see Esth 9:18; Fox 2009, 687). People love festive occasions. In preparing to go to a feast a person anoints the body with oil and dresses up. One wants to appear festive at a dinner of rich food and costly wine, served in abundance. This proverb warns that a person who is given to the pursuit of pleasure **will never be rich**.

Affirming: Wicked / Dealers of Treachery (21:18)

■ **18** In a season of judgment God delivers **the righteous** by punishing **the wicked**, identified as **the unfaithful** or *treacherous*. The punishment of the wicked is described as **a ransom** [*kōper*] **for the righteous**. It is the reason that the righteous can be delivered in God's economy.

A similar description is found in Isa 43:3-4. God accepts other nations as the ransom of Israel. This concept is not explained in the OT. It is not vicarious punishment, for only the righteous servant can bear the punishment due the guilty (Isa 53). In Isa 43 and presumably in this text the wicked are punished for their wrongdoings. But in their being punished God is able to deliver the righteous. Since God loves the righteous and punishes the wicked, it can be said that **the wicked become a ransom for the righteous**. (See Prov 11:8; 13:8.)

Better-than: A Desert Place than Living with a Contentious Wife (21:19)

■ **19** (See 21:9.) This proverb reaffirms the principle that it is **better to live** somewhere else, even in the **desert**, a hot, dry, desolate land, such as is found to the southeast of the hill country in Israel, than with **a quarrelsome and nagging** or ***ill-tempered*** wife. This proverb instructs youths and parents that finding a wife with a good temperament is critical to escape an intolerable situation.

Opposing: Wise Store / Fools Devour (21:20)

■ **20** ***Stores of*** choice food and olive oil are found ***in the dwelling of*** the wise. That is, they maintain a storehouse for keeping grain, wine, oil, and other valuable commodities. The wise have these treasures, for they know how to get and use commodities judiciously for the clan's welfare. Fools, however, wantonly ***consume*** everything of value. Soon all is gone. (See 1 Chr 9:29; Jer 40:10; Hag 2:12.)

Advancing: Pursuit of Righteousness (21:21)

■ **21** Whoever pursues **righteousness** and ***loyal*** love (ḥesed) receives the grand rewards of **life, prosperity** [ṣĕdāqâ] **and honor**. A person so rewarded has high standing in the community. The person's success accrues to the benefit of the entire community. The MT reads ***one pursuing righteousness . . .*** **finds . . . *righteousness***, which the NIV renders **prosperity** (though some omit the second occurrence as dittography, for the second line is too long and the omission has support from the LXX). Certainly a long life and honor are the highest rewards in this life according to the wisdom tradition.

Advancing: Wise Attack a City / Pull It Down (21:22)

■ **22** In this proverb ***a*** wise ***person***, either a resourceful warrior or king, attacks a fortified city guarded by strong warriors. He finds a way to ***scale the wall*** and **pull down the stronghold** in which the people had put their trust. This proverb teaches that people need to put trust in wisdom rather than in human-built fortifications, for wisdom enables a cunning person to develop a plan that is able to get through the most elaborate fortifications. (See Prov 24:5.)

Teachers relished telling stories about a wise person who was able to defeat a powerful foe by the use of wisdom. Qohelet gives the story of a wise man who dwelt in a small city. When his city was attacked by a powerful king, that wise man found a way to thwart the attack and deliver the city (Eccl 9:13-15).

There is an account of a wise woman's rescuing a city from being assaulted by Joab, David's general, because Sheba, a rebel, had taken refuge in that city (2 Sam 20:14-22). Joab set siege to the city and threatened to destroy the wall. A wise woman called out from the city, asking Joab if he would be satisfied with the head of his enemy. Joab agreed. Shortly afterward she threw down Sheba's head. Joab lifted the siege. That wise woman rescued her city from a horrendous fate.

Advancing: Controlled Speech / Avoiding Sorrow (21:23)

■ **23** This saying is dominated by the participle **those who guard/keep**, standing at the head of both lines. They **guard** or ***keep*** their mouths and . . . **tongues** from misspeaking by using words skillfully and judiciously (see Prov 10:16; 13:3). Thereby they **keep themselves from *troubles***. It is not that these people never experience pain or loss, but they are not continually getting into troubling situations by misspeaking.

Affirming: The Arrogant Mocker / Excessive Pride (21:24)

■ **24** There is a chiastic element in this aphorism, beginning with **proud** (*zēd*) and ending with ***pride*** (*zādôn*). This proverb describes the obnoxious nature of an exceedingly **proud** person. The Hebrew *zēd* describes a person as thinking that no one, not even God, is superior (see Mal 3:15). Such a person, called ***a mocker***, is characterized as presumptuous or **insolent** (*yāhîr*).

Viewing himself as far superior to everyone, this kind of person acts most audaciously (lit. ***in angry outbursts of pride***). His actions are exceedingly cruel. Such arrogance is seen in false prophets who, though acting on their own, claim that God has given them the words that they are speaking to the people, leading them astray (Deut 18:20-22).

Advancing: Desire of Lazy / Refuses to Work (21:25)

■ **25** The term ***desire*** (*taʾăwâ*) connects the next two proverbs. ***A lazy person*** has strong ***desires*** or cravings. But cravings in a lazy person are dangerous. **Because his hands refuse to work**, he never has the means of satisfying any longing. As a result he languishes in great frustration. Thus, his cravings **will** eventually **be *his*** death. (See 2 Thess 3:10.)

Opposing: One Who Craves / Those Who Give (21:26)

■ **26** A person dominated by ***desire*** or ***craving*** is contrasted with **the righteous**. The first person is beset by cravings **all day long**. His desires never slumber. By contrast, **the righteous give without *restraint***. They see a need and respond to it by sharing whatever is at their disposal, trusting God to supply their future needs. Generosity and interest in others are traits of the righteous. Generosity and genuine concern for others keep them from being dominated by the cravings of the flesh.

Advancing: Sacrifice of the Wicked / Offered with Calculation (Line *a* = 15:8*a*) (21:27)

■ **27** Here is one of the few references to sacrifice in Proverbs. **The sacrifice** presented by **the wicked is detestable**, the most pejorative word in the wisdom tradition (→ sidebar "Yahweh Detests or Abomination to Yahweh" at end of

6:16-19). The reason their sacrifice is so appalling is that they present it with cunning motivation as conveyed by the term *zimmâ* (**evil intent**). That is, the wicked bring a sacrifice for personal gain, such as gaining honor in the community or to conceal a foul activity. In making such a sacrifice they are using the means God gave for worship and maintaining a right relationship with him for their own benefit without any thought of humbling themselves before God.

Opposing: False Witness / A Person of Hearing (21:28)

■ **28** A false witness in a legal case **will perish**. This saying does not establish the time frame between giving **false** testimony and being punished. But it asserts that a person's **false** testimony will be discovered, leading to that person's demise.

Since the wording in the second line is obscure, there are various interpretations. The subject (*'îš šômēa'*) describes a person who listens well and is able to give accurate testimony as to what had been said. As a result in a legal contest he speaks successfully (*lānesaḥ* from *nṣḥ* [*be victorious*]), attested in Rabbinic Hebrew (so Aquila and Vulgate [Waltke 2005, 164, n. 44; Fox 2009, 692]). But others take this word from *neṣaḥ* (**endlessness, forever**). The gloss, then, is **speak continually**. With that meaning the line may be saying that **the listener** will not be silenced in giving testimony. In antiquity one could win a legal case by speaking so long and forcefully that one silences an opponent.

Opposing: The Wicked Has a Bold Posture / The Upright Understand Their Ways (21:29)

■ **29** The wicked and the upright are contrasted in regard to their bearings. **The wicked** display confidence by *putting* up a bold front (lit. *makes his face strong*). A brazen countenance hides their scheming by which they seek to dupe people. They bear themselves in a way that leads people to place confidence in what they say. Proverbs 7:13 gives the example of the seductress who approaches a man boldly with a brazen countenance.

But **the upright give thought to their ways**. They consciously make sure that they are on the true path and that they are conducting themselves properly. For the upright, behaving properly is far more important than projecting a particular image in order to be honored, an approach that is counter to current Western culture.

Continuation: Yahweh's Supremacy (21:30)

■ **30** The next two proverbs contrast the plans that humans make with the outcome determined by God (see 16:1-4, 9). The first proverb sets out a principle and the following proverb illustrates that principle by a battle victory. The first proverb points to the vast chasm between human **wisdom**, *understanding*, and *counsel* and Yahweh's. Yahweh's wisdom is so superior that no earthly wisdom *can stand* or **succeed against** it. This saying underscores the vital importance of listening to Yahweh's counsel in order to succeed in any matter, but especially when facing opposition.

In contemporary society there are numerous ideologies that espouse programs and standards of conduct that are contrary to the teaching of divine wisdom. These ideologies claim greater insight into dealing with complex contemporary problems such as the great disparities among nations. While current thinkers are extoled for more advanced insights on ways to enhance the living standards of the multitudes than the authors of Scripture, the insights they offer are flawed and will not prevail against Yahweh's wisdom.

Opposing: Battle: Military Preparation / Victory from Yahweh (21:31)

■ **31** This proverb contrasts human preparations for war with Yahweh's guiding the outcome of the battle. Warriors work hard in training horses for battle. This is a synecdoche for all the preparations an army makes for battle. Since the horse charges into battle fearlessly (see Job 39:19-25), it was a major force in ancient battles. Its role in battle may be compared to that of tanks today.

An army, believing that it is better equipped than its foe, goes forth to battle confident of victory. But this proverb says that no matter how extensively an army prepares, it is Yahweh who gives the **victory**. This principle was especially true for Israel since she was in covenant with God. Also this proverb does not undercut the need of preparing for battle, but it does seek to curtail the prideful bluster of those who win a major victory at great effort, that is, the braggadocio of the king and generals over a victory. (See Ps 33:16-17.)

M. Proverbs 22:1-16

OVERVIEW

This small collection of proverbs concludes the second section of division two. Its character aligns with this section as seen in the distribution of the structures of the proverbs: eleven are advancing, three opposing, and two affirming. Two proverbs are formulated as imperatives (vv 6, 10), giving greater urgency to their content. Yahweh, being referenced four times (vv 2, 4, 12, 14), is active in human affairs by guarding words of knowledge (v 12) and guiding the punishment of those under his wrath (v 14). Fearing Yahweh brings wealth, honor, and life (v 4).

The dominant theme is wealth and poverty (vv 1, 2, 7, 9, 16). Wealth, a benefit of wisdom (v 4), is downplayed in the saying that the rich and the poor have the same inherent value because Yahweh is the Maker of both (v 2) and in the saying that attributes greater value to a good reputation and honor than to wealth (v 1). Blessing attends those who share food with the poor (v 9), but poverty is the destiny of those who seek to become wealthy at the expense of the poor (v 16). Another proverb cautions against borrowing, pointing out that the borrower becomes a servant to the lender (v 7).

Other topics are speech (vv 11, 14), educating children (vv 6, 15), and the king (v 11). This collection reiterates five dangers to avoid: thorns and snares on one's path (v 5), borrowing (v 7), sowing injustice (v 8), laziness (v 13), and the seductive speech of a foreign woman (v 14).

IN THE TEXT

Affirming: Reputation / Favor (22:1)

■ **1** Although wisdom promises wealth, other things, though intangible, are **more desirable than great *wealth***. Two of them are *a* **name** (i.e., good reputation) and ***high esteem*** (i.e., honor). Wesley describes esteem or favor as "a good report among men, especially good men, and that hearty kindness which attends it" (1975, 1871). Building a solid reputation takes a long time. Officials, such as the king or district governors, and employers seek out people who have a stellar reputation for taking counsel and for employment. (See Eccl 7:1.)

Advancing: God Is Maker of Rich and Poor (22:2)

■ **2** *The* **rich and *the* poor**, living in different areas of the community, seldom interact. Whenever they do ***meet***, they are on the same plane in ***Yahweh's*** sight since he is **the Maker** of both. (See Prov 14:31.)

This foundational statement is in accord with the account that God created all humans, male and female, in his image (Gen 1:26). All humans, then, are God's work. The account of their origin means that everyone has inherent worth and is on the same plane before God, even though society puts people on different levels according to their wealth, intelligence, skills, possessions, and position.

Job, having this view of human worth, claimed that he never rejected any complaints against him from his servants, for he recognized that the one who had made him in the womb also made them (Job 31:13-15).

This proverb is a gem, for it lauds the inherent worth of all persons, thereby discounting any view or ideology that exalts any person or race or nationality as superior. This principle is foundational to a democratic society.

Opposing: Prudent / Simple (22:3)

■ **3** (See 27:12.) When by chance people come on ***trouble*** or **danger, the prudent** respond very differently from **the simple**. When an ***astute person***, being constantly vigilant as to the surroundings, notices something untoward taking place on the path ahead, such as people arguing boisterously, that person inconspicuously changes course in order to avoid becoming engaged in that conflict.

But when **the simple** see something improper taking place on the path ahead, they **keep going** on their way hoping that nothing bad will happen to them. As a result of their insolent attitude, they ***suffer harm***. The wording ***suffer harm*** or **pay the penalty** intimates that a government official punishes them. Possibly an official assumes that they have been involved in whatever was taking place. Alliteration dominates the first line: ʿārûm rāʾâ rāʿâ (Clifford 1999, 196).

Advancing: Benefits of the Fear of Yahweh (22:4)

■ **4** The rewards of **humility** and **the fear of _Yahweh_** are **riches, honor and life**, the best possible earthly rewards. These rewards, standing in ascending order of value, are the result of Yahweh's active engagement in the lives of those who fear him. The coupling of humility with the fear of Yahweh is unusual. Humility here points to a person's having an attitude that is open to learning from a rebuke, a loss, or a setback. It is the opposite of being proud and unresponsive to input.

Advancing: Traps in the Path / Avoiding Traps (22:5)

■ **5** The path of _the perverse_, those who are crooked in their dealings, is full of **snares and pitfalls**, metaphors for all kinds of harmful obstacles (i.e., difficult situations, losses, and setbacks that one has to face) on life's path. **But those who would preserve their life,** that is, those who are alert to possible dangers lying on the path (see v 3), are diligent to **stay far _away_ from them**. However, the perverse are prone to engage in risky activities, being overly confident that they can avoid any reprisals for cheating others. This proverb warns them that in time one of those snares will trap them. (See 15:19.)

Advancing: The Value of Educating Children (22:6)

■ **6** Cast as an exhortation, this proverb advocates the education of children. Children not only learn quickly but retain what is learned throughout life. Thus, it is crucial to form in them sound habits, virtues, and good attitudes so that these qualities become deeply engrained in their character.

In pondering this saying it is important to keep in mind that this type of proverb does not make a promise, but states a principle. Given that children have widely varying dispositions, the outcome of education for a specific child cannot be guaranteed. Above all there are no grounds for reading this proverb inside out to accuse parents for being the cause for a child's departing from the way of wisdom (see Longman 2006, 404-5).

Affirming: Rich / Borrower (22:7)

■ **7** This saying is descriptive, not prescriptive, of a persistent pattern in society. **The rich rule over the poor**. Their wealth keeps them in power. The second line reveals a major reason that they maintain this position—**the borrower is slave to the lender**. Until a loan is repaid the borrower is beholden to the lender, partially because the borrower has to put up security, such as land, to receive the loan. Furthermore, a loan often carries conditions such as the lender might determine what crops the borrower is to plant or when to harvest them. In a variety of ways lenders have great influence over borrowers.

The distress caused by lenders is heard in Jeremiah's lamenting that he had become a man of strife, even though he had never been a lender nor a borrower (Jer 15:10). His lament shows that harsh feelings often develop between borrowers and lenders. Thus, this proverb alerts the poor to be very judicious in borrowing lest they come into bondage.

Advancing: Sowing and Reaping (22:8)

■ **8** The metaphor of sowing and reaping is frequently employed to express the certainty of retribution. One who **sows injustice** or ***wickedness*** (ʿawlâ), an abstract term, covering actions condemned by God, **reaps calamity** or misfortune (ʾāwen); there is a play on the sound of these two terms.

The exact sense of the second line, **the rod they wield in fury will be broken,** is unclear. Possibly the sower's **fury** strikes out like **a rod** against the trouble he is reaping, but that rod fails, that is, is broken, by the trouble. The sower will not be able to overcome the trouble.

Advancing: Generous Person / Sharing Food (22:9)

■ **9** Those who are **generous** [lit. ***have a good eye***] **will . . . be blessed.** Those with a good eye, the opposite of those with an evil eye, that is, stingy or envious persons (Prov 23:6; 28:22), are those who compassionately **share their food with the poor.** They are doubly blessed, by those whom they help and by God (Lennox 1998, 230-31).

Advancing: Drive Out Mocker / End of Strife (22:10)

■ **10** Various types of people have a powerful impact on the community, either for good or for ill. By scoffing at the values a community holds, **the mocker** stirs up **strife,** threatening the community's solidarity. That is why this proverb is formulated as an exhortation: **drive out the mocker,** for the removal of such a person causes **strife** ***to cease*** as well as **quarrels,** possibly legal disputes, and **insults,** such as defamatory slurs hurled at people.

Advancing: King Is a Friend to One with a Pure Heart (22:11)

■ **11** A person **who loves a pure heart** (Fox 2009, 700), that is, one who maintains impeccable integrity, and **speaks** ***graciously*** becomes **a friend** *of* the **king.** That is, the king entrusts such a person with significant responsibilities.

In 1 Kgs 4:5 Zabud, an official under Solomon, is identified as a priest and friend of the king, that is a personal adviser. In the Roman Empire a trusted ruler under the emperor had the title "friend of the emperor." (See Prov 16:13.)

Opposing: Yahweh Guards Knowledge / But Frustrates the Words of the Treacherous (22:12)

■ **12** Knowledge properly used promotes the well-being of a community, but the words of the ***treacherous*** cause a community great harm. Therefore, **Yahweh** diligently **watches** over **knowledge** spoken by the wise so that their words may guide and encourage people. On the other hand, **He** ***subverts*** **the words of** ***one who deals treacherously*** (bôgēd), that is, one who deceives people by setting out grandiose plans and making promises that entice people to buy into his proposals—plans that have virtually no chance of ever becoming a reality. Yahweh, therefore, seeks to keep the people from falling for such bogus schemes by exposing the treachery hidden in them.

Advancing: An Excuse Used by the Lazy (22:13)

■ **13** (See 26:13.) A lazy person is highly skilled at making up farfetched excuses to avoid working. This proverb offers an example of such an excuse. Responding to a proposal to do a job, a sluggard insolently says, **"There's a lion outside!"** He immediately gives a reason: **"I'll be killed in the public square!"** The roar of the lion may be heard in the verb *'ērāṣēaḥ*, **I'll be killed** (Clifford 1999, 198).

While several references to lions in the OT indicate that they inhabited regions of ancient Israel, the sluggard is offering a ridiculous excuse to keep from having to work. This proverb vividly ridicules the kind of excuses and the demeanor of the lazy. (See 19:24; 26:13-15.)

Advancing: Words of Adulteress / God's Wrath (22:14)

■ **14** *A foreign* woman is an outsider who lives as a streetwalker, is skilled at speaking seductively. Thus, her mouth is described as **a deep pit**, a trap from which escape is virtually impossible. A person who is under Yahweh's wrath **falls into** that trap. This seductress's speech becomes "an instrument of divine wrath" (Yoder 2009, 226).

Advancing: Folly in a Child / Discipline Drives It Away (22:15)

■ **15** From birth **folly is bound up in** *a child's mind*, that is, a child has a natural inclination to pursue foolish behavior. Therefore, parents have to work skillfully and diligently at overcoming this inclination. A means frequently advocated by the wise for *driving* **it far away** is **the rod of discipline**. Proper discipline must be applied early in a child's life, for once folly lodges in a youth it is virtually impossible to drive out (27:22; see 1:7*b*; 13:24).

Opposing: Two Paths Leading to Poverty (22:16)

■ **16** This proverb, having an elliptical structure, has led to various attempts to gain a sound reading, but none are compelling. The NIV applies **come to poverty,** found in the second line, to both lines. This proverb describes two different paths taken **to increase wealth** (i.e., **oppressing the poor**) and *giving* **gifts to the rich**.

Certainly oppressing the poor increases one's income. A variety of tactics for cheating the poor are mentioned in the prophets and proverbs, including overcharging them, giving them less than they paid for, and selling them into bondage for a small debt (Amos 2:6*b*, 7; 4:1; 5:11; 8:6; Prov 14:31; 28:3). Another scheme used against the poor is offering a loan at high interest and with a heavy penalty for failure to pay on time.

Another person **gives gifts to the rich** in hope of winning their favor and sharing in their wealth. A possible ploy of giving gifts is to encourage a rich person to sponsor a business adventure. But the rich, being very protective of their wealth, are reluctant to enter into uncertain business adventures or be easily influenced by gifts.

Both those who oppress the poor and those who give gifts to the rich **come to poverty**, because their focus is on money rather than the well-being of others regardless of whether they are rich or poor.

III. INSTRUCTIONS OF THE WISE: 22:17—24:34

The third section of the book of Proverbs has two parts. In Part A (22:17—24:22), a sage instructs his son or apprentice. This instruction is remarkable in that an Israelite sage drew on ideas, metaphors, and themes from the Instruction of Amenemope, an Egyptian wisdom text (ca. 1188-945 BC). Part B (24:23-34) is a small collection of sayings that an Israelite sage has preserved by placing them after the longer section titled Sayings of the Wise.

A. Sayings of the Wise (22:17—24:22)

OVERVIEW

Sayings of the Wise is the title of Part A. A sage has composed a manual of instruction for a son or an apprentice as a guide to becoming an honored government official.

The sage begins the instructions by exhorting either his son or an apprentice under him to "pay attention . . . to the sayings [he] *is going to* teach" (22:17, 21). The sage's pedagogical approach is heard in his addressing the son or the student directly with the second-person pronouns "you" and "your," occurring eleven times in the introduction (vv 17-21 HB). Then in the body of the instruction the sage addresses the student as "my son" five times (23:15, 19, 26; 24:13, 21). In order that his instruction be heard, the sage is appealing to the close bond between himself and the son or the apprentice.

Being an instruction the sequence and the style of the sayings differ from those in Section II. Only six proverbs in this collection consist of only two lines (22:28, 29; 23:9, 12; 24:7, 10), the predominant form of the sayings in Section II. The sayings in the instruction vary in length, being visible in the units the NIV identifies: fifteen sayings of four lines (22:22-23, 24-25, 26-27; 23:10-11, 13-14, 15-16, 17-18; 24:1-2, 3-4, 5-6, 8-9, 15-16, 17-18, 19-20, 21-22), two of five lines (23:4-5; 24:13-14), four of six lines (23:1-3, 19-21, 26-28; 24:11-12), two of eight lines (23:6-8, 22-25), and one of ten lines (22:17-23). The longest saying has eighteen lines (23:29-35). Another stylistic difference between these two sections is that seventeen of these instructions are admonitions, while Section II, a considerably longer segment, only has two admonitions (20:13, 22; Murphy 1998, 169).

The sage's key exhortation to the son is to seek wisdom (23:12, 22-23; 24:13-14). His growing in wisdom will bring joy to his parents (23:22-24), and it carries the promise that he will rise in the ranks of nobility and in time come to "serve before kings" (22:29). His future is bright because wisdom will provide him essential skills such as the ability to design and build a house (24:3-4), to develop a strategy for success in battle (24:5-6), and to be sufficiently astute in raising a child so that the child will avoid an early death (23:13-15). Moreover, it is important that the youth learn proper table manners so that he will know how to conduct himself properly at official banquets (23:1-3, 6-8).

In general, the youth must avoid activities that will anger, demean, or exploit the common people, activities like crushing the poor (22:22-23), moving boundary stones (22:28; 23:10-11), or raiding the property of a righteous person (24:15-16). Personally he must never become the guarantor of another's loan (22:26-27). There are attitudes that must be avoided, particularly cynicism (24:17-18), pride that leads him to advance himself by foolish schemes (24:8-9), and envy of the riches of the wicked (24:1-2, 19-20).

The sage further advises his son or apprentice that there are various types of people he must avoid lest he take on their behavioral patterns and thereby tarnish his reputation and deter his growth in wisdom: "a hot-tempered person" (22:24-25), a stingy person (23:6-8), and a fool (23:9; 24:7). Moreover, he needs to avoid the company of "drunkards and gluttons" (23:20-21). The sage also cautions the youth against wearing himself down by overwork in order to become rich (23:4-5).

On the affirmative side the youth is to fear God and the king (24:21-22; see 23:17-18). Proper fear of God will motivate him to help people as well as give him the courage to deliver any who are being wrongfully "led away to death" (24:11-12). This fear gives the youth confidence that whatever challenging situation he faces, wisdom from God will guide him and keep him from faltering (24:10).

BEHIND THE TEXT

The remarkable feature of this wisdom instruction is its close affinity with the Egyptian text the Instruction of Amenemope (ca. 1188-945 BC; Washington 1994, 11-24), particularly in 22:17—23:11. The similarities between the two documents indicate that one sage was influenced by the other. For decades it was debated as to which author was dependent on the other. This issue has been settled with the discovery of a copy of the Instruction of Amenemope that predates the establishment of a strong central government in Israel under Solomon. Now it is certain that the Israelite author drew on the Egyptian document.

Nevertheless, the Israelite sage composed his own instruction. This claim is supported by several facts. Only the material in Prov 22:17—23:11, about a third of this instruction, has been influenced by the Instruction of Amenemope. The sage has ordered the sayings free from the influence of other wisdom texts (Plöger 1984, 207). In particular, the Israelite sage has not clearly identified the units as Amenemope did.

Furthermore, the Israelite author is thoroughly committed to the fear of Yahweh as the foundation of wisdom, having placed references to Yahweh at the beginning, the middle, and the end of the instruction (22:19; 24:21; see 22:23; 23:17; 24:18). While Amenemope is also a devout sage, he does not advocate reverence for a particular god as the basis of wisdom.

I. The Meaning of an Unusual Word in Proverbs 22:20 and Comparison with the Instruction of Amenemope

Since the rare Hebrew term *šilšôm/šālîšîm* in v 20 has puzzled interpreters across the centuries, it has received a variety of glosses in English translations. When the first Hebrew word has the meaning *formerly*, it is always joined by *tĕmôl* "yesterday and the day before." However, *tĕmôl* is missing in this verse.

Since **formerly** does not fit this context, many scholars follow the oral tradition and read *šālîšîm* as **military officers**. That sense, however, is not congruent with the context. Therefore, many who accept this word as the best reading posit that it functions as a metaphor for "excellent things" (Murphy 1998, 169 n. 20a). That view, however, carries little weight since this term never has that sense.

When it became clear that this instruction was strongly influenced by the Instruction of Amenemope and that the Egyptian work consisted of thirty chapters, scholars emended the MT to read *šĕlôšîm* as **thirty**. This emendation is the best one that has been offered to date. It requires only a small change, that is, reading the letter *waw* as *yod*, two letters written so similarly in some stages of Hebrew script that confusion between them is frequent, a confusion similar to that of "i" and "e" in handwritten English texts (see Waltke 2005, 219-20, n. 113, 217-88; Clifford 1999, 199-200). This solution has led many commentators and English translations to identify thirty sayings in 22:17—24:22 (e.g., McKane 1970, 371-406; Waltke 2005, 217-88; Fox 2009, 705-7, 753-69). The NIV follows this approach. It identifies each of the thirty units by placing a space between them.

Some scholars, however, are not persuaded that this instruction consists of thirty units (e.g., Plöger [1984, 266-68], Whybray [1994a, 323-25], and Murphy [1998, 169]). They offer several reasons for rejecting this division. (1) There is no consensus among translations or commentators on the makeup of the thirty units. If the Israelite author had sought to compose thirty sayings as is found in the Instruction of Amenemope, it is expected that he would have employed some signal to identify each unit, especially since each chapter in the Instruction of Amenemope is clearly marked with a heading composed of the term "chapter" plus a number. In addition, Amenemope opens ch 30 with the exhortation "look to these thirty chapters" (27:6). But there is no stress on the number of units in this Hebrew instruction.

(2) The biblical author only drew on the Egyptian text in composing 22:17—23:11, twenty-four out of the seventy verses, around 35 percent of his work.

(3) The introduction to this instruction has wording that is similar to the introduction in the Instruction of Amenemope. However, it is much shorter, ten lines in contrast to forty-five. But those who identify thirty units in the biblical text include the introduction as one of the units (Prov 22:17-21), except for McKane (1970, 372, 374-77). In the Instruction of Amenemope, however, the introduction precedes ch 1. Consequently, those who count the introduction in the biblical text as a chapter are conceding that the Israelite author was not following the structure used by Amenemope.

(4) The length of the units identified in the Hebrew text vary widely as do the chapters in Amenemope. But the variation is different. In the biblical text the sayings vary from two lines to eighteen lines, while the chapters in

Amenemope vary from six (ch 28) and eight lines (chs 3; 12; 14; 23; 24) to thirty-two lines (ch 9).

If the Israelite sage was influenced by the organization of the Instruction of Amenemope, he would have composed more longer units similar to the triad on drunkenness, which has eighteen or nineteen lines (23:29-35). The difference in the length of units adds force to the position that the Israelite sage was not influenced by Amenemope's structuring of his instruction. Given these arguments this commentary does not identify thirty units in the biblical instruction.

Therefore, there must be another reason for the use of **thirty** in 22:20. It is possible that the Israelite scribe used this number for the symbolic significance it had in Egypt. The significance of thirty in Egyptian culture is attested by the fact that both the visceral court and the court of deities, which judged the dead were composed of thirty judges (Fox 2009, 711). Thirty, then, appears to be the ideal number for achieving a just decision.

The Israelite scribe used **thirty** symbolically to convey that this instruction offers the son excellent, reliable instruction for achieving success as a government official. This suggestion receives additional support in that **thirty** is used as a substantive rather than modifying another word.

2. Times When an Israelite Could Have Become Acquainted with the Instruction of Amenemope

Another issue is to identify a period in Israel's history when an Israelite sage could have become acquainted with this Egyptian text. Two periods are most favorable.

The first period is the flourishing of wisdom under King Solomon in the tenth century BC as attested in 1 Kgs 3:1; 5:12; 10:28-29; 11:17-40. Since there was no dominant power in the Levant in that era, the region was free of major wars. That peaceful environment freed Solomon to engage commercially and culturally with several other peoples (1 Kgs 10:23-29). He married an Egyptian princess (1 Kgs 9:16), hired a Phoenician architect for his building projects (1 Kgs 5:1, 7-12, 18), and entered into international commerce with the Phoenicians (1 Kgs 10:22, 28-29).

During this time rulers and sages engaged in the pursuit of wisdom, a pursuit that included international exchanges as attested by the Queen of Sheba's visiting Jerusalem to discover for herself Solomon's skill in wisdom (1 Kgs 10:1, 10, 13).

A second favorable period for an Israelite sage having access to Egyptian wisdom texts was the end of the eighth century BC. Pharaohs became active again in Israel and Judah, for they wanted to stay the advance of the Assyrian army into the western Levant. Therefore, they made several military excursions into Palestine and established alliances with various peoples in that region. Egypt's influence in Palestine continued into the sixth century.

During that time Aramaic became the international language in the Middle East. It is quite possible that various Egyptian literary texts were translated into Aramaic. The Instruction of Amenemope was a strong candidate for translation since it was a text favored by Egyptian scribes as attested by the number of copies that have survived from the seventh through the fourth centuries BC. An Israelite sage would have had the opportunity to become acquainted with the Instruction of Amenemope in a language that was very similar to ancient Hebrew.

Judah's famous king in this period was Hezekiah (727-697 BC). Having a burning zeal for Yahweh, he promoted a revival of the true worship of Yahweh (2 Kgs 18:5-8; 2 Chr 29:1—31:21). His zeal led him to invite northern Israelites to participate in the annual festivals at Jerusalem as he sought to reunite northern Israel with Judah. Hezekiah was also actively engaged in international relations, especially since Assyria's aggression threatened the survival of Judah (2 Kgs 20:12-19).

It is likely that Hezekiah's zeal led him to promote the collecting and editing of Israelite wisdom sayings as stated in Prov 25:1. It was critical that such copies be made after Ahaz, his predecessor who entered into alliances with Assyria and promoted the worship of foreign gods. Texts that taught faith in Yahweh and true wisdom were needed for training an army of government officials in the fear of Yahweh. These officials could fill numerous government positions throughout Judah. From their positions they were able to reestablish justice and promote reverence for Yahweh throughout the land. Their fidelity to the covenant would lead the people to have confidence in the government. These leaders were essential for spreading reform throughout the nation.

3. The Significance of an Israelite Sage's Drawing from an Egyptian Wisdom Text

It is significant that an Israelite official composed a document to instruct an Israelite youth that included insights from a foreign wisdom text. This fact attests to the Israelite sages' recognition that judicious insights and sound principles could be found in the writings of other peoples. This view was grounded on their belief that God had created the world in wisdom. That belief meant that all peoples have access to wise insights through their observations of patterns in nature and in society. The Israelite sages also realized that ideas, principles, and practices learned from foreign sages need to be grounded on the foundation of all wisdom, the fear of Yahweh, in order for these insights to offer sound guidance to Israelite youths.

From another perspective it need not be surprising that a biblical text contains material that is also found in an Egyptian text. Throughout history wisdom has been an international enterprise, for sages are inherently curious about the teachings of other peoples.

240

The international character of education has flourished in today's world. Numerous programs and grants, many funded by governments and universities especially in developed countries, support students and professors studying in other countries. Multiple disciplines host international conferences for the exchange of ideas among scholars from countries throughout the globe. That such sharing, though certainly not of the present magnitude, took place in antiquity is attested in the Queen of Sheba's traveling to Jerusalem to engage Solomon in dialogue. Other evidences of intellectual exchange in antiquity have been documented by the discovery of foreign literary texts at numerous key cities throughout the Levant. For example, a fragment of the Epic of Gilgamesh, a Babylonian text about a legendary ruler, was found at Megiddo, a major fortress in northern Israel.

The connection between this canonical text and the Instruction of Amenemope shows that those who fear God may gain significant insights from the literature and sayings of other peoples. Whatever is learned, though, needs to be placed on the foundation of wisdom, the fear of Yahweh, so that the insights build character and faith.

IN THE TEXT

The length of the units identified in commenting on this instruction follows the NIV. Since many sayings are longer than a couplet, a brief description of the style of the parallelism of each saying in this section is placed at the head of the comments rather than in the title line as in Section II.

Introduction (22:17-21)

■ **17-21** A high government official opens his instruction with an introduction of ten lines. In typical fashion the sage begins by exhorting the son or apprentice to **pay attention and *listen* to the sayings of the wise**. The double imperative underscores the importance of the exhortation. The phrase **the sayings of the wise**, which identifies the genre of this document, most likely was originally the title of this section like the title before 24:17.

The student is challenged to **apply *his mind*** or **heart** to **the knowledge** that the teacher will share. The instruction is motivated by the reward that ***keeping*** the sayings ***will be pleasing in his belly***. That is, in pondering these sayings so that they become part of his deepest thoughts as represented by the term ***belly***, the son or apprentice will find as much pleasure as from eating a delicious meal. The metaphor also encourages the student to digest these sayings so that they will be readily available **on *his* lips**. Whenever he recalls this teaching, it will provide him guidance for dealing with all kinds of circumstances, especially those that require a perceptive approach.

Above all the teacher desires the student to place ***his* trust . . . in Yahweh**. The expression of this goal at the outset of the instruction reveals the

241

Israelite teacher's commitment to the foundation of Israelite wisdom: the fear of Yahweh.

The sage goes on to affirm that he *has* written *excellent* sayings that convey *truthful and reliable* sayings of counsel and knowledge (→ above, "The Meaning of an Unusual Word in Proverbs 22:20 and Comparison with the Instruction of Amenemope"). By learning these instructions the youth will be equipped to *formulate sound* or *reliable* reports to the one who *has* sent him on an assignment. This advice indicates that the teacher is instructing a youth in training to become a government official. It also suggests that as an apprentice the youth is serving as a courier. In this role he must guard the privacy of the messages and bring back accurate **reports to those *who sent* him.** By adhering to this standard, he will gain the respect of the officials he serves.

Robbing the Poor (22:22-23)

■ **22-23** The youth is enjoined not *to* **exploit the poor because they are poor.** Since the poor lack the means for challenging a government official, an official may be tempted to devise a scheme to exploit them, such as demanding high fees for a small infraction or confiscating valuable objects from the needy as a form of extortion. That this proverb condemns an official's use of legal means to win a judgment against a poor person is conveyed by two phrases, **in *the gate*** where **court** is held (v 22*b*) and **take up *a*** case (*yārîb rîb* [v 23*a*]). Adherence to this admonition is motivated by the assertion that **Yahweh** will take up *the* case of the poor and by the threat that Yahweh **will exact life for life.** Even though an official has the power to use legal means to oppress the poor, he will find his life in danger before Yahweh's judgment.

Affirming: Against Friendship with an Angry Person (22:24-25)

■ **24-25** The lines in v 24 are affirming, and those in v 25 are advancing. Verse 25 gives the motivation for the prohibition in v 24. The first couplet is structured chiastically, prohibition:object::object:prohibition.

The apprentice is admonished **not *to* make friends with a hot-tempered person.** In fact, it is prudent **not** even to **associate with one easily angered.** Friendship with an angry person is very fragile. Out of anger that friend is likely to utter sharp, hurtful words, thereby damaging the relationship. Such words ring in the memory of the person rebuffed for years. Moreover, it is hard, if not impossible, to correct the impact of those words (Lennox 1998, 235). Or **a hot-tempered person** may suddenly begin to act erratically, thereby causing serious injury to a friend. Amenemope likewise exhorts against befriending and engaging in conversation with a heated person (Amenemope 11:13-14). This is a frequent topic in Egyptian instructions (e.g., Any 5:6).

This admonition is supported by a double motive. First, in befriending **a hot-tempered** person one is likely to **learn** that person's **ways.** Over time one begins to think and act like that angry person. Second, in making such an association the youth *sets a trap* for *his own life.* One day that trap will unexpectedly **ensnare** him. Amenemope lists various ills that befall an angry person, especially one who provokes quarrels (12:1—13:9): becoming worthy of a beating for speaking hurtfully, bringing misfortune on his children as a result of being charged with a crime, causing strife in the family, and being forced into hiding as a result of making people despondent.

Do Not Become Security for Another's Debt (22:26-27)

■ **26-27** The couplet in v 26 is affirming, and the one in v 27 is advancing. Verse 27 is advancing in relationship to v 26.

The youth is counseled **not** to **shake** hands, i.e., agree to become security for a loan taken out by another person. A handshake gives the creditor access to one's finances (Hossfeld and Reuter 1999, 56-57). Neither should he **put** up security for another's **debts** (see 6:1-5; 11:15; 17:18; 20:16; 27:13). In becoming the guarantor of another person's loan, a youth places his own holdings at risk. If the borrower fails to repay the loan and the youth is unable to pay it, the youth stands in jeopardy of losing his **very bed**, possibly his last possession. In antiquity having a bed was a bonus, for most people slept on the floor or the ground (Murphy 1998, 101). A description of the terrible plight of people unable to repay loans is recounted in Neh 5:3-11.

Advancing: Boundary Stones Not to Be Moved (Line *a* = 23:10*a*) (22:28)

■ **28** This saying is structured in advancing style. The son is admonished **not** *to* move an ancient boundary stone (see Deut 19:14; 27:17; Amenemope 7:12-19). A greedy person moves a boundary marker in order to gain more acreage for cultivation.

An Israelite family's land was inalienable under the terms of the covenant. This standard is referenced by the phrase **an ancient boundary stone set up by your ancestors**. The intent of the law was to provide every family land as a means of support. It particularly protected the land of the poor and the weak from being swallowed up by the rich, thereby keeping the less fortunate from being uprooted from their land.

Advancement of a Skilled Person (22:29)

■ **29** This verse has three lines. The second and third lines are affirming; together they are advancing in relationship to the first line. The grammatical structure of the last two lines forms a chiastic pattern: prepositional phrase:verb:verb (same one negated):prepositional phrase.

The sage encourages a youth to pursue the discipline necessary for becoming a scribe with the promise that *those* skilled [*māhîr*] **in their work** . . . **will serve before kings**. The term *māhîr* refers to a highly skilled professional. A skilled scribe was competent at keeping records and interpreting the laws (see Amenemope 27:16-17). Ezra, in particular, is identified as a scribe skilled in the Mosaic law (Ezra 7:6).

Kings, high officials, and landowners were continually looking for promising, young apprentices. This promise of high office, even *serving* before

kings, motivates the son to work diligently at learning well the skills of writing and accounting and at developing interpersonal skills in order that one day a high official or the king will assign him to an administrative job.

This saying brings to mind Joseph's experiences in Egypt. Not long after having been sold as a slave to Potiphar, he rose to become the overseer of Potiphar's businesses, a captain in Pharaoh's guard (Gen 39:1-6). Then after serving time as a prisoner as a result of false charges, he rose to become a special assistant to Pharaoh, one of the highest offices in Egypt (Gen 41:39-45).

Advancing: Controlling One's Appetite at an Official Banquet (23:1-3)

■ **1-3** Each of the three couplets is structured as advancing. Verse 2 is advancing in relationship to v 1. The lines in v 3, another admonition, are advancing.

An integral component in the training of an official was learning well the rules of etiquette so that he conducts himself properly at official functions, especially banquets. Anyone who fails to practice self-discipline in speaking and eating at such occasions could easily disgrace himself and harm his career. Similar encouragement is found in Egyptian instructions, e.g., Ptahhotep, lines 119-30 (*AEL*, 1:65), and Amenemope 23:13-20.

At a royal banquet a young bureaucrat needs to pay careful attention to where he is seated. That awareness includes his being alert to the order and the station of those seated at the same table, the table's settings, and the food **before him**. It is important that he passes the food properly and that he does not take a large portion of any dish. Above all he must not **crave** *a delicacy* so much that he tries to get some before those of higher standing have been served.

Since all kinds of delicious, highly desirable foods that are not a part of his daily fare would be on the table, the novice must discipline himself not to eat too much rich food. The youth needs to realize that such rich **food is deceptive**. That is, it looks very delicious, but it may be hard for him to digest. Or there may be foods that appear irresistible but which turn out to be repulsive to the taste. Also he must not take so much food that he leaves a lot on his plate.

This instruction gives frank counsel to a youth who loves to eat. He must realize that it would be far better for him *to put a knife*, an eating utensil not a dagger (Clifford 1999, 209), **to *his* throat** than to yield to a strong craving, either by taking some food before a high official has been served or by taking too much of that particular food. The metaphor of the knife to the throat is very forceful as the sage seeks to impress on the youth the necessity of observing proper table etiquette.

Jesus likewise employed a very bold metaphor in the saying that if one's eye causes one to stumble, it is better to gouge it out than to fall into sin (Matt 18:9, see v 8). Everybody has a penchant that must be harnessed, especially at high public gatherings. If one fails to manage that tendency, one is likely to behave in a way that will gravely damage one's career.

Admonition against Desiring Wealth (23:4-5)

■ **4-5** The two lines in v 4 are advancing. The second two lines in v 5 are affirming; together they are advancing in relationship to the first line. Verse 5 is advancing in relationship to v 4.

A youth is warned against *wearing himself* out by working long and hard to *become* rich. He needs to stop thinking that he can work day and night without harming himself by relying on his own **cleverness** or *understanding* (see Amenemope 9:10—10:15). A person who is exhausted from overwork is unable to enjoy the results of that labor. Also a body worn down by excessive work is susceptible to illness.

This exhortation is motivated by calling attention to the reality that *wealth* is fleeting. In fact, it may disappear in **a glance**. Wealth, by its very nature, is relative. Each society places different values on goods. In one society a particular object may bring a high price, but that object may have little or no value in another society. For example, many peoples of the ancient Middle East, particularly the Babylonians and the Persians, placed a premium on purple garments.

Many ancient Middle Eastern governments had laws that permitted only the nobility to wear purple or scarlet garments. As a result of the value placed on purple, those skilled in producing purple dye, especially the Phoenicians, became exceedingly wealthy (see Ezek 28). But centuries later, when the Middle East came under the rule of Muslims, a people who placed no value on purple, the economy of those cities that produced purple dye collapsed. In fact, the technology used in making the dye was lost. The complete collapse of the purple industry illustrates well the saying that **riches . . . will surely sprout wings and fly off to the sky like an eagle.**

This saying certainly applies to personal wealth. Throughout history many have seen their wealth vanish in a very brief time span. In fact, the sudden loss of wealth continues to be the experience of many who live in a capitalistic system. Numerous businesses and industries undergo sudden shifts, from boom to bust. At the beginning of the twenty-first century some prestigious financial firms in the West disappeared overnight. It is not surprising that Jesus taught his disciples not to lay up treasures where thieves break through and steal and rust rots, but to place their treasure in heaven (Matt 6:19-20).

PROVERBS

23:4-5

Wealth and Wisdom

The admonition against overworking to become wealthy stands in some tension with proverbs that speak of wealth as one of the benefits of diligently searching for wisdom (e.g., Prov 8:18). A closer reading finds that these sayings teach that wealth is a by-product of growing in wisdom. In other words, there is a dynamic connection between wealth and wisdom, not a causal connection. Wealth is never to be viewed as the goal either of seeking wisdom or of fearing

Yahweh. Rather, it is a gift that often attends the acquiring of wisdom and the fear of Yahweh.

Today it needs to be underscored that biblical proverbs do not encourage the relentless pursuit of wealth. Rather they teach that the fear of God brings God's blessing. That blessing may be experienced in a variety of ways, such as good health, succeeding at one's work, or increasing in wealth.

Further, the richness of God's blessing may be experienced for a brief season or for decades, as God chooses. In all cases the benefits brought by God's blessing empower a person to use them for God's glory, particularly in sharing the fruits of those blessings with others, above all those who are less fortunate and those who are suffering.

Avoid Eating the Food of a Begrudging Host (23:6-8)

■ **6-8** The two lines in v 6 are affirming. Each of the lines in vv 7 and 8 are advancing. Verse 7 is advancing in relationship to v 6, and v 8 is advancing in relationship to vv 6-7.

The youth is exhorted **not *to* eat the food *nor crave the delicacies* of a begrudging host,** that is, a person characterized as having *an evil eye.*

After receiving an invitation to a banquet from a tightfisted person of high standing, a youth is excited, believing that the host is genuinely extending a hospitable invitation. But in reality that host **is always thinking about the cost.** At the banquet he politely encourages the youth to **"Eat and drink."** But being stingy, his heart is not in his words, watching closely to make sure he does not eat too much. Moreover, that host has no intention of establishing a friendship or a patronage with the youth. Rather than helping that youth advance professionally, he relishes seeing that youth flounder.

If that host's behavior becomes too oppressive, the tone at the banquet is likely to become so revolting that it turns the youth's stomach, causing him to **vomit . . . the little *he has* eaten**—a very shameful situation in the presence of the upper class. The ancients believed that such was the response of a person who has come under the evil eye of a miser (Elliott 1991, 154). Amenemope pictures a person's vomiting twice: as a result of hungering for a poor person's bread (14:7-8) and of having one's flatteries soundly rebuked by curses and blows (14:13-19).

As a metaphor in this proverb, it likely pictures the youth's repulsion at a request or a proposal that the host makes. Having to turn down the host, the youth will leave the dinner greatly upset, so upset that he feels like vomiting. His efforts at winning that person's favor with **compliments will have been wasted.** There is deep irony in this description. The very mouth that heaped praise on the host becomes the source of the youth's humiliation before that host (see Murphy 1998, 175).

Amenemope warns against coveting the property of a poor person under the metaphor of not consuming a poor person's bread. The instruction is motivated with the warning that while eating such bread it will get stuck in the greedy person's throat, making him vomit.

This metaphor means that such wealth will publicly expose the covetous person in a way that will greatly shame him. He will be shown to be guilty before his superiors. The shame will so befuddle him that he will not have any resources to deal with it. Any pleas he makes for lenience will be answered by a curse and a beating. What he gained will be totally lost as is also conveyed by the metaphor of vomiting. This picture serves as a strong motivation to avoid coveting a poor person's goods (14:5-19).

Advancing: Avoid Speaking to Fools (23:9)

■ **9** The two lines are advancing. An apprentice is admonished **not** *to* **speak to fools**. The admonition is motivated by calling attention to the inclination of fools *to* **scorn** wise counsel, even **prudent words** offered out of kindness (see 26:4; Ptahhotep, lines 575-79, *AEL*, 1:74).

In general a youth needs to realize that not everyone, especially a fool, wants to hear his keen insights, even though in his mind they are very valuable. Jesus set forth similar counsel: "Do not give dogs what is sacred; do not throw your pearls to pigs. If you do, they may trample them under their feet, and turn and tear you to pieces" (Matt 7:6; see Prov 26:4-5).

Against Moving Boundary Stones (23:10*a* = 22:28*a*) (23:10-11)

■ **10-11** The lines in v 10 are affirming and those in v 11 are advancing. Verse 11, giving the reason for the admonition, is advancing in relationship to v 10.

The prohibition **not** *to* **move an ancient boundary stone** is restated. It is given sharper focus than it was in Prov 22:28. Anyone who seeks to gain control of the land of *orphans* commits a serious offense because such action is against those who are unable to muster a defense that prevails over such a covert theft.

Given the vulnerable standing of orphans, the prohibition is made even stronger. A person is not even to **encroach on the fields of the fatherless**. This warning addresses a person who is planning to walk through the acreage of a weak person in order to identify either the most desirable land to take or a parcel that would be easiest to gain by stealthily moving the boundary stones. By preventing a person from entering the land of a weak person, the wise seek to preempt plans to gain control of that land.

An aggressor was emboldened to take such action because he assumed that an orphan lacked a relative who would act as his redeemer. In ancient Israelite law a redeemer was a close relative who came to the assistance of a family member who was in very difficult straits.

A common situation that led a relative to act as a redeemer was a relative's having to pay a debt by either entering servitude or leasing out the family's land (Lev 25:25-30, 47-55). In this case a redeemer paid the debt, thereby securing either the relative's release from servitude or his regaining control of the land.

Another way that a kinsman could act as redeemer was as a relative's legal defense; this role is attested in two texts—Job 19:25 and Lam 3:58-59. The use of **case** (*rîb*) in this saying indicates that the redeemer recovers land taken from an orphan by an aggressor's moving a boundary stone by a court decision.

These two prohibitions are supported by an assertion that functions as a warning: orphans have *a redeemer* who **is strong**. This wording implies that God is their Redeemer.

The Instruction of Amenemope (7:1—9:8) contains an extended passage against moving boundary stones, especially those of a widow's property. That instruction is motivated by the assertion that whoever commits such an act will be caught by the moon god or will be overcome by a terrible hardship.

God as Kinsman-Redeemer

In several OT texts God is lauded as Israel's Redeemer (*gô'ēl*) above all for delivering her from Egyptian bondage (e.g., Exod 15:13; Ps 78:35; Isa 43:14; 48:17; 49:7). The use of this title for God encouraged the weak and the afflicted to look to God as their source of help in dealing with difficult situations (Ps 103:3-4). While lamenting his affliction, Job came to believe that God, being true to justice, would serve as his *gô'ēl*, that is, his defense attorney, and prove that he was not guilty of any wrongdoing that had led to his suffering (Job 19:23-27).

Affirming: Applying Oneself to Learning (23:12)

■ **12** The lines in this couplet are affirming. At this point in the instruction the reliance on the Instruction of Amenemope ceases. This shift is signaled by a new appeal (with a cohortative) for the son or apprentice addressed as "you" to pay attention. Such an appeal often signals a new section (Fox 2009, 733). In addition, this saying is connected with the next one by the key word "discipline" or **instruction** (*mûsār*).

The youth is exhorted to **apply** his *mind* **to instruction** by *listening closely* **to words of knowledge**, that is, the instruction of the wise. **Apply your mind** directs him to learn the disciplines well, and *listen closely* encourages him to receive *the* **instruction** gladly rather than chafe against it.

Advancing: The Value of Disciplining a Child (23:13-14)

■ **13-14** The lines in both couplets are advancing. The instruction in Prov 23:14, supporting the admonition in v 13, is advancing.

A parent or a teacher is admonished **not *to* withhold discipline from a child**, a common theme in Proverbs (13:24; 19:18; 22:15; 29:15-17). Some children require a measure of physical punishment administered appropriately in order to correct bad attitudes or wrongful behaviors. Certainly striking a youth must be done circumspectly both in regard to the forcefulness of the blow and the place that receives the blow. The phrase **they will not die** is not to be taken as implying that a flogging might be so severe that it leaves the youth on the verge of death. Rather, it conveys that the discipline will keep children from engaging in activities or habits that have the potential of leading to an early death (Fox 2009, 733; Waltke 2005, 252). This reading is confirmed by the parallel statement *you will deliver their lives* from death (lit. *Sheol*).

Appropriate **discipline** will discourage a youth from engaging in immoral activities such as yielding to the allure of a prostitute that leads to terrible outcomes (23:22-28). Without firm direction from an adult many youths make wrong choices, choices that lead to their having to bear heavy consequences, some that afflict them throughout life. Thus, all children need a strong figure who cares enough for them to use firm methods of guidance in order that they may grow up to become confident adults who benefit their families and the community.

On a spiritual plane this proverb encourages a parent to use appropriate discipline in order to deliver a child from both an early death and Sheol. In light of Jesus' teaching about eternal life, this motivation is even more compelling for Christians than it was for the ancient Israelites. That is, appropriate discipline has the potential of keeping a child from eternal death.

Advancing: A Parent Rejoicing at a Child's Wisdom (23:15-16)

■ **15-16** Each of the couplets is formulated as advancing, and each couplet affirms the other. These two sayings are arranged chiastically. The outer lines speak of wisdom in association with *the* heart and *the* lips (vv 15*a*, 16*b*). The inner lines (vv 15*b*, 16*a*) stress the joy that a parent or a teacher experiences when *a* son or a student displays wisdom.

The youth, addressed as **my son**, is informed that in becoming **wise**, particularly in developing the skills of logical *thinking* and *speaking* what is **right**, he makes the father or the teacher **glad**. The teacher's deep sense of joy is conveyed by *rejoicing* in his **inmost being** (lit. *kidneys*). The ancient Israelites located a person's deepest emotions in the kidneys. This wording conveys that the son's moral and intellectual competence gives the father the greatest joy that a human can receive.

It is important to read the last three sets of instructions, v 12, vv 13-14, and vv 15-16, together. The exhortations are designed to persuade parents to be persistent and consistent in the disciplines they use in raising their children. They need to interact with their children in a way that helps the children open their ears for receiving "instruction," as exhorted in v 12. For children who are receptive, proper "discipline" guides them in becoming **wise** adults. Parents who guide their children well **rejoice** greatly.

For a Future Hope Avoid Jealousy (23:17-18)

■ **17-18** The lines in the first couplet are opposing and those in the second couplet are affirming. Verse 18 is advancing in relationship to v 17.

The son is exhorted **not *to* envy sinners**. This admonition is crucial, even more so in today's culture, since sinners are often portrayed as models of those who have the best possessions and the most fun (see Pss 37; 73). A youth who **envies** sinners is likely to take drastic steps to get what it appears they have. To counter such a strong temptation a youth is urged to **always be zealous *in* the fear of *Yahweh*.** A youth who focuses his affection on Yahweh finds that the apparent advantages of sinners lose their appeal (see Ps 73:15-17). No longer envying sinners, the youth comes to realize that those who **fear *Yahweh*** have **hope** for a bright **future,** *a* hope that **will not be cut off.** Rewards that attend fearing Yahweh are often realized very slowly, but their value is superior and enduring. (See Prov 20:1; 31:1-9.)

Avoid Drunkenness and Gluttony (23:19-21)

■ **19-21** This instruction of eight lines consists of an exhortation (v 19), an admonition (v 20), and a motivation (v 21). The lines in each of these three couplets are affirming. Verses 20-21 are advancing in relationship to v 19. Verse 20 is a prohibition that is supported by the reasons in v 21; thus v 21 is advancing in relationship to v 20. The prohibition is a particularization of the principle set out in v 19.

This saying is headed by the exhortations **listen, my son, and *become* wise.** The father or teacher appeals to the youth to pay careful attention to the following instruction, for in heeding this admonition the son ***will keep his*** heart *focused* **on the right path.**

The youth is specifically admonished not to associate with those who are partygoers, that is, those who **drink . . . wine** freely and **gorge . . . on meat.** Gorging on rich food and drinking large quantities of wine lead to two bad consequences. First, it makes ***one* poor** because **wine** and **meat** are expensive. Second, the overconsumption of **wine** dulls the mind, hindering one from thinking deeply, and the excessive consumption of rich food makes the body sluggish. After indulging in feasting and drinking, a person has difficulty staying focused on a task. Thus, one's productivity is greatly reduced. Bondage to these habits keeps a person from earning a good wage and from enjoying life. The eventual result is that one ***becomes clothed*** in rags. (See 20:1; 23:29-35; 31:1-9.)

In Deut 21:20 gluttony and drunkenness, the same words as here, are viewed as the causes of a person's becoming obstinate and rebellious, especially toward one's parents.

Listening to One's Parents (23:22-25)

■ **22-25** This cluster is framed by reference to the father who begot (v 22*a*) and the mother who gave birth (v 25*b*). The references to father (vv 22*a*, 24*a*, 24*b*, 25*a*) and mother (vv 22*b*, 25*a*, 25*b*) stand in an interchanging pattern. Verses 24 and 25 are tightly connected by being placed in a chiastic pattern: **has great joy** (*gîl*):**rejoices** (*śāmaḥ*)::**rejoice:be joyful.**

The youth is exhorted, **listen to your father**, the source of your **life** and **do not despise your mother when she is old**. In antiquity not listening to one's parents was deemed to be very disrespectful. It was to be avoided by a youth throughout life (see Sir 3:12-16).

In the context of honoring one's parents the youth is exhorted: ***acquire truth and do not sell it***. By gaining and holding on to truth, the student advances in **wisdom, instruction and insight** or ***understanding***, thereby honoring both father and mother. In order to acquire wisdom the youth must study diligently, accept discipline or instruction, and obey his parents and teacher.

A son who heeds this exhortation causes his **father** to ***rejoice greatly*** in his child becoming **righteous** and **wise**. These two qualities are frequently coupled in proverbs. Wisdom guides the youth, providing insight that leads to righteous living. The joy that such a child brings both parents is stressed by reaffirming that both **father and mother rejoice**.

The mother's ***rejoicing*** is underscored by her being mentioned with the father in v 25*a* and then being described as **she who gave** him **birth** in v 25*b*. In observing her son's attainment of wisdom she recalls that joyful day when she **gave** *him* **birth** as she now rejoices in his having attained wisdom.

Warning against the Enticements of an Adulteress (23:26-28)

■ **26-28** The couplets in Prov 23:26 and 27 are structured as affirming. The two lines in v 28 are advancing. Verse 27 is advancing in relation to v 26, and v 28 is advancing in that it is a particularization of v 27.

The youth, again addressed as **my son**, is exhorted: **give me your heart and let your eyes *keep to* my ways**. That is, pay close attention to what I am going to say so that you may stay on the straight path. Whybray (1994a, 339) interprets the appeal as demanding that the son submit to the father's will. The use of **heart** and **eyes** alerts the youth to the critical role these organs play in the temptation that needs to be shunned. The father particularly urges **the son** or the student to focus his sight on the way he conducts his life in order to stay on the upright course.

The father proceeds to alert the son who has little experience in sexual pleasure to the powerful allure of ***a strange*** or ***alien*** woman (reading *zārâ* for the MT *zônâ* [***prostitute***] with Fox 2009, 738; Waltke 2005, 247 n. 35). He wants the naive youth to perceive the importance of fending off her enticement to sexual pleasure. ***Strange*** indicates that this woman is another man's wife, and ***alien*** (*nokriyyâ*; see 6:24) that she is a foreigner. Sages viewed an adulteress as more dangerous than a prostitute (Fox 2009, 738; see 6:23-35), because a youth who comes under her influence not only faces the danger she poses but is also likely to face the wrath of her husband. This woman is clearly "off-limits" for the son (Murphy 1998, 177).

The teacher stresses that although this woman appears very desirable, in reality she is **a deep pit**, verily **a narrow well**. In antiquity a pit or a well, not being screened off, held grave danger, especially for young children running about the village. Anyone who fell into one of these cavities might die unless someone discovered the victim and proceeded to rescue him or her. The danger of a deep pit is a vivid analogy for the danger of joining with a harlot. Such a liaison may cost a youth his life (7:26-27; 9:18). In the meantime such a liaison wrecks a man's deepest relationships, husband-wife and disciple-Lord, for these relationships are built on loyalty, trust, and love, the moral qualities that such a union decimates.

The teacher proceeds with a description of a harlot's tactics for seducing a youth. No longer pictured as a passive danger as conveyed by the metaphor **pit** (Fox 2009, 739), she is pictured as a cunning aggressor, stealthily seeking out a passerby that she might entice to join her. **Like a bandit she lies in wait** for a victim (see Gen 38:13-16). Her skill at seduction **multiplies** the number of **men** *who behave treacherously*. The term *treacherous* carries great force. It conveys that after succumbing to an adulteress a male immediately begins to act deceptively in an effort to conceal his unfaithfulness. Loyalty is no longer at the center of his character.

References to adultery in ancient sources usually focus on the harm done to the woman's husband and ignore the harm done to the husband's wife. But in that this man's deed is described as a treacherous act, it discloses the harm that he has done to her. Given the nature of acting treacherously, this husband has to confess his unfaithfulness, make a genuine apology, and work toward reconciliation with his wife to escape from the pit of leading a deceptive life.

This saying is most appropriate for contemporary youths who are seeking wisdom and growing in righteousness. On that spiritual journey a male is likely to meet a woman who, though neither a prostitute nor an adulteress, is so strongly drawn to him that she seeks to become his companion. If he yields to her appeals for companionship, he starts down a dangerous path that is likely to lead him to fall into a deep pit. It will likely take him a long time to find a way out of that pit and recover his standing in his family and in the community of faith.

A parallel danger awaits a woman who is zealously serving God. A man, claiming to be spiritual, may entice her into a close relationship with no intention of caring for her after his lust is satisfied.

These dangers are especially prevalent for those preparing for or who are engaged in the ministry. The forces of wickedness seek to undermine one's zeal for building God's kingdom by becoming entangled in an illicit relationship. Such an entanglement undercuts a person's integrity and is likely to take a person out of the ministry for many years.

Against Intoxication (23:29-35)

This epigram (Fox 2009, 740) or mocking song (Waltke 2005, 262) on the dangers of intoxication opens with six short "who" questions. These questions are structured in affirming style (Prov 23:29) and are followed by an answer consisting of two lines, also in affirming style (v 30). An admonition of three lines cast in affirming style follows (v 31). Each of the couplets in vv 32-34 is formulated as affirming. In describing the outcome of failing to heed the admonition in v 31, they stand as advancing in relationship to that verse. The epigram concludes with the youth deliriously talking to himself (v 35). This verse has four lines. The first two are structured as affirming and the last two as advancing.

This vivid description of a youth's becoming intoxicated is tragically humorous. The teacher is using humor to capture the son's imagination in order to overcome his natural resistance to being admonished against drinking wine. The details create a vivid picture of the powerful effects that alcohol has, especially in robbing a person of wisdom. In other words, drinking too much wine has the potential to undo years of instruction given by the teacher. (See 20:1; 31:4-7.)

Delirious Questions and a Straightforward Answer (23:29-30)

■ **29-30** The teacher leads the student to consider the physical agonies that attend the excessive consumption of wine with a series of short questions. The questions cast in staccato style cause the student to hear in his imagination the delirious condition that results from becoming intoxicated. *To whom* woe [*'ôy*]? *To whom alas* [*'ăbôy*]? **Who has strife? Who has complaints?** These questions also draw attention to the complaints made against a drunk's erratic behavior.

The next set of questions centers on the physical agony that besets a drunk person: **Who has needless bruises? Who has bloodshot eyes?**—better, *whose* eyes *appear dark red?*

The teacher provides the answer to these questions: **Those who linger over wine, who go to *inspect* bowls of mixed wine**. The youth is filled with **woe** as a result of drinking wine from many bowls over several hours. The length of time is conveyed by the term **linger**. *Sampling* indicates that the youth has been avidly tasting various wines, including **mixed wine**, that is, wine that has been made more potent.

Exhortation against Being Seduced by Wine (23:31)

■ **31** Because of wine's ability to overpower a person, the teacher admonishes the student: **Do not gaze at wine when it is *deep* red, when it sparkles in the cup**. Whenever a youth begins to sense the strong draw of the wine, he needs to look away from it. Literally the text reads: *when it gives its eye in the cup*. Fox (2009, 741) unpacks this metaphor in the following way. As the youth gazes at the wine, the wine looks back. That is, the youth sees his own eyes looking back at him as he stares into the wine—a dark red wine like merlot reflects the drinker's eyes. The bond between the wine and the eyes is even tighter in that the wine will make his eyes dark red. While staring at the wine, the youth ponders how delicious it will taste and how **smoothly *it will*** *go* **down.** Letting such thoughts run through his mind unchecked, the youth eventually yields to the wine's seductive power.

Consequences of Excessive Drinking of Wine (23:32-34)

■ **32-34** In the stomach the sparkling wine bites like **a** poisonous **snake,** causing the youth to feel as though he had been bitten by **a viper.** The alcohol makes him delirious. His head begins to swim. He sees **strange sights.** All kinds of *bizarre images* pass before his **eyes.**

While sleeping off the stupor, an inebriated person feels as though he *is* **sleeping on the high seas** or **lying on top of** a boat's **rigging,** desperately holding on to keep from going overboard. This picture captures well the inability of one who is drunk to maintain balance.

The Youth Talks to Himself (23:35)

■ **35** When the youth awakens from the drunken stupor, he feels as though he has been in a boxing match. Instead of feeling ashamed, he brags as though he were triumphant: **"They hit me, . . . but I'm not hurt! They beat me, but I don't feel it!"** Even though he feels pain throughout his body as though he had been in a brawl, he boasts that he has **not** *been* **hurt.** Drunkenness leads to a denial of reality. Regardless of the youth's confidence that he is in control, wine has a strong hold on him. Its power is visible in his next assertion: **"When will I wake up so** *that* **I can find another drink?"** As he is becoming sober, the youth foolishly declares that when he is awake he will satisfy his desire for **another drink.** Unawares, he is becoming enslaved to alcohol.

Egyptian wisdom texts also warn against the ill consequences of drunkenness; for example, the prohibition against indulging in drinking beer in the Instruction of Any (4:6-11).

FROM THE TEXT

In antiquity the bondage of alcoholism could not be easily broken. Fortunately today there are numerous clinics and hospitals with intensive programs to assist an alcoholic in recovering from this illness.

This picturesque instruction against becoming enslaved to alcohol is applicable to other addictions, such as pornography, gambling, or drugs. An addiction robs a person of a vibrant life as an outside force takes control of one's desires. Such robbery is very tragic for a youth who has started to travel the path of wisdom. Because these addictions are virtually impossible for a person to overcome without professional help, anyone so enslaved needs to seek out a center or an institute known for success in delivering people from the particular addiction being faced. (See 21:17; 23:21; Eccl 10:17.)

Envy of the Wicked (24:1-2)

■ **1-2** The lines within each verse are structured as affirming. Verse 2 is advancing in relationship to v 1.

This saying opens with a double prohibition: **Do not envy the wicked, do not desire their company**. Often a youth is drawn to the company of those who are becoming wealthy by shady tactics or of those who boast about enjoying grand adventures even though they are illegal. A youth longs to get in on the excitement, experience the camaraderie, and have access to extra cash (see 1:10-19).

These admonitions are supported by a description of the distorted thinking of the wicked. **Their *minds* plot *violent deeds***, deeds that destroy property wantonly and harm innocent people. They relish devising ingenious schemes for disrupting society and exploiting people. They constantly challenge each other to come up with outrageous schemes for wreaking havoc. This description of the demented conversations of the wicked seeks to show a youth that the wicked are unworthy of his envy. Rather than longing to become allied with the wicked, a youth needs to be drawn to the company of those who pursue righteousness, those who are blessed because they do not walk in the counsel of the wicked or stand in the way of sinners or sit in the seat of mockers (Ps 1:1). (See Prov 23:17-18; 24:19-20.)

Wisdom Needed for Building a House (24:3-4)

■ **3-4** The lines in v 3 are affirming; those in v 4 are advancing. Verse 4 advances the premise set out in v 3.

Wisdom is essential for ***building*** a house. Before starting such a complex project a person must draw on the skill of strategic planning provided by wisdom for drawing up detailed plans of the desired structure. Next one needs to be astute in hiring craftsmen with **understanding** to construct the house well. After the house has been built, **knowledge** is needed for decorating the **rooms** so that each has a special ambience that enhances the display of **rare and beautiful treasures**. Wisdom turns a building into a beautiful home.

The Power of Wisdom for Waging War (24:6a = 20:18b and 24:6b = 11:14b) (24:5-6)

■ **5-6** The lines in each couplet are affirming. Verse 6 stands in an advancing relationship to v 5.

Because of **knowledge the wise** have greater **power** for overcoming difficult situations than those who rely on brute force. Qohelet tells a story of a wise person who was able to deliver a city besieged by a strong king through his wisdom (Eccl 9:13-16). That story illustrates the adage "wisdom is better than strength" (Eccl 9:16a).

Before ***waging*** war, a **wise** commander takes counsel with **many** skilled **advisers**, recognizing that the development of a strategic battle plan is essential for achieving **victory**. Victory is attained more often by a clever strategy than by sheer force. The value of drawing up a strategic plan before starting a task is applicable to every situation. (See Prov 11:14; 15:22; 20:18.)

A Fool Cannot Reach Wisdom (24:7)

■ **7** This couplet is structured as advancing. **Wisdom is too high for fools** to grasp. Consequently, whenever they take a seat **at the** *city* **gate**—the place in antiquity where people gathered to discuss events, make plans, and try cases—they are silent. Frequently in Proverbs fools are described as talkative (12:23; 13:16; 15:2; 20:3). But when a serious discussion is taking place, **fools** have nothing to contribute.

A Mischief-maker (24:8-9)

■ **8-9** The couplets in both verses are structured as advancing. Verse 9 is advancing in relationship to v 8. A person **who** plots evil becomes **known as a schemer** (*ba'al mĕzimmôt*). This title is not desirable, for **the schemes of folly are sin**.

Being in the habit of debunking all things that people value highly, such as temple rituals, festivals, and officials, **a schemer**, also known as **a mocker** (*lēṣ*), **is** deeply *detested* (*tô'ēbâ*). The stream of caustic remarks pouring out of that person so irritates people that they exclude the person from community gatherings. It is rare in Proverbs that the verb **detest**, one of the strongest terms of denunciation (→ sidebar "Yahweh Detests or Abomination to Yahweh" at 6:16-19), has a subject other than God.

Faltering in a Time of Trouble (24:10)

■ **10** The lines in v 10 are structured as advancing. Does this verse serve as a heading to vv 11-12? Interpreters are divided on this issue. It seems best to take v 10 as a distinct saying since it addresses a different situation than presented in the next two verses.

In a time of trouble people are faced with numerous challenges. Those who are resourceful discover ways to deal with these problems. A few even prosper. However, the majority **falter**, showing that they have *little* **strength** and ingenuity. This saying underscores the critical need for wisdom in order to cope during troubled times.

Rescuing People Being Led to Death (24:11-12)

■ **11-12** The lines in v 11 are affirming. In v 12 the second and third lines are structured as affirming. The second line advances the first, and the fourth advances the third. Verse 12 is advancing in relationship to v 11.

Rather than faltering in a time of trouble, this proverb calls for displaying courage in rescuing people from death. The precise nature of the situation that threatens people's lives is unclear, because the terms are general. In a situation in which people *are* **being led away to death** those who fear God are exhorted to **rescue** them by *holding* **back those** who *are* **staggering toward slaughter**. Although "wrongly" is not used to describe the reason these people are being led away, it is implied.

The next verse presents a possible defense offered by those who observe such a tragic scene taking place but fail to rescue those who are **being led away**

to death. Most ordinary citizens intentionally ignore what is taking place out of fear for their own lives and the lives of family members. They excuse their shortcoming by saying, **"We knew nothing about this."** They hope to escape reproach by claiming ignorance as to what has been taking place.

To those who offer such a defense the sage puts forth three challenging, rhetorical questions. **Does not** God **who weighs the heart** [i.e., evaluates people according to their inner motives] **perceive *this*? Does not he who guards your life know it?** The implied answer to these two questions is "Certainly!" The third question is even more condemning. **"Will he** [i.e., God] **not repay *each human* according to what *he* has done?"** Again the implied answer is "Yes."

It is difficult to know the type of situation(s) this saying is addressing especially in Israel's history. There were various times when a leader slaughtered large numbers of people to advance his position. In northern Israel Jehu, a general, rebelled against King Jehoram. To establish his rule he orchestrated massive slaughters. At the outset he had all the members of Ahab's house put to death (2 Kgs 10:1-17). Then he orchestrated a religious festival and invited hundreds of ministers, prophets, and priests of Baal. After making the sacrifices, he had all those who served Baal killed (2 Kgs 10:18-25).

Another example took place in Judah following the murder of Ahaziah, the king, by Jehu. Taking advantage of this situation, Athaliah, the queen, ordered every member of the royal family killed so that she could capture the throne of David (2 Chr 22:10-12). Courageously Jehosheba, Ahaziah's sister, hid Joash, the sole surviving son of Ahaziah. With the help of the priests, she raised the child. When Joash turned eight years old, Jehoida, the high priest and husband of Jehosheba, organized a revolt to depose Queen Athaliah, a worshipper of Baal, and enthrone Joash (2 Chr 23:1-15).

Whether this saying has situations of mass slaughter like these in view is difficult to know. In any case this saying seeks to inspire those who witness the illegitimate incarceration and killing of people to respond courageously by rescuing people who are marked to be put to death. In the last two centuries in various parts of the world there have been many cases of genocide, sometimes referred to as ethnic cleansing. When the Nazis were herding Jews into concentration camps and putting large numbers of them to death, most people in Germany and other nearby countries looked the other way. Nevertheless, several brave citizens of various European countries displayed great courage in rescuing thousands of Jews from being herded off to these camps. Today many of those brave heroes are honored by trees planted in their honor along the Avenue of the Righteous Among the Nations at Yad Vashem in Jerusalem. These heroes are premiere examples of those who have heeded the exhortation in Prov 24:11.

24:11-12

257

Sweetness of Honey and of Wisdom (24:13-14)

■ **13-14** The lines in v 13 are affirming. The second and third lines of v 14 are affirming; these two lines are advancing in relationship to the first line of v 14. The saying in v 14 is an application of the exhortation set out in v 13.

The student or *the* **son** is exhorted to **eat honey, . . . for it is good**. He is to dig out **honey from the comb** because it *tastes* sweet. The son is being prodded to take delight in the good, nutritious, sweet things the creation provides.

This analogy serves to encourage the observation of the next exhortation: **know that wisdom is *sweet to*** one's ***whole being*** (*nepeš*). Just as one's palate desires the sweet taste of honey, a person's psyche has a deep longing for wisdom. Just as one gains pleasure and a burst of energy from eating honey, *finding wisdom* heartens one's disposition (*nepeš*). Newly acquired wisdom excites one's deepest thinking. Therefore, wisdom needs to be diligently sought, especially in that it offers the son **hope** for **a future,** *a* hope that **will not be cut off**. Wisdom is the gyroscope that keeps one traveling on the right path, a path that leads to a delightful future.

The connection between wisdom and hope is vital. Hope motivates a person to face with courage the numerous challenges that confront one throughout life (see v 10). It inspires a person to overcome gigantic obstacles, and it empowers one to endure appalling situations. There are inspiring accounts of those who survived the horrendous conditions experienced as prisoners of war, for example, Senator John McCain, a prisoner of war in Vietnam; missionary Jake DeShazer, a Japanese prisoner of war in China; and Victor Frankl, a Jewish Viennese psychiatrist who was incarcerated in three German concentration camps. Frankl developed the philosophy of logotherapy: a person who has a deep sense of meaning is able to survive any situation, no matter how horrible. By drawing on his own philosophy, he was able to survive the dreadful conditions of these concentration camps and help other prisoners survive as well.

Against Raiding the Dwelling of a Righteous Person (24:15-16)

■ **15-16** The lines in v 15 are affirming, and those in v 16 are opposing. Verse 16 is advancing in relationship to v 15. The terms **fall** and **stumble** in vv 16 and 17 connect this saying with the following one.

The saying opens with two admonitions: **Do not lurk like *a wicked person* near the house of the righteous** and **do not plunder *the resting* place** or *fold* of his flocks. Spoken to a person who is aspiring to be a government official, this admonition addresses a temptation to use legal means to deprive a righteous person of his property or flocks. That official may be motivated to take such action because that person has angered him or has refused to do something that the official believes should be done, such as refusing to sell grain during a time of hunger (see 11:26).

The admonition is supported by stating a key retribution principle: **though the righteous fall seven times, they rise again** (see Job 5:17-19). **Seven**, the ideal number, conveys that no setback can keep the righteous down. Therefore, this official who wants to harm a righteous person needs to realize that the righteous endure because of God's protection. By contrast, *a misfortune causes* the wicked *to* stumble. After falling, the wicked are unable to rise. Such is the fate of an official who strikes out at a righteous person.

An Adjustment to the Text of the First Line of Prov 24:15

In the MT this prohibition is addressed to *a wicked man* (*rāšā'*), standing as a vocative. Based on this view, this saying is a warning against such a person's planning to defraud the righteous (Longman 2006, 439). However, this instruction is clearly addressed to "my son" (23:15, 19, 26), a youth in training to become a government official (22:17-21). Therefore, it is unlikely that *a wicked person* is being addressed. Possibly the word "wicked" was a marginal notation made by a scribe in an effort to make sense of this prohibition, for one would not think that an official in training needed to be instructed against lying in wait to enter a righteous person's property.

The NIV's solution is to render *rāšā'* **like a thief,** but the term **like** is not in the Hebrew text, and **thief** is an unusual rendering for *rāšā'* ("wicked"). A better approach is to omit this word as a marginal note that entered the body of the text during its transmission history (Fox 2009, 749).

Another possible solution is to interpret the proverb as an admonition to the youth in training not to be tempted to join with those who plan to raid a righteous person's property. In that case it is similar to the warning against yielding to enticements to join a gang that raids the property of others and shares the loot (1:10-19; see 24:1-2). More importantly, by lauding the resilience of a righteous person faced with troubles the line serves to encourage the youth to pursue righteousness (Longman 2006, 439).

Inappropriate Joy at an Enemy's Fate (24:17-18)

■ **17-18** The lines in v 17 are affirming. Those in v 18 are structured as advancing. Verse 18 is advancing in relationship to v 17.

The son is admonished **not** *to rejoice* when *an* enemy **falls**, not even in the privacy of *his own mind.* The reason is that **Yahweh** will see him *gloating* at the enemy's misfortune and **disapprove**, considering such an attitude *inappropriate* or *bad* (*ra'*). **Yahweh** may *withdraw* his **anger** from that enemy. The precise situation addressed by this proverb is hard to reconstruct, for in various songs, such as Exod 15:1-18, God's people enthusiastically celebrate the defeat of an enemy.

This proverb does not condemn rejoicing at the defeat of the wicked. Rather, it counsels against gloating at the misfortunes that befall a foe. It is important to observe that this counsel stands after the description of the great resilience of the righteous. The righteous have such resilience as a result of

God's mercy. Those who have been richly blessed need to be aware that their gloating over the ill fate of the wicked has the potential of leading to an arrogant smugness.

Smugness makes a person calloused to the sufferings of others. Thus, it is crucial to temper taking pleasure at the terrible suffering of the wicked to prevent such a result. Waltke (2005, 284) wisely comments that by repudiating improper attitudes as smugness, insensibility, and cynicism, a person guards against suddenly committing a wrongful deed, one that is out of character.

The importance of this prohibition is underscored by the motivation that God **will withdraw** his **wrath** from the enemy. This proverb advances the theme that vengeance belongs to God (Longman 2006, 440; see Rom 12:17-21). In addition, it is important to note that the sages strongly encourage those pursuing wisdom to be aware of their innermost feelings and attitudes, for these feelings shape one's character and influence one's actions (Fox 2009, 750).

Against Being Distressed by Evildoers (24:20*b* = 13:9*b*) (24:19-20)

■ **19-20** The couplets in both verses are affirming. Verse 20 is advancing in relationship to v 19.

The youth is admonished **not** *to* **fret**, that is, *be strongly agitated at* or *be out of sorts with* the success of **evildoers**, such as at their becoming wealthy or receiving high positions. He is not to **be envious of the wicked**. Harboring resentment at them produces negative attitudes that erode one's moral strength.

This admonition is supported by a strong assertion: **the evildoer has no future**. Indeed, **the lamp** [i.e., the life force] **of the wicked will be snuffed out**, even before they have grown old. Whenever the son is troubled by the prosperity of the wicked, he needs to reflect on the terrible fate to which they are headed. Their destiny is the dark, dreary abode of Sheol. Being mindful of their fate causes his irritation at their acclaim to dissipate (see Ps 73:16-20). (See Prov 23:17-18; 24:1-2.)

Fear Yahweh and the King (24:21-22)

■ **21-22** The lines in v 21 are opposing; the lines in v 22 are affirming. Verse 22 is advancing in relationship to v 21.

This exhortation most fittingly closes this extended wisdom instruction for a son or an apprentice. It challenges the student or *the* **son** to **fear Yahweh and the king**: Yahweh because he is the sovereign Lord and the king because he is Yahweh's earthly representative charged with governing Yahweh's people. A disposition of reverence provides a firm foundation for a wise person to work diligently and with integrity in serving the king and the people.

Whenever the son becomes disheartened either with royal decisions or his job, he is admonished to squelch any impulse to do something foolish like *joining* with **rebellious officials**, for such an affiliation would anger both lords. This admonition is motivated by a description of the absolute power of both rulers in punishing an adversary in their respective realms. Either of them is capable of suddenly causing *a disaster* to befall the **rebellious**. This ability of these rulers to inflict punishment is underscored by the rhetorical question: **Who knows what *misfortunes either of them can cause*?** No one can imagine the kind of *trouble* God or the king might **bring**. (See 16:14; 19:12; 20:2.)

B. Additional Sayings of the Wise (24:23-34)

OVERVIEW

This small collection of sayings of the wise consists of three admonitions (vv 27, 28, 29), two proverbs (vv 23b-25, 26), and an epigram (vv 30-34). One proverb has two lines (v 26) and one admonition three lines (v 27). There is also an admonition that has four lines (vv 28-29). Two sayings are longer, five lines (vv 23b-25) and eleven lines (vv 30-34). The latter may be classified as an epigram (Fox 2009, 773-74). The wide variations in the length of these sayings correspond to the variations in Section IIIA and may be a secondary reason for this collection's placement.

Themes addressed in this collection include the pleasure provided by "an honest answer" (v 26), the importance of prioritizing one's work (v 27), poverty that attends laziness (vv 30-34), and the importance of impartiality in judging (vv 23b-25). There is also an admonition not to testify falsely against a neighbor, especially as an act of vengeance (vv 28-29).

BEHIND THE TEXT

This brief collection of twenty-three lines has been placed after the instructions for becoming a respected scribe (Section IIIA) and given the title "these also are sayings of the wise" (24:23a). This title is similar to the one that heads the preceding instruction (22:17).

Nothing is known about this small collection's origin. It is possible that a scribe while editing wisdom sayings came across one or two sheets of papyrus from a scroll on which these sayings were written. Wishing to preserve them, he placed them after the above instruction and gave them a similar heading. That these sayings have been consciously placed here as an addition is clearly signaled by the use of the term "also" or "further" (*gam*) at the head of v 23.

IN THE TEXT

Just Verdicts (Verse 23b = 28:21a [less the phrase "in judging"]) (24:23-25)

■ **23-25** The title (v 23a) is followed by a saying of five lines (vv 23b-25). The first line states a fundamental legal principle (v 23b). The results of violating or adhering to that principle are set out in vv 24-25. The lines in v 24 are advancing, and those in v 25 are affirming. Verse 24 is advancing in relationship to v 23b in that it gives the consequences of violating the basic principle. Verse 25 is opposing in relationship in v 24.

The initial proverb states the principle that *showing* partiality in judging is not good (see Deut 1:17; 16:19). **Not good** is a litotes for a very bad, even intolerable situation. Partiality in judging destroys a community's solidarity. To uphold justice a court must be impartial in deciding a case. This standard underlies the contemporary saying, "Justice is blind." True justice has no regard for the high or low standing of either a plaintiff or a defendant.

Whenever a judge or an official **says to *a wicked person*** [rāšāʿ], "**You are innocent,**" people will be so distressed at such a perversion of justice that they **will *curse*** that judge or official. Even **nations *will denounce*** an Israelite court for a travesty of justice. In general, people realize that the release of a guilty person is a threat to that community and also to surrounding nations.

Conversely, **it will *be pleasant*** for **those who *argue a case*** so convincingly that **the guilty *are convicted***. The defenders of justice will be honored in the community and ***will receive a*** rich blessing from God. Their recognition will encourage all to be diligent in working to see that wrongdoers are punished appropriately regardless of their position in the community.

An Honest Answer (24:26)

■ **26** A person, especially a leader, who offers *a straightforward* **answer** or *response* to a contentious issue produces such delight in the hearer(s) that it is comparable to the pleasure of **a kiss on the lips**. Direct, insightful, **honest** words build relationships.

Advancing: Importance of Prioritizing One's Work (24:27)

■ **27** The head of a household must prioritize his **work** according to the principle that urgent work must be attended to before undertaking important projects, even though the latter provides greater satisfaction.

The social setting behind this instruction is life in an ancient village. For protection from wild animals and bandits people lived close together in a walled village. Early each morning family members left the village to work in the fields and shepherd the flocks, returning at sundown.

This proverb exhorts a young husband to be diligent in working in his **fields**, particularly in preparing them for planting in the fall. Only after the fields have been plowed and the seed planted may he remain in the village during the day and **build *a*** house. Of course, he must interrupt such a project whenever the field needs tending to or at harvesttime. This instruction makes clear that a family must have a source of food or income before the father spends time working on other important matters.

Affirming: Avoid Giving Deceptive Testimony and Taking Vengeance without Reason (24:28-29)

■ **28-29** Both couplets in vv 28 and 29 are affirming. Verse 29 presents the thinking that leads to the behavior described in v 28.

According to this admonition a person should not go to court and **testify against *a*** neighbor **without cause**. In fact, a person should never speak *decep-*

tively, in or out of court. Lies and deceit destroy trust among neighbors. This was especially the case in an ancient community that lacked a police force. Solidarity was essential for the community to be safe and prosperous.

When a person feels slighted or mistreated by a neighbor, he may be tempted to **make false charges** against *that* neighbor without *due* cause, thinking **"I'll do to them as they have done to me."** That offended person wants to **pay them back** by causing them as much or even greater grief than he feels he has incurred. Whenever tempted to take revenge, a person needs to remember the wise counsel: wait for Yahweh to correct matters (20:22*b*). (See Lev 19:18.)

The desire to seek vengeance is laden with the potential of adverse outcomes. Besides robbing one's peace of mind, it carries the potential of leading to a long-standing feud between neighbors. A feud forces members of both families to be continually on guard. Neighbors can no longer live beside each other peaceably.

A Parable of a Lazy Farmer (24:30-34)

■ **30-34** A parable or an epigram consisting of eleven lines closes this small collection. Whybray (1994a, 356) labels it "a teaching story." The teacher describes the condition of a downtrodden **field** he walked by (vv 30-31). After pondering the significance of what he has seen (v 32), he composes a saying about laziness (v 33).

The first five lines are structured as affirming. Verse 31 advances v 30 by describing what the sage has seen. The sage's reflection (v 32), with lines that are affirming, advances the parable. Each of the couplets in vv 33 and 34 are structured as affirming. Verses 33-34 together are advancing in relationship to v 32, presenting the results of the sage's reflection.

A sage passed by **the field** and **the vineyard** of *a lazy person*, a person *devoid of common* sense. He was shocked by the sad state of the field as he recalled the hard work of the owner's ancestors in clearing the land, building a stone wall, planting the vines, and tending them over many years so that they would produce a bountiful yield.

The passerby noticed that the field had become overgrown with **thorns.** The grain had wilted, and the vines were dying. Since **the stone wall was in ruins,** the vineyard was no longer protected.

The passerby stopped to ponder the reasons for the field's run-down condition. His reflecting, conveyed by four verbs (v 32)—*perceive* (*ḥāzâ*), *consider* (*šît lēb*, lit. *take to heart*), *see* (*rāʾâ*), and *receive instruction* (*lāqaḥ mûsār*)—led to a valuable **lesson.** He discerned that the owner had spent too much time *sleeping* and *slumbering*. Rather than picking up a hoe and working diligently to remove the weeds and instead of repairing the wall, that owner merely *folded his arms and rested*. His frequent naps lengthened into hours of slumber.

The lesson the sage gained from reflecting on what he saw is that sloth brings **poverty** and **scarcity like an armed *vigilante***. Whenever a farmer fails to attend diligently to the fields, they soon appear as though they have been overrun by a marauding troop. The sluggard's laziness has led to ruining the foundation of the family's livelihood.

This epigram also provides motivation for the earlier proverb that advises the importance of prioritizing one's work (v 27). It also shows that in teaching with parables Jesus was truly a teacher in the Israelite wisdom tradition.

IV. SECOND SOLOMONIC COLLECTION: 25:1—29:27

OVERVIEW

Section IV, which consists of five chapters, preserves additional proverbs from the time of Solomon. These sayings were copied and arranged by sages at Hezekiah's court. Section IV has two parts, Part 1 (chs 25—27) and Part 2 (chs 28—29).

Part 1 is distinguished by numerous proverbs constructed around an analogy. Frequently a metaphor or a word picture stands in the first line, and the topic is in the second line. Often the metaphor functions like a riddle (Fox 2009, 775). As the key element it prods the hearer to figure out what it represents. For example, Prov 25:12 opens with the metaphor "like an earring of gold or an ornament of fine gold." On hearing these two metaphors, a person ponders what is like beautiful gold jewelry. The answer comes in the second line: "the rebuke of a wise judge to a listening ear." Other proverbs in this collection introduce the analogy with the preposition "like" (*k*) in the first line and the topic introduced with "thus" (*kēn*), either in the second line or a following verse (26:1, 2, 8, 18-19; 27:8, 19; Fox 2009, 775). Two of these proverbs, however, lack the term "thus" (25:13; 26:11). The use of metaphors has virtually vanished in Part 2 except for two in ch 28: driving rain (v 3) and a lion (v 15).

265

In Part 1 seven proverbs are formulated as commands (25:4, 5, 16-17, 21-22; 26:5; 27:11, 13) and five as prohibitions (25:6-7, 8, 9-10; 26:4; 27:10). In addition, four proverbs offer wise counsel in a style that resembles a warning (25:16 + 17; 26:5, 24-26; 27:23-24). This style of instruction is missing in Part 2 except for the prohibition in the third line of 28:17.

The length of the proverbs in Part 1 varies. Besides several couplets, four proverbs consist of three lines (25:13, 20; 27:10, 22), eight of four lines (25:4-5, 6-7b, 7c-8, 9-10, 16-17, 21-22; 26:18-19; 27:15-16), and one of six lines (26:24-26). These variations in the length of the proverbs is somewhat similar to the variations in Section IIIA. However, ch 26 deviates in this regard, for all but two proverbs are couplets, the main style found in Section II and in Part 2. Furthermore, the majority of the proverbs in ch 26 are clustered around a topic: a fool (26:1-12 [except v 2], 17-19), a lazy person (26:13-16), and types of persons who speak maliciously (26:18-26 [except v 20], 28).

In Part 2 all the sayings are couplets except for two that have three lines (28:10, 17). The dominant structure of the sayings in this part is opposing—eighteen in ch 28 and fourteen in ch 29. Chapter 28 stands out for the number of sayings on piety (28:5, 6, 14, 18, 20, 25, 26, 27).

Many proverbs in Section IV, especially in Part 2, offer direct counsel to the king and/or high officials (25:2, 3, 4-5, 6-7, 15; 28:2, 3, 12, 15, 16, 28; 29:4, 12, 14, 18, 26). The king is viewed as a human who needs to strive for wisdom so that he may establish justice and promote prosperity. Malchow (1985, 238-45) has identified this material as a manual for future rulers. Clearly, there is a concentration of sayings offering guidance to the king and court officials. However, Egyptian and Babylonian instructions addressed to a future ruler focus more on issues unique to a ruler than is the case with this material (Fox 2009, 818).

Another significant topic in Part 2 is the impact that the people's character has on the nation's morale. Sayings that contrast the righteous (*ṣaddîqîm*) and the wicked (*rāšāʿ*) frame this section (28:1; 29:27) as is evident in these terms standing in a chiastic pattern: "wicked":"righteous" (28:1)::"righteous":"wicked" (29:27; Malchow 1985, 239). Ten proverbs laud the contribution of the righteous or the wise to the security and the prosperity of the nation (28:1b, 4b, 5b, 12a, 28b; 29:2a, 7a, 8b, 16b, 27a), thirteen sayings bring out the fear, agony, and discord caused by the wicked (28:4a, 5a, 8, 12b, 15, 28a; 29:2b, 7b, 8a, 10, 16a, 22, 27b). In addition, issues of economics are the topic of eight proverbs in ch 28 (6, 8, 19, 20, 22, 24, 25, 27). The concluding epigram (27:23-27) in accord with the economic theme lauds shepherding as an occupation capable of sustaining a growing clan indefinitely. It may also be interpreted as providing counsel to the king, who is often referenced as a shepherd in several ancient Middle East cultures (Malchow 1985, 243-45).

BEHIND THE TEXT

The heading to Section IV (25:1) records that scribes at King Hezekiah's court searched out and transcribed (*he'tîqû*) proverbs from the Solomonic era. According to Fox (2009, 777), it is appropriate to render the Hebrew verb *he'tîq* as ***transcribe*** given that the subject is plural and that this small collection could easily be copied by one scribe. Presumably a government official came across a collection of sayings, distinct from those in the official volume that housed Israelite wisdom (25:1) and then took steps to have them included in the official canon of Israelite wisdom. The use of ***too*** (*gam*) clearly indicates that this collection has been appended to an existing corpus of proverbs, possibly those found in Section II.

In sponsoring this effort Hezekiah was acting like other Middle Eastern monarchs at the end of the first half of the second millennium BC. Realizing the importance of promoting the national heritage, several kings initiated programs to preserve the national literature. They commissioned scribes to travel throughout the empire in search of literary texts. Copies were made and stored in a national library or repository.

A ruler famous for such an effort was Ashurbanipal (668-627 BC), the last major emperor of Assyria. He commissioned scribes to search for documents throughout the empire. Copies were made and housed in the great library that he established at Nineveh. Egyptian Pharaohs also supported a House of Life for preserving Egyptian literature. That house had a school, library, and scriptorium (Fox 2009, 777).

It is likely that Hezekiah, one of Judah's most devout kings, commissioned the collecting and copying of proverbs from the Solomonic era as an integral aspect of his program to promote the true worship of Yahweh throughout Judah and into the former northern Israel. Realizing that in order for belief in Yahweh to become strong again throughout the land, it was critical that a large number of officials be trained in wisdom and in the fear of Yahweh. This was especially the case after the aggressive apostasy of his predecessor Ahaz. The need to preserve Israelite literature about the worship of Yahweh was also urgent at this time because Assyria was now ruling areas of northern Israel (722 BC) and had deported many northern Israelites to various parts of the Assyrian Empire.

Newly trained scribes and sages in Israelite wisdom would fill numerous government positions throughout the provinces. From their post they would be able to establish genuine justice and carry out administrative tasks in ways that would reestablish the people's confidence in the government's commitment to Yahweh as the true God. For this training copies of Israelite Wisdom literature needed to be made. It is possible that while meeting this need this group of proverbs from the time of Solomon were found.

A. Proverbs 25:1-28

OVERVIEW

The most prominent feature of the proverbs in ch 25 is the number structured around a vivid analogy (vv 4-5, 11, 12, 13, 14, 18, 19, 20, 23, 25, 26, 28). This rich repository of metaphors includes: "apples of gold in settings of silver" (v 11), "earrings of gold" (v 12), "snow" (v 13), "rain" (v 14), "wind" (v 14), "bone" (v 15), "honey" (vv 16, 27), weapons—"club," "sword," "sharp arrow" (v 18), "a broken tooth" (v 19), "a lame foot" (v 19), "vinegar" (v 20), "coals" (v 22), the "north wind" (v 23), "cold water" (v 25), "a muddied spring" (v 26), "a polluted well" (v 26), and a breach in a city's wall (v 28). In addition there are some recurring terms: **honor** (v 2 [2x]), "search" (vv 2, 3), lawsuit/"court" (vv 8, 9 [2x HB]), dealing with a "neighbor" or "friend "(vv 8, 9-10), "honey" (vv 16, 27), and "glory" (vv 2 [2x], 27 [2x HB]).

In regard to structure and genre, this chapter has six sayings that consist of two couplets (vv 4-5, 6-7b, 7c-8, 9-10, 16-17, 21-22). There are three exhortations (vv 4, 5, 17) and three prohibitions (vv 6, 8, 9). Also there are two better-than sayings (vv 6-7b, 24). Furthermore, the first set of sayings, vv 2-15, are grouped around three topics: proper behavior in the presence of the king (vv 2-7), guidance for taking a case to court (vv 8-10), and the value of good speech (vv 11-15).

Many of the proverbs in the second portion of the chapter (vv 16-27) advise against indulging in behaviors that lead to very undesirable consequences: promising to give a gift and failing to do so (v 14), eating too much honey (vv 16, 27), taking advantage of a friend's hospitality (v 17), committing perjury against a neighbor (v 18), trusting a faithless person (v 19), and singing to a heavy heart (v 20). Similar counsel is heard in the proverb against betrayal in v 9. Other proverbs in the second portion draw attention to harmful traits that need to be avoided: speaking with a sly tongue (v 23), having a quarrelsome demeanor (v 24), giving way to the wicked (v 26), seeking one's own honor (v 27), and lacking self-control (v 28). In vv 21-22 is the well-known exhortation to give food and water to a hungry and thirsty enemy.

The next to the last verse of this chapter is formulated to unite the two sections. "Honey" (vv 16a, 27a) forms an inclusio for the second portion. Words from the roots *ḥqr* (**seek**) and *kbd* (**honor**) (v 27b) are present in the opening two couplets (*kěbôd* [v 2a, 2b], *ḥāqōr* [v 2b], *ḥēqer* [v 3b]) respectively. Also the root *kbd* as a verb begins v 2, and the noun *kābôd*, **honor**, is repeated at the end of v 27 (HB). That is, these two roots in v 27b stand in a chiastic pattern to their placement in vv 2-3. Moreover, the root *ḥqr* stands twice at the beginning and once at the end of the chapter while the root *kbd* stands twice in the first couplet and twice at the end of v 27 (see Bryce 1972, 153-54). The final verse provides a general statement that underscores the danger inherent in failing to correct the various kinds of improper behaviors described in the second section of this chapter.

IN THE TEXT

Opposing: God / King (25:1-3)

■ **1-3** These two proverbs, which exalt the majesty of God and laud the insightful skill of the king, are connected by forms of the Hebrew root *ḥqr* (**search** [*ḥăqōr*] and **unsearchable** [*'ên ḥēqer*]), standing in the second line of each couplet. **The glory of God *is* to conceal a matter, *and* . . . the glory of kings *is to search out a matter*.**

Because God ***concealed*** his wise designs deep in the structure of the created order, many aspects of creation remain a mystery to humans. These mysteries bear witness to **the glory** of God's wisdom. The hidden aspects of creation also challenge kings to discover God's ways. By searching, a king becomes wiser. That search makes a king more resourceful and wiser in administrating the affairs of the nation and in resolving disputes and problems. One way that a king discloses an insight gained in his search is by composing a proverb. Such display of insights achieved by **kings** leads the people to give them **glory**.

As for the people, they find that the ***minds*** **of kings are** as **unsearchable** as **the heavens are high and the earth is deep**. In the OT ***beyond searching*** (i.e., unfathomable) is usually applied to God's activity, especially in creation and judgment (Job 5:9; 9:10; Ps 145:3; Isa 40:28). Only here is it used in reference to the king (Waltke 2005, 312-13). This descriptor attests the exalted status of kings in antiquity.

The people's glorifying the king may be compared to the praise contemporary people give to those who achieve great feats, such as swimming the English Channel, climbing Mount Everest, or reaching the North Pole. Also the ancients took pride in the great building projects promoted by their kings, particularly the construction of magnificent buildings such as temples, palaces, and grand mausoleums. These monuments bore witness to a king's wisdom and greatness. Solomon's building of the magnificent temple in Jerusalem brought him great glory. That feat is forever associated with his name.

The wisdom of kings is also manifested in their rendering insightful judicial decisions that offer a precedent for dealing with difficult cases. Solomon is famous for resolving the identity of the real mother in a dispute between two women as to the identity of the living baby (1 Kgs 3:16-28). Skillfully Solomon devised an approach to discover which one was the mother. As a result of his arriving at the truth "all Israel . . . held the king in awe" (v 28). (See Prov 16:10-15.)

25:1-3

Analogy: Establishing the King's Throne (Line 5*b* = 16:12*b*) (25:4-5)

■ **4-5** This saying addresses the king's having a secure throne. The analogy at the front of this proverb is a word of instruction addressed to a smith: **remove the dross from the silver *ore*.** By heeding this instruction the smith gains refined silver, silver that can be worked into a beautiful vessel or an exquisite piece of jewelry. This picture encourages leaders to **remove wicked officials,** being compared to dross, **from the king's presence.** In order that a king might have an effective and honorable government, all corrupt officials must be removed because their practices corrupt the operation of the government just as dross prevents silver from being molded into a vessel. When the wicked are removed, the king's **throne will be established through righteousness.** Wicked officials, that is, those who advance their own position and power at the expense of the citizens, cause the people to lose confidence in the crown. Thus, a king must remove such office holders to avoid the loss of public confidence in his administration.

Better-than: Avoid Self-Exaltation (25:6-7*b*)

■ **6-7*b*** In the first colon there are two admonitions. Similar phrases standing at the end of the first and the fourth line—*before a king* and **before . . . nobles**—enclose the proverb. In addition, the first bicolon is arranged chiastically according to grammatical units: negative command:adverbial phrase::adverbial phrase:negative command.

In an honor-based society everyone must keep to one's station. No one was ever to assume a higher station than that person had in the system. Such was especially the case at royal functions. Nobles and honored guests took their seats according to their status. The highest officials sat nearest the king. Based on this custom this proverb admonishes against ever taking a higher seat at a royal function. Such behavior would be viewed as most audacious. A person who was so brazen as to sit down in a higher seat would be quickly ushered to a lower seat, thereby being publicly disgraced.

That some people were bold enough to take a higher seat at a high occasion is evident by Jesus' giving the parable against taking a high seat of honor at a wedding feast (Luke 14:7-11). A more prudent course for an official was to take a lower seat. One day he would be greatly honored by being ushered to a more prominent seat.

FROM THE TEXT

While attending a dinner at the house of a prominent Pharisee, Jesus observed that the guests carefully took their seats at the table according to rank (Luke 14:1-11). This led him to tell a parable that counseled against presumptuously taking a higher seat at a wedding feast, for whoever did would be ushered to a lower seat, when the person who had that seat arrived, thereby suffering humiliation. Jesus counseled that the wise course is to take the lowest seat at a wedding feast on the principle **for all those who exalt themselves will be humbled, and those who humble themselves will be exalted** (Luke 14:11). The audience who heard Jesus speak this parable would have immediately recalled this proverb.

Affirming: Lawsuit (25:7c-8)

■ **7c-8** The last three words in the Hebrew text of v 7 (seven words in the NIV) are placed with v 8 to make a saying of four lines, the style of the preceding proverbs and the one that follows.

This proverb admonishes against **hastily** initiating a lawsuit against a neighbor based on something one has just seen that appears to be out of order. A prudent person realizes that he may not have had a good vantage point for being able to determine accurately what had taken place. What one sees or what one thinks one sees and what actually takes place are frequently very different, especially if the action has been viewed from a poor angle. For example, one may think that a person struck another, but in reality the assumed aggressor was actually reaching out to prevent a person from falling. In addition, the beholder of the action has no idea of the actor's motives.

Another downside of going to court quickly is coming to realize during the proceedings that one lacks sufficient evidence to establish one's position. Or the plaintiff might realize that the defendant is able to refute the poorly supported allegation so convincingly that the complaint is dismissed. If it is discovered that an accuser has pursued a frivolous lawsuit or has shared wrong information about a trusted member of the community, the plaintiff will endure disgrace for many years. It is from this perspective that Jesus gives the advice: settle a dispute quickly with an adversary while on the way to court rather than taking the matter to a judge, for the judge might have the defendant thrown into prison (Matt 5:25-26).

Advancing: Do Not Betray Confidence (25:9-10)

■ **9-10** This proverb admonishes, **do not betray another's confidence** while *arguing a case with a* neighbor. Once confidential information is disclosed, even in support of a position being argued in court, that information spreads quickly through the community, bringing **shame** on that person for betraying another person's confidence. Moreover, **the charge against you will stand**. Despite sharing confidential information, that person fails to win the dispute. Therefore, a person who is unlikely to win *a* case at court needs to realize that it is wiser to settle the dispute with a neighbor out of court. (See Matt 18:15.)

Analogies: A Ruling Rightly Given and an Appropriate Rebuke (25:11-12)

■ **11-12** Two vibrant similes underscore the powerful impact of **a ruling rightly given** by the king. A right **ruling** establishes justice and promotes stability in a community. The people respond joyfully. Such **a ruling** is comparable to viewing a beautiful display, as **apples of gold in settings of silver**, a display that adds elegance to a room.

Similarly, a person who has **an open** ear, that is, being receptive to criticism, welcomes **the rebuke of a wise judge**. The rebuke will prod him to be more becoming in his conduct. The value of such a rebuke in that person's judgment is comparable to **an earring of gold or an ornament of fine gold**. Just as fine jewelry enhances one's appearance, the rebuke will enhance this person's conduct. Examples of beautiful jewelry owned by ancient Israelites have been discovered at numerous archaeological sites.

Noteworthy in this proverb is the play on sound: *ring* (*nezem*) with **ear** (*'ōzen*) and **gold jewelry** (*ḥălî kātem*) with **reproof** of a wise **person** (*môkîaḥ ḥākām*) (Clifford 1999, 224).

Analogy: A Reliable Messenger (25:13)

■ **13** A **snow-cooled drink** provides refreshment to harvesters working under the hot sun. The setting for this metaphor is harvesttime, which takes place from mid-April through May. The reference to snow suggests that the setting is upper Galilee or the Metulah Valley, a valley close to Mount Hermon, the highest mountain in Israel. Mount Hermon receives snow during winter that lasts into spring. But getting snow from there would take great effort. Perhaps the reference is to **snow** that has been stored underground for cooling liquids. In any case the metaphor underscores the refreshing impact that a **trustworthy messenger** has on **the spirit of his master**. Because of the messenger's reliability he feels confident that the communiqué will be delivered.

Sibilants enliven this saying; for example, the first line ends with *qāṣîr* (**harvest** or *summer*) and the second begins with *ṣîr* (**messenger**); *šeleg* (**snow**) in the first line is balanced by *šôlěḥāyw* (*sending* him) at the end of the second line, both having the consonants *š* and *l*.

Analogy: A Braggart Who Fails to Give a Promised Gift (25:14)

■ **14** This proverb states the opposite of the preceding one. It describes the way that a boaster causes keen disappointment. A person who is inclined to making big promises, promises **gifts** to a needy family. That family becomes excited just like those who live in a dry land become excited when they see **clouds** gather in the sky and feel *the* **wind** pick up, thinking it is going to rain. But as they watch the **clouds** drift away, they are keenly disappointed. Their disappointment serves as an analogy for the dashed hopes that family feels when the **gifts** promised never arrive. Likely on seeing a needy family the braggart responded impulsively by promising gifts. Since this person is merely a talker, he never gets around following through on what was promised.

Advancing: Patience in Persuading / Use of Soft Words (25:15)

■ **15** When presenting a complaint to or making a request of *a civil official* (Mic 3:1, 9), a person increases the chance of being heard by being *patient* and speaking in **a gentle** *voice*. If the request has merit, **a ruler** is more likely to see that merit than if that person acts impatiently and speaks loudly. Indeed, words are powerful, so powerful that a person who has developed the skill of speaking softly is able to achieve mighty deeds as conveyed by the metaphor **a gentle tongue *breaks* a bone**. Words do not have to be shouted to achieve a desired outcome.

Advancing: Self-Control and Friendship (25:16-17)

■ **16-17** These two proverbs advise moderation in engaging in a pleasurable activity in order to escape the ill consequences that attend overindulgence. This point is illustrated with the metaphor of having access to **honey**, a prized treat since it was one of the few sweets available in ancient Israel. It also appears to have been scarce. When bees were domesticated and in what regions of Israel is unknown. Since the honey is described as *found*, the reference is likely to wild honey such as Samson found in a lion's carcass while on his way to Philistia (Judg 14:8-9). Such a find was a most pleasant surprise in antiquity. But anyone who gorges on honey is likely to become so sick that soon he *disgorges* it. One's exuberance at the discovery quickly turns to disgust.

The principle conveyed by this saying applies to overindulging in any pleasures. A specific application is stated in the next saying. It is prudent for a person to refrain from frequenting **a neighbor's house** lest that neighbor becomes so fed up with seeing that visitor that he comes to **hate** him. In antiquity genuine friends likely had open access to each other's homes—a far different standard of welcome than found in large Western cities. Nevertheless, even in antiquity familiarity bred contempt.

The wisdom tradition advises against taking liberties with a friend. A person who demands much of a friend may irritate that friend to the degree that the friendship dissolves. Friendship requires careful nurturing to survive the complexities of life.

Analogies: Giving False Testimony against a Neighbor / Relying on Treachery to Escape Trouble / Seeking to Console One Who Is Despondent (25:18-20)

■ **18-20** In the next three proverbs, bold, vivid analogies underscore harsh consequences that come from acting brazenly or deceptively. The first proverb highlights the devastating impact that results from *giving* **false testimony against a neighbor**, a violation of the ninth commandment (Exod 20:16). Giving false testimony is comparable to striking a person with **a club or a sword or a sharp arrow**, weapons that produce deep, even lethal wounds. The metaphor is appropriate, for if the court finds a neighbor guilty on the basis of false testimony, that neighbor's standing in the community and quite possibly his ability to support his family are destroyed.

The next proverb (Prov 25:19) illustrates the bitter consequences experienced by **reliance on *a person who is* unfaithful in a time of trouble.** When turning to an unreliable person in a time of desperate need, a person in trouble is likely to find that person is incapable of providing real help. Looking to such a person is like having *a* **broken tooth or a lame foot**. About the only way in antiquity to treat such a tooth was to pull it out, an action that carried risks. Likewise, **a lame foot** prevents a person from escaping trouble.

The third proverb (v 20) calls attention to the negative impact of seeking to console a despondent person, that is, one with **a heavy heart** in a seemingly good way, such as *singing* songs. But there are times when a person's singing grates against the nerves of a despondent person, making that person even more miserable. Such singing is likened to the burning pain of **vinegar poured on a wound**. Instead of consoling, the singing is very irritating. This analogy shows that using an inappropriate approach to console a sad person makes that person more despondent.

Two Analogies

Two analogies at the beginning of v 20 are very uncharacteristic for a proverb. This may have come about by a scribe's accidentally recopying letters from v 19. The line about *taking* **away a garment on a cold day** is missing in the LXX and may be overlooked (Clifford 1999, 225; Fox 2009, 786).

Affirming: Against Taking Vengeance (25:21-22)

■ **21-22** Whenever *an* **enemy is hungry** and/or **thirsty**, one who fears Yahweh needs to set aside hatred and display kindness by *giving* that foe **food** and **water**. Extending compassion to an enemy yields two consequences. First, one *heaps* **burning coals on** the foe's **head**. Understandings of this analogy vary.

One interpretation is this expression of kindness makes the enemy feel such shame that it produces a strong burning sensation deep inside him (see Fox 2009, 787). Or it may mean that one day God will appropriately punish that enemy. Second, Yahweh **will reward** the person who shows kindness. The implied reward is Yahweh's blessing. (See 20:22; 24:17-18, 29; Sir 28:1-7; also Exod 23:4; Lev 19:18.)

Coals of Fire

In the OT there are several references to **burning coals** (*gaḥălê ʾēš* or *geḥālîm*); for example, Prov 6:28; 26:21; Ps 18:12 [13 HB]. Ancient warriors used them as lethal weapons (Ps 120:4). Thus, it is not surprising that the OT pictures Yahweh, the divine warrior, as employing burning coals to punish the wicked (Ps 140:10 [11 HB]). Since Yahweh fiercely hates deeds of violence, he rains coals of fire on those who commit vile deeds (Ps 11:4-6).

Ezekiel describes Yahweh as coming to earth, borne by the cherubim, to punish Jerusalem (chs 9—11). Beneath the cherubim was a hearth with burning coals. When the cherubim were at the south side of the temple, Yahweh ordered a cherub to take some of the coals and put them in the hands of the person clothed in linen so that he could scatter them over Jerusalem, presumably to punish the wicked. According to Fuhs (1975, 465), Yahweh's use of glowing coals reveals the intensity of his anger, and the burning heat from the coals conveys that there is no escaping his judgment.

The metaphor *heaping* **burning coals on** an enemy's **head** describes Yahweh's punishing the wicked so that they no longer trouble the righteous (see Pss 140:9-11 [10-12 HB]; 120:1-4). **On the head(s)** means that specific evildoers, not humans in general, are punished (see Ps 11:5-6). Their punishment will be severe, if not fatal.

FROM THE TEXT

In a series of exhortations to believers whose minds have been transformed by offering themselves as living sacrifices to Christ (Rom 12:9-21), Paul provides specific guidance for displaying genuine love in daily living. His guidance is rooted in Israelite wisdom (Dunn 1988, 738). This is especially the case with the admonition "Do not take revenge . . . but leave room for God's wrath" (v 19a). Paul supports this injunction by quoting this proverb. Instead of taking vengeance, believers are to leave whatever punishment is due the offender to God. Punishment is God's prerogative, not a human's (see Schreiner 1998, 675-66).

Paul concludes these instructions on transformed living with the injunction, "Do not be overcome by evil, but overcome evil with good" (v 21). What evil is overcome by a good deed? Is it the evil of contemplating retaliation or is it an enemy's malicious attitude? In light of 2 Esd 16:53, the enemy's hostility will be punished (ibid.).

Is another reading possible, given that Paul often extols love's redemptive power? The question is, can an act of kindness overcome an evildoer's enmity? Paul's response is "yes." Drawing on this proverb, he asserts that God is able to use a believer's tangible expression of love to transform a foe's hateful attitude (see Dunn 1988, 751; Murray 1965, 142-44).

IN THE TEXT

Analogy: The Impact of Deceptive Speech (25:23)

■ **23** Just as **the** wind blowing out of **the** north . . . **brings unexpected rain,** so **a sly tongue** . . . **provokes a** *furious* **look.** The undesirable effect of **a sly tongue** is as despised as rain brought by the north wind. The interpretation of this analogy is difficult because in Palestine it is the west wind rather than the north wind that brings rain. In any case it is describing an unexpected rainstorm that comes at the wrong time of the season, greatly damaging the crops.

Another interpretation finds that the analogy resides in a play on the secondary sense of *hidden* contained in the semantic range of both ṣāpôn (**north**) and sāter (*secrecy, hiding place*). The latter term as a modifier of **tongue** yields the phrase **a sly tongue.** A person who speaks cleverly, that is, deceitfully, produces **a** *distraught* **look.**

The metaphor is that just as a *hidden* wind suddenly turns the sky dark by bringing in a layer of thick, gray clouds, twisted speech darkens the faces of those who have been duped with dismay (see Whybray 1994a, 368-69; Murphy 1998, 195-96). Or, as van Leeuwen (1997, 220) states, "Rain storms and emotional storms can both rise from unexpected (hidden) sources." The viability of this interpretation is strengthened by the fact that these two phrases are placed chiastically at the front and at the end of the proverb. Nevertheless, this interpretation fails to account for the people becoming morose at *the* north wind *bringing* rain.

A simpler solution is offered by Fox (2009, 789). He posits that **north** is used for northwest on the basis that a popular proverb does not use geographical terms precisely. However, this proposal is weak given that people who live close to the soil are very aware of weather patterns.

Another interpretation based on taking the verb *těḥôlēl* to convey *twist, whirl* (Vg., Clifford 1999, 237) holds that the north wind drives the rain clouds away from the thirsty land, dampening the people's excitement that it was going to rain.

A contrasting view offered by Waltke (2005, 333) holds that a north wind may unexpectedly bring a cold rain that severely damages the crops. This position explains why the people would become furious at the north wind blowing as implied by the second line. Thus, the blowing of the north wind serves as a poignant analogy of the destructive effects of **a sly tongue**, either in damaging reputations or in leading people so far astray that they suffer significant losses. When people discover that they have been duped, they become so *distraught* that their *faces* turn dark and morose.

None of these solutions is compelling. The view that posits a play on the sense of *hidden* deserves careful consideration, but it fails to account for the people becoming dismayed at the north wind bringing rain. Since Waltke's view provides a viable connection between the analogy and the tenor of the proverb, it is tentatively adopted.

Better-than: A Contentious Wife (= 21:9) (25:24)

■ **24** Living with a *contentious* or quarrelsome wife in a small house is so unbearable that her husband finds it better to retire to a corner of the roof than having to listen to his wife's continuous tirades. In the ancient Middle East houses had flat roofs that offered extra living space.

Analogy: Good News from a Distant Land (25:25)

■ **25** Receiving good news, especially from a distant land, produces great joy. This was especially the case in antiquity, for it took several weeks to receive any word about the welfare of a family member or a servant who was on a journey to a distant land. When good news from or about that person arrived, it brought great relief to the family or the master. The joy that news produced is comparable to the relief a weary *person* experiences from a drink of cold water. This proverb encourages travelers to be diligent in sending back word to family members or an employer (Lennox 1998, 265-66).

Analogy: Righteous Yielding to the Wicked (25:26)

■ **26** Water is a very precious commodity in a dry land like Israel. Anyone traveling through a dry region needs to know the location of good water sources. When a traveler arrives at a reliable water source and finds that it has been **polluted** or **muddied** by animals or careless sojourners, he is extremely disheartened. The lack of clean water is a threat to his life. Similarly, a community is seriously disheartened when **the righteous . . . give way to the wicked**. Whenever the wicked outwit the honorable, their impact on a community increases, threatening the well-being of all.

This proverb provides a corrective to the many proverbs that assert that the righteous never fail (e.g., 10:30*a*; 12:3*b*; Ps 55:22 [23 HB]). It needs to be remembered that proverbs state general principles, not categorical truths. Therefore, each proverb needs to be interpreted in light of the corpus of a people's wisdom sayings.

Analogy: Use Compliments Sparingly (25:27)

■ **27** *Eating* a small amount of a sweet food like **honey** gives a person great delight, but gorging on rich food may make a person sick (see v 16*a*). The Hebrew of the second line is very obscure. In light of the first line, it describes something that is very good as long as it is not done in excess, thereby causing distress. The words *seek* or **search** and *honor*, repeated twice, are clearly present. A possible reading is, "nor is it honorable to search for honor" (NJPS; see Yoder 2009, 253; Longman 2006, 460). It certainly **is *not* honorable to *seek one's own honor*.** Honor gained by manipulation rings hollow. This is only a possible reading of this verse due to the obscurity of the Hebrew text.

Analogy: Self-Control (25:28)

■ **28** Ancient cities were enclosed with walls for protection from wild animals, bandits, and enemies. Consequently, a large breach in the **walls** left a city vulnerable. The breaches needed to be repaired quickly to restore the city's security. This picture offers a vivid analogy for the insecurity felt by a person who is unable to manage a deep passion or a solemn mood. **A person who lacks self-control** is unable to work effectively. Furthermore, such a person often develops a lifestyle that is likely to lead to poor health, thereby taking the path to an early death.

B. Proverbs 26:1-28

BEHIND THE TEXT

In this chapter the court compiler has joined many sayings by a key term or theme. The first twelve verses center on the characteristics of a fool (*kĕsîl*), except for v 2. Next there are four clusters, each describing a human character type, that is, a lazy person (vv 13-16), **a maniac** who deceives a neighbor (vv 17-19), **a gossip** (vv 20-23), and a malicious person (vv 24-26). The chapter concludes with two sayings about things that result in harm (vv 27-28).

Two proverbs have four lines (vv 18-19, 24-25), a frequent pattern in the first chapter of the Hezekiah collection. Most of the proverbs are built on an analogy. Nine are constructed as advancing (vv 4-5, 13-16, 24-26). Yahweh is not mentioned in any of these proverbs.

The first section about a fool is structured as a chiasm (vv 1-12). At the center are sayings about the inability of a fool to grasp the insights present in the sayings of the wise (vv 7-9). On either side are proverbs that counsel against hiring a fool to do an important task, for that will most likely lead to embarrassment or even worse financial harm (vv 6, 10). On the outside are proverbs concerning a fool (vv 1-5, save for v 2), and the ingrained nature of folly (vv 11-12). The structure of vv 13-26 is clear. The proverbs in vv 13-19 address two topics, a lazy person (vv 13-16) and **a maniac** who deceives a neighbor (vv 17-19). The proverb in v 19 functions as a bridge to the concluding group of proverbs in vv 20-28, which are concerned with strife, deceit, and deviousness. This last group of proverbs are set in couplets held together by key words: vv 20-21 + 22, 23 + 24, 25 + 26.

OVERVIEW

In this set of proverbs the fool (*kěsîl*) is thoroughly castigated. The fool, lacking the skill for handling a proverb (vv 7, 9, 11, 12), uses them in ways that wound others (v 10). Since he brings disgrace on the community, a fool is never worthy of honor (vv 1, 8). Such a person needs to be sternly disciplined, even with a whip (v 3).

Another character trait is a lazy person, one who is unproductive and quick to avoid work with incredible excuses (v 13). Even though the lazy think that they are intelligent (v 16), they tend to get stuck in meaningless, repetitive routines (v 12).

Other proverbs in this collection give instructions on dealing with quarrels. One should not meddle in a quarrel (v 17), nor should one stoke a dispute with whispers (vv 20, 22). The prudent course is to let a quarrel die out (vv 20–21; see v 17). Moreover, it is ill advised to play a joke on a neighbor (vv 18-19). Neither should one trust the smooth, enticing words of a person prone to hatred (vv 24–26). The chapter closes with two somber warnings: one may be hurt by the nature of the work one is doing (v 27) and flattery works ruin (v 28).

This collection is a repository of rich metaphors: snow (v 1), sparrow (v 2), whip (v 3), bridle (v 3), rod (v 3), being lame (v 7), sling-stone (v 8), thorn-bush (v 9), archer (v 10), dog (vv 11, 17), lion (v 13), door on hinges (v 14), throwing or shooting firebrands (v 18), wood and charcoal for fire (vv 20-21), sweet morsels (v 22), silver coating on pottery (v 23), digging a pit (v 27), and a rolling stone (v 27).

Analogy: Against Honoring a Fool (26:1)

■ **1** It **is not fitting for a fool** (*kĕsîl*) to receive **honor**. Such recognition has negative consequences. It encourages a fool to continue acting foolishly, and it inspires the naive to model their behavior after the fool. An occasion when a fool is honored is likened to **snow** falling **in summer**, a virtual impossibility in Palestine, or to **rain** at **harvest**—in late April into May for barley and the end of May to the first of June for wheat. Rain falling at harvesttime would severely damage the crop as well as greatly increase the labor in cutting and winnowing the grain.

While it is very unlikely that in Palestine there would be rain during wheat harvest, there is a slight possibility for some rain during barley harvest in April. On a rare occasion there could be a rainstorm during wheat harvest, which is several weeks later (see 1 Sam 12:17-18). This account makes it very clear that such a storm was sent by God as a sign of his displeasure at the people's having chosen a king. Honoring a fool is so unfitting and troubling that it should be as impossible as the coming of snow or rain at the wrong season.

Analogy: An Undeserved Curse (26:2)

■ **2** A **curse** uttered *for no reason* (*ḥinnām*) has no power; that is, the harm specified in the curse will not take place. This assertion is underscored by the analogy of the behavior of **a fluttering sparrow or a darting swallow**. These small birds dart about at random, leaving no impact on the land. Similarly, an ungrounded curse will not have any impact on its target.

Analogy: Beating a Fool (Line *b* = 10:13*b*; 19:29*b*) (26:3)

■ **3** A **horse** is prodded to run faster by **a whip,** and *a* **donkey** is harnessed with **a bridle** for pulling a heavy load. These analogies show that the only way to get **fools** (*kĕsîl*) to do something productive is by striking them *on the back* with **a rod**. That is, a fool must be compelled by strong force to turn from folly. This proverb serves as a warning to youths not to be obstinate in learning. (See Prov 10:13; 19:25, 29.)

Individually Advancing; Together Opposing: Answering a Fool / Results (26:4-5)

■ **4-5** The stark contradiction in these two proverbs, formulated subtly in the Hebrew, is intentional. It grabs the reader's attention, motivating a person to contemplate the better way to respond to a fool in a particular situation. Being placed back to back, these two proverbs illustrate the character of individual proverbs; they offer general guidance rather than specific guidelines. Therefore, when drawing on a proverb for guidance, a person must skillfully apply it to the particular situation.

By nature **a fool** (*kĕsîl*) speaks **folly** (*'iwwelet*). Sometimes a fool's reasoning is so outrageous that an astute person is aghast, being tempted to respond with a similar line of absurd logic with the hope that the fool may see the ridiculousness of his reasoning. But there is danger in speaking or reasoning like a fool. One who uses a fool's line of reasoning might later discover that distorted line of logic, lodging in his mind, leads him to make a foolish response at an inopportune time. This proverb, thus, counsels against ever reasoning or gesticulating like a fool.

The second proverb exhorts a wise person *to* **answer a fool according to his folly**. In so doing a fool is confronted with the audaciously illogical character of his reasoning. Since pride motivates a fool to keep acting foolishly, this tactic hopes to get a fool to see the faultiness of his reasoning and thus to keep him from ***being* wise in his own eyes**.

Fox (2009, 794) points out that when two similar proverbs are juxtaposed, the second one serves to restrict the application of the first one. So while there is peril in answering a fool according to the first proverb, there are times when the wise must show the fool the absurdity of his reasoning as advised in the second proverb. Wesley (1975, 1880) comments, "So as his folly needs and requires, convincing him strongly, reproving him sharply, and exposing him to just shame."

Analogy: The Potential Harm of Hiring a Fool as a Messenger (26:6)

■ **6** Before the days of postal services and telecommunications, communicating with people at a distance was done by a messenger who carried either a written message or was entrusted to relate an oral message. In the latter case the messenger had to repeat the message precisely, not adding or deleting any words. If the message was written, the messenger was responsible for keeping its content confidential. Clearly, anyone who needed to send a message knew that it was critical to hire a dependable messenger.

This need is underscored by a shockingly bold analogy. An official who sends a message by a fool is compared to a person's **cutting off *his* feet**, severely limiting his mobility, or to **drinking poison**, that is, putting himself directly in the way of peril. These two graphic analogies motivate a government official or a business person not to ever consider **sending a message by *a* fool** due to the grave consequences that would result from the messenger's failing to keep the message confidential. (See 10:26; 13:17.)

Analogy: Fool with a Proverb (Line *b* = 26:9*b*) (26:7)

■ **7** While **a fool** may quote **a proverb**, his ability to understand it or to apply it ***properly*** is deficient. It is comparable to **the useless legs** of *a* lame *person*. Just as a lame person cannot walk, a fool is unable to handle a proverb.

Analogy: Fools Being Honored (26:8)

■ **8** Wise counsel teaches that one should not **honor . . . a fool** (see v 1), for such recognition only emboldens a fool to act foolishly. This counsel is supported by an analogy, but the Hebrew in the first line is obscure, making it difficult to understand the nature of the danger conveyed by the metaphor. Is the danger a stone shot from a sling or from a sling that functions improperly?

Another possibility is that a slingshot is rendered useless by **tying a stone in a sling**; then the stone cannot be propelled. Since it is doubtful that anyone would bind a stone in the sling's pouch, Fox (2009, 795) argues for the first option, pointing out that it calls attention to the danger of hurling stones from a sling without care. Likewise, honoring a fool carelessly holds the potential of significant danger. Wesley (1975, 1880) notes, "No less absurd is he that giveth to a fool that honour which he is not capable of using aright."

Ancient Slings

An ancient sling was a hollow pouch made of cloth or leather to which were attached two cords. Holding the cords, the warrior twirled the sling rapidly above his head; at the right moment he released one cord, propelling the stone with deadly accuracy. Stones were hurled with speeds reaching over a hundred miles per hour. Archaeologists have found rounded sling stones, made out of both flint and mud; also stones shaped like almonds have been found (Yadin 1963, 2:364; Hoffmeier 1988, 4:1040; King and Stager 2001, 228-29).

Analogy: Fool with a Proverb (Line *b* = 26:7*b*) (26:9)

■ 9 This proverb calls attention to the danger in the manner that **a fool handles a proverb**. It supports the point with a vivid analogy of **a thornbush in a drunkard's hand**. The precise analogy, however, is unclear. Possibly the picture is a drunk person grabbing hold of a thornbush, unmindful of the pain being inflicted by the thorns, and swinging it wildly, endangering all innocent bystanders. His absurd action is comparable to **a fool** speaking a proverb randomly, endangering any of those listening should they apply a proverb as interpreted by a fool.

Fox (2009, 795) offers an insightful explanation: the type of proverb referenced here is different from those preserved in the book of Proverbs. It is a saying spoken repeatedly to stir up people. An example is the people shouting, "Saul has slain his thousands, and David his tens of thousands" (1 Sam 29:5). This saying aroused Saul's envy, propelling him to be obsessed with seeking David's death.

Another example is the exiles complaining, "the parents eat sour grapes, and the children's teeth are set on edge" (Ezek 18:2). With this saying the exiles passed blame for their being in exile on to the forefathers, thereby keeping themselves from taking responsibility for their condition and repenting of their actions that had angered God. Repeating a hurtful saying may lead to unexpected harmful responses, such as a drunkard's twirling a thornbush.

Another way to read this proverb is that just as an inebriated person does not feel pain from grabbing a thornbush, neither does a fool feel the prick of the counsel offered by a proverb that encourages forsaking folly.

Analogy: Hiring a Fool (26:10)

■ **10** When shooting a weapon, a person must be very mindful of all that is taking place around him as well as the target. A foolish **archer**, though, may be so intent on shooting arrows that he shoots them indiscriminately, *wounding* people *randomly*. Similarly, an official must be discerning in hiring a worker. If the official randomly **hires a fool or *a* passer-by**, that hire likely leads to a disastrous outcome, for a fool will be careless in doing the job. For example, if the task is building a wall, the wall may not be sturdy; one day it falls over, injuring those standing nearby.

Analogy: Fools Reflecting Folly (26:11)

■ **11** Failing to learn from past bungling, **fools** (*kĕsîl*) keep doing the same foolish thing over and over, even appearing to enjoy the activity. Their behavior is likened to **a dog *returning* to its vomit** instead of searching for nourishing food. Similarly, fools are unmindful of the lack of accomplishment that attends continuously repeating foolish behavior. (See 2 Pet 2:22.)

Comparison: Self-wisdom (Line *b* = 29:20*b*) (26:12)

■ **12** A gifted person who receives frequent commendation may come to think of oneself as exceedingly **wise**. But self-conceit leads to self-deception, making such a person worse off than **a fool**. The thick barrier of conceit prevents such a person from realizing personal limitations. Thus, **there is more hope for a fool** (*kĕsîl*) to overcome folly than for a self-aggrandized person to become wise. Today a person who acquires superior knowledge in a particular field, like computer technology, may come to believe oneself more brilliant than others. But this special knowledge only concerns a small aspect of complex postmodern technological culture. That is, anyone who develops a high view of one's own knowledge and ability in a very limited aspect of a subject faces the danger of self-delusion as to one's own brilliance. (See Prov 22:29*ab*.)

Advancing: Lazy (26:13-16)

■ **13-16** A group of four proverbs characterize *a lazy person* (*ʿāṣēl*) or a **sluggard**. The structural patterns of these proverbs are affirming, analogy, advancing, and comparison. The lazy person's lack of effort increases with each of the first three sayings: the sluggard does not leave the house (v 13), won't get out of bed (v 14), and won't expend the effort to eat (v 15; Waltke 2005, 355).

In the first proverb **a sluggard** is quick to make up farfetched excuses to avoid work. Since he does not want to go outside to do a chore, he makes the excuse that there is *a lion cub* [*šaḥal*] *in the way*, even a . . . lion [*ʾărî*] **roaming the streets**. By appealing to the prudent course of self-protection, he gives what he thinks is a compelling reason for staying inside, but his excuse is blatantly absurd. The lazy person always seeks for ways to avoid work. (See 22:13.)

The second proverb pictures the lazy person lying in bed, tossing and turning, like **a door . . . on its hinges**, getting nothing done. This sluggard lacks the motivation to get up, get dressed, and get busy. So he never goes anywhere.

The third proverb shows how absurdly lazy **a sluggard** may become. While eating, he **buries his hand in the dish** and is so dim-witted that he fails **to bring it back to his mouth**. This saying brings out how a lazy person brings harm on himself in becoming malnourished. (See 19:24.)

The fourth proverb counters the assumption that a lazy person has no self-esteem. In fact, he has such a high self-view that he considers himself **wiser than seven *learned persons*** who display their wisdom by ***answering*** inquiries **discreetly**. This **sluggard** has such high self-confidence as conveyed by the number seven that it is impossible to enlighten him. (On a sluggard see 6:6-11; 24:30-34.)

It is important to note that both teachings, about a fool (vv 1-12) and about a lazy person (vv 13-16), end by castigating such a person as being ***wise*** **in *one's*** **own eyes.**

Analogy: Meddling in Quarrels (26:17)

■ **17** The next two proverbs (vv 17, 18-19) address the issue of arousing needlessly another person's disgust. When a person who likes to meddle in whatever is taking place comes on a group disputing a matter vigorously, he joins in the dispute even though it has nothing to do with him. His intruding is likened to **one who grabs a stray dog by the ears**. Anyone who does such a foolish thing gets into a tussle with that dog, risking serious injuries.

Since the ancient Israelites, especially village dwellers, had little regard for dogs, the dog in this proverb is likely a stray (*'ōbēr*) dog. Thus, there is a play on a stray dog and a passerby. The analogy, then, conveys that the parties disputing will turn on the meddler like a dog turns on the one who pulls its ears. Either reading teaches that it is best to stay out of a quarrel just as the course of prudence is to leave a stray dog alone.

Analogy: Against Playing a Joke on a Neighbor (26:18-19)

■ **18-19** This proverb, covering two verses, underscores the folly of a person who plays a cruel joke on a neighbor. Since the course of wisdom is to maintain good relationships with neighbors, one must be very discrete in playing any kind of prank on a neighbor. The better course is not even to entertain such a hoax.

This proverb advises against shocking a neighbor with a made-up story, especially a story about something very dear to that neighbor like a favorite horse, and saying after seeing the neighbor's startled, anxious reaction, "**I was only joking!**" Doing such a prank is likened to **a maniac shooting flaming arrows of death** at innocent passersby, just for the fun of it. **Arrows** and **death** are a hendiadys, ***deadly arrows*** (Waltke 2005, 341).

The term **maniac** (*mitlahlēah*), a Hitpalpel participle, describes a person who repeatedly engages in reckless behavior (Sir 32:14, 15). The erratic conduct of a seemingly mad person infuriates neighbors. Such a prankster will discover that it is very hard to overcome the hostility his pranks produce. (See 26:28.)

Analogy: Gossip Feeds Strife (26:20-21)

■ **20-21** The next three proverbs treat gossip and quarreling; *nirgān* ("slanderer," "a gossip") stands in v 20*b* and v 22*a*. Quarrels generate such intense "heat" that they are comparable to a roaring fire. The first proverb stresses that when **a gossiper** ceases spreading gossip **a quarrel dies down** (*šātaq*) just like **without wood a fire goes out.** The Hebrew *šātaq* stands for very forceful action. It is used to describe the calming of the raging sea (Ps 107:30; Jonah 1:11, 12).

According to the second proverb (Prov 26:21), just as adding **charcoal to embers and . . . wood to fire** makes it burn hotter, so too **a quarrelsome person** stokes a quarrel with inflammatory rhetoric. He wants to keep it going by making it hotter. The focus of this saying is on the character of **a quarrelsome person** as one who relishes keeping strife going in the community.

Analogy: The Juicy Character of Gossip (= 18:8) (26:22)

■ **22** The third proverb emphasizes the tastiness of the juicy tidbits of information that a gossip shares. They are **like choice morsels,** pieces of savory meat, or slices of sweet bread. Such choice details, particularly unwholesome comments about another, **go down** *into a hearer's* **inmost parts,** where they lodge for a long time. Juicy gossip is well remembered; most of those who hear it act toward those talked about for a long time as though what they heard was true.

In other words, gossip plays a significant role in formulating people's long-lasting opinions of those talked about. Attitudes based on gossip, however, are often wrong, leading to unfounded prejudices and hostilities toward people, even by those who were formerly friends. It is difficult for those who have been misjudged to overcome such unfounded prejudice.

Analogy: Fervent Speech Designed to Deceive (26:23)

■ **23** The next two proverbs, v 23 and vv 24-26, warn about being beguiled by eloquent speech spoken with malicious intent. Several terms tie these verses together: **lips** (vv 23*b*, 24*a*) plus "speech" (*qôl*; *voice* [v 25*a*]), **heart** (*lēb* [vv 23*b*, 25*b*]) plus *qereb* (*inner person, heart* [v 24*b*]). Also they are tied together both by the similar sounds of the terms "enemies" (*śōnēʾ* [v 24*a*]) and "malice" (*śinʾâ* [v 26*a*]) and the assonance of key terms in the warning: *hatred* or "malice" (*śinʾâ*) is echoed in **guile,** "deception" (*maśśāʾôn* [v 26*a*]) and "be exposed [*tiggāleh*] in . . . assembly" (*qāhāl* [v 26*b*]; Clifford 1999, 234). This combination of words and sounds captures the beguiling effect of eloquent rhetoric spoken by those who have evil minds.

But such energized rhetoric carries no lasting value. It is likened to *a clay pot* that has been given **a coating of silver dross** to make it appear elegant and expensive. But its appearance is a facade. That vessel is nothing more than a cheap clay pot. Similarly, the great promises heard inspire people's imagination to expect great things by doing what the speaker encourages them to do will prove to be worthless like that pot. They are only hollow words.

Advancing: Beguiling Speech (26:24-26)

■ **24-26** This saying, an extended proverb of six lines, begins by describing *hateful* or *malicious persons*, enemies whose agenda is to deceive a person or a community with **charming** *speech*. Their skillful rhetoric *disguises* their intent to gain control of what others possess. They make great promises, often by appealing to human greed by painting beautiful word pictures of the success that those who join their scheme will experience.

This proverb warns people against **believing** such schemers, because they **harbor deceit** *in their minds* (*lēb*). Consequently, nothing they say may be trusted. This point is stressed by describing **their hearts** (*lēb*) as filled with **seven abominations**. Given that seven conveys totality and **abomination** (*tôʿēbâ*) is the highest censure in Proverbs (→ sidebar "Yahweh Detests or Abomination to Yahweh" at 6:16-19), the words of these *hateful* people are totally corrupt or deceptive.

This saying also alerts the upright, above all community leaders, that they must assess the character and the intent of those who enter a town's forum and seek to motivate the people with eloquent speech (Waltke 2005, 364).

Nevertheless, there will be a day when their conniving speeches **will be exposed in the assembly**, that is, a public forum held to deal with such dissemblers (v 26). God does not tolerate those who speak so maliciously in the community of those who fear him.

Affirming: Danger Inherent in Certain Activities (26:27)

■ **27** Sometimes an activity that a person is intensely engaged in suddenly results in harming the worker. A common illustration of this situation is that of *digging* a pit, likely to catch an animal that has been disrupting village life. Suddenly the person digging the pit *falls into that pit*, suffering serious injury (see Pss 7:5 [6 HB]; 9:15-16; 35:7-8; 57:6 [7 HB]; 141:10; Eccl 10:8-9). In another example a worker struggles hard to *roll* a stone up a grade; suddenly losing control of the stone, it *rolls* back, crushing him (see Eccl 10:8-9 and Sir 27:16).

In these illustrations a worker suffers harm from an essential aspect of the hard work at which he is expending great effort. Some view these pictures as implying that the doer is punished for being deceitful, but there is no hint in the wording that such is the case. Rather, this proverb calls attention to the chance of incurring harm while engaged in work that holds an inherent danger.

Affirming: Lying / Flattery (26:28)

■ **28** A person given to **lying** is characterized by the phrases *a false tongue* and its parallel *a mouth that utters smooth words*, that is, a **flattering mouth**.

Certainly **a lying tongue hates those it hurts**. In making a person feel good about the self, flattery lowers that person's defenses against subtle deception. In this way a flatterer **works ruin**.

The precise meaning of this proverb is hindered by the uncertainty of the meaning of the final two words in the second line; *ya'ăśeh midḥeh* may mean *give a shove* (Fox 2009, 802). The picture, then, is that the flatter says something that suddenly shoves the person, figuratively speaking, making the person fall for the deceptive scheme.

C. Proverbs 27:1-27

OVERVIEW

This chapter has three sections; the first two are set off by a tricolon (vv 10, 22). The central topic of the first section is friendship (vv 1-10), and in the second section it is loyalty in friendship (vv 11-22). The third section is a short poem lauding the advantages of shepherding as an occupation (vv 23-27).

Most proverbs in this chapter are couplets; a few are longer: three lines (vv 10, 22), four lines (vv 15-16, 23-24), and ten lines (vv 23-27). Seven are formulated as admonitions (vv 1, 2, 10, 11, 13, 22, 23-27), while three are formulated as opposing proverbs (vv 6, 7, 12) and two as better-than sayings (vv 5, 10c). Parallel structure, however, is absent in vv 14 and 22. Some proverbs are connected by a catchword: "praise" (*hallēl* [vv 1 and 2]); "love," "friend" (*'ōhēb* [vv 5 and 6]); "friend" (*rēa'* [vv 9 and 10]); and "human" (*'ādām* [vv 19 and 20]).

Many proverbs employ a metaphor to gain insight into a theme or topic: stone (v 3), sand (v 3), honey (v 7), a bird (v 8), incense (v 9), perfume (v 9), rain dripping (v 15), wind (v 16), oil (v 16), iron (v 17), fig tree (v 18), crucible (v 21), furnace (v 21), mortar (v 22), and pestle (v 22). Two recurring topics are friendship (vv 6, 10, 17) and the fool (vv 3, 21-22). Also considered are the powerful emotions of anger, fury, and jealousy (v 4).

A distinctive feature of three proverbs is a statement that calls attention to a reality that is the opposite of what is expected: a stranger's commendation is better than self-praise (v 2), open rebuke is better than hidden love (v 5), the wounds of a friend are preferable to the kisses of an enemy (v 6). Curiously, Yahweh does not appear in any of the sayings.

BEHIND THE TEXT

Many lines in these proverbs echo sayings found elsewhere in this book. Plöger (1984, 320) takes this fact as evidence that this collection has its own origin; that is, this chapter existed independently from other collections found in the other sections of Proverbs.

Advancing: Presumption about the Future (27:1)

■ **I** The first two proverbs are connected by the nodal term *hll* **boast**, *praise*. The chapter opens with an exhortation *not to* **boast** about what one will do **tomorrow**, that is, the near future, for a person does not know what opportunities, challenges, or obstacles will turn up on a new day. Challenges not only interrupt what one has planned on doing but may even prevent the planned activity from taking place. This proverb does not discourage planning or visionary thinking, rather, it cautions against being presumptuous as to what one will accomplish in the near future. This proverb is well known for James reaffirms its counsel for believers (4:14).

This proverb encourages the prioritizing of duties and goals in order to work at the tasks God has laid on one's heart. That is, one needs to live each day circumspectly, keeping focused on one's highest goals. While the contingencies that a day presents must be faced, a wise person faces them in ways that will not lead to derailment from the highest goals that God has given. Wesley states, "*The day* is said to *bring forth*, what God by his almighty power either causes or suffers to be brought forth or done in it" (1975, 1882).

Affirming: Avoid Self-Praise (27:2)

■ **2** Some people like to receive praise so much that they frequently engage in self-praise. But frequent self-praise lowers a person's respect in the community as people tire of hearing one continually vaunting the self. People also tend to distrust the perspective of a person who is always commending oneself. Moreover, self-praise feeds pride, a major sin condemned in Proverbs (e.g., 6:17). The better course is to let *a stranger* offer one **praise**. Compliments from a stranger are genuine, for that person has little, if any, self-interest in extending commendations.

Analogy: Weight of a Fool (27:3)

■ **3** *Anguish* or provocation (*ka'as*) produced by a fool (*'ĕwîl*) is a very heavy burden for a community to bear, even *heavier* than a huge **stone** and *a load of* **sand**. This saying implies that a fool burdens the community by the proclivity of causing grief over everything that the community seeks to do. The weight of a **fool's** objections and boisterous behavior moves the people to cry out to God in anguish, seeking relief. Job uses the word "anguish" for his horrific suffering, saying that it is heavier than the sands of the seas (Job 6:2-3).

Advancing: Anger / Envy (27:4)

■ **4** Human emotions are powerful; **anger, fury,** and *envy* are three of the strongest. **Anger** or *wrath* (*hēmâ*) is cruel, and **fury** (*šeṭep 'āp*), that is, *overwhelming anger*, propels a person to do painful deeds without any consideration of the extent of the harm they may cause.

Even more deadly than anger is *envy* (*qin'â*). Envy is a deep, hidden emotion that eats away at one's psyche over a long period of time, even years, before impelling one to commit a hostile act against the person envied. Envy is so deadly because a person believes that something that rightly belongs to him or her has been wrongfully taken by or given to another person. Whereas wrath may lead to wanton violence, envy motivates a person to inflict serious harm on the one envied, in a cold, calculating way in order to gain what that person believes is rightly his or hers. Envy is very hard to assuage (6:34-35).

Jealousy and Envy

The Hebrew root *qn'* may be glossed with **zeal**, **jealousy**, or **envy**. Jealousy is anger over another's seeking what one considers or desires to be one's own, while envy is deep hatred at a person who is perceived to have taken what one views as rightfully one's own. The wording **who can stand before** favors the stronger gloss **envy** for *qin'â*.

Better-than: Open Rebuke over Concealed Love (27:5)

■ **5** The next two sayings call attention to the fact that something that is ordinarily considered to be unfavorable may be better than that for which one usually longs. Clearly, people prefer a gesture of love over an **open rebuke**. **Hidden love**, however, has little value. Hidden love is never reciprocated, since the one loved has no awareness of the other person's feelings. But a person who takes the risk of rebuking another so that the person does not suffer loss or harm as a result of a peculiar trait or habit, expresses genuine concern for that person. If one gives heed to the rebuke, one will avoid embarrassment or one's life will improve.

Opposing: Wounds of a Friend / Kisses of an Enemy (27:6)

■ **6** No one likes to be wounded, either physically or emotionally, but there are times when **wounds** are better than **kisses**. While kisses are expected from a friend and wounds from a foe, there are occasions when a true friend risks the danger of calling a person's attention to a flaw or an error, even if the words will be considered **wounds**, thereby expressing genuine love. By contrast, **an enemy** heaps compliments on a person, even making public displays of affection like **kisses**, but these displays of affection are designed to hide contempt for that person.

Kisses in this context reference the cultural custom of enthusiastically greeting with an embrace and kisses to both cheeks. Much more reliable than receiving a display of affection in public are the **wounds** inflicted by **a friend** (*'ôhēb*). This saying is marked by two oxymorons: **wounds from a friend** and *kisses of* an enemy. (See Lev 19:17-18.)

Opposing: Satiated / Hungry (27:7)

■ **7** A person's emotional and physical states greatly influence one's attitude. Honey, a very pleasant sweet, was highly prized in ancient Palestine since the ancients had few sweets available. This delight is seen in Samson's finding honey in a lion's carcass while walking on the road to Philistia (Judg 14:8-9). But even honey *is despised* (for MT *bûs* **trample on,** *bûz* **despise, scorn** is read [Fox 2009, 806]) by a person whose *appetite is satiated* (see Prov 5:3).

The term *nepeš*, which heads each line, means either **person** or **appetite.** But *a person* who is **hungry** finds even **bitter *food*** to be so palatable that it **tastes sweet.** This proverb calls attention to the value of perceiving a person's disposition so as to know how a person will respond to an object or a situation. It also points out that something treasured may come to be viewed as common or even despised.

Analogy: Straying Bird for a Straying Person (27:8)

■ **8** A person who likes to *wander* from home rather than staying with the clan is compared to **a bird that flees from its nest,** thereby placing itself in harm's way. In antiquity a wanderer was most likely a person who had been compelled to leave the clan (Waltke 2005, 377). Such a person, lacking support of the clan, was vulnerable to numerous dangers, including bandits, hunger, and lack of shelter.

While in contemporary life wanderlust is quite common, even romanticized, it still comes at a high cost, including loneliness, lack of identity, and a sense of disorientation or lostness. A solitary person is very vulnerable. Humans need to be part of a family that serves as an anchor point for dealing with the vicissitudes of life.

Analogy: Joys: Ointments / Advice (27:9)

■ **9** Numerous small things—such as odors, tastes, and smells—provide great joy. *Oil* or **perfume** offers pleasure, both in giving off a pleasant smell and soothing a person's skin. The fragrance of **incense** fills a room with a pleasant smell as it covers unpleasant smells.

Unfortunately, the meaning of the second line, having a strange combination of words and lacking a verb, is unclear. The various English translations seek to produce an intelligible line, but their efforts are only conjectures.

The first two words suggest that the subject is *the sweetness or* the **pleasantness of *friendship*,** that is, joy from a good friendship. Such friendship is sweeter than oil or perfume. According to Longman (2006, 478), the next words may convey that this joy is greater than one's own counsel.

This reading may be improved by understanding the first words of the second line to function as a homonym for both *sweetness* and advice = *sweet advice* (Fox 2009, 807). Waltke (2005, 378) interprets *sweetness* as being both a metonym for something that is pleasant and agreeable and a metaphor for that which delights a person. He offers the translation "the sweetness of one's friend comes from passionate counsel" (2005, 368). Waltke's reconstruction has the advantage of being supported by the theme of the next proverb.

Exhortation + Better-than Saying: Don't Forsake a Family Friend / Such a Friend Is Better than a Distant Brother (27:10)

■ **10** A friend is one of life's greatest treasures, providing help and counsel throughout life. By offering support in a trying time, a friend enables a person to circumvent or confront a menacing situation. Therefore, a person is warned against *forsaking* **a friend or a friend of** *one's* **family**. Longstanding family friendships are a reliable resource for assistance and counsel. These people are a tremendous resource in caring for one's parents as they age; they help one fulfill the commandment to honor one's parents.

The next injunction says **do not go to your relative's house** *in a time of* **disaster**. The reason for this advice is not immediately clear.

The third line of this proverb, which may be an independent proverb (Fox 2009, 808), underscores the counsel of the first line: **better** is **a neighbor nearby than a relative far away**. It may clarify the second line by pointing out that in a time of great need a nearby friend is able to offer immediate help while a relative who lives at a distance is unable to provide help quickly or for an extended period of time. Another possible reason for elevating the role of a neighbor may be that the relative's family is also in deep sorrow as a result of the disaster.

Advancing: A Wise Son, a Joy / Empowers the Father (27:11)

■ **11** A parent exhorts a child, or possibly a teacher a student, to **be wise**, offering the motive *make his* **heart** *rejoice*. The father or teacher adds another motivation, namely that he will have confidence *to give an* **answer** *to*, that is, withstand, anyone who **treats** him **with contempt**, presumably about his family. Children who act wisely provide a parent support in resisting any complaints made against the family, possibly a charge against the behavior of a son. Fox (2009, 808) says, "When a man is disparaged, he can boast of his son." (See 10:1; Ps 127:3-4 [4-5 HB].)

Opposing: Response to Danger: The Prudent / The Simple (27:12)

■ **12** (See Prov 22:3.) While traveling or working *a* **prudent** (*'ārûm*) person is constantly alert to what is taking place in the surrounding environment. That person sees a threatening situation and gets out of the way of potential danger. However, *a naive person*, unaware of what is taking place, *continues* blissfully along the way and unexpectedly *pays* the penalty (lit. *is punished*).

A contemporary example of the value of being alert to what is taking place about a person is that of driving on a freeway. A prudent driver needs to be constantly aware of the traffic on all sides. When another vehicle moves erratically or shows signs of trouble, a shrewd driver slows down or changes lanes to avoid possible danger. But the naive driver continues in the same lane at the same speed, only to bear the consequences if the erratic driver gets into an accident.

Affirming: Take a Pledge from One Who Makes Security for an Outsider (27:13)

■ **13** This proverb is virtually the same as in Prov 20:16. (→ 20:16.)

Advancing: Greeting Loudly in the Morning / Considered a Curse (27:14)

■ **14** It is appropriate to greet a neighbor pleasantly **early in the morning**. But *to bless a* neighbor **loudly**, especially at that time of day, is most inappropriate. Such a greeting, being both too loud and too early, would be received as very irritating (Lennox 1998, 284). Such behavior would be deeply despised in an honor-based society. In fact, the neighbor would be so embarrassed that he would consider the greeting **a curse**. This proverb is especially applicable to Americans, who are notorious for being boisterous and impolite, especially by peoples who conduct themselves quietly in public.

Analogy: Contentious Wife + Affirming: Analogies for Restraining Her (27:15-16)

■ **15-16** A **wife** who has a **quarrelsome** demeanor is compared **to the dripping of a leaky roof in a rainstorm. Dripping *rain*** is a vivid analogy for her continual complaining given that a steadily repeated sound easily gets on a person's nerves, often leading to an angry outburst. The analogy underscores how intolerable a wife's bickering is to those who live in the house with her.

Any attempt to restrain her is shown to be virtually impossible by two analogies of things that humans cannot do: **restraining the wind** and **grasping oil with the hand**, that is, the texture of oil prevents a hand from holding on to it. (See 21:9, 19; 25:24.) (→ sidebar "Textual Difficulties in Prov 27:16" below.)

Textual Difficulties in Prov 27:16

It is difficult to determine the contextual meaning of the Hebrew verbs in this verse. The NIV glosses the verb (*ṣāpan*) in the first line with **restraining**, but that sense applies more to the wind than the woman. *Ṣpn* means literally **to hide, conceal**, but how does one conceal **the wind**? Fox (2009, 810) and Longman (2006, 480) use "hides," the usual gloss for the verb; "he who hides her hides the wind." This wording provides a clearer picture in that **wind** serves as a metaphor for the woman's boisterous quarreling.

The verb in the second line, *yiqrāʾ*, means **call**. But how does oil *call*? Waltke (2005, 369) takes *yiqrāʾ* from *qrʾ II* (**meet**) and renders the line "oil meets his right hand." Some, as the NIV, employ the gloss **grasp**, which offers a good sense but lacks linguistic support. Fox (2009, 811) keeps the MT and emends *šmn* (**oil**) to *šĕmô* (**his name**) with support from the LXX and gains the reading, "He is called, 'Right.'" In any case the intent of these lines is to provide analogies of actions that humans are unable to do to underscore the impossibility of changing a quarrelsome wife.

Analogy: Sharpening of the Mind (27:17)

■ **17** An **iron** blade is sharpened by briskly rubbing a block of iron over it. Similarly, a person's thinking is sharpened by having a brisk exchange of ideas with another person, face to face (lit. *a man sharpens the face of a friend*). Assertions, challenges, and counter responses made in thoughtful exchange are key to sharpening one's reasoning and developing the skill of substantiating a position. *Face*, thus, functions as a paronomasia, referencing both the blade of a knife and the face of a debating partner.

Analogy: Diligent Care / Reward (27:18)

■ **18** A farmer who *tends* a **fig tree** is rewarded by having an abundance of fruit to **eat**. Similarly, an official who has been taught by the wise needs to *protect* the interests of *his* master. He will share in his master's honor.

This saying teaches that a prominent person needs to be tended to similarly to the care shown to a fruit tree. Over many years such care empowers the official to excel and be duly honored. Certainly throughout life every person needs to learn and be nourished in order to continue to be mentally and spiritually healthy, bearing the fruits of the Spirit.

Analogy: Reflection in Water / Reflection of a Heart (27:19)

■ **19** The next two proverbs are connected by the term *man* or *human* (*ʾādām*), standing in the second line of each in the Hebrew. The first proverb is expressed tersely, allowing for breadth of interpretation. The analogy is the reflection a person sees of one's face in a clear pool of **water**. In antiquity mirrors were very primitive, often made out of polished metal. Most people, thus, only saw their own faces reflected in clear water.

The second line says that one gains insight into the true nature of one's **heart** by reflecting on the texture of one's life. Thereby one discovers attitudes that need to be reinforced, refined, or altered. Another way to read this line is that a person gains a true understanding of self by looking into one's own heart (Plöger 1984, 25-26); that is, self-understanding comes through self-reflection (Whybray 1972, 158).

Analogy: No Satisfaction: Sheol / Eyes (27:20)

■ **20** Just as the appetite of the grave, to which the Hebrews gave the names *Sheol* and *Abaddon*, or **Death** and **Destruction** (see 30:15*b*-16; Isa 5:14), is never full, so too a person's **eyes** are never satisfied with seeing (Eccl 1:8*b*; 4:8). A person never tires of looking at beautiful, amazing, or captivating sights, both natural and man-made. Viewing a sunset is never dull. The insatiable appetite of the eye is a major reason people take long trips to far-off places; they anticipate beholding new, exotic sights. One adventurous trip, of course, never satisfies. Thus, lack of satisfaction applies to all human desires. One needs to learn how to gain a sense of contentment with what one has.

Analogy: Being Tested by Praise (Line *a* = 17:3*a*) (27:21)

■ **21** This saying and the next are similar in being built on analogies about the process of separating a valuable product. Ore containing silver or gold has to be heated in order to gain gold or silver that can be worked by a smith. It is also important for a leader to assay a person's character in order to know one's skills and temperament. A person's character can be assessed by evaluating the response to praise. A person who is inspired by praise to work energetically at a task has a noble character and can be trusted with great responsibility. But if praise leads a person to arrogant and obstinate behavior, that person's character is seriously flawed.

Analogy: A Fool Is Incorrigible (27:22)

■ **22** The incorrigible nature of a **fool** (*ĕwîl*) is underscored. **Folly** (*'iwwelet*) is so engrained in a **fool** that there is no way to remove it. This assertion is supported by the analogy of pulverizing hard grains **in a mortar . . . with a pestle**, the hard task by which the ancients made meal. But removing **folly** from a **fool** cannot be done. Folly cannot be pounded out of a fool by any pedagogical method.

Affirming Internally and Advancing between the Two Couplets: Knowing the Flock / Wealth Does Not Last (27:23-24)

Verses 23-27 form a poem or epigram that commends herding over other occupations, such as trading hard assets or mining (v 24). The poem begins with a strong exhortation supported by a reason (vv 23-24), then there is a description of the advantages of herding (vv 25-26). It concludes with a euphoric picture of the abundance that comes to a shepherd's family (v 27).

This poetic description of shepherding may serve as an analogy for a wise ruler, for rulers are frequently referred to as shepherds in the OT (see Ps 78:71). The wise ruler cares for the citizens like a shepherd cares for the flock. Such care will lead to an increase in population and abundance for the families under his rule. In turn his rule will be long and prosperous. A stable population is the bedrock of a long rule.

■ **23-24** A shepherd is exhorted to **know** well **the condition of** *the* flocks. **Flocks** may reference sheep or sheep and goats, while the parallel term **herds** includes sheep, goats, and cattle. **Know** means that the shepherd is familiar with the traits of every member of the flock and meets the needs of every animal in a caring manner. A shepherd needs wisdom for leading the flock to water in the morning and evening and to good, safe grazing areas throughout the day. In addition, a shepherd needs special skill at breeding the flock so that its numbers increase annually, like Jacob who was very skilled in greatly increasing Laban's and his own flocks (Gen 30:35-43; 31:5-12). Indeed, shepherding draws on the many skills that wisdom offers: planning, insight, shrewdness, guiding, and professional skills (Waltke 2005, 391).

The advantage of shepherding is supported by noting that **riches** [i.e., stored wealth, such as silver, gold, and gems] **do not last indefinitely.** Once that kind of wealth is spent, it is gone; hard assets are not renewable. Another danger is that they may be lost or stolen. This possibility is underscored by noting that valuable jewelry (such as a crown, a family heirloom of high value) does not survive throughout **the generations**. This comparison to hard assets serves to encourage a shepherd to faithfully do the hard work of tending the flock daily.

Advancing: Shepherding

■ **25-27** The benefits from shepherding are highlighted. In late spring a shepherd gathers hay growing on the hills and stores it for the flock when grazing areas become sparse. The next spring new growth appears on the steppe, allowing the flock to graze freely. Well-fed **lambs** yield an abundance of wool, *providing* the clan **with clothing,** and **the goats** provide plenty of rich milk. The income from selling wool, meat, and milk enables a shepherd to purchase **a field** just like Abraham was able to buy the Cave of Machpelah (Gen 23). The benefits are underscored by picturing the goats giving an abundant supply of **milk**, sufficient to **feed** the entire family and *the* **female servants.** In a semiarid land goats are easier to maintain than cows; also their milk is richer and more nutritious.

FROM THE TEXT

Jesus identified himself as "the good shepherd," knowing every sheep by name (John 10:1-16). He promises to protect them, aggressively resisting wolves, thieves, and robbers. Also he promises to lead those who believe in him to good pasture so that they may be well fed, healthy, and reproduce abundantly. From the context of this poem on shepherding in Proverbs, it is to be inferred that Jesus as the good shepherd is exceedingly wise and shows that wisdom in caring for the flock.

D. Proverbs 28:1-28

OVERVIEW

This chapter is framed by proverbs contrasting the wicked with the righteous (Prov 28:1, 28). Close to the center (v 12) stands a similar proverb. The dominant structure of the proverbs is opposing (nineteen), while seven are constructed as advancing. There is one better-than saying (v 6), and two are built on analogies (vv 3, 15).

In contrast to the preceding chapters in the Hezekiah collection (chs 25—27), this chapter lacks the numerous rich metaphors except for driving rain (v 3) and a lion and a bear (v 15). Two proverbs in this collection are composed of three lines (vv 10, 24). Also vv 13 and 14 are connected chiastically. At the center is the blessed person and the outside frame concerns a hardened sinner. Three verses (16-18) are connected by words from the roots 'šq (*oppress*) and 'qš ("perverse").

Some proverbs bring out exceptions to general principles underscored in many other proverbs. Rain is described as harmful (v 3). The teaching that the wise become wealthy is counterbalanced by the aphorism that it is better to be a poor person with integrity than to have riches (v 6; see v 11). None of the proverbs are grouped around a common theme as in the preceding part of the Hezekiah collection (Plöger 1984, 32).

A distinctive topic in this group is piety. Living faithfully is stressed in three aphorisms (vv 6a, 18a, 20a). The faithful are those who fear, seek, or trust Yahweh (vv 5b, 14a, 25b). Understanding justice well (v 5b), they "walk in wisdom" and integrity (v 26b). As a result, they will be "kept safe" (vv 18, 26), be blessed (v 14a), and prosper (vv 19a, 25b, 27). By confessing and renouncing sin a person "finds mercy" (v 13b). Two proverbs speak of keeping the law, that is, the teaching of the wise (vv 4b, 7a). The righteous are mentioned in two proverbs. They are "as bold as a lion" (v 1b), and "when the righteous triumph, there is [glory or] elation" (v 12a).

There are a few references to sin, a force that blocks Yahweh's blessings from being realized. Thus, anyone who "conceals . . . sins does not prosper" (v 13a) and the prayers of one who disregards instruction are not heard (v 9). Children are the focus of two proverbs. A wise son who keeps the Law (v 7) is contrasted with a son who is "a companion of gluttons" (v 7b) and with one who steals from his parents (v 24).

Rulers are the focus of six proverbs. The cruelty of wicked rulers (vv 3, 15, 16a) pushes citizens into hiding for protection (vv 12b, 28a). When the authority of the strong central government collapses, local tyrants assert control over small districts (vv 2, 3, 12, 15, 16, 28). Conversely, a land ruled by a leader with understanding has stability (v 2b); as a result, the righteous work openly and thrive (v 28b).

Another significant topic is economics. Patient labor plus God's blessing produces abundance, but greed (v 8), bribery, and deception lead to want. Those who seek quick wealth or use oppressive means to acquire wealth eventually become poor (vv 8, 21), but those who seek Yahweh prosper (v 25). The latter have a long life since they hate unjust gains (v 16b). Riches, however, carry with them the danger of making their owner proud (v 11a). Those who are in haste to become rich will be punished (v 20b), and the greedy stir up dissention (v 25).

Thus, it is better to be poor with integrity than to be rich and deceitful (v 6). In fact, a poor person with discernment sees through the facade of the rich (v 11b). Nevertheless, the poor may even act oppressively (v 3). One cause of poverty is the pursuit of vain goals (v 19b). Those who give to the poor are blessed and do not lack, while those who ignore the poor receive curses (v 27). It is important to remember that the pursuit of quick wealth carries its own peril (v 20b).

Opposing: Confidence: Wicked / Righteous (28:1)

■ **I** The wicked (*rāšā'îm*) are very apprehensive about having their deeds exposed. Whenever they suspect that someone has observed them doing wrong, ***they run*** even **though no one pursues *them***. Such skittishness comes from a deep fear of being caught and punished (see Lev 26:17, 36). Consequently, the wicked never feel secure. **The righteous**, by contrast, **are as bold as a lion**. They go about their daily activities with confidence. Having done nothing askew, they have no fear of exposure.

Opposing: Many Rulers / Stable Rule (28:2)

■ **2** When a land is beset by internal conflicts, local princes and warlords take advantage of the social unrest and assert authority over various local regions. Such was the case in Egypt during the two Intermediate Periods. It was also the situation in northern Israel near the end of the kingdom when there was a rapid change of kings, alternating between those who opposed Assyria and those who became allies of Assyria, which was extending its empire into Palestine (2 Kgs 15:8-31; 17:1-6; Hos 8:4). But a land with an understanding and knowledgeable **ruler** has stability. One reason is that stable leadership promotes a strong economy. Unfortunately, the Hebrew text of the second line is beset by obscurities.

Analogy: Oppressor of the Poor (28:3)

■ **3** The poor are ordinarily generous and helpful, especially to others who are poor. But during an oppressive environment even ***a poor person*** (*rāš*, the reading in the margin of the NIV) **oppresses the poor** (*dallîm*). Such an upside down situation is compared to a land's being hit by **a driving rain**, which, instead of nourishing the crops, wipes out much of the harvest. Torrential rains not only ruin the harvest but also remove topsoil. Thus, rain, which is usually a blessing, especially in a dry land like Palestine, can fall so hard that it is destructive. This proverb calls attention to a variety of things that sometimes produce an affect that is inverse to what is usually the case.

Opposing: Forsakers of Instruction / Those Who Heed It (28:4)

■ **4** This proverb sets out that the ways that people respond to the law greatly affects the wicked. **Those who forsake instruction** [i.e., the teaching of the wise] **praise** [i.e., cheer on] **the wicked**. That is, they encourage them to break the law boldly. Conversely, **those who heed it resist** (*yitgārû*) the wicked and thereby curtail their influence.

Opposing: Justice: Wicked Do Not Understand / Seekers of Yahweh Understand (28:5)

■ **5** Since ***the wicked*** do not grasp the principles of **what is right** or ***just***, they fail to understand that a just decree is essential for fostering personal dignity and a secure community. But **those who seek *Yahweh* understand it fully.** **Fully,** in modifying the verb **understand,** is very general; content for this term is gained from its being parallel to ***justice.*** That is, those who follow Yahweh have insight into applying justice to the various dimensions of life (see 1 Cor 2:15). They understand well the critical role justice has for maintaining a vibrant community.

Better-than: The Poor and Blameless / The Rich and Perverse (28:6)

■ **6** (See 19:1.) Many proverbs speak of wealth as a benefit for keeping the Law and/or being wise. Nevertheless, this principle does not work categorically as this proverb points out in saying that **the poor whose walk is blameless** are better than **the rich whose ways are perverse.** This proverb shows that the wise knew that there were those who lived a blameless life and yet were poor. A poor person contributes to the community's well-being by serving God faithfully, while one who is wealthy, but dishonest, detracts from the community's well-being.

Opposing: Children: Keeping the Law / Companion of Gluttons (28:7)

■ **7** One who diligently **heeds instruction,** that is, the teaching of the wise, is **a discerning *child,*** bringing honor to the parents. But a youth who likes to run about with **gluttons *shames* his father** (see Deut 21:18-21). In the Deuteronomy text a rebellious child is labeled a glutton. Echoes of the parable of the prodigal son (Luke 15:11-32) are heard in this proverb. (See Prov 20:13.)

Advancing: Increasing Wealth by Taking Interest / Wealth of the Poor (28:8)

■ **8** One tactic often used for ***acquiring*** wealth is making loans at ***high*** interest. Another approach is to include a provision in the loan that the lender must share a percentage of the profit made from the loan; for example, if the loan was for the borrower to purchase seed, the lender receives a share of the profit from the harvest along with the interest due on the loan.

While it is accurate that the Law forbade loaning at interest to a fellow Israelite (Exod 22:25; Lev 25:36; Deut 23:19), this restriction did not apply to loans made to foreigners (Deut 23:20). How these laws in Deuteronomy were regulated when Israel became a nation is not attested. Certainly the laws in the Torah condemned loaning at excessive interest, today called "usury." In any case this proverb uses two terms for interest: *nešek* (lit. ***bite***), the interest taken out of the loan at the outset; and *tarbît* (lit. ***increase***), an amount added to the loan. Possibly the first term references a loan used to purchase seed or equipment and the second was for a loan of money (see Vaux 1965, 170).

Moneylenders who use shrewd methods for enhancing their wealth are unaware that in God's economy they do so only to give their increase to the poor. This principle, being found in various wisdom texts, holds that the wealth a miser stores up is eventually distributed by a generous person, perhaps the executor of the miser's estate, to aid the poor (Prov 14:31; Eccl

2:21). Longman notes that the implied assumption is that such gain would be returned to the poor in God's providence (2006, 490).

Unfortunately, the manner in which such redistribution took place is nowhere described in the OT. The force of the inverted outcome in the second line is enhanced by a wordplay between the terms *lĕḥônēn* (**be kind**) in the second line with *hônô* (*his* **wealth**) in the first line and by the fact that *lĕḥônēn* is the more forceful word (Lennox 1998, 291). (See Prov 13:22*b*.)

Advancing: Prayer (28:9)

■ **9** (See 15:8, 29.) The **prayers** of one who **turns a deaf ear to . . . instruction**, that is, refusing to obey the teaching of the wise, are **detestable** (→ sidebar "Yahweh Detests or Abomination to Yahweh" at 6:16-19). In turning to God for help through prayer and at the same time turning away from God by not keeping his word is a mockery of God that God does not brook. In reality this kind of person is using God rather than honoring God, no matter how fervent his **prayers**.

Three Lines: Two Are Advancing and the Third Is Opposing: Misleading the Upright / Falling into a Trap / Receiving a Good Inheritance (28:10)

■ **10** Anyone who seeks to *lead* **the upright** [*yĕšārîm*] **along an evil path will fall into their own trap**. The picture is that of a deceptive person setting a trap along a path by digging a pit and then camouflaging it in order that a passerby falls into it. This deceptive person entices an upright person to take this path in order to capture the upright person. But in God's providence this conniving person falls into the very trap that was set. Conversely, *those of integrity* [*tĕmîmîm*] **receive a good inheritance**. This saying underscores retribution with a cluster of words for traveling on a path: mislead, way, fall, and pit (Clifford 1999, 245).

Opposing: The Self-confident Rich / The Poor with Discernment (28:11)

■ **11** This proverb brings out a situation that is the opposite of numerous wisdom sayings. Since riches were usually taken as a sign that their owner is wise, there are people who become rich and then point to their wealth as proof that God is favoring them. Such a high sense of self-worth, however, robs them of a true sense of their relationship with God.

An example of a self-confident rich person was Nabal (lit. *fool*), a rich farmer in the Negev during the days when David, a fugitive from Saul, was maintaining order in the Negev. One day David asked Nabal for basic supplies to feed his men, but Nabal refused (1 Sam 25; compare Prov 19:12; 20:2). A few days later when Nabal learned that his wife, Abigail, had helped David, he fell ill and died ten days later. His arrogance was so shocked by a family member's helping David that he keeled over.

By contrast, *a* **poor** *person* who is **discerning sees** through the facade put on by a rich, proud person. This proverb brings out that the skill of discernment is not tied to social status or wealth. It also shows that the teaching about the wise was more nuanced than stating that the wise always become wealthy.

Nevertheless, the emphasis of aphorisms on the connection between wisdom and wealth lead many to despise the wisdom of the poor as seen in Eccl 9:16. This proverb belongs to those that counter such a wrong judgment.

Opposing: Righteous / Wicked (Line *b* = 28:28*b*) (28:12)

■ 12 When the righteous [*ṣaddîqîm*] triumph [*ˁālaṣ*, **to exalt at a triumph**], there is **an abundance of** elation throughout the land. That is, people as a whole are cheerful and optimistic. But **when the wicked rise to power, people go into hiding**, seeking to avoid facing them or to being conscripted into coerced labor or to suffering oppression. The harsh social conditions under the rule of the wicked drive people to conduct their affairs in an underground economy.

Advancing: Hiding Wickedness / Confessing Sins (28:13)

■ 13 The next two proverbs are arranged chiastically: consequence of concealing sin (v 13*a*): finding mercy by confessing sin (v 13*b*)::blessing for dreading evil (v 14*a*):consequence of hardening the heart (v 14*b*).

Renouncing sin or evil stands at the center and is the focus of the saying. The opposite attitude, concealing sin, stands at the outer frame; this attitude is shown to carry severe consequences.

This saying sets forth two ways of dealing with transgressions, a very rare topic in Proverbs. One way is to *cover up* or *conceal any wrongdoing*, hoping that it will never be discovered. But most attempts at a coverup eventually fall apart. The wrong done comes to light, leading to harsh consequences. Even before discovery that person becomes tentative in his work, possibly out of fear of discovery, and **does not prosper.**

The proper way of dealing with a wrong is to *confess* it and to *renounce* such behavior. A value of public confession is that it enhances one's resolve never to commit such a wrong again. Through confession one **finds mercy.** This statement implies that one who makes a confession receives forgiveness both from God and the community. This is the only proverb in the book that advocates making a confession for doing wrong. (See Ps 32:1-5.)

Opposing: One who Fears / One Who Hardens One's Heart (28:14)

■ 14 The first line states a blessing (*ˀašrê*). **Blessed is the *person* who *dreads*** (*mĕpaḥēd*) or **trembles** or *fears continually*. *Paḥēd* is a very strong term for fear. Although the object of the fear is not identified, the NIV assumes it is God. Fox (2009, 826), however, holds that the implied object is *rāˁâ*, **evil,** *misfortune*, since in the OT *paḥēd* never has God as an object. One who dreads evil has a deep fear or respect for **God** as the Holy One. This principle is clearly present in this proverb though the precise meaning of all the words is not certain. Conversely, the self-confident person **hardens *his* heart** and **falls into trouble**. It is impossible for a human to escape some kind of punishment for wrongdoing.

Analogy: Wicked Ruler (28:15)

■ **15** The tyrannical approach that **a wicked *ruler*** takes in governing **a help-less people** is compared to **a roaring lion or a charging bear**. The lion is a metaphor for the king's wrath in Prov 19:12 and 20:2. An angry ruler preys on his own people. He will suddenly trouble a particular person or group just because they are in his way and are unable to defend themselves. Under such a tyrant the people have little recourse except to hide from him.

Opposing: A Tyrant / A Ruler Who Hates Bribes (28:16)

■ **16** The root *ʿāšaq* (*oppress, exploit*) connects the next two proverbs. The Hebrew text is disturbed, so the meaning of some lines is not clear. This saying appears to contrast two types of rulers. One type of ruler **practices extortion,** cruelly oppressing the people. As a result, graft and perversion of justice flourish throughout the land. The opposite type of ruler **hates**, that is, ***refuses to allow***, any practice of exacting any ***unjust* gain** from the people. His stance for honesty brings God's blessing as is evidenced in that ruler's having a long reign. Life abounds for the people under this ruler.

Advancing: A Fugitive for Murder / Not to Be Supported (28:17)

■ **17** A person **tormented** [*ʿāšaq*] **by the guilt of murder *seeks* refuge in the grave** (lit. ***pit***) out of fear of being found by the avenger of blood (Deut 19:11-13), a manslayer ***seeks* refuge in *a pit*. No one** in the community is **to hold *him* back**, that is, provide him protection.

Seeking refuge in ***a pit*** may be a euphemism for attempting to commit suicide. Or ***pit*** may carry a double sense. The fugitive hides from an avenger of blood in a pit and that pit becomes his **grave**—in some texts ***pit*** means ***grave*** (Pss 88:6 [7 HB]; 143:7). Though the wording is difficult, this proverb clearly warns that whoever sheds blood faces a ghastly fate.

Opposing: Integrity / Perversion (28:18)

■ **18** The wisdom tradition frequently views life as a journey (see Prov 4:11-12). **One *who walks in integrity* is kept safe** from any traps or dangers along the path. That kind of person finds help from others who fear God or from God himself for dealing with difficult situations. But **one whose ways are perverse will fall**. That path's unevenness and its curves make it impossible to negotiate without stumbling and falling.

Opposing: Worker / Wanderlust (= 12:11) (28:19)

■ **19** These two lines make a play on the verb ***be satisfied or satiated*** (*śābaʿ*). A farmer who diligently ***works his* land** will reap a harvest that ***will satisfy*** his household with **food**. But ***a person* who *chases vain* or *empty activities*** [i.e., those that produce no yield] ***will be satiated*** with **poverty**. This proverb lauds industrious work and castigates being engaged in multiple activities that yield no product.

Opposing: Blessing for Faithfulness / Poverty Attends Hasty Wealth (28:20)

■ **20** One who faithfully engages in one's work receives *abundant blessings* over time. The term **faithful** (*'ĕmûnôt*), being in the plural, has superlative force; it describes a person who is consistently faithful in every aspect of life. The person treats all well—fellow workers, employees, and clients. As a result, over time the person becomes wealthy. But a person who is **eager to get rich will** not *escape punishment*.

This wording implies that a person who is driven to accumulate wealth quickly compromises virtues by engaging in various kinds of deceptive schemes. After a time these crooked practices lead to his suffering heavy losses, the direct opposite of his desire. The losses are punishment for his cheating people. The wisdom tradition frowns on striving for quick wealth. Rather, it teaches that a genuine person who is faithful comes to wealth as a by-product of being faithful.

Opposing: Showing Partiality / Doing Wrong for a Piece of Bread (Line *a* [less the phrase "in judging"]= 24:23*b*) (28:21)

■ **21** This proverb is formulated as a "not good" saying. Being the inverse of a better-than saying, it sets forth a strong negative judgment. The general judgment is supported by an example in the second line.

The principle here is that any show of partiality, especially in administrating or judging, is not good. The example that illustrates the principle is of a person stooping so low that the person does **wrong** for the slightest gain, merely **a piece of bread**.

This saying counsels against ever compromising one's integrity, for one will lose far too much to gain so little. Any such compromise shows that the doer has lost respect for justice. As Wesley comments, "When a man hath once accustomed himself to take bribes, a very small advantage will make him sell justice" (1975, 1885).

Advancing: Miser (28:22)

■ **22** *A person with an evil eye* (*a* stingy *person*), that is, one who seeks to control a situation or people through magical powers, *works quickly* to take advantage of a situation for personal gain, even if one's actions are harmful to another. That one is so focused on the quick gain that one is unaware that the very schemes used for gaining wealth will lead to personally suffering *want* or **poverty**.

Opposing: Rebuke / Flattery (28:23)

■ **23** A person needs to relate to others with integrity and concern. Some situations require a person to *rebuke* another for that person's own good, for the person who does not correct behavior or attitude will incur loss. Anyone who takes courage and offers a rebuke will in time **gain *more*** favor from the one rebuked than if he *had flattered* him (see 19:25; 25:12; 27:5, 6). No one enjoys receiving a rebuke; but one who learns from a rebuke is grateful to the one who offered the rebuke.

Advancing: Robbery of Parents (28:24)

■ **24** A descendant who **robs *a* father or mother** and then excuses such untoward action by claiming that the act was not really wrong is labeled *a companion of a destroyer*. The scenario behind this proverb may be a son's or daughter's taking control of a parent's assets under the guise of helping the parent in old age. But in reality that child takes control of the parent's finances for personal gain.

Such a descendant, acting in a way that avoids breaking the Law technically (Whybray 1972, 165), offers the excuse, **"It's not wrong."** Nevertheless, that person has clearly violated the very spirit of the Law. Such treatment of one's parents is so grievous that this kind of person is labeled *a companion of destroyers*, a name indicating that these actions threaten the parent's livelihood as well as the solidarity of the family. Clearly, one engaged in such behavior has violated the fifth commandment to honor one's parents. (See 1 Tim 5:4, 8.)

Opposing: Greedy / Trusting (28:25)

■ **25** The key term *trusting* (*bôṭēaḥ*), heading v 25*b* and v 26*a*, connects the next two proverbs. **The greedy**, referenced by the metaphor *wide throat*, that is, having an *unbridled appetite* (Clifford 1999, 247), **stir up conflict** (see 15:18). Through that conflict they hope to gain more for themselves, but in the long term they will not prosper. Rather, it is those who **trust in Yahweh**, being generous rather than greedy, who **prosper** (lit. *become fat*) by implication through Yahweh's blessing. They avoid causing conflict.

Opposing: Fool / Wise (28:26)

■ **26** Those who trust in *their own thinking* [lit. *heart*] are fools. No person has sufficient mental powers to construct a productive life without guidance from the wise. By contrast, **those who walk in wisdom are kept safe**; being wise, they rely on Yahweh. In light of the preceding proverbs, the wise escape loss, harm, and punishment. As a result, they have a blessed life.

Opposing: Generous / Miser (28:27)

■ **27** Those who give to the poor will lack nothing. The premise of this assertion is that judicious generosity brings blessings on the giver. In other words, as a result of God's blessing, those who are generous will not lack any basic need. This claim is built on the belief that God blesses those who are generous. By giving generously a person expresses trust in God rather than in wealth. By contrast, others walk past those in need *with* their eyes *turned upward* so as not to notice them. Such a calloused attitude leads to receiving **many curses**, presumably from the needy.

Opposing: Wicked / Righteous (Line *b* = 28:12*b*) (28:28)

■ **28** This saying describes radically contrasting conditions in society similar to v 12. When **the wicked** assert themselves and gain control of a city or a region, **people** [i.e., ordinary citizens] **go into hiding**. Daily tasks are done at unusual times in order not to be observed, lest one be abused or imprisoned. Other activities are done in secret or darkness, such as prayer. But when **the wicked perish, the righteous** [*ṣaddîqîm*] **thrive**, being free to work openly without any fear of oppression. Consequently, they increase, gain wealth, and rise in positions of leadership (Fox 2009, 835).

This proverb encourages the righteous to hold on to their integrity under an oppressive regime for in time the political climate will change radically, allowing them to again assume roles of leadership in the community and prosper in their occupations. (See 29:2.)

E. Proverbs 29:1-27

OVERVIEW

This chapter concludes the Solomonic collection edited by scribes at Hezekiah's court. The structure of the proverbs is balanced: twelve are constructed as opposing (vv 3, 4, 6, 7, 8, 10, 15, 18, 23, 25, 26, 27) and thirteen as advancing (vv 1, 5, 9, 11, 12, 13, 14, 16, 17, 19, 20, 21, 24). Only two are in affirming style (vv 2, 22).

The principal topics are similar to those in Section II: the king/ruler (vv 2, 4, 12, 14, 26), the contrast between the righteous and the wicked (vv 2, 6, 7, 16, 27), the contrast between the wise and the fool or scoffer (vv 8, 11), the advantage of discipline (vv 15, 17, 19), and concern for the poor (vv 7a, 13, 14). In addition, two aphorisms laud the joy parents receive from a child who loves wisdom (vv 3a, 17) and one emphasizes the shame a foolish child brings (v 15b). Attention is also given to the discord that anger produces (vv 8, 9, 11, 22).

In this collection is found the famous saying "where there is no vision, the people perish" (v 18a KJV). All communities need a visionary to remain vibrant. The second line describes as blessed one who keeps the Law (v 18b). There are also three Yahweh sayings (vv 13, 25, 26). The conviction that all humans are equal before God is highlighted by calling attention to the reality that Yahweh gives sight to both the poor and the oppressor (v 13).

Three proverbs concerning Yahweh—as the giver of sight (v 13b), the giver of justice (v 26b,) and the protector of those who trust him (v 25b)—stand in proximity to those that speak of the king (vv 12, 14, 26a), thereby showing that Yahweh is more favorable to the people than the king (see Whybray 1994a, 398).

Amazingly the rich metaphors that characterize proverbs in the other chapters in Section IV have diminished to only three: net (v 5b), snare (vv 6a, 25a), and the safety of a high place (v 25b).

To signal that this chapter concludes the collection of Solomonic proverbs added by the scribes at Hezekiah's court, the initial word begins with 'alep, the first letter of the Hebrew alphabet, and the lead words of both lines of the last couplet begin with *tāw*, the last letter of the Hebrew alphabet (Clifford 1999, 256).

IN THE TEXT

Advancing: Stiff-necked from Many Reproofs / Consequences (29:1)

■ **I** Ignoring genuine reproofs is unwise. It may even prove fatal. *A* **stiff-necked person** is one who becomes very hardened as a result of constantly shrugging off well-intended rebukes (see Deut 10:16). The more hardened that person becomes, the more that person is in danger of becoming immune to heeding a timely rebuke. One day such a person **will be suddenly broken**—without remedy. The cause of death may be a heart attack or a stroke. An example of such a sudden death in the OT is Eli's tragic fate. When Eli learned of the death of his sons and the loss of the ark of the covenant to the Philistines, he fell backward from his chair. Breaking his neck, he died immediately (1 Sam 4:18).

A **stiff-necked *people*** is a metaphor used several times in the OT for Israel's stubborn refusal to hear God's warnings. This metaphor describes the attitude of the Israelites in making the golden calf at Mount Sinai (Exod 32:9; 33:3, 5; 34:9). Some prophets used this metaphor in an effort to awaken Israel to her resistance to God's word (Isa 48:4; see 2 Chr 30:8).

Affirming: Righteous / Wicked (29:2)

■ **2** The quality of life in a community is heavily influenced by the moral character of its leaders. When **the righteous** [*ṣaddîqîm*] **thrive** or ***increase in number*** and exercise leadership, as implied by the parallel term **rule** in the second line, **the people rejoice**, for the righteous bring blessings on the community. But **when the wicked rule, the people groan**, since they live under oppressive conditions. They fear harm from such unprincipled leaders. (See Prov 28:12, 28.)

Opposing: A Lover of Wisdom / A Companion of Harlots (29:3)

■ **3** A person, presumably a youth, **who loves wisdom** develops a principled lifestyle that **brings joy to his father**. As he grows up, he increases in wisdom, bringing honor to the family. As a responsible adult, he will care for his parents in their old age. But a youth who spends **his wealth**, possibly from an inheritance received early, in ***consorting with* prostitutes,** quickly **squanders *that* wealth**. Most bad habits are expensive, for example, gambling, partying, and carousing. Engaging in such activities absorbs one's income and usually puts one into such debt that it may be a burden throughout that person's life. With such encumbrances a son is unable to offer his parents much help in their old age.

When Jesus told the parable of the prodigal son, this proverb would have come to the minds of many in the audience. Thus, they would have been very astounded at the father's welcoming back this wayward son who had shamed him so deeply with such joy that he held an elaborate celebration

(Luke 15:11-24). In this parable Jesus sets out the radical thought that God's grace surpasses standards imposed by an honor-based society, standards that the community believes give honor to God.

Opposing: Just King / Bribery (29:4)

■ **4** In this saying a righteous king is contrasted with a corrupt official (see Prov 29:14). **A king** [who rules **by justice**] **gives a country stability.** As a result the citizens enjoy security, prosperity, and peace. It is unlikely that there will be an uprising during his reign. But a leader who is so driven by greed that he shows favoritism to those who are generous to him, that is, those who give him *gifts* (*těrûmôt*), undermines the people's confidence. Deeply troubled by such bold corruption, they lose confidence in the government. Visible opposition to such a leader may break out at any time. Injustice that attends favoritism *tears down* a country.

The Term "Gifts"

The meaning of *těrûmôt* in this context is unclear. Elsewhere in the OT it references only **sacred gifts**. The NIV has the gloss **bribes**, but the gloss **contributions** is closer to its usual force. Given the context, some take it as referring to taxes (e.g., Longman 2006, 502), but that meaning is not attested elsewhere. It is doubtful that any government official would be opposed to taxes. Fox (2009, 834-35) takes a different path by identifying the form in the MT as a variant spelling of *tarmît* (**deceit**), that is, **a deceitful ruler.**

Since this term is used for gifts made to the sanctuary, it is possible that an official co-opts this term in an effort to make his corrupt method of enriching himself appear legitimate. The misuse of government funds undercuts **the rule of justice.** Despite the difficulty of determining the precise sense of this term, it is clear that the issue is a high official's using his position to squeeze money out of citizens.

Advancing: Flattery / Spreading a Net (29:5)

■ **5** The imagery of trapping connects the next two sayings. Humans enjoy receiving praise. Taking advantage of this human trait, a flatterer commends *a neighbor* profusely in an effort to influence the neighbor inappropriately. Such use of flattery is comparable to **spreading *a net*** to capture an animal. When an animal unwarily treads on that net, it falls into the pit and becomes trapped. Similarly, a flatterer leads a neighbor to make a purchase or to enter into a deal that the neighbor soon comes to regret (see 2:16; 5:3; 6:24; 7:5, 21; 26:28; 28:23). A wise person is always on guard against being beguiled by flattery.

Opposing: A Wicked Person / A Righteous Person (29:6)

■ **6** This saying pictures *an evil person* being caught in a snare *set* by *one's* own sin. Its goal is to challenge the confidence of the wicked that they can escape harm from wrongdoing. Despite their presumption, they will be ensnared in time. The righteous, on the other hand, **shout for joy** as they travel the path of life. Whenever they see a wicked person fall, they are especially **glad**, because the teaching that the wicked fall because of doing evil is confirmed. (See 1:19; 12:13; 26:27.)

Opposing: The Righteous / The Wicked (29:7)

■ **7** This proverb is framed by two words from the root *yd'* (**know**)—*yôdēaʿ* (**know** or **care**) and *daʿat* (**knowledge** or concern)—framing the proverb as the first and last words. The Hebrew **know** has a wide range of senses. In this context it means far more than knowledge of the laws regarding the poor. It carries the sense **have** concern **for**. The righteous care about [*yôdēaʿ*] **the legal standing** or **rights** [*dîn*] **of** the poor. As their advocates, they take steps to see that they receive justice. **The wicked**, however, **do not understand**, that is, **have no such concern**, for the poor.

Opposing: Social Unrest: Mockers / The Wise (29:8)

■ **8** Mockers (*ʾanšê lāṣôn*), **people of a tongue** (1:22; Isa 28:19), are contrasted with **the wise** in regard to their impact on community life. They **inflame** [*pûaḥ*] **a city** by heaping insults on officials and shouting inflammatory words. Metaphorically the verb *pûaḥ* (**blow**) pictures their rhetoric as a blast of wind that fans a small flame into a roaring fire (see Prov 26:21). Thus, their rhetoric sometimes leads to conflict among factions in a community. On the other hand, the wise function as a strong, stabilizing force in a community. When people are aroused, **the wise** speak in ways that cool their **anger**.

Advancing: A Dispute with a Fool (29:9)

■ **9** When **a wise person** *gets into a dispute* [*nišpāṭ*] **with a fool, the fool rages and scoffs**. *Dispute* may reference either an argument or a lawsuit. Fox (2009, 837) and Clifford (1999, 251) hold that it is a debate, not a legal case; otherwise anger would not be an issue. However, in support of its being a lawsuit is the use of the verb *nišpāṭ*, **enter into a controversy** (**before the court**) (1 Sam 12:7; Jer 2:35; Ezek 17:20; 20:35-36).

During a lawsuit a fool seeks to keep a wise person from presenting his position in an orderly fashion by ranting and laughing sarcastically, constantly interrupting the wise person's presentation. The wording may also suggest that when speaking in self-defense the fool employs inflammatory words, seeking to divert attention from the merits of the plaintiff's arguments. The fool's disruptive behavior prevents a reasonable resolution of the dispute. (See Eccl 9:17.)

Opposing: Violent People / The Upright (29:10)

■ **10** The bloodthirsty—people given to shedding blood—**hate** *those who are principled* (*tām*), that is, those who live by the high standards of wisdom (see Prov 26:28; 29:27b). By contrast, **the upright** seek to preserve lives. In so doing they are the light and the salt of a community.

The Meaning of the Second Line of Prov 29:10

The Hebrew in the second line is very difficult. The idiom *yĕbaqšû napšô* (*seek one's life*) may mean **seek to kill**. In that case the line reads **the blood-thirsty . . . seek to kill the upright** (Waltke 2005, 438). That meaning is not congruent with **the upright** being the subject of **seek** in the Hebrew text. It is possible that the idiom means "to help someone," i.e., "preserve one's life" (Clifford 1999, 251-52; Fox 2009, 837), rather than having its usual sense *kill someone* (e.g., Exod 4:19). In that case the line says *the upright seek to preserve their lives*.

Longman (2006, 504) offers another reading: "the virtuous seek their lives," that is, the lives of the bloodthirsty, in order to put an end to violence. Definitely the upright would make an effort to stop bloodshed, but the righteous are not pictured as aggressively seeking to put the wicked to death elsewhere in Proverbs. Thus, the gloss *preserve life* is tentatively accepted.

Determining whether this couplet is structured as affirming or opposing would help in deciding between these options, but that identification is made difficult due to the lack of context. Since opposing proverbs are prominent in this chapter, it seems better to read the second line as presenting a concept that opposes the first line. Therefore, the rendering *preserve one's life* is followed.

Advancing: Passion: A Fool / A Wise Person (29:11)

■ 11 The actors, *a fool* and *a wise person*, are emphasized by their placement next to each other at the center of the proverb. The difference in the way these two kinds of people express deep emotions is described. *A fool* [*kĕsîl*] *gives* full vent to *his deepest feelings* (*rûaḥ*). *Feelings* is preferred to **rage** for the Hebrew *rûaḥ* stands for a person's temperament, which may be expressed by various emotions, such as anger, haughtiness, patience, and steadfastness. Whenever *a fool* becomes very upset, he loudly *vents* his distress.

Conversely, *a wise person*, having good self-control, expresses ideas judiciously, succinctly, and calmly, even under pressure. The uncertainty of the meaning of the unique phrase *bĕʾāḥôr* (*back, in the end*) in the second line leads to various readings. One reading is that *a wise person* has the ability to hold back or to control his emotions (Fox 2009, 838). A second reading is that *a wise person* stills the anger of the wicked (Waltke 2005, 439). In favor of this reading is the force of the verb *šābaḥ*, a term used for Yahweh's stilling the raging sea (Pss 65:7; 89:9).

Advancing: Ruler / Impact on Officials (29:12)

■ 12 A ruler who *gives heed to* [i.e., commends] *a false report* encourages all . . . officials under him to become wicked. By accepting, commending, and acting on fabricated information, a ruler signals that he does not esteem the truth. Lesser officials, observing that those who give distorted reports are rewarded, follow suit in fabricating their reports in order to receive greater recognition. Over time these officials become more brazen, even becoming engaged in doing wrong. This proverb discloses that corruption among high officials has a way of permeating every office in the government. The proverb is dominated by the sound *š*: *mōšēl maqšîb ʿal dĕbar šāqer kol mĕšortāyw rĕšāʿîm* (Fox 2009, 838). (See Ps 101:6b-8; Prov 25:5.)

Advancing: Poor and Oppressor Enlightened by Yahweh (29:13)

■ **13** Various proverbs describe the economic disparity between the poor and the rich (e.g., 22:2). This proverb takes a different direction by emphasizing a valuable aspect of life that both *an* oppressor and *a* poor *person* have in common. The phrase oppressor (*ʾîš tĕkākîm*) occurs only here in the OT. It stands for the brutal character of a tyrant since it likely comes from the root *tōk* (*oppression, violence*), which in its three occurrences in the OT stands in conjunction with *mirmâ* (*deceit, fraud*) (Pss 10:7; 55:11) and *ḥāmās* (*violence*) (Ps 72:14). In Ps 55:11 *tōk* is used for the corruption that takes place in a town's marketplace, thereby ruining that town.

The formulation of the first line suggests that this saying is a riddle. *An* oppressor and *a* poor *person* have something in common. What is it? The answer, though it is not easy to come by, is a key teaching in the OT: **Yahweh** gives the marvelous sense of **sight** to **both** of them. Consequently, whenever these two types of people meet, they need to respect each other. On the one hand, a poor person should recognize that he has as much value in God's sight as the oppressor because God has favored him with the gift of sight. This insight can provide a poor person the self-confidence to stand up to an oppressor.

The oppressor, on the other hand, needs to realize that a poor person is on the same level, for God has also gifted that person with sight. Thus, he needs to treat the poor with respect. This awareness should lead the oppressor to dampen contempt for one who is poor. Furthermore, he needs to realize that he must not continue to take advantage of the poor for personal gain.

One example of applying the principles set forth in this proverb is arranging a meeting between a criminal and that one's victim. When the two have a face-to-face meeting, the criminal may come to recognize that the victim is not a well-off person who can easily afford to part with excessive property. It is also hoped that the criminal will come to realize the loss and emotional distress inflicted on a real person.

The victim too faces a real person and may discover that attitudes toward the criminal need to become more compassionate. Such encounters often produce real changes in the attitudes of those from different walks of life. By gaining respect for each other the behavior of both parties may change, thereby improving relationships between segments of a community.

Advancing: King / A Secure Throne (29:14)

■ **14** The tenor of a king's rule greatly affects the attitudes of the people. The ideal in Israel was for *the* king to *judge* the poor *in truth*, that is, **with fairness**. This ideal is a key element in the prayer to be sung at the enthronement of a

Davidic king (Ps 72). A petition reiterated in that prayer calls for the king to administrate justice for all, especially the poor (Prov 29:4, 12-14).

This petition is founded on the conviction that the **throne** of **a king** who **judges the poor** justly **will be established forever.** This position confronts the natural inclination of rulers to curry the favor of the rich and the powerful, the very ones who are inclined to influence the king to show them favoritism, a favoritism that is often bestowed at the expense of the poor.

Opposing: Discipline / Lack of Discipline (29:15)

■ **15** A youth *gains* wisdom by learning that is encouraged by a **rod** *and reproof.* Disciplines, though administered differently today, speed up learning, especially given the natural resistance of all humans to changing their thinking or behavior, changes necessary for becoming wise, productive adults. But *a youth* who is free to do whatever the youth wants tends to pursue foolish ways, bringing *disgrace on the* **mother**. Reference to the mother's shame underscores the appalling consequences faced by the parents as a result of that child's wayward behavior. (See 13:24; 22:15; 23:14-15; Sir 30:1.)

Advancing: The Wicked / The Righteous (29:16)

■ **16** This saying offers hope to people who live in a society in which **the wicked thrive** or *increase*. When **the wicked** *increase, crime* greatly increases. During such a time **the righteous** must act shrewdly and diligently in order to survive. They take consolation in their confidence that they **will see** *the* **downfall** of the wicked. Their hope resides in their belief that God will intervene, giving them a ruler who will lead a reform based on the standards of the covenant. (See 28:12, 28; 29:2.)

Advancing: Discipline / Delight (29:17)

■ **17** Parents are exhorted to bring up *a child* with the proper use of **discipline**, for a well-guided child *will provide* them *rest (nûaḥ)*. **Discipline** administered in love produces in a child respect for the parents. As a well-trained child grows up, the child rewards the parents with *many* **delights**, lit. *delicacies for your appetite*. (See Gen 49:20; Prov 10:1; 19:18; 23:13.)

Opposing: Lack of Vision / Keeping the Law (29:18)

■ **18** A community needs *a vision* or *a* revelation, that is, a divine word from its leader, a prophet, or a sage, in order to prosper and have a strong sense of direction. Just as a prophet receives a word from God, so too may a leader or a sage (see Eliphaz's vision report [Job 4:12-21]; Waltke 2005, 446). A leader who has a word from Yahweh, either personally or through counselors, inspires the people to live righteously and guides them in working together for the benefit of all.

But when the leaders fail to set forth *a vision*, the people **cast off restraint** and do what they want. When the people no longer have regard for the law, there is a breakdown in civil order. Such was the case for the Israelites as they traveled through the Sinai wilderness.

While Moses was on the mountain, the people pressured Aaron to make them a god (Exod 32:1-6, 17-25). He asked for donations and from them made the golden calf. The people celebrated wildly before it (Exod 32:25). Their revelry so angered God that he became intent on wiping them out (Exod 32:9-10). Only by Moses' intercession were the Israelites spared. Other scriptures refer to a time when there was no true prophet in the land or when a word from Yahweh was rare (1 Sam 3:1; Ps 74:9; Lam 2:9). During those times the people faced frightful hardships, such as famine and lawlessness.

Conversely, **whoever** heeds wisdom's instruction, either the Torah or the instruction of the wise, is **blessed** (*'ašrēhû*). They are blessed because God promotes the community's well-being.

Advancing: Correcting a Servant / A Servant Who Does Not Respond (29:19)

■ **19** This saying and the next are connected by having the phrase **with words** (*bidbārîn*) in the first stich. **A servant**, today a worker, needs specific guidance from time to time in order to comply with the standards required by the nature of the work, both to be productive and to work safely. This proverb informs a master or a manager to use tactics other than **mere words** to get a servant or a worker to change unacceptable behavior, for most servants or workers do not readily accept a reproof.

In antiquity a master could gain compliance by administering a beating, which the law specified limits. A master who punished a servant so harshly that he caused an injury was to be punished (Exod 21:20-21, 26-27). Today supervisors must use a variety of creative ways to have workers comply with a business's safety regulations.

Wesley (1975, 1886) describes the servant as one "who is so not only in condition, but also in the temper of his mind, disingenuous and stubborn."

Advancing: Speaking in Haste (Line *b* = 26:12*b*) (29:20)

■ **20** Since speech has the power to build up relationships or to tear them down, it is important that a person think before speaking. But there are people who are prone **to speak** in haste. Making quick assumptions about what is taking place or what another person is talking about, they interrupt a conversation, offering an opinion, whether or not it is well-grounded. But **speaking in haste** often leads to making statements that are faulty or offensive, for the one speaking has not taken the effort to grasp the nature of the issues being discussed nor discerned the mood of those engaged in a dispute. Consequently, **there is more hope for a fool than for** a person given to speaking without reflection. Since proverbs hold little hope for a fool, this comparison strongly condemns uttering words **in haste**. (See Prov 12:23; 14:3.)

Advancing: A Pampered Servant / Brings Grief (29:21)

■ **21** In antiquity many slaves or servants, especially those born in a household, were raised or trained by their master (Exod 21:4). If a master *pampers* [*pannēq*] *a* servant . . . from youth, that servant, on becoming an adult, will become **insolent**. That servant possibly turns out to be a poor worker, lacking sufficient stamina to endure long hours of hard labor. Or, that one may have a stubborn disposition (see Prov 22:6), either refusing to do various chores or doing them poorly.

It is not prudent to comment further on this verse, for the meaning of two key words is unknown. The verb *pannēq*, rendered *pampers*, occurs only here in the Hebrew Bible. It has the sense "pamper" in later Hebrew. The term *mānôn* in the second line has three homonyms: **insolent**, *weakling*, and *pained* (*DCH* 5:240). The versions fail to give insight into its sense here. The sense of the proverb is well stated by Yoder (2009, 276): "the servant is unruly and the master is miserable."

Affirming: Anger: Dissension / Sin (Line *a* = 15:18*a*) (29:22)

■ **22** This proverb uses two phrases to characterize a person obsessed with anger: *a person of anger* (*'îš 'ap*) and *a person dominated by wrath* (*ba'al ḥēmâ*). **An angry person** delights in *stirring* up conflict. The more heated and boisterous the conflict, the more that person enjoys the squabbling. Furthermore, **a hot-tempered person commits many *crimes***. Anger drives such a person to commit violent acts in total disregard for the law, such as destroying property wantonly. An example today is a person who enters a workplace and begins shooting a weapon at random, killing and wounding anyone in sight. (See 15:18; 21:25; 28:25.)

Opposing: Pride Brings Low / Sincerity Leads to Honor (29:23)

■ **23** This proverb has a chiastic structure. At the center stand words from the root *špl* (*below*): *hišpîl* (*bring low*) and *šāpal* (**lowly**). At the edges are descriptors of people who have radically different demeanors: *prideful* (*ga'ăwâh*) and *humble*, that is, *contrite of spirit* (*šĕpal rûaḥ*).

A proud person is so overconfident that he expects great results from everything he does. Such a person also expects enthusiastic commendations from everyone. But an obnoxious attitude leads to being deeply despised by all. In time he will have his comeuppance. The very pride that drove him to promote himself will get him into a situation that **brings *him* low**. He will be greatly humiliated in public.

In contrast, a sincere person, one who is graciously deferring, *gains* honor. A person with a considerate disposition shows genuine interest in others. For example, that kind of person listens attentively to what others have to say. People, being drawn to such a person, give him or her **honor**, the type of recognition that a proud person craves. (See 11:16; Matt 23:12.)

Advancing: Accomplice of a Thief / Failure to Testify (29:24)

■ **24** Anyone who becomes *an accomplice of a thief* in order to share in that criminal's unjust gains puts personal well-being in jeopardy. In making such an alignment one reveals that one *hates one's own self.*

The second line presents a situation in which such a person is forced into being *his own enemy.* The wording reflects a practice used by an ancient community, without a police force, to deal with a crime. In an effort to find the perpetrator of a crime or an act of violence, the community leaders called a public assembly. At the assembly they had everyone take an oath that compelled any person who knew something about the crime to inform the leaders. Anyone who failed to testify became subject to the curse (Lev 5:1). At such an assembly the accomplice of a thief would take the oath. If he *failed to* testify to what he knew, he placed himself under that curse. Thereby he acted as *his own enemy*, for that curse would consume him (see Zech 5:2-4). (See Prov 16:19.)

Opposing: Fear of Humans / Trust in Yahweh (29:25)

■ **25** *Trembling* (*hărādâ*) before *a person* is contrasted with *trusting* in *Yahweh* (see Jer 17:5, 7). A person who is so intimidated by another that he trembles in that one's presence feels that he must do whatever that person demands, even if the action demanded is dishonest.

A picture of such dread is seen in the terror that was felt by Joseph's brothers when they discovered in Benjamin's sack the silver that they had paid the Egyptian overlord for grain (Gen 42:28). They were caught between the demands of the Egyptian overlord and their father's fear of losing Benjamin, his only living son by his beloved wife Rachel. The terror of Jacob's sons caused the family great distress as they sought to cope with the famine.

Fear of another *person proves* to be a snare. It robs a person of the courage to do what is right. By contrast, **whoever trusts in** *Yahweh* **is kept safe** (*yĕśuggāb*). The Hebrew *śāgab* means *to be set on a high place*, that is, a secure refuge. *Trust* in *Yahweh* rests on the fear of Yahweh. This proverb brings out the radical difference between *dread* that enslaves and a proper fear of God that produces trust, the foundation of genuine confidence (see Jer 17:5-7).

Opposing: Justice Sought from King / Justice Received from Yahweh (29:26)

■ **26** Whenever a king holds **an audience**, there is a long line of people waiting to present the king a request. Only a few of those in line get an audience with the king. When David was king, many citizens, being unable to present their issues to him, became disgruntled. Absalom, David's son, took advantage of the people's dissatisfaction by promising to those who failed to get an audience with David that if he were judge, they would receive justice (2 Sam 15:1-4).

After winning the support of these disgruntled citizens, he led a revolt against David, compelling the king to flee Jerusalem (2 Sam 15:10-37).

This proverb, however, counsels those who **seek an audience with a ruler** in order to have an issue resolved that **it is from *Yahweh*** that *a person* gets justice rather than from an earthly ruler.

Opposing: Righteous / Wicked (29:27)

■ **27** People on the opposite sides of the moral spectrum strongly **detest** each other. **The righteous detest *a person who commits iniquity*, and the wicked detest *a person of integrity*,** literally ***those who follow a straight path***. The term **detest** is the strongest possible word for despising something. It is used frequently in Proverbs for Yahweh's hatred of evil (e.g., Prov 3:32; 6:16) (→ sidebar "Yahweh Detests or Abomination to Yahweh" at 6:16-19).

At the end of this collection of proverbs collected by scribes at Hezekiah's court is placed a saying that asserts that on earth there are two irreconcilable orientations to moral living. Awareness of this reality emboldens those who trust in Yahweh to be firm in withstanding evildoers. Such citizens make for a strong, upright society.

Those who have moral courage do not cower before the wicked (29:25*a*). They hold evildoers accountable for their wrongdoings, confident that Yahweh will keep them safe (v 25*b*). Such citizens are the foundation for a healthy, dynamic, secure nation. They make the king's throne secure.

V. APPENDIX: 30:1—31:9

A. The Sayings of Agur (30:1-33)

OVERVIEW

The extent of Agur's sayings is not easy to determine. Interpreters have assigned various portions of this chapter to him: vv 1-9 (Van Leeuwen 1997, 251; Fox 2009, 850), vv 1-14 (based on the LXX having a new heading at v 14: "words of the wise" [compare 24:23a], Whybray 1994a, 148-50; Plöger 1984, 356), and the entire chapter (Yoder 2009, 278; Steinmann 2001, 59-66). Since the book of Proverbs has section titles at 1:1, 10:1, 24:23a, and 25:1, the heading is accepted as standing for the whole chapter.

This chapter has two sections: (1) Agur's sayings (30:1b-9) and (2) a collection of sayings that range from two (vv 10, 15ab) to ten lines (vv 11-14, 24-28). Numerical sayings are dominant in this collection. One employs only one number in its heading (vv 24-28). Four are based on the pattern three/four (vv 15b-16, 18-19, 21-23, 29-31). Set among the numerical sayings are three epigrams: characterization of a generation (vv 11-14), against greed (v 15ab), and against acting like a fool (vv 32-33). The placement of these epigrams is based on a catchword.

315

IN THE TEXT

1. Agur's Self-Introduction and Prayer (30:1-9)

a. Heading (30:1ab)

■ **1ab** The heading identifies this collection as **the sayings of Agur son of Jakeh**. No information about either Agur or Jakeh has survived. The next word, *hammaśśāʾ*, may be taken either as a noun, **an inspired utterance**, or as a place name, **Massa**. If it is the latter, Agur may have belonged to an Ishmaelite clan (Gen 25:12-14). Ishmael was Abraham's son by Hagar (Gen 16:15-16; 1 Chr 1:29-31). In support of its being a toponym is the fact that Lemuel is identified as King of Massa (31:1 NJPS, REB). Accepting that reading, the appendix preserves two wisdom sayings representative of northern Arabian wisdom. It also accounts for the inclusion of these two collections in the appendix. The inclusion of non-Israelite wisdom in Proverbs is not surprising, for wisdom is an international enterprise as is evident in the influence of the Instruction of Amenemope on Prov 22:17—23:11.

Agur's words are also identified as **this man's utterance** [*nĕʾum*] **to Ithiel**. Utterance or *oracle* authenticates Agur's words as inspired. It is used six times in the headings to Balaam's utterances (e.g., Num 24:3-4, 15-16). **Agur** addresses **Ithiel,** an unknown person. In the Hebrew text the term **Ithiel** is repeated and joined with **Ukal** (NIV mg.). It is possible that these two words are the names of two people Agur addresses (NJPS). Many English versions, such as the NIV, however, render them **I am weary, God, but I can prevail** or *I am worn out* (see REB). Translated in this manner, they provide a good lead into Agur's apology.

b. An Apology (30:1c-4)

■ **1c-4** Agur begins with a very self-deprecating apology. He identifies himself as **a brute** (*baʿar*) rather than as **a learned man**. He adds that he is lacking in **human understanding**, that is, **understanding** common to most *humans*, and **has not learned wisdom**. This last statement may mean that he has not studied under a prominent sage. Or it may mean that he has diligently studied the wisdom of the sages but fails to understand their insights. A similar self-deprecation is spoken by a psalmist: "When my heart was grieved and my spirit embittered, I was senseless [*baʿar*] and ignorant; I was a brute beast before you [God]" (Ps 73:21-22). Agur denies *having* attained . . . **the knowledge of the Holy One**. That is, he either lacks profound insight into the nature of God or has never received a special revelation. Only those who witnessed the creation have extensive wisdom (Prov 8:22-31; Job 15:7-8).

In support of his claiming to lack wisdom, Agur asks a series of rhetorical questions to discover the identity of anyone who has had a unique experience giving him wisdom. **Who has gone up to heaven and come down** or *has*

PROVERBS

30:1-4

gathered . . . the wind in his *palms* or has wrapped up the waters in a cloak or has established all the ends of the earth? The obvious answer is "no one, but God, not even one of God's **sons**," that is, a member of the heavenly court. God is truly wholly other. With these questions Agur honors God's power and wisdom. He also shows his devotion by using four names for God in this apology: **Holy One** (v 3*b*), **God** (*ĕlôah* [v 5*a*]), **Yahweh** (v 9*b*), and **God** (*ĕlōhîm* [v 9*d*]). Not having any of these experiences is solid evidence that Agur is lacking wisdom.

In this apology Agur is following the ancient custom of debasing himself as a backdrop to his exaltation of God.

c. The Words of God (30:5-6)

■ **5-6** Agur affirms that **every word of God** is *refined*, that is, accurate and trustworthy (Ps 18:30 [31 HB]). Also he asserts that **God** like **a shield** protects **those who take refuge in him.**

Out of high respect for what God has revealed, Agur admonishes: **Do not add to his words**. This admonition is at home in ancient Middle Eastern treaties; it is a warning against anyone adding terms to a formal document (see Deut 4:2; 12:32 [13:1 HB]). Agur is affirming that what God has revealed is sufficient. It does not need to be changed or qualified. A twofold penalty supports the admonition: *being rebuked* by God and *being proven* a liar.

d. A Prayer (30:7-9)

■ **7-9** Agur offers a brief prayer, the only prayer in Proverbs. His prayer reflects the modesty he has expressed in his denials. It shows that he earnestly desires to live a godly life.

Agur *asks Yahweh* to grant him **two things** before **he dies**. He wants to keep from dishonoring God by either becoming proud or by sinning. He specifically *asks Yahweh*: **keep falsehood . . . far from me**. Agur is aware that if he *lies* or acts dishonestly, he would dishonor God, thereby disrupting his relationship with God. Next Agur prays that he never face **poverty *or*** have **riches**. He asks simply that he *be given his* **daily** bread (see Matt 6:11). **Daily** is literally *appropriate portion* (*ḥōq*).

Agur recognizes that he only needs sufficient *food* for each day. He motivates his petitions by mentioning the temptations that attend becoming **rich** or **poor**. If he *has* **too much,** he would be tempted to **disown God.** That is, being comfortable, he would live each day without honoring **Yahweh** (see Hos 13:6). Acting in that way he would *betray* (*kiḥēš*) God. In antiquity atheism, far different than it is today, was a denial that God had any effect in one's life or in human affairs. Conversely, if he *should* **become** so **poor** that he lacks **daily bread**, he would feel compelled to **steal**. Such behavior would **dishonor the name of . . . God.**

PROVERBS

317

2. A Collection of Numerical Sayings and Epigrams (30:10-33)

a. Admonition against Slander and Description of a Corrupt Generation (30:10-14)

An independent admonition is followed by an epigram of four verses. They are connected by the key word "curse." The epigram characterizes a perverted generation. It has three verses of two lines each and a fourth of four lines. Each of the four verses begins with *generation* (*dôr*), rendered "those who"/"those whose" in the NIV. Each time it is modified by an extended noun clause. Only the fourth description states the repulsive goal of this corrupt generation.

■ **10** Agur begins with an admonition against *defaming* a servant. The Hebrew term is a verbal form of the word *tongue*. Being a general term, it includes stating something about **a servant** to his **master** with the intent of putting him in a negative light, even if what is reported is basically accurate.

This admonition implies that the speaker is more intent on harming the servant than on making a viable comment. Anyone who says something harmful about a servant has little fear of retaliation, for **a servant** is powerless. The only recourse available to him is to **curse** the talebearer. This warning would carry some weight in antiquity, for the ancients believed that curses brought harm on the person cursed.

■ **11-14** These verses list the characteristic of a *generation*. Each verse is headed by the word *generation* (*dôr*; **those who/whose**). Today sociologists assign a name to the coming generation of young adults based on their dominant characteristics. In this epigram *the generation* is characterized as **those who curse their fathers and do not bless their mothers**.

Possibly they feel that their parents have treated them poorly or have been excessively strict. In the Law treating parents in this way was a capital offense (Exod 21:15, 17; Deut 27:16; see Prov 20:20). But those of this *generation* are impervious to the seriousness of their behavior, for they believe that they are **pure**. However, in reality they are dirty with their own *excrement* (see 2 Kgs 18:27; Isa 4:4; 36:12). *Excrement* functions as a metaphor for a repulsive, nasty attitude. They also are **haughty**, expressing their superior attitude with *uplifted* eyes. With their **glances** (lit. *eyelids*), they express their disdain of others. In many societies and possibly in ancient Israel it was customary to focus one's eyes slightly downward (see Fox 2009, 867).

This *generation* is further characterized as having a hostile demeanor. It is described by vivid metaphors: their **teeth are swords** and their **jaws are set with knives**. They use very sharp rhetoric to deny the poor a place in society (see Prov 28:12, 28). They keep the poor relegated to a ghetto, out of view and out of contact with people in the community. The metaphorical description of their mouths indicates that their words inflict great pain on **the poor**. They act so cruelly toward them in order to increase their own wealth and power.

b. A Series of Numerical Sayings and Three Epigrams (30:15-33)

OVERVIEW

The dominant form in the remainder of this chapter is numerical sayings. These sayings give a list of items that share specific traits. The first line states that a certain number of items have a particular trait. The second line, structured as affirming, raises that number by one and adds a second descriptor. The following lines list the items that meet both characteristics. The dominant pattern in this collection is three/four (vv 18-19, 21-23, 29-31).

The purpose of a graded numerical saying remains a conjecture. They may have served as riddles. A person or a small group was challenged to name a certain number of items having both characteristics. Friends might have taken turns trying to stump each other in naming the requested number of items.

In this collection other aphorisms have been inserted. Between the first and second numerical saying (vv 15c-16, 18-19) is a saying about an eye that mocks one's parents (v 17). Between the second and third numerical sayings (vv 18-19, 21-23) is a saying about an adulterous woman (v 20). It may have been inserted at this place since the preceding line speaks of the way of a man with a woman. The concluding aphorism of five lines (vv 32-33) gives advice on curtailing a strong impulse to engage in wrongdoing.

Numerical sayings are used primarily to classify a variety of things that have something in common, for example, animals, actions, social relationships, classes of people, and particular behaviors. These lists inspire people to notice ways in which aspects of nature are similar (Murphy 1998, 237-38).

The first numerical saying may have three advancing numbers: two, three, and four. If that is the case, it is unique in the OT. More likely an independent saying (v 15ab) has been placed before the graded numerical saying because it has the number two and it appears to deal with a theme similar to the numerical saying.

That it was not originally part of this numerical saying is confirmed by the fact that its number modifies the subject instead of being part of the introduction and because its theme is different: a disposition, i.e., "greed," rather than an aspect of nature, is insatiable. It is also different in presenting a moral; that is not a concern of the following saying (Fox 2009, 868).

The Leech (30:15*ab*)

■ **15*ab*** **The leech has two daughters. Daughters** refer to the two suckers at each end of its body. They keep drawing blood from its host until the leech is fully bloated. **"Give, give," they cry. They cry**, absent in the Hebrew, is inserted in some English translations to make a sentence. This independent saying has been placed here for two reasons: (1) It contains the number two, making a connection with three/four in the next couplet; (2) it describes a creature that is never satisfied.

Four Things Never Satisfied (30:15c-16)

■ **15c-16** This numerical saying identifies **three/four** things **that are never satisfied.** They **never say, "Enough!"** First is **the grave.** Ancient texts personified **the grave** as having a voracious appetite. It is always hungry for more victims (27:20; Isa 5:14). Second is **the barren womb.** A woman who is **barren,** feeling incomplete and vulnerable, constantly pleads for a child. Her crying never ceases until she gives birth. Two devout women who were so troubled by barrenness that they made a vow to motivate God to give them a child are Leah (Gen 30:14-24) and Hannah (1 Sam 1:9-20). A third example is Lemuel's mother (Prov 31:2*a*).

Third, **land, which is never satisfied with water.** This is especially the case in Israel, a semiarid region. Fourth, **fire, which never says, "Enough!"** A *fire's* appetite for brush and wood is insatiable. Only when it has devoured everything in its path does it die out.

This numerical saying seeks to have people recognize that various aspects of life are insatiable. It encourages discovering ways to cope with such desires, including entreating God's help, lest they be tormented throughout life.

Mocking One's Parents (30:17)

■ **17** This independent saying describes the horrible fate of a person who **mocks a father** and **scorns an aged mother** with **the eye** (see 19:26; 20:20). *Eyes* are very expressive of one's deepest feelings. With **the eye** this person expresses contempt, possibly out of deep-seated envy at the parents (see Sir 14:9; 31:13). The ancients viewed the **eye** as possessing special powers. They speak of an evil eye, that is, an eye that has power to inflict harm on a person, even death. Perhaps this person is cursing the parents with an evil **eye.**

Although the age of the offspring is not given, the penalty indicates that the *mocker* is an adult. Displaying such an attitude is counter to the commandment to honor one's father and mother (Prov 23:22; Exod 20:12). The penalty for such behavior was severe. A possible reason for displaying such contempt for a parent is greed, desiring to gain access to one's inheritance. That may account for placing this saying after the numerical saying about not being satisfied (Fox 2009, 870).

In this saying the punishment befalls the organ that expresses the dishonor. Birds of prey, **ravens** or **vultures,** *peck* out and *devour* the ill-wishing **eye.** Consuming that **eye** destroys its powers, breaking the curse (Prov 20:20). Proverbs 24:19-20 presents a similar picture. As a result of envy "the lamp"— a term that functions similarly to **the eye** of the wicked in this proverb—is "snuffed out." "Snuffed out" corresponds to the implication that such an ungrateful offspring does not receive a proper burial. That was a terrible disgrace in ancient Israel. Consequently, one who treats a parent so shamefully suffers an even worse disgrace.

Four Amazing Things (30:18-19)

■ **18-19** This **three/four** numerical saying lists **four** things that have an **amazing** characteristic beyond the sage's ability to **understand**. The term **way** heads each of the four lines in v 19. **Way** stands for the unique, **amazing** manner of the movement of each item in the list. The list names two animals (**an eagle** and **a snake**), a means of transportation (**a ship**), and the manner of a relationship (**a man** *and* a . . . **woman**).

People marvel at **the way** . . . **an eagle** soars high **in the sky**, leaving no trace. It circles about, spots its prey, and swoops down on it at an amazing speed. People are also intrigued by **the way** . . . **a snake** warms itself **on a rock**. This behavior does not mean that a snake is lazy, for in the blink of an eye it grasps a small animal or darts away from danger. Today it is known that snakes are cold-blooded and relish the warmth provided by the sun and a warm rock.

Watching **a ship** glide gracefully and swiftly through the waves is a pleasant sight. Also amazing is the ability of such a heavy object to move through the water, leaving no trace, especially since heavy objects placed on water immediately sink. The items in this list cover three spheres: **sky**, land, and *sea*.

The fourth marvel is **the way of a man with a young woman**. The subtle gestures of a man's seeking to win the affection of a woman are amazing to observe. At the outset of a relationship a couple communicates deep affection for each other with slight gestures and delicate words. Also youths are amazed at the strong attraction they suddenly feel for a person of the opposite gender, especially since most of their lives they have been shy of the opposite gender.

The Way of an Adulteress (30:20)

■ **20** This independent saying has been placed here to serve as a bold contrast to the tender discovery of love between a man and a woman. It portrays the cold, brazen demeanor of **an adulterous woman**. After having sex with a man, most likely for a fee, she nonchalantly **eats** something **and wipes her mouth**. Her eating, especially *wiping* **her mouth,** is evidence that she does not attach any importance to the sexual encounter. Sex has no more meaning to her than *wiping* her mouth. She underscores her callous attitude by boldly *saying*, "I've done nothing wrong." Being focused on herself and her power over men, she has no sense of remorse for engaging in casual sex or for enabling a man to dishonor his wife. She is oblivious to the reality that her immoral activity harms others and that she shares in the responsibility for that harm.

Four Things that Make the Earth Tremble (30:21-23)

■ **21-23** This **three/four** saying lists situations that are so troubling that **the earth trembles**. The preposition **under** (*taḥat*) begins each line of the heading and the first line in vv 22 and 23. The NIV does not translate this word in the last two verses.

Earth in this saying stands for the social order, and *tremble* captures people's becoming very unsettled by inversions in that order. They fear that drastic changes will lead to the loss of everything they own. They also fear for their own safety. Other texts in the OT lament social upheaval, such as Job 12:14-25 and Eccl 10:5-7. This theme is common in eschatological and apocalyptic texts (e.g., Isa 24:1-3). It is also attested in Egyptian texts such as the Admonitions of Ipuwer.

The most startling inversion stands first. **A servant . . . becomes king** (see Prov 19:10; Eccl 10:5-7). Only a peasant uprising would produce such a reversal. Peasants overpower the ruling class, likely because those in authority are too inebriated and out of touch with the people's distress at their rule. After gaining control of the government, the leader of the revolt becomes **king**. Having been **a servant,** he lacks the training and experience to govern well. Also he often has control of only a portion of the country. Thus, regions remain in turmoil.

The second inversion is that a ***hardened* fool** [*nābāl*] becomes ***well fed***. This type of person is very obstinate and does not even believe in God (Pss 14:1; 53:1 [2 HB]). The general principle in proverbial sayings is that such a person faces hardships, possibly poverty. But now a ***hardened* fool** has **plenty to eat**. Such a state of affairs was very disturbing to the sages because they taught that abundance comes from hard work (Prov 20:13; 28:19). They also believed that such an inversion in the social order undercuts the drive to be industrious (Fox 2009, 874).

The third inversion is **a contemptible [lit. *hated*] woman who gets married**. It is unclear why this woman was ***hated***. One suggestion is that she was the unfavored wife in a polygamous marriage. Another view holds that she was a divorcée (see Deut 22:13, 16; 24:3, Elephantine papyri). But the text at hand does not hint at either divorce or remarriage. Another view is that she has a repulsive demeanor, such as being contentious (see Prov 19:13*b*; 21:9, 19; 25:24). Another suggestion is that she is an older, less attractive woman who gets married late in life to the community's amazement. That view, though, is highly unlikely, for it reflects a modern, Western perspective of marriage.

A more viable view is that a less favored wife becomes the head of the house. The ***earth's trembling*** resides in her gaining authority over the household. This view is favored, for it is in accord with the theme of the other situations (Fox 2009, 876).

The fourth inversion is similar to the first. **A female servant displaces her mistress**. In such a reversal **the** servant is inclined to make life difficult for **her** former **mistress**. The tension between women in a polygamous setting is vividly described in the accounts of Sarah and Hagar, her servant (Gen 16; 21:8-14). After Hagar bore Abraham a son, at Sarah's instigation, Sarah felt so humiliated by Hagar's success that she treated Hagar cruelly, eventually banishing her.

However, this saying may describe a more hostile situation since **displaces** possibly means ***disinherits***. In that scenario the **servant** manipulates the husband to gain part or all of the inheritance that belongs to the first wife, causing the **displaced** wife a major setback (Fox 2009, 877).

This numerical saying underscores the importance of maintaining the hierarchical order in society.

Four Small Things that Are Wise (30:24-28)

■ **24-28** The introduction to this numerical saying has only one number. It is a list of **four things on earth** that **are small** and **extremely wise**. This list provides evidence that the ancients made keen observations of nature and were beginning to record their observations in wisdom texts (Whybray 1994a, 419).

Ants head the list. Though they are very small and have **little strength,** they work continuously throughout **the summer** *storing up food* for the winter (see Prov 6:6-8). Given their size, they travel *very* far to get **food.** Often they form two columns, one moving to a food supply and the other returning. Sometimes an ant is seen carrying a bit of food that is larger than its body.

Hyraxes, or *rock badgers*, large rabbit-like creatures, appear to have **little *might*. They make their home in the crags.** Having thick, soft padding on the soles of their feet, they easily scramble among the crevices. The rocks keep them safe from predators (Ps 104:18*b*).

Migratory **locusts**, moving in a large swarm, appear to **advance . . . in ranks** even though they lack a **king**. They settle on a field, quickly devouring everything. Ancient authors such as Joel use **locusts** as a metaphor for picturing the terrible devastation that an invading army causes (see Joel 1:4; 2:4-9; Nah 3:15).

A **lizard** or *a gecko*, though it darts about, may be caught by **hand**. Yet these small, often loathed reptiles find their way into **palaces,** residing with royalty. Humorously they gain no benefit from taking up residence among royalty (Whybray 1994a, 419). Another suggestion for this rarely attested word is *spider*.

This list shows that *wisdom* has greater value than **strength**. Thus, it encourages humans to overcome physical limitations by mental acuity.

Four Stately Animals (30:29-33)

■ **29-31** This **three/four** numerical saying lists four creatures **that are stately in their stride** and **move with stately bearing: a lion, . . . a strutting rooster, a he-goat, and a king.** Each of them has a distinctive manner and a gait that conveys bold confidence. The **lion** is given the principal place. It is named first and described as **mighty** and refusing to *retreat*. Its strength, prowess, and courage are legendary.

The next two animals are **a strutting rooster** (*zarzîr*) and a *male* goat. The identity of the *zarzîr* remains uncertain. A **he-goat** struts about the herd, displaying its authority over the herd. Similar to these animals, **a king** has a stately bearing that exudes confidence as he leads his troops into battle. Since **a king** is often compared to **a lion** (2 Sam 1:23; Prov 19:12; 20:2), this line is closely connected with the first.

32-33 The final saying counsels against ever acting like *a* **fool**. Sometimes a mood settles over a person or one becomes so upset that even a wise person feels strongly inclined to act foolishly in order to ***vaunt*** oneself. In such a mood a person may even be inclined to ***plot*** doing something **evil**.

Whenever such a mood comes on a person or such cunning thoughts occupy the mind, it is critical for that person to gain self-control. One way is with a dramatic gesture such as ***clapping a*** **hand over *the*** mouth. This gesture keeps a person from speaking words the person will soon regret. Often words spoken in haste impel a person to do something untoward. Thus, a person needs to do something forceful enough to startle the mind in order to gain self-control.

The following metaphors vividly describe the harsh consequences that result from yielding to a foolish impulse. Each consequence begins with the term *mîṣ*, ***press*** or ***squeeze***. It is rendered **churning, twisting,** and **stirring up** as required by its respective objects. ***Pressing*** something ***hard*** produces a dramatic effect: **churning *milk*** produces ***curds***; **twisting** *a person's* nose *causes* blood *to flow*; **stirring up anger produces strife**. These metaphors vividly illustrate that a foolish or **evil** deed arouses such anger in people that the doer is likely to suffer harsh consequences.

B. The Sayings of Lemuel (31:1-9)

OVERVIEW

The sayings of Lemuel (31:1-9) connect well with the sayings of Agur (30:1-9). Both men, being identified with Massah, may represent northern Arabian wisdom. Lemuel presents the teaching of his mother. The wisdom of the queen mother connects well with the portrait of the noble wife (31:10-31). Both texts are examples of the insights and skills Wisdom gives to women of valor. Both women counsel a man: a son and a husband.

King Lemuel records for future kings the wise counsel of his mother (Fox 2009, 884). The value Lemuel places on his mother's teaching is in accord with the exhortations in Section I to listen to a mother's instructions (e.g., 1:8; 6:20).

The inclusion of the sayings of Agur and Lemuel in Proverbs is important. It shows that Israelite sages acknowledged that the insights of non-Israelites and women are valuable for instruction.

Nothing else is known about King Lemuel. The first line in the Hebrew text is unclear. Does Massah identify him with a clan of Ishmaelites, a north Arabian tribe (Gen 16:15-16), or is it the word meaning "an inspired utterance" (30:1)? Does "king," which stands before *maśśā'*, modify Lemuel, "King Lemuel" (NRSV), or is it part of a phrase: the "king of Massa" (NJPS) or "King Lemuel of Massa" (REB)? Since the Hebrew text is unclear, these options are only conjectures.

The queen mother exhorts her son to focus his attention on his people, making sure that the poor receive justice rather than spending his vigor or wealth on women and partying. Such advice from anyone other than the queen mother would likely have been considered offensive by the young king. Clifford (1999, 271) notes, "[Her] exhortation is applicable to all who are tempted to turn authority into privilege."

IN THE TEXT

I. Superscription (31:1)

■ **I** This instruction belongs to the genre of royal instruction. It is the only extant example of this genre from a woman (Whybray 1994a, 422). In many monarchies the queen mother played an important role in the palace. She kept her son aware of what was taking place in the palace, especially among the servants and the women in the harem. She also advised the king on a variety of matters. Her unwavering loyalty to him made her a trusted source of counsel.

2. The Exhortations of Lemuel's Mother (31:2-9)

a. Opening Exhortation (31:2-3)

■ **2** Lemuel's mother passionately and lovingly entreats her son to **listen** to her. Her passion is heard in the threefold repetition of **what** or **listen**. With another threefold repetition she addresses him affectionately: **my son, the son of my womb, the son of my vows**. The last phrase reveals that when she had difficulty conceiving, she prayed to God and supported her entreaty with **a vow** (see 1 Sam 1:10-11). God **answered** her **prayers** with the birth of Lemuel. Feeling very close to her son, she earnestly desires that he rule wisely and justly. Therefore, she counsels him not to engage in improper behaviors (Prov 31:4-7) and to help the **destitute** (vv 8-9).

■ **3** She warns him **not** to **spend** *his* **strength on women**, for they **ruin kings**. The word for **strength** also means **wealth** (NIV mg.). She is alerting her son to the cunning designs of women who relish their position in the palace. They enjoy manipulating the king for personal gain. For example, they seek gifts of jewelry and clothing and possibly use their charms to obtain their own houses. They also desire special privileges. Consorting with many **women** could prove very costly to him. The queen mother does not want to see the state's funds used so frivolously, for such use would limit its resources for helping the poor.

The queen mother motivates this counsel by describing such women as those who **ruin kings**. In an indirect way she is alerting Lemuel to the danger of becoming preoccupied with **women**. Jealousies may develop within the harem, leading to conflicts and intrigues. It is possible that some might even plot to assassinate the king (see the Egyptian Instruction of King Amenemhet).

b. Exhortation against Drunkenness (31:4-7)

■ **4-5** Continuing to use a repetitive style for emphasis and to capture her son's attention, she addresses him by name. The queen mother advises **Lemuel** that **it is not for kings to drink wine *nor* to crave beer**. Since the ancients had few, if any other beverages, it is unlikely that she is frowning on serving **beer** and **wine** with meals. Rather, she is warning her son against sponsoring drinking bouts at the palace.

Should he engage in the excessive consumption of **beer** and **wine**, his thinking may be clouded. On an occasion when he is hearing a case, he is likely to **forget *the decrees*** of the land. Or he may not be able to focus his attention in order to grasp specific details about the case being presented. As a result, he would render an unjust verdict, depriving **the oppressed of their rights**. When justice is thwarted, citizens become angry and resistant to the king's rule.

■ **6-7** Abruptly the queen mother shifts the focus of her counsel regarding beer and wine. She advises that these drinks **be *distributed to*** **those who are perishing** or **are in anguish**. Since the verb **be *distributed*** or be given is plural, she is no longer directly addressing Lemuel. Rather, she is recommending that the government provide these beverages to those who are very sick. Her counsel reflects a deep concern for those who are suffering. Recognizing that they need solace to cope with their conditions, she believes that providing them beer and wine will help them **forget their poverty** and **their misery** (see 1 Esd 3:18-24; Fox 2009, 887).

In evaluating this counsel, it needs to be kept in mind that in antiquity people had few means for relieving pain, such as aspirin and ibuprofen. Alcohol was one source they had available to ease relentless pain.

c. Exhortation to Defend the Poor (31:8-9)

■ **8-9** Lemuel's mother concludes by exhorting her son to be an aggressive advocate for ***the* destitute**, . . . **the poor and needy,** those who lack the skills and the resources for defending themselves in legal disputes. He is to **speak up** for them, that is, to be their advocate. As king he is to **judge** their cases **fairly** and to **defend** their **rights.** In order for their **rights** to be honored, **the poor** need a powerful defender (Amos 5:10-15).

VI. CAPSTONE: THE NOBLE WIFE: 31:10-31

BEHIND THE TEXT

This capstone focuses on the activities that take place in a stable, ideal, productive household. It gives a picture of a family in a village or city that has become prosperous and gained status as the result of hard work, high morals, and fearing Yahweh (Whybray 1994a, 426). This accords with the connection between wisdom and her building a house (Prov 9:1; 14:1). Thus, this poem broadens the role of Woman Wisdom from training sages and leaders (chs 1—9) to giving wisdom to women and men to accomplish well daily activities. Families led by Wisdom are essential for Israel's stability and prosperity.

This poem provides a splendid capstone to the book of Proverbs. It offers a concrete example of the intellectual acumen and practical skills Woman Wisdom provides devout women. The poem is not to be read as saying that Wisdom gives every woman all these abilities; rather, it illustrates the skills and virtues Woman Wisdom instills in those who fear Yahweh.

In this portrait Wisdom empowers the wife of valor to manage her household, engage in local commerce, teach her children, and support her husband. She is a concrete example of the realization of the promise in various proverbs that encourage finding a wise wife (12:4; 18:22; 19:14).

The motif of a house is a setting that binds the two portraits of a woman of strength: Woman Wisdom (chs 1—9) and the noble wife (31:10-31). In the house she has built Wisdom prepares a banquet (9:1-6). She sends out invitations by some of her servants while others prepare the meal. Those who come to the banquet will learn wisdom. The noble wife likewise manages her household well, including her servants (31:15, 21, 27). Like Wisdom's mouth (8:7-8), her mouth, being full of wisdom, enables her to teach her family (31:26).

Furthermore, several details show that the portrait of the noble wife has been constructed to connect with the portrait of Woman Wisdom in Section I (Camp 1985, 179-208; Yoder 2009, 290). The fear of Yahweh is central to both women (1:7, 29; 8:13*a*; 9:10; 31:30). Both are known at the city gate (1:21*b*; 8:3; 31:23, 31). They provide followers and family security (1:33; 2:12-14; 3:23; 31:11-12, 25, 27*a*). Both work diligently (1:20; 8:1-3; 31:17-19, 27), make a profit (3:14; 8:18; 31:18*a*, 24), and acquire wealth (8:18, 21; 31:11*b*). They teach or speak wisdom (1:23, 25; 8:4-16, 32-34; 31:26). Both extend their hands to help those in need (1:24*b*; 31:20). Both experience joy from their work and their deeds of kindness (8:30-31; 31:25*b*). Wisdom bestows honor (4:8-9), and the noble wife is honored (31:29-31). Because both women are unsurpassable (3:13-18; 31:29), their value is priceless (3:13-15; 8:11; 31:10).

Thus, this poem functions as an inclusio with the role of Woman Wisdom in Section I. Whereas Wisdom moves about a city, inviting all to follow her, the noble wife works at home, managing the household and performing many chores. She goes to the market to purchase food and supplies and to sell the wares made at her household. In this regard her portrait is closer to that of Woman Wisdom's hosting a grand banquet at the house she has built and manages (9:1-6). She goes out to evaluate a field for sale and then proceeds to purchase it.

This poem may be identified as an encomium (Fox 2009, 902-3), a poem of lofty praise for a specific person or a particular type of person (see Ps 128). It lauds the noble wife as a woman of strength. She embodies the skills and the astute virtues Wisdom promises to pour out on those who follow her (Prov 1:23). From another perspective she is the incarnation of the promises presented in the instructions and wise sayings found throughout Proverbs. She truly is the crown of her husband (12:4) and a model of a wise person. The portrait of the wife of strength indeed corresponds to that of Woman Wisdom in Section I (1:20-33; 8:1-36; 9:1-6).

The encomium is structured as an alphabetical acrostic; each successive line begins with the next letter of the Hebrew alphabet, which has twenty-two letters. The classic example of an alphabetical acrostic is Ps 119, having twenty-two sections with eight couplets, each beginning with the same letter of the alphabet. Ben Sira likewise concludes his volume on wisdom with an alphabetic acrostic. This style enhances the role of the encomium as the conclusion to Proverbs.

The acrostic structure, however, contributes to the lack of symmetry in the poem's order. This unevenness has been countered by repetition of key words and other poetic devices, including two chiasms. The one with **hands** and **palms** stands near the center (vv 19-20). The other, at the extremities of the poem, the noble wife (v 10*a*):her husband (v 11*a*)::her husband (v 28*b*):noble (v 29*a*; Clifford 1999, 273). The poem also has a clear structure: the wife's value (vv 10-12), her skills (vv 13-27), and her worth (vv 28-31; Waltke 2005, 515).

This encomium honors a woman whom Wisdom has endowed with multiple skills that equip her to manage a large household well. It illustrates that any woman who responds to the call of Wisdom will receive skills and insights for maintaining a stable home with a sound income. This encomium serves to laud the skills Wisdom provides a noble wife rather than functioning as a model every woman should strive for.

Moreover, this portrait of the woman of valor is a realistic description of outstanding women in ancient Israel. These women acted courageously, gave sound advice, and influenced society. Some were warriors like Deborah (Judg 4—5). Others like Jehosheba worked covertly to preserve the Davidic line (2 Kgs 11:1-3). Queen Bathsheba skillfully guided events so that her son was crowned to succeed David (1 Kgs 1—2).

Abigail insightfully sized up the danger her husband put his household in by spurning David's request for food (1 Sam 25:14-39). She responded quickly, aggressively, and shrewdly. After assembling a large quantity of food, she organized a supply train to transport it to David. When her company reached David, she appeased his wrath and bravely entreated him not to take revenge on Nabal, her husband (1 Sam 25:24-31).

There is the idyllic story of Naomi and Ruth overcoming hardships and poverty (Ruth 1—4). The Shunammite woman advised her husband to build a room for Elisha to stay in when he passed that way (2 Kgs 4:8-10). Other women of position counseled their husbands. Queen Jezebel counseled Ahab (1 Kgs 21:5-7), and Queen Esther skillfully appealed to the Persian monarch, enabling her people to escape a pogrom (Esth 7—8). In the above examples there is no indication that a husband objected to his wife's counsel.

OVERVIEW

This poem renders praise not only to the wife of strength but also to every woman of high character. The description of the activities of the noble wife is both realistic and idealistic, with a touch of hyperbole. Her many skills enable her to perform well a wide variety of tasks. As a result her household becomes wealthy.

This portrait is sufficiently realistic in that even a current reader thinks of his or her mother on hearing this poem. However, even a brief reflection on all the activities the noble wife does leads to the realization that no woman is able to accomplish all these tasks. The goal of this poem is not to encourage women to become workaholics. Rather, it is to honor the variety of skills women have. It also closes this book by honoring Woman Wisdom as the giver of these skills to those who heed her call. Thus, the poem operates on two levels (Alonso-Schökel 1988, 114).

IN THE TEXT

A. The Wife of Strength (31:10-12)

■ **10** The introductory rhetorical question that demands a negative answer asserts that **a wife of noble character** is priceless because of her acumen, stamina, compassion, and productivity. No emphasis is placed on her appearance, attitudes, or feelings (Wolters 1988, 454). Her stellar character makes her priceless (Fox 2009, 852).

A Wife of Noble Character

This woman is identified as "a woman of valor or strength" (*'ēšet ḥayil*). The Hebrew *ḥayil* carries the senses "power, strength, valor, wealth, capability." The term *'ēšet ḥayil* occurs three times in the OT (Prov 12:4; 31:10; Ruth 3:11). This title corresponds to the titles used for men of distinction, those known for exceptional bravery: *gibbôr ḥayil* or *'iš ḥayil* (**a powerful warrior**), *'iš milḥāmâ* (**a man of war** [1 Sam 16:18]). When a tribe or village was harassed by a strong foe, such a person rallied the people to resist the enemy, even against great odds. After defeating the foe, he became the leader of a tribe or the nation. The premiere example is David (1 Sam 16:18). This title is also used for a wealthy leader within a tribe (1 Sam 9:1; 2 Kgs 15:20).

When this title is used for a woman, it emphasizes her stamina, industry, management skills, courage, determination, and resourcefulness. Interestingly, in this description of **the woman of valor**, terms associated with a warrior are embedded in the poem: **value** (*šālāl*; lit. **spoil** [Prov 31:11]), **food** (*ṭerep*; lit. **prey** [v 15]), and **girding the loins** (v 17; Yoder 2009, 293).

A noble wife's management skills and industry make her household prosperous. She is skilled at dealing with difficult situations such as a famine or a raid by an enemy. Clearly, her **worth *is* far more than** that of **rubies** (3:15; 8:11). This is a realistic metaphor for her worth. That worth is achieved by her skills and her diligent labor throughout the day.

Not only is she skilled at many tasks, but she is also a strong manager, guiding servants to produce a variety of products such as apparel and bedding. She sells the surplus at the market. Her husband is honored at the city gate where he sits with the elders. Because of his wife's success, he has time to be a leader in the community, a role inspired by Woman Wisdom (8:16).

Is the poem to be read as showing that the wife's hard work enables her husband the pleasure to do as he likes? Hardly. Her many skills illustrate the wisdom that Wisdom gives a woman who accepts her call. These skills enable her to lead a household that provides every member a sense of security. The husband's role symbolizes the skills Wisdom gives a leader to serve the community with keen insights. The highest honor in this poem goes to the wife of valor rather than the husband because she embodies wisdom and her honor is the basis of his honor.

Their household was a small estate that included a large tract of land for farming and herding and some sheds for various activities, such as spinning, weaving, and making garments. An example of a household that included a number of small businesses was Potiphar's, which Joseph managed (Gen 39:4-6).

■ **11-12** Given her loyalty and skills, **her husband has full confidence in her. She brings him good** [i.e., **benefits**], **not harm** throughout **her life**. Thus, **he** lacks nothing of value (*šālāl*), for her business aptitude provides a steady stream of income. The literal meaning of the Hebrew term is **spoil** (*šālāl*), the valuables a valiant warrior collects after a battle.

B. Activities of the Noble Wife (31:13-27)

■ **13** The noble wife is skilled at purchasing or producing **wool and flax** (see Prov 31:21-22). The best fibers of flax, being soft and flexible, are used to make linen. The coarser fibers are used for twine and ropes. In fact, the production of linen was a key industry in ancient Israel (King and Stager 2001, 150). The noble wife's hands do this work **willingly**. It brings her joy and a deep sense of satisfaction. The context indicates that she also supervises servants in the making of clothing.

■ **14** She goes to the market to purchase a variety of **foods** for the household, including delicacies imported from distant lands as suggested by the reference to **merchant ships**. These ships dock at a port, then transport their merchandise to sell at markets in nearby cities (see Neh 13:16).

■ **15** Disciplined and energetic, the noble wife **rises while it is still dark**. She plans **the** food (*ṭerep*; lit. **prey**) to be prepared for the day. She assigns her servants their tasks so that the food will be ready at the various times for meals. She also has **portions** prepared **for her female servants**, possibly for them to take along as they go to their places of work. In antiquity and still today in many parts of the world, meal preparation consumes a large part of the day. Most families, even among the poor, have at least one servant to help with this chore. The noble wife's preparing **portions** for the **servants** is evidence of her concern for them.

■ **16** On occasion the **noble wife** goes to assess **a field** that is for sale. If she finds it desirable, she negotiates its purchase. In this case she determines that

31:11-16

the land she purchases will make **a** good **vineyard**. Later **she** will oversee *the planting of the* **vineyard**. That involved extensive work: clearing the field of stones, plowing and tilling the soil, planting choice vines, hewing out a wine vat, erecting a hedge around the field, and possibly building a watchtower in it (Isa 5:2). She pays for this work *from* **her earnings**. Perhaps when it is completed, she employs tenants to care for *the* **vineyard**. Such practice was common for the rich, as attested in some of Jesus' parables (e.g., Luke 20:9).

■ **17** The noble wife engages in arduous **work**. Like a warrior she adjusts her clothing (lit. *girds her loins*) to keep it from restricting her as she works.

■ **18** Being skilled as a businesswoman, **her trading is profitable**. A literal reading of this line is **she** *examines her wares*, making sure they *are good*. She takes pride in selling products of high quality. Not only does she rise early (Prov 31:15), but she also works late into the evening by the light of *a* **lamp**. This is expressed by the hyperbole **her lamp does not go out at night**.

■ **19** She is skilled at spinning wool into yarn and then weaving the yarn into fabric. These may be two of the tasks she does at night. In ancient Middle Eastern texts spinning and weaving serve as symbols of a woman's skill; noble women and queens are pictured holding a **spindle** (see Judg 16:13-14; Yoder 2009, 293).

■ **20** The *noble wife* has a spirit of compassion. She takes food and clothing **to the poor** and **the needy** with *open* arms (see Prov 11:24; 28:27). In Deut 15:7-8 *open hands* is a metaphor for showing generosity to the poor.

A chiastic pattern binds Prov 31:19-20: *hands:palms::palm*:hands. The chiasm emphasizes that the very **hands** by which the noble wife makes a profit reach out to help those in poverty. Her ample earnings do not make her greedy.

■ **21-22** When the weather turns cold and **it snows**, the exquisite garments she has made keep everyone in **her household** warm (vv 13, 19). For keeping warm in **bed she *has made* coverings**. Even though Israel's hills seldom receive snow, the winters are infamous for their bone-chilling cold because of dampness and a stiff wind.

Her family is clothed in expensive garments of **scarlet** (2 Sam 1:24), **fine linen** (Esth 8:15), **and** *red*-**purple** (Ezek 27:7, 16). Besides using the **linen** produced at her household (Prov 31:13), she may have imported **fine linen** from Egypt. **Purple** and **scarlet** dyes or dyed cloth was imported from Phoenicia. The noble wife and her family are dressed like royalty. Incidentally, this is the only reference in the poem that shows that she does not neglect herself (Fox 2009, 896).

■ **23** Because of her skillful management of the household and success at manufacturing, **her husband** (see v 11) sits **at the city gate . . . among the elders**. He is highly **respected**, both for his role in the council and for his wife's skills. Since his wife is a skilled seamstress, one can be assured that he is well-dressed. **At the city gate** he participates in council meetings, hears disputes, and may oversee business activities, both those of his household and those of other merchants. His official role brings honor to his wife.

■ **24** This additional reference to her *making* **linen garments** reveals that her household produces garments to *sell*. **She** also **supplies . . . merchants with sashes.** Selling these products is a major source of her household's income.

■ **25** The theme of clothing is now employed as a metaphor. The noble wife is **clothed with strength and dignity.** The term **clothed** functions to convey that these qualities have become ingrained in her character (see Job 29:14; Isa 11:5). Self-assured, **she** *laughs* **at** the future. She is confident of being able to cope with anything unexpected that might befall her or the family. Her poise provides the family and servants a strong sense of security, increasing their productivity.

■ **26** Because the wife of valor **speaks with wisdom,** her **instruction** or *teaching* her children, supervising her servants, and advising her husband is characterized as *kind* or **faithful** (*hesed*; → sidebar "Loyal Love or *Hesed*" at Prov 3:3-4). Her words are identified as *teaching* (*tôrâ*; see 6:20 where *tôrâ* is used for a mother's teaching); thus, they are authoritative. Another way to understand the phrase is her *teaching* about *kindness* or *faithfulness* (Yoder 2009, 296).

■ **27** The noble wife vigilantly **watches over the affairs** taking place at **her household.** Unlike the lazy farmer (24:30-34), she never stops working long enough to **eat the bread of idleness.** Because of her diligence no one in her household needs to be anxious that something is not being attended to.

C. Praise of the Noble Wife (31:28-31)

■ **28-29** In recognition of her skills, virtues, and vigilance, **her children arise and call her blessed** (*'aššēr*; → sidebar "A Beatitude" in overview for 3:13-20). Most likely she is praised at a public ceremony. Her children's *rising* captures the enthusiasm of the praise her family extends to her. On this occasion **her husband** especially **praises her,** for he realizes that she is the driving force behind his wealth and his high standing in the community. Their praise proclaims: **Many women do noble things** [*hayil*]**, but you surpass them all.** This word of praise places her among the *valiant* (*hayil*) women.

■ **30-31** The poet concludes the encomium with a principle and an exhortation. First, the poet cites a saying about a woman's genuine worth: **charm is deceptive, and beauty is fleeting; but a woman who fears Yahweh is to be praised.** People are prone to extol beautiful, charming women profusely. But **beauty is fleeting** and **charm is deceptive.** The latter is the case because **charm** provides no indication of a woman's true character or the depth of her devotion to **Yahweh.**

A woman who **fears Yahweh** is worthy of high praise. Her devotion to God has exceedingly more enduring value than her appearance. Over time a charming woman loses her power of attraction. But public admiration for a woman deeply devoted to Yahweh increases as she ages. At the end of Proverbs as at the beginning, ***the fear of Yahweh*** is the bedrock on which an honorable life is built (1:7; 9:10).

The poet concludes by exhorting the community to **honor her for all that her hands have *produced***. Their rising as she enters the marketplace located inside **the city gate** is an expression of high praise. There **her works *will*** also **bring her praise**. People in the community will express admiration for the high quality of the clothing she has made. At the end of Proverbs the woman of strength is present **at the city gate**. This corresponds to Woman Wisdom's presence at the city gate in the opening instruction (1:20-21). Thus, the conclusion of the encomium functions as an inclusio for the book of Proverbs.

FROM THE TEXT

An encomium to the noble wife, a woman of valor, is a fitting close to Proverbs. Her activities and leadership provide a concrete example of the way Wisdom works in the life of a person who fears Yahweh, equipping her with many skills. These skills enable her to manage a large household. Her business skills provide a sound income. Wisdom instills in her virtues. She shows genuine concern for her servants and also reaches out to help the poor. In this secure setting she teaches her children wisdom and the fear of Yahweh. Because of Wisdom's presence in her life, she is highly honored by her family and the community.

This encomium encourages young men who are learning wisdom to entreat God for a wife who fears Yahweh and seeks wisdom rather than one who is attractive and charming. It encourages young women to strive to become women of strength, acumen, compassion, and devotion. They may be confident that Wisdom will give them the skills for managing their homes well, leading to their becoming highly respected in the community.

Not only does this poem honor the wife of valor, but it encourages every God-fearing wife in the pursuit of wisdom and in working diligently to provide a stable, active home. It also encourages families to have occasions for honoring a noble wife.